Real World MACRO

TWENTY-FIRST EDITION

edited by

Daniel Fireside, John Miller, Amy Offner

and the

Dollars & Sense Collective

REAL WORLD MACRO
TWENTY-FIRST EDITION

ISBN: 1-878585-46-0

Published by:
Economic Affairs Bureau, Inc.
Dollars and Sense
740 Cambridge Street
Cambridge, MA 02141
tel: 617-876-2434
e-mail: dollars@dollarsandsense.org
web: www.dollarsandsense.org

Real World Macro is edited by the *Dollars & Sense* collective, publishers of *Dollars & Sense* magazine and *Real World Micro, Real World Globalization, Current Economic Issues, Real World Banking, The Environment in Crisis, Introduction to Political Economy, Unlevel Playing Fields,* and *The Wealth Inequality Reader.*

The 2004 Collective: Ben Boothby, Beth Burgess, Esther Cervantes, Chuck Collins, Daniel Fireside, Ellen Frank, Amy Gluckman, Erkut Gomulu, Lena Graber, Maryalice Guilford, John Miller, Laura Orlando, Alejandro Reuss, Brian Riley, Adria Scharf, Chris Sturr, Todd Tavares, Chris Tilly, Ramaa Vasudevan, Rodney Ward, Thad Williamson, Jeanne Winner, James Woolman, Jane Yager.

Manufactured by Capital City Press
Printed in U.S.A.

CONTENTS

CHAPTER 6: UNEMPLOYMENT AND INFLATION

CHAPTER 7: PERSPECTIVES ON MACROECONOMIC POLICY

CHAPTER 8: INTERNATIONAL TRADE AND FINANCE

STATISTICAL APPENDICES

INTRODUCTION

THE TWO ECONOMIES

It sometimes seems that the United States has not one, but two economies. The first economy exists in economics textbooks and in the minds of many elected officials. It is an economy in which no one goes for long without work, families are rewarded with an ever-improving standard of living, and anyone who works hard can live the American Dream. In this economy, people are free and roughly equal, and each individual carefully looks after him- or herself, making uncoerced choices to advance their own economic interests. Government has some limited roles in this world, but it is increasingly marginal, since the macroeconomy is a self-regulating system of wealth generation.

The second economy is described in the writings of progressives, environmentalists, union supporters, and consumer advocates—as well as honest business writers who recognize that the real world does not always conform to textbook models. This second economy features vast disparities of income, wealth, and power. It is an economy where economic instability and downward mobility are facts of life. Jobs disappear, workers suffer long spells of unemployment, and new jobs seldom afford the same standard of living as those lost. As for the government, it sometimes adopts policies that ameliorate the abuses of capitalism, and other times does just the opposite, but it is always an active and essential participant in economic life.

If you are reading this introduction, you are probably a student in an introductory college course in macroeconomics. Your textbook will introduce you to the first economy, the harmonious world of self-regulating stability. *Real World Macro* will introduce you to the second.

WHY "REAL WORLD" MACRO?

A standard economics textbook is full of powerful concepts. It is also, by its nature, a limited window on the economy. What is taught in most introductory macroeconomics courses today is a relatively narrow set of concepts. Inspired by classical economic theory, most textbooks depict an inherently stable economy in little need of government intervention. But fifty years ago, textbooks were very different. Keynesian economic theory, which holds that government action can and must stabilize modern monetized economies, occupied a central place in introductory textbooks. Even Marxist economics, with its piercing analysis of class structure and instability in capitalism, appeared regularly on the pages of

those textbooks. The contraction of economics education has turned some introductory courses into little more than celebrations of today's economy as "the best of all possible worlds."

Real World Macro, designed as a supplement to a standard macroeconomics textbook, is dedicated to widening the scope of economic inquiry. Its articles rub mainstream theory up against reality by providing vivid, real-world illustrations of economic concepts. And where most texts uncritically present the key assumptions and propositions of traditional macroeconomic theory, *Real World Macro* asks provocative questions: What are alternative propositions about how the economy operates and who it serves? What difference do such propositions make? What might actually constitute the best of all possible macroeconomic worlds?

For instance, *Real World Macro* questions the conventional wisdom about economic problems such as inflation, asking who is hurt and who benefits. While mainstream textbooks readily allow that inflation favors debtors over creditors, they create the impression that inflation is equally bad for workers, employers, and investors. But a fast-growing economy that pushes up prices also tightens labor markets, strengthening the economic position of workers and threatening investors, whose asset values are eroded by rising prices.

Similarly, when the Fed prioritizes price stability over employment, monetary policy does not serve us all, as most textbooks suggest, but puts the interests of owners and bondholders ahead of the interests of workers and job-seekers. Those policies come at a considerable human cost. Researchers have found that with every one percentage point increase in the U.S. unemployment rate, 920 more people commit suicide, 650 commit homicide, 20,000 suffer heart attacks, 500 die from heart and kidney disease and cirrhosis of the liver, 4,000 are admitted to state mental hospitals, and 3,300 are sent to state prisons.

William Vickery, the Nobel-prize winning economist, used his 1993 presidential address to the American Economics Association to advocate macroeconomic policies that would lower the unemployment rate to roughly 2%. Genuine full employment, Vickery argued, would bring about "a major reduction in the incidence of poverty, homelessness, sickness, and crime." We think that policies like this, and the alternative propositions that lie behind them, are worth debating—and that requires hearing a range of views.

WHAT'S IN THIS BOOK

Real World Macro is organized to follow the outline of a standard economics text. We have specifically keyed our table of contents to David Colander's *Economics* (5th edition) and its *Macroeconomics* "split," but since the topics covered by all major texts are similar, this reader is a good fit with other textbooks as well. Each chapter leads off with a brief introduction, including study questions for the entire chapter, and then provides several short articles from *Dollars & Sense* magazine that illustrate the chapter's key concepts—52 articles in all. In many cases, the articles have been updated or otherwise edited to heighten their relevance.

Here is a quick walk through the chapters.

Chapter 1, Measuring Economic Performance, starts off the volume by taking a critical look at the standard measures of economic activity. What do those measures actually tell us about the quality of life in today's economy, and what crucial aspects of economic life do they leave uncounted?

Chapter 2, Wealth and Inequality, examines these two end products of today's economic growth. *Dollars & Sense* authors show who is accumulating wealth and who isn't, and argue that inequality is not a prerequisite to economic growth.

Chapter 3, Savings and Investment, peers inside the pump house of economic growth and comes up with some provocative questions. Do more corporate profits and higher stock prices actually mean more investment? What public policies have proven track record of promoting investment? And why have household savings disappeared?

Chapter 4, Fiscal Policy, Deficits, and Debt, assesses current government spending and taxing policies. The chapter's authors argue that tax cuts for the rich, the new military buildup, and proposals to privatize Social Security won't stimulate economic growth, but have already squandered budget surpluses that could have provided for social needs.

Chapter 5, Monetary Policy and Financial Markets, explains how the Fed conducts monetary policy in the "new world of banking" dominated by giant financial holding companies. It asks whose interests the Fed serves: those who hold financial assets, or the rest of us.

Chapter 6, Unemployment and Inflation, reveals how macroeconomic policy that prioritizes price stability over employment puts the interests of owners and bondholders ahead of the interests of workers. The chapter begins with a critique of the "natural rate" of unemployment. It also looks at the effects of unemployment, infla-

tion, and "New Economy" productivity growth on workers' bargaining power and living standards.

Chapter 7, Perspectives on Macroeconomic Policy, introduces alternatives to classical-inspired macroeconomic theory. It begins with a critical analysis of the New Classical economics claim that the macroeconomy is inherently stable, and moves on to discuss Keynesian, Marxist, and feminist perspectives on macroeconomics.

Chapter 8, International Trade and Finance, critically assesses the prevailing neoliberal policy prescriptions for the global economy. The articles criticize development strategies based on "free trade" and financial liberalization. They also look at proposals to reform international financial institutions, eliminate sweatshop conditions, and lighten the deadening impact of debt on developing economies.

KEY TO COLANDER

In each chapter introduction, we provide a key that links our text to David Colander's *Economics*, 5th edition, and its macroeconomics "split," *Macroeconomics*, 5th edition. Professors and students using other textbooks should, of course, feel free to ignore these keys. Here is the summary key for the entire table of contents.

Here and in the individual chapter keys, *Economics* Chapter 1 will be abbreviated "E1," and *Macroeconomics* Chapter 1 will be abbreviated "M1."

Chapter 1—Colander chapters E2, E22, E23; or M2, M6, M7.

Chapter 2—Colander chapters E22-E26; or M6-M10.

Chapter 3—Colander chapters E24-E26, M34; or M8-M10, M19.

Chapter 4—Colander chapters E25-E26, E30-E31, E34; or M9-M10, M14-M15, M19.

Chapter 5—Colander chapters E27-E28, E34; or M11-M12, M19.

Chapter 6—Colander chapter E29; or M13.

Chapter 7—Colander chapters E22, E25-E26; or M6, M9-M10.

Chapter 8—Colander chapters E21 and E32-E33; or M16-M18.

CHAPTER 1

Measuring Economic Performance

INTRODUCTION

Most macroeconomics textbooks begin with a snapshot of today's economy as seen through the lens of the standard measures of economic performance. This chapter provides a different view of today's economy, one far more critical of current economic policy and performance that asks what the standard measures of economic performance really tell us.

In "High and Dry: The Economic Recovery Fails to Deliver," John Miller tracks the current economic recovery that began in November 2001. Despite its length and a heavy dose of economic stimulants—everything from tax cuts, record low interest rates, and massive military spending—job creation in this recovery remains the worst on record. Miller argues that the recent growth spurt has done little to resolve the underlying problems of the post-bubble U.S. economy and is unlikely to create self-sustaining growth that will better the lives of most workers (Article 1.1).

Real GDP, or Gross Domestic Product adjusted for inflation, is the economist's measure of the value of economic output. Increases in real GDP define economic growth, and for economists, rising real GDP per capita shows that a nation is enjoying an improving standard of living. Our authors are not convinced. Jonathan Rowe argues that GDP actually counts environmental destruction, worsening health, and ruinous overconsumption as contributions to economic growth and national well-being (Article 1.2). While Rowe worries that GDP includes the wrong things, Lena Graber and John Miller discuss what it excludes: work in the home that is essential to

economic well-being. They report that counting home-based work—from cleaning to child care—would add 33% to 112% to the GDP of industrialized economies and even more to the GDP of developing economies (Graber and Miller, Article 1.3). Finally, in "Unemployment Rate Deception," Eoghan Stafford argues that the official unemployment rate is artificially low and that a more accurate measure would increase the July 2003 rate by more than half (Article 1.4).

DISCUSSION QUESTIONS

1) (Article 1.1) How has the current economic expansion of the U.S. economy done when it comes to economic growth and creating jobs? Compare the outlook for the U.S. economy in "High and Dry" with the predictions for the U.S. economy of the most recent *Wall Street Journal* survey of blue-chip economists (published in the beginning of January and July of every year in the *Wall Street Journal*).

2) (Article 1.1) In what ways have the post-bubble U.S. economy and policy responses been similar to or different from those in Japan after that country's economic boom ended? Have U.S. policymakers been effective in counteracting the threat of economic stagnation and in improving the economic prospects of most people?

3) (Article 1.2) How is GDP is measured, and what does it represent? What are Rowe's criticisms of GDP? Do you find them convincing?

4) (Article 1.2) Rowe discusses the Genuine Progress Indicator (GPI) as an alternative measure of economic progress. What are the differences between GDP per capita and the GPI? Which do you think provides a better measure of economic progress, and why?

5) (Article 1.3) Wages for housework might sound outlandish, but what are the economic justifications for valuing work in the home? Do you find them persuasive?

6) (Article 1.3) Suppose we decided that home-based work should be included in macroeconomic measures. That still leaves some practical questions. How should it be counted? And should work in the home be paid? If so, by whom?

7) (Article 1.4) Calculate the traditional Bureau of Labor Statistics (BLS) unemployment rate and describe how this measure treats involuntary part-time workers and people who want work but aren't actively looking. Show how the BLS unemployment rate can be adjusted to account for workers marginally attached to the labor force and for part-time workers who would prefer full-time work. Which unemployment rate do you think better represents the extent of unemployment, and why?

KEY TO COLANDER

"E1" means *Economics* chapter 1.
"M1" means *Macroeconomics* chapter 1.

This chapter is designed to be used with chapters E2 and E22-E23, or M2 and M6-M7.

Chapter E22 or M6 contains sections on dating business cycles and economic performance (the topic of Article 1.1) and measuring unemployment rates (the topic of Article 1.4).

Article 1.2 and 1.3 complement the section "Some Limitations of National Income Accounting" in chapter E23 or M7. Both Rowe and Colander discuss the Genuine Progress Indicator.

March/April 2004

HIGH AND DRY

THE ECONOMIC RECOVERY FAILS TO DELIVER

BY JOHN MILLER

This economy is pumped. Boosted by economic stimulants—military spending, tax rebates, interest rate cuts, and a spate of mortgage refinancing—the U.S. economy expanded at an 8.2% annual rate in the third quarter of 2003, its fastest pace in nearly two decades, and at a respectable 4% rate in the fourth quarter. The Dow is back over 10,000. Corporate profits are up. Business investment is improving, and consumer confidence is holding.

Predictably, the *Wall Street Journal*'s editors spent the winter holidays chortling about "the merry economy." The 55 blue-chip economists the *Journal* surveyed predict that economic growth will exceed 4% and the economy will create 1.5 million jobs this year, just in time for George W. Bush's election campaign.

Despite this ginned-up sense of economic well-being, the specter of stagnation—that the United States could go the way of Japan and sink into a decade-long economic funk—continues to haunt the U.S. economy.

The current wave of frenetic economic activity has done nothing to solve the underlying flaws of the post-bubble economy. Overcapacity, especially the hangover from the collapse of manufacturing and the dot-coms, oppressive consumer debt burdens, an ever-widening trade deficit, burgeoning budget deficits, and unprecedented inequality—all are still with us. And even after a heavy dose of economic stimulants, job creation in this recovery remains the worst on record.

The Bush administration has expended a lot of fiscal firepower to stimulate this recovery. But the administration's stimulants of choice are not generating a cumulative and self-sustaining economic expansion. What's more, the prescription on many of them is about to expire. Future tax cuts will go ever more exclusively to the well-to-do, resulting in less new consumer spending. The Fed has little room left to cut short-term interest rates. Higher long-term rates have already slowed mortgage refinancing. And that is to say nothing of the toxic side effects of the Bush team's economic antidepressants: they gut public-sector social spending and support an economic growth that does surprisingly little to improve the living standard of most people.

EIGHT MONTHS DOWN, THREE YEARS SIDEWAYS

Last July, the National Bureau of Economic Research (NBER) —the nation's official arbiter of the business cycle—declared that the recession that began in March 2001 had ended way back in November of that year, only eight months later. The 2001 recession was neither long nor deep. The average duration of post-World War II recessions is 11 months. And the output lost in the 2001 recession, measured by the decline in real Gross Domestic Product (GDP, the broadest single measure of economic output), was less than a third of the drop-off during the 1990-91 recession.

Why did it take the NBER's economists 20 months to recognize a recovery that was already underway? Because this recovery has been so weak that the NBER hesitated to declare the recession over. The economy fell for just eight months, but it has crawled sideways for nearly three years. Real personal income (income of households adjusted for inflation) has grown much more slowly than in past recoveries, and the economy has continued to lose jobs long after a typical recovery would have returned to pre-recession job numbers.

Instead of a robust recovery, the economy has entered "a twilight zone—growing fast enough to avoid an official recession but not fast enough to create jobs," according to Paul Krugman, economist and *New York Times* columnist. Economic growth averaged just 2.6% from the official end of the recession in November 2001 through the second quarter of 2003. Economic journalist William Greider warned that the U.S. economy was flirting with something far worse, "a low-grade depression." (See "The Japan Syndrome," page 10.)

RUNNING ON FUMES

At this January's World Economic Summit in Davos, Switzerland, Stephen Roach, chief economist at Morgan Stanley investment bank in New York, warned business leaders that "the main engine of the global economy, the ... U.S., is right now running on fumes." Tax cuts, home sales and mortgage refinancing fueled by low interest rates, and Iraq-driven military spending—not self-sustaining job and wage growth—fueled the 2003 growth spurt. Each of those additives to the economic fuel tank will be less able to power future economic growth, either because it's now in short supply or because it has gummed up the economic engine.

Take monetary policy. Interest rate cuts were key to keeping the weak, post-bubble economy out of a deep recession: they helped underwrite last year's surge in consumer spending on durable goods, especially housing and automobiles.

But the Fed will be hard pressed to coax more spending out of the economy. With the federal funds rate at 1%, there is not much room left for further rate cuts. In addition, interest rates on home mortgages are already rising. This will slow the spate of mortgage refinancing that put money in consumers' pockets in 2002 and 2003: over the last two years, half of all U.S. homeowners refinanced $4.5 trillion in mortgage debt.

On top of that, consumers are up to their eyeballs in debt. Debt service now claims a record 13% of disposable income, despite the interest rate cuts. Three years of a bear market have put a real dent in people's net worth, and less mortgage refinancing will do nothing good for the value of their homes. With employment lower than three years ago and wages stagnant, consumers sooner or later will stop spending, as Roach warns. In fact, by the end of last year the surge in consumer spending, especially for automobiles, had already cooled.

Fed interest-rate cuts never bolstered investment spending as much as consumer spending. Lingering excess productive capacity across the economy left businesses reluctant to make new investments. During much of the recovery, corporations have used the lower interest rates to pay down short-term debt and to buy back their own stock, not to add to capital spending.

Business investment did pick up considerably in the second half of 2003, posting its strongest gains since the first quarter of 2000. Robert Shapiro, economist with the centrist Progressive Policy Institute, says that "with consumer spending slowing, improved business fixed investment is now the strongest private sector support for the expansion in 2004." But even with the recent upswing in corporate spending, investment levels are quite modest. During the red-hot third quarter of last year, real business investment, as Shapiro himself emphasizes, was still 7% lower than it was in 2000 and was even below its average level during the 2001 recession.

Fed interest-rate cuts were also supposed to fix another obstacle to sustained economic growth and job creation: the gaping U.S. trade deficit. But the fix hasn't worked too well. (See "That Pesky Trade Deficit," page 12.)

FISCAL POLICY MISSES THE MARK

Fiscal policy, the manipulation of government spending and taxing policies, is just as problematic for sustaining economic growth as monetary policy. For the Bush administration, fiscal policy usually means just one thing: cutting taxes for the well-to-do. Three rounds of tax cuts for the rich, combined with last year's military spending for the Iraq war and its aftermath, have indeed shifted the government's fiscal status in a big way: the federal budget went from a $236 billion surplus in fiscal year 2000 to a $521 billion projected deficit in fiscal year 2004.

Such a powerful fiscal swing, the equivalent of about 7% of GDP, was sure to lift economic growth over the short term, almost regardless of the particulars. And Bush's fiscal policy did goose economic growth rates in 2003. When the invasion of Iraq gave rise to the biggest quarterly increase in military spending since the Korean War, GDP growth rates during the second quarter picked up from 2.0% to 3.1%, with economic analysts attributing three-quarters of the spike to government spending. Similarly, tax rebates over the summer added to the consumer spending that drove the third quarter GDP growth spurt.

But the limitations of the Bush team's attempt to punch up a sluggish economy for the election year have already begun to show. First off, future tax cuts will do less to add to consumer spending because they go ever more exclusively to the well-to-do, who spend a smaller share of their income than other taxpayers. Even in 2003, nearly half of taxpayers (49%) got $100 or less back in lower taxes, reports Citizens for Tax Justice. In 2005, that number rises to three-quarters of taxpayers, and it continues up from there. At the same time, nearly two-fifths of the Bush tax cut goes the richest 1%.

Second, the Bush stimulus package has done little or nothing to relieve the pressure on state and local budgets. With 30 states still facing between $39 and $41 billion in budget shortfalls in fiscal year 2005—the equivalent of 8% of their expenditures—more cutbacks in state spending are inevitable. Those state budget cuts are sapping the stimulative effect of any federal deficit spending. Nicholas Johnson, director of the State Fiscal Project at the Center on Budget and Policy Priorities, estimates that the state fiscal crisis is "taking at least half a percentage point out of the growth rate of the national economy."

The administration's failure to address the budget crisis in the states is not only trimming economic growth; it's also destroying critical programs. State budget cuts have hit working people and the poor especially hard. The federal government has shifted responsibility for social spending onto the states, and that is what's being cut. California, for instance, cut spending by $12 billion in the two years prior to last fall's recall election; schools there now go without computers, and public libraries are unable to purchase books. Nationwide, 34 states have cut programs such as Medicaid and the Children's Health Insurance Program

> DURING THE RED-HOT THIRD QUARTER OF 2003, REAL BUSINESS INVESTMENT WAS STILL 7% LOWER THAN IT WAS IN 2000 AND EVEN BELOW ITS AVERAGE LEVEL DURING THE 2001 RECESSION.

THE JAPAN SYNDROME: COULD IT HAPPEN HERE?

It isn't only left-leaning journalists sounding the alarm bells. Even the *Wall Street Journal* asked, "Is the U.S. economy at risk of emulating Japan's long swoon?"

During the 1980s, Japan enjoyed an economic boom as heady as the one the United States saw in the 1990s, complete with a soaring stock market and a red-hot housing market. But when the bubble burst, the Japanese economy sank into a decade-long economic slump. Japanese income growth slowed, falling behind the United States'. The Nikkei, Japan's major stock market index, lost three-quarters of its value from its peak in 1989. The Japanese real estate boom collapsed in 1991; in 2003, a house in Tokyo cost less than half of what it did in 1991. A tanking real estate sector and a slowing economy saddled Japanese banks with bad loans. Excess capacity, especially high for Japanese automakers, discouraged new investment and ensured that the slowdown would persist.

The 1990s boom in the United States came to a similar if less severe end. By 2000, the U.S. stock market bubble had burst. Broad measures of stock values lost about one-third of their peak values over the next two years. Manufacturing had already hit the skids. Industrial production fell steadily, contributing to a general excess of industrial capacity. Today, capacity utilization rates still hover at about 75%, and the manufacturing sector has shed jobs for some 42 straight months. The new economy fared no better. The NASDAQ, the high-tech stock index, melted down, losing nearly three-quarters of its value from March 2000 to July 2002, and gaggles of dot-com firms folded, putting plenty of white-collar workers out of work.

Only the continued strength of the U.S. real estate market, along with the willingness of debt-strapped U.S. consumers to spend, seemed to stand between the U.S. economy and Japan's fate. The Fed would add one more fac-

that provide health care to low- and moderate-income families.

And while fiscal stimulus might be pumping up measured growth rates, the Bush administration is running large deficits likely to be sustained even if investment spending continues to improve and labor markets eventually tighten. Those long-term structural deficits, as economists call them, could provide the political justification for further cutbacks in social and infrastructure spending necessary to put economic growth on a more solid footing. In fact, if the Bush tax cuts are made permanent, there would be no room in the federal budget for *any* domestic discretionary spending in just eight years, according to a recent study by Eugene Steuerle, a senior fellow at the Urban Institute. By 2012, entitlements (Social Security, Medicare, and Medicaid), military spending, and interest on the growing government debt would have absorbed all remaining federal revenues, leaving not a dollar for education, job training, housing, environment, community development, energy, public infrastructure, or other domestic programs. That would be a disaster not only for working families and children, as the Urban Institute emphasizes, but for the productivity of the U.S. economy as well.

JOBLESS RECOVERY TO JOB-LOSS RECOVERY

Whatever administration and Fed policies have done to produce an uptick in measured economic growth, they have done little to create jobs—the key to sustaining wage growth and a self-perpetuating economic expansion. And the Bush administration sure did promise new jobs. With the 2003 tax cut in place, the president's Council of Economic Advisors insisted, the economy would create 306,000 jobs a month from July 2003 to December 2004.

Hardly. When economic growth picked up in the final five months of 2003, the recovery finally stopped losing jobs. But the economy added a total of just 278,000 new jobs in those five months, with 80% of those job gains concentrated in temporary staffing, education, health care, and government. That is fewer jobs than the Bush team's promised *monthly* total.

Job creation in this recovery does not fall short just with respect to the administration's inflated promises, but by any reasonable measure. Even with those new jobs in the last five months of the year, the economy lost a net 331,000 jobs for 2003 on top of 1.5 million lost in 2002. The last time payroll employment declined for two consecutive years was in 1944 and 1945 as war production wound down. And that is a far cry from the average 300,000 new jobs per month the U.S. economy posted from 1995 to 2000.

Since the recession began 33 months ago, 2.4 million U.S. jobs have disappeared. Following every other post-World War II recession, jobs had fully recovered to their pre-recession levels within 31 months of the start of the recession. Worse yet, as a recent study by economists at the

New York Federal Reserve Bank shows, a far larger share of recent layoffs have been permanent, rather than the temporary cyclical layoffs dominant in most previous recessions.

The current recovery can't even stack up to the only other "jobless" recovery on record, the 1991-92 recovery that cost Bush's father re-election. *Business Week* calculates that to equal the job creation record of the early 1990s rebound, the economy would need to have *added* 3 million more private sector jobs by now, including 1,547,000 more manufacturing jobs and 707,000 more information technology jobs.

Jesse Jackson warned the 2000 Democratic Convention to "Stay out of the Bushes"—advice that should be taken seriously by anyone concerned with holding onto a job or finding a new one. We have gone from a jobless recovery under the elder Bush to a job-loss recovery under the younger Bush.

Employers are unwilling to add new jobs because they remain unconvinced that the economic recovery is sustainable. Instead of hiring new workers, bosses are squeezing more out of the old ones. This, along with corporate restructuring and layoffs, has produced rapid increases in productivity—the economy's output per hour of labor input. For instance, during the last two years, the hourly output of U.S. workers has gone up at a 5.3% pace, exceeding the "new economy" productivity growth rate of 2.6% from 1996 to 2001. For the first time in a postwar recovery, productivity is growing far faster than the economy.

Manufacturing has been especially devastated. Factory productivity has gone up by 15%, versus a 9% rise in the comparable period in the early 1990s. That has helped produce the longest string of manufacturing layoffs since the Great Depression. Ohio, Michigan, and Pennsylvania have each lost 200,000 or more manufacturing jobs since January 2001.

Another drain on U.S. job creation is the increasing number of jobs lost to global outsourcing. Not only manufacturing jobs are going abroad, but also white-collar work, from backroom office operations (bookkeeping, customer service, and marketing) to engineering and computer software design. Increased competition engendered by the Internet has allowed formerly non-tradable jobs to escape abroad in this latest bout of corporate cost-cutting. How many jobs are being lost to this global arbitrage, as economists call it, is a matter of dispute. There are no official data, but estimates range from 500,000 to 995,000 jobs since March 2001, or somewhere between 15% and 35% of the total decline in employment. Gregory Mankiw, the politically tone-deaf chair of Bush's Council of Economic Advisors, recently assured Americans that outsourcing is "a plus for the economy in the long run"—cold comfort for those who have seen their jobs move offshore.

Stephen Roach puts IT-enabled "offshoring" at the top of his list of possible explanations for the inability of this recovery to create jobs. "In my discussions with a broad

tor that insulated the U.S. economy against a Japan-style economic collapse: monetary policy. Ironically, it was the Fed's own repeated interest rate hikes in the second half of 1999 and the first half of 2000, along with the Clinton administration's downsizing of the federal government, that contributed mightily to bringing on the economic slowdown in the first place.

In the summer of 2002, the Fed devoted its annual retreat in Jackson Hole, Wyoming, to the threat of Japanese-style stagnation. Fed members and their boosters ended up assuring themselves that they had averted the threat by acting more quickly than Japanese central bankers had. While the Japanese central bank (CBJ) had waited nearly two years after the bubble burst to act, it then set about furiously cutting short-term interest rates, from 6% in 1991 to under 1% in 1995. The Fed did act more quickly than its Japanese counterpart, dropping the federal funds rate on overnight loans to commercial banks from 6.25% to 1.25% in just two years.

Has the Fed saved the day? That the U.S economy has muddled through the last three years with slow growth and is now in the midst of a growth spurt is enough for many to conclude that the threat of stagnation is behind us. But that would be a mistake. Japan's economy did not collapse into stagnation but slid gradually, as the Japanese bankers attending the Jackson Hole retreat emphasized. At the same time, economic forecasters repeatedly predicted that Japanese economic growth rates would soon pick up. Most ominously, Japan's real estate bubble burst a couple of years after its stock market bubble. If the housing market does fall apart, U.S. banks could end up in critical condition much as they did during the mid-1980s banking crisis that gripped much of the nation. And with U.S interest rates already close to zero, Pam Woodall, economics editor of the conservative British weekly the *Economist,* worries that "a housing bust might therefore nudge the economy into deflation."

THAT PESKY TRADE DEFICIT

The U.S. trade balance has steadily worsened during this recovery, as imports rose rapidly while exports did not. U.S. exports are just now topping their pre-recession levels. At a comparable point following the 1990-91 recession, exports were up 18%. Last year, the U.S. current account deficit, the broadest measure of the balance of trade in goods and services, surpassed 5% of GDP—the level financial analysts traditionally use as sign of financial distress in a developing economy.

The Fed's interest rate cuts were supposed to help. By lowering interest rates, the Fed would bring down the value of the dollar, making U.S exports cheaper for foreign purchasers. The value of the dollar has indeed fallen by about 12% since early 2002, with the largest drop occurring against the euro, but we have yet to see any improvement in the current account deficit.

What's more, depreciating the dollar is tricky business. Lower interest rates make U.S. bonds less attractive to investors. But financing this record trade deficit depends on the willingness of foreign investors to accumulate dollar assets almost without limit. Foreigners already supply 42% of the funds borrowed by U.S. households, businesses, and government. For instance, in 2002, foreigners purchased 58% of new Treasury debt. And foreign lenders are likely to demand higher compensation as the value of their dollar-denominated assets declines, driving up interest rates. Alternatively, some large foreign creditors might dump their dollar holdings, triggering a full-blown dollar crisis that would cause interest rates to spike and the U.S. stock and bond markets to tumble. Either way, the current account deficit is sure to dampen U.S. economic growth.

cross-section of business executives," reports Roach, "I was hard-pressed to find any who weren't contemplating white-collar offshoring."

Typically, economic stimulus policies activate "multiplier effects" that sustain economic growth over time. Higher government spending calls forth more output. Employers in turn hire more workers. New jobs put money in workers' pockets and empower workers who already have jobs to press for higher wages. And that fuels consumption. But without new jobs, that internally generated fuel is all but absent in the current upturn. Outsourcing and other trends

are eroding the bargaining position of U.S. workers; predictably, wage and salary disbursements are currently running some $350 billion below the path of previous upturns. With cost-saving productivity gains and the offshoring of jobs showing no sign of abating, there is little reason to believe that this recovery will soon be able to run on its own steam. More likely, the economy will continue to grow slowly but create few new jobs.

FACING UP TO OUR ECONOMIC PROBLEMS

This is no time to balance the budget. Dimitri Papadimitriou, president of the Levy Institute, a progressive economics think tank, estimates that the government sector as a whole (federal, state, and local) will have to run a deficit of 7% to 8% of GDP to keep the economy growing.

The public sector must both provide immediate economic stimulus and move to correct the economy's underlying problems through policies that will counteract economic stagnation and spread the benefits of economic growth more widely. Economic stimulus need not be toxic. Alternative policies are fully capable of jogging the economy back to life and at the same time creating jobs and making the economy stronger rather than weaker over the long haul.

Here is some of what has to happen. First, the Bush administration's pro-rich tax cuts, which provide less bang for the buck than more broad-based tax cuts, have to go. With 80% of taxpayers now paying more in payroll taxes than in income taxes, lowering payroll taxes would do more to boost consumer spending than cutting income taxes. But even payroll tax cuts, dollar for dollar, do less to stimulate economic growth than government spending. A one-dollar payroll tax cut adds just 90 cents to output in the following year, while a hike in unemployment benefits would generate $1 in output for each dollar the government spends, and one dollar in federal government spending to build up infrastructure would add an additional $1.80 in output over the next year, estimates David Wyss, chief economist at Standard & Poors.

There is still room for additional government outlays, especially if the Bush tax cuts for the super-rich are repealed. Relative to the size of the economy, the federal government is still no larger than its postwar average. And there is much to be done. To begin with, temporary federal unemployment benefits that were allowed to expire in December 2003 must be reinstated. Otherwise, by the middle of this year, an estimated two million unemployed people will see their benefits expire. The Bush budget proposal for fiscal year 2005 will cut another $6 billion in support for the states, but as much as an additional $100 billion in federal aid is needed to support cash-strapped states in the coming years.

Public investment, which has fallen to about *one-half* its levels during the 1960s and 1970s relative to the size of the economy, must be restored to maintain the nation's economic competitiveness. That means increased public investments in education, job training, and child care as well as in basic infrastructure, the environment, energy, and research and development. Many of these programs, especially spending on the environment and natural resources and on job training and employment services, have suffered deep cuts since 2000.

"In the end," as economist Anwar Shaikh points out, "government expenditures need to provide not only demand stimulus but also social stimulus." Otherwise, while GDP growth may be momentarily high(er), the well of sustained expansion and broad-based economic gains will stay dry.

Sources: "Jobless Recovery? Not in 2004, Economists Say," *WSJ*, 1/2/03; Jacob M. Schlesinger and Peter Landers, "Parallel Woes: Is the US Economy At Risk of Emulating Japan's Long Swoon?" *WSJ*, 11/7/01; Pam Woodall, "House of Cards," *The Economist*, 5/29/03; Nicholas Johnson and Bob Zahradnik, "State Budget Deficits Projected For FY2005," Center on Budget and Policy Priorities, 1/30/04; Louis Uchitelle, "Red Ink in States Beginning to Hurt Economic Recovery," *NYT*, 7/28/03; "The Hurting Heartland," *Business Week*, 12/15/03; "JobWatch," Economic Policy Institute, 1/04; Louis Uchitelle, "A Statistic That's Missing: Jobs That Moved Overseas," *NYT*, 10/5/03; James C. Cooper and Michael J. Mandel, "So Where Are The Jobs?" *Business Week*, 1/26/04; Jacob Schlesinger, "Bush's Early Electoral Edge: It's Not His Father's Economy," *WSJ*, 1/12/04; Stephen Roach, "False Recovery," *Morgan Stanley Global Economic Forum*, 1/12/04; Anwar Shaikh et al., "Deficits, Debts, and Growth: A Reprieve But Not a Pardon," Levy Economics Institute, 10/03; Randall Wray and Dimitri Papadimitriou, "Understanding Deflation: Treating The Disease, Not the Symphthoms," Levy Economics Institute, Winter 2004; Robert J. Shapiro, "Economic Recovery Remains Vulnerable to Setbacks," Center for American Progress, 12/22/03.

ARTICLE 1.2

July/August 1999

THE GROWTH CONSENSUS UNRAVELS

BY JONATHAN ROWE

Economics has been called the dismal science, but beneath its gray exterior is a system of belief worthy of Pollyanna.

Yes, economists manage to see a dark cloud in every silver lining. Downturn follows uptick, and inflation rears its ugly head. But there's a story within that story—a gauzy romance, a lyric ode to Stuff. It's built into the language. A thing produced is called a "good," for example, no questions asked. The word is more than just a term of art. It suggests the automatic benediction which economics bestows upon commodities of any kind.

By the same token, an activity for sale is called a "service." In conventional economics there are no "dis-services," no actions that might be better left undone. The bank that gouges you with ATM fees, the lawyer who runs up the bill—such things are "services" so long as someone pays. If a friend or neighbor fixes your plumbing for free, it's not a "service" and so it doesn't count.

The sum total of these products and activities is called the Gross Domestic Product, or GDP. If the GDP is greater this year than last, then the result is called "growth." There is no bad GDP and no bad growth; economics does not even have a word for such a thing. It does have a word for less growth. In such a case, economists say growth is "sluggish" and the economy is in "recession." No matter what is growing—more payments to doctors because of worsening health, more toxic cleanup—so long as there is more of it, then the economic mind declares it good.

This purports to be "objective science." In reality it is a rhetorical construct with the value judgments built in, and this rhetoric has been the basis of economic debate in the United States for the last half century at least. True, people have disagreed over how best to promote a rising GDP. Liberals generally wanted to use government more, conservatives less. But regarding the beneficence of a rising GDP, there has been little debate at all.

If anything, the Left traditionally has believed in growth with even greater fervor than the Right. It was John Maynard Keynes, after all, who devised the growth-boosting mechanisms of macroeconomic policy to combat the Depression of the 1930s; it was Keynesians who embraced these strategies after the War and turned the GDP into a totem. There's no point in seeking a bigger pie to redistribute to the poor, if you don't believe the expanding pie is desirable in the first place.

Today, however, the growth consensus is starting to unravel across the political spectrum and in ways that are both obvious and subtle. The issue is no longer just the impact of growth upon the environment—the toxic impacts of industry and the like. It now goes deeper, to what growth actually consists of and what it means in people's lives. The things economists call "goods" and "services" increasingly don't strike people as such. There is a growing disconnect between the way people experience growth and the way the policy establishment talks about it, and this gap is becoming an unspoken subtext to much of American political life.

> THERE IS A GROWING DISCONNECT BETWEEN THE WAY PEOPLE EXPERIENCE GROWTH AND THE WAY THE POLICY ESTABLISHMENT TALKS ABOUT IT.

The group most commonly associated with an antigrowth stance is environmentalists, of course. To be sure, one faction, the environmental economists, is trying to put green new wine into the old bottles of economic thought. If we would just make people pay the "true" cost of, say, the gasoline they burn, through the tax system for example, then the market would do the rest. We'd have benign, less-polluting growth, they say, perhaps even more than now. But the core of the environmental movement remains deeply suspicious of the growth ethos, and probably would be even if the environmental impacts somehow could be lessened.

In the middle are suburbanites who applaud growth in the abstract, but oppose the particular manifestations they see around them—the traffic, sprawl, and crowded schools. On the Right, meanwhile, an anti-growth politics is arising practically unnoticed. When social conservatives denounce gambling, pornography, or sex and violence in the media, they are talking about specific instances of the growth that their political leaders rhapsodize about on other days.

Environmentalists have been like social conservatives in one key respect. They have been moralistic regarding growth, often scolding people for enjoying themselves at the expense of future generations and the earth. Their concern is valid, up to a point—the consumer culture does promote the time horizon of a five-year-old. But politically it is not the most promising line of attack, and conceptually it concedes too much ground. To moralize about consumption as they do is to accept the conventional premise that it really is something chosen—an enjoyable form of self-indulgence that has unfortunate consequences for the earth.

That's "consumption" in the common parlance—the sport utility vehicle loading up at Wal-Mart, the stuff piling up in the basement and garage. But increasingly that's not what people actually experience, nor is it what the term really means. In economics, consumption means everything people spend money on, pleasurable or not. Wal-Mart is just one dimension of a much larger and increasingly unpleasant whole. The lawyers' fees for the house settlement or divorce; the repair work on the car after it was rear-ended; the cancer treatments for the uncle who was a three-pack-a-day smoker; the stress medications and weight loss regimens—all these and more are "consumption." They all go into the GDP.

Cancer treatments and lawyer's fees are not what come to mind when environmentalists lament the nation's excess consumption, or for that matter when economists applaud America's "consumers" for keeping the world economy afloat. Yet increasingly such things are what consumption actually consists of in the economy today. More and more, it consists not of pleasurable things that people choose, but rather of things that most people would gladly do without.

Much consumption today is addictive, for example. Millions of Americans are engaged in a grim daily struggle with themselves to do less of it. They want to eat less, drink less, smoke less, gamble less, talk less on the telephone—do less buying, period. Yet economic reasoning declares as growth and progress, that which people themselves regard as a tyrannical affliction.

Economists resist this reality of a divided self, because it would complicate their models beyond repair. They cling instead to an 18th-century model of human psychology—the "rational" and self-interested man—which assumes those complexities away. As David McClelland, the Harvard psychologist, once put it, economists "haven't even discovered Freud, let alone Abraham Maslow." (They also haven't discovered the Apostle Paul, who lamented that "the good that I would I do not, but the evil that I would not that I do.")

Then too there's the mounting expenditure that sellers foist upon people through machination and deceit. People don't choose to pay for the corrupt campaign finance system or for bloated executive pay packages. The cost of these is hidden in the prices that we pay at the store. As I write this, the *Washington Post* is reporting that Microsoft has hired Ralph Reed, former head of the Christian Coalition, and Grover Norquist, a right-wing polemicist, as lobbyists in Washington. When I bought this computer with Windows 95, Bill Gates never asked me whether I wanted to help support a bunch of Beltway operators like these.

This is compulsory consumption, not choice, and the economy is rife with it today. People don't choose to pay some $40 billion a year in telemarketing fraud. They don't choose to pay 32% more for prescription drugs than do people in Canada. ("Free trade" means that corporations are free to buy their labor and materials in other countries, but ordinary Americans aren't equally free to do their shopping there.) For that matter, people don't choose to spend $25 and up for ink-jet printer cartridges. The manufacturers design the printers to make money on the cartridges because, as the *Wall Street Journal* put it, that's "where the big profit margins are."

Yet another category of consumption that most people would gladly do without arises from the need to deal with the offshoots and implications of growth. Bottled water has become a multibillion dollar business in the United States because people don't trust what comes from the tap. There's a growing market for sound insulation and double-pane windows because the economy produces so much noise. A wide array of physical and social stresses arise from the activities that get lumped into the euphemistic term "growth."

The economy in such cases doesn't solve problems so much as create new problems that require more expenditure to solve. Food is supposed to sustain people, for example. But today the dis-economies of eating sustain the GDP instead. The food industry spends some $21 billion a year on advertising to entice people to eat food they don't need. Not coincidentally, there's now a $32 billion diet and weight loss industry to help people take off the pounds that inevitably result. When that doesn't work, which is often, there is always the vacuum pump or knife. There were some 110,000 liposuctions in the United States last year; at five pounds each that's some 275 tons of flab up the tube.

It is a grueling cycle of indulgence and repentance, binge and purge. Yet each stage of this miserable experience, viewed through the pollyanic lens of economics, becomes growth and therefore good. The problem here goes far beyond the old critique of how the consumer culture cultivates feelings of inadequacy, lack, and need so people will buy and buy again. Now this culture actually makes life worse, in order to sell solutions that purport to make it better.

Traffic shows this syndrome in a finely developed form. First we build sprawling suburbs so people need a car to go almost anywhere. The resulting long commutes are daily torture but help build up the GDP. Americans spend some

MEASURING PROGRESS

Far from being a true measure of economic (and human) progress, the GDP thrives on bad news. The GDP soars when the government spends millions to clean up a toxic waste site or to treat those suffering from cancer who lived nearby. And the GDP can drop from some very good news. For instance, it is good news for a family if a parent can afford to cut back on work and devote more hours at home. But because she is working less, spending less money on day care, and earning less, the GDP measures it as a drop in economic activity.

In the mid-1990s, the San Francisco group Redefining Progress created an alternative GDP that measures the costs as well as the benefits of economic growth. The "Genuine Progress Indicator," or GPI, accounts for how production and consumption create social ills like inequality, and creates environmental problems that threaten future generations, such as global warming and the depletion of natural resources. It adjusts the GDP downward to account for each of these aspects of economic activity, along with underemployment and the loss of leisure time. It would adjust the GDP upward if there had been more leisure time and social progress.

The result: while the GPI rose somewhat between 1950 and the early 1970s, it has been falling ever since. By 1994 the GPI was 26% lower than in 1973. During the same period, the GDP was growing.

$5 billion a year in gasoline alone while they sit in traffic and go nowhere. As the price of gas increases, this growth sector will expand.

Commerce deplores a vacuum, and the exasperating hours in the car have spawned a booming subeconomy of relaxation tapes, cell phones, even special bibs. Billboards have 1-800 numbers so commuters can shop while they stew. Talk radio thrives on traffic-bound commuters, which accounts for some of the contentious, get-out-of-my-face tone. The traffic also helps sustain a $130 billion-a-year car wreck industry; and if Gates succeeds in getting computers into cars, that sector should get a major boost.

The health implications also are good for growth. Los Angeles, which has the worst traffic in the nation, also leads—if that's the word—in hospital admissions due to respiratory ailments. The resulting medical bills go into the GDP. And while Americans sit in traffic they aren't walking or getting exercise. More likely they are entertaining themselves orally with a glazed donut or a Big Mac, which helps explain why the portion of middle-aged Americans who are clinically obese has doubled since the 1960s.

C. Everett Koop, the former Surgeon General, estimates that some 70% of the nation's medical expenses are lifestyle-induced. Yet the same lifestyle that promotes disease also produces a rising GDP. (Keynes observed that traditional virtues like thrift are bad for growth; now it appears that health is bad for growth too.) We literally are growing ourselves sick, and this puts a grim new twist on the economic doctrine of "complementary goods," which describes the way new products tend to spawn a host of others. The automobile gave rise to car wash franchises, drive-in restaurants, fuzz busters, tire dumps, and so forth. Television produced an antenna industry, VCRs, soap magazines, ad infinitum. The texts present this phenomenon as the wondrous perpetual motion machine of the market—goods beget more goods. But now the machine is producing complementary ills and collateral damages instead.

PEOPLE DON'T CHOOSE TO PAY SOME $40 BILLION A YEAR IN TELEMARKETING FRAUD. THEY DON'T CHOOSE TO PAY 32% MORE FOR PRESCRIPTION DRUGS THAN DO PEOPLE IN CANADA.

Suggestive of this new dynamic is a pesticide plant in Richmond, California, which is owned by a transnational corporation that also makes the breast cancer drug tamoxifen. Many researchers believe that pesticides, and the toxins created in the production of them, play a role in breast cancer. "It's a pretty good deal," a local physician told the *East Bay Express*, a Bay Area weekly. "First you cause the cancer, then you profit from curing it." Both the alleged cause and cure make the GDP go up, and this syndrome has become a central dynamic of growth in the U.S. today.

Mainstream economists would argue that this is all beside the point. If people didn't have to spend money on such things as commuting or medical costs, they'd simply spend it on something else, they say. Growth would be the same or even greater, so the actual content of growth should be of little concern to those who promote it. That view holds sway in the nation's policy councils; as a result we try continually to grow our way out of problems, when increasingly we are growing our way in.

To the extent that conventional economics has raised an eyebrow at growth, it has done so mainly through the concept of "externalities." These are negative side effects suffered by those not party to a transaction between a buyer and a seller. Man buys car, car pollutes air, others suffer that "externality." As the language implies, anything outside the original transaction is deemed secondary, a subordinate reality, and therefore easily overlooked. More, the effects upon buyer and seller—the "internalities," one might say—are assumed to be good.

Today, however, that mental schema is collapsing. Externalities are starting to overwhelm internalities. A single jet ski can cause more misery for the people who reside by a lake, than it gives pleasure to the person riding it.

More importantly, and as just discussed, internalities themselves are coming into question, and with them the assumption of choice, which is the moral linchpin of market thought.

If people choose what they buy, as market theory posits, then—externalities aside—the sum total of all their buying must be the greatest good of all. That's the ideology behind the GDP. But if people don't always choose, then the model starts to fall apart, which is what is happening today. The practical implications are obvious. If growth consists increasingly of problems rather than solutions, then scolding people for consuming too much is barking up the wrong tree. It is possible to talk instead about ridding our lives of what we don't want as well as forsaking what we do want—or think we want.

Politically this is a more promising path. But to where? The economy may be turning into a kind of round robin of difficulty and affliction, but we are all tied to the game. The sickness industry employs a lot of people, as do ad agencies and trash haulers. The fastest-growing occupations in the country include debt collectors and prison guards. What would we do without our problems and dysfunctions?

The problem is especially acute for those at the bottom of the income scale who have not shared much in the apparent prosperity. For them, a bigger piece of a bad pie might be better than none.

This is the economic conundrum of our age. No one has more than pieces of an answer, but it helps to see that much growth today is really an optical illusion created by accounting tricks. The official tally ignores totally the cost side of the growth ledger—the toll of traffic upon our time and health, for example. In fact, it actually counts such costs as growth and gain. By the same token, the official tally ignores the economic contributions of the natural environment and the social structure; so that the more the economy destroys these, and puts commoditized substitutes in their places, the more the experts say the economy has "grown." Pollute the lakes and oceans so that people have to join private swim clubs and the economy grows. Erode the social infrastructure of community so people have to buy services from the market instead of getting help from their neighbors, and it grows some more. The real economy—the one that sustains us—has diminished. All that has grown is the need to buy commoditized substitutes for things we used to have for free.

So one might rephrase the question thus: how do we achieve real growth, as opposed to the statistical illusion that passes for growth today? Four decades ago, John Kenneth Galbraith argued in *The Affluent Society* that conventional economic reasoning is rapidly becoming obsolete. An economics based upon scarcity simply doesn't work in an economy of hyper-abundance, he said. If it takes a $200 billion (today) advertising industry to maintain what economists quaintly call "demand," then perhaps that demand isn't as urgent as conventional theory posits. Perhaps it's not even demand in any sane meaning of the word.

Galbraith argued that genuine economy called for shifting some resources from consumption that needs to be prodded, to needs which are indisputably great: schools, parks, older people, the inner cities and the like. For this he was skewered as a proto-socialist. Yet today the case is even stronger, as advertisers worm into virtually every waking moment in a desperate effort to keep the growth machine on track.

Galbraith was arguing for a larger public sector. But that brings dysfunctions of its own, such as bureaucracy; and it depends upon an enlarging private sector as a fiscal base to begin with. Today we need to go further, and establish new ground rules for the economy, so that it produces more genuine growth on its own. We also need to find ways to revive the nonmarket economy of informal community exchange, so that people do not need money to meet every single life need.

In the first category, environmental fiscal policy can help. While the corporate world has flogged workers to be more productive, resources such as petroleum have been in effect loafing on the job. If we used these more efficiently the result could be jobs and growth, even in conventional terms, with less environmental pollution. If we used land more efficiently—that is, reduced urban sprawl—the social and environmental gains would be great.

Another ground rule is the corporate charter laws. We need to restore these to their original purpose: to keep large business organizations within the compass of the common good. But such shifts can do only so much. More efficient cars might simply encourage more traffic, for example. Cheap renewable power for electronic devices could encourage more noise. In other words, the answer won't just be a more efficient version of what we do now. Sooner or later we'll need different ways of thinking about work and growth and how we allocate the means of life.

This is where the social economy comes in, the informal exchange between neighbors and friends. There are some promising trends. One is the return to the traditional village model in housing. Structure does affect content. When houses are close together, and people can walk to stores and work, it encourages the spontaneous social interaction that nurtures real community. New local currencies, such as Time Dollars, provide a kind of lattice work upon which informal nonmarket exchange can take root and grow.

Changes like these are off the grid of economics as conventionally defined. It took centuries for the market to emerge from the stagnation of feudalism. The next organizing principle, whatever it is, most likely will emerge slowly as well. This much we can say with certainty. As the market hurtles towards multiple implosions, social and environmental as well as financial, it is just possible that the economics profession is going to have to do what it constantly lectures the rest of us to do: adjust to new realities and show a willingness to change.

July/August 2002

WAGES FOR HOUSEWORK

THE MOVEMENT AND THE NUMBERS

BY LENA GRABER AND JOHN MILLER

The International Wages for Housework Campaign (WFH), a network of women in Third World and industrialized countries, began organizing in the early 1970s. WFH's demands are ambitious—"for the unwaged work that women do to be recognized as work in official government statistics, and for this work to be paid."

Housewives paid wages? By the government? That may seem outlandish to some, but consider the staggering amount of unpaid work carried out by women. In 1990, the International Labor Organization (ILO) estimated that women do two-thirds of the world's work for 5% of the income. In 1995, the UN Development Programme's (UNDP) Human Development Report announced that women's unpaid and underpaid labor was worth $11 trillion worldwide, and $1.4 trillion in the United States alone. Paying women the wages they "are owed" for unwaged work, as WFN puts it, would go a long way toward undoing these inequities and reducing women's economic dependence on men.

Publicizing information like this, WFH—whose International Women Count Network now includes more than 2,000 non-governmental organizations (NGOs) from the North and South—and other groups have been remarkably successful in persuading governments to count unwaged work. In 1995, the UN Fourth World Conference on Women, held in Beijing, developed a Platform for Action that called on governments to calculate the value of women's unpaid work and include it in conventional measures of national output, such as Gross Domestic Product (GDP).

So far, only Trinidad & Tobago and Spain have passed legislation mandating the new accounting, but other countries—including numerous European countries, Australia, Canada, Japan, and New Zealand in the industrialized world, and Bangladesh, the Dominican Republic, India, Nepal, Tanzania, and Venezuela in the developing world—have undertaken extensive surveys to determine how much time is spent on unpaid household work.

THE VALUE OF HOUSEWORK

Producing credible numbers for the value of women's work in the home is no easy task. Calculating how many hours women spend performing housework—from cleaning to childcare to cooking to shopping—is just the first step. The hours are considerable in both developing and industrialized economies. (See Table 1.)

What value to place on that work, and what would constitute fair remuneration—or wages for housework—is even more difficult to assess. Feminist economists dedicated to making the value of housework visible have taken different approaches to answering the question. One approach, favored by the UN's International Research and Training Institute for the Advancement of Women (INSTRAW), bases the market value of work done at home on the price of market goods and services that are similar to those produced in the home (such as meals served in restaurants or cleaning done by professional firms). These output-based evaluations estimate that counting unpaid household production would add 30-60% to the GDP of industrialized countries, and far more for developing countries. (See Table 2.)

A second approach evaluates the inputs of household production—principally the labor that goes into cooking, cleaning, childcare, and other services performed in the home, overwhelmingly by women. Advocates of this approach use one of three methods. Some base their calculations on what economists call opportunity cost—the wages women might have earned if they had worked a similar number of hours in the market economy. Others ask what it would cost to hire someone to do the work—either a general laborer such as a domestic servant (the generalist-replacement method) or a specialist such as a chef (the specialist-replacement method)—and then assign those wages to household labor. Ann Chadeau, a researcher with the Organization for Economic Cooperation and Development, has found the specialist-replacement method to be "the most plausible and at the same time feasible approach" for valuing unpaid household labor.

These techniques produce quite different results, all of which are substantial in relation to GDP. With that in mind, let's look at how some countries calculated the monetary value of unpaid work.

UNPAID WORK IN CANADA, GREAT BRITAIN, AND JAPAN

In Canada, a government survey documented the time men and women spent on unpaid work in 1992. Canadian women performed 65% of all unpaid work, shouldering an especially large share of household labor devoted to preparing meals, maintaining clothing, and caring for children. (Men's unpaid hours exceeded women's only for outdoor cleaning.)

The value of unpaid labor varied substantially, depending on the method used to estimate its appropriate wage. (See Table 3.) The opportunity-cost method, which uses the average market wage (weighted for the greater proportion of unpaid work done by women), assigned the highest value to unpaid labor, 54.2% of Canadian GDP. The two replacement methods produced lower estimates, because the wages they assigned fell below those of other jobs. The specialist-replacement method, which paired unpaid activities with the average wages of corresponding occupations—such as cooking with junior chefs, and childcare with kindergarten teachers—put the value of Canadian unpaid labor at 43% of GDP. The generalist-replacement method, by assigning the wages of household servants to unpaid labor, produced the lowest estimate of the value of unpaid work: 34% of Canadian GDP. INSTRAW's output-based measure, which matched hours of unpaid labor to a household's average expenditures on the same activities, calculated the value of Canada's unpaid work as 47.4% of GDP.

In Great Britain, where unpaid labor hours are high for an industrialized country (see Table 1), the value of unpaid labor was far greater relative to GDP. The British Office for National Statistics found that, when valued using the opportunity cost method, unpaid work was 112% of Britain's GDP in 1995! With the specialist-replacement method, British unpaid labor was still 56% of GDP—greater than the output of the United Kingdom's entire manufacturing sector for the year.

In Japan—where unpaid labor hours are more limited (see Table 1), paid workers put in longer hours, and women perform over 80% of unpaid work—the value of unpaid labor is significantly smaller relative to GDP. The Japanese Economic Planning Agency calculated that counting unpaid work in 1996 would add between 15.2% (generalist-replacement method) and 23% (opportunity-cost method) to GDP. Even at those levels, the value of unpaid labor still equaled at least half of Japanese women's market wages.

HOUSEWORK NOT BOMBS

While estimates vary by country and evaluation method, all of these calculations make clear that recognizing the value of unpaid household labor profoundly alters our perception of economic activity and women's contributions to production. "Had household production been included in the system of macro-economic accounts," notes Ann Chadeau, "governments may well have implemented quite different economic and social policies."

For example, according to the UNDP, "The inescapable implication [of recognizing women's unpaid labor] is that the fruits of society's total labor should be shared more equally." For the UNDP, this would mean radically altering property and inheritance rights; access to credit; entitlement to social security benefits, tax incentives, and child care; and terms of divorce settlements.

For WFH advocates, the implications are inescapable as well: women's unpaid labor should be paid—and "the money," WFH insists, "must come first of all from military spending."

Here in the United States, an unneeded and dangerous military buildup begun last year has already pushed up military spending from 3% to 4% of GDP. Devoting just the additional 1% of GDP gobbled up by the military budget to wages for housework—far from being outlandish—

TABLE 1
WOMEN'S TIME SPENT PER DAY PERFORMING HOUSEHOLD LABOR, BY ACTIVITY, IN HOURS:MINUTES

Country	Childcare Time	Cleaning Time	Food Prep Time	Shopping Time	Water/Fuel Collection	Total Time[a]
Australia (1997[b])	2:27	1:17	1:29	0:58	n.a.	3:39
Japan (1999)	0:24	2:37	n.a.	0:33	n.a.	3:34
Norway (2000)	0:42	1:16	0:49	0:26	0:01	3:56
U.K. (2000)	1:26	1:35	1:08	0:33	n.a.	4:55
Nepal (1996)	1:28	2:00	5:30	0:13	1:10	11:58

Note: Some activities, especially childcare, may overlap with other tasks.

[a] Totals may include activities other than those listed.

[b] Only some percentage of the population recorded doing these activities. Averages are for that portion of the population. Generally, figures represent a greater number of women than men involved.

Sources: Australia: <www.abs.gov.au/ausstats>; Japan: <www.unescap.org/stat>; Norway: <www.ssb.no/tidsbruk_en>; United Kingdom: <www.statistics.gov.uk/themes/social_finances/TimeUseSurvey>; Nepal: INSTRAW, *Valuation of Household Production and the Satellite Accounts* (Santo Domingo: 1996), 34-35; <www.cbs.nl/isi/iass>.

TABLE 2

VALUE OF UNPAID HOUSEHOLD LABOR AS % OF GDP, USING OUTPUT-BASED EVALUATION METHOD

Country	% of GDP
Canada (1992)	47.4%
Finland (1990)	49.1%
Nepal (1991)	170.7%

Source: INSTRAW, *Valuation of Household Production and the Satellite Accounts* (Santo Domingo, 1996), 62, 229.

TABLE 3

VALUE OF UNPAID HOUSEHOLD LABOR IN CANADA AS % OF GDP, 1992

Evaluation Method	% of GDP
Opportunity Cost (before taxes)	54.2 %
Specialist-Replacement	43.0%
Generalist-Replacement	34.0%
Output-Based	47.4%

Source: INSTRAW, *Valuation of Household Production and the Satellite Accounts* (Santo Domingo: 1996), 229.

would be an important first step toward fairly remunerating women who perform much-needed and life-sustaining household work.

Resources: Ann Chadeau, "What is Households' Non-Market Production Worth?" *OECD Economic Studies* No. 18 (Spring 1992); Economic Planning Unit, Department of National Accounts, Japan, "Monetary Valuation of Unpaid Work in 1996" <unstats.un.org/unsd/methods/timeuse/tusresource_papers/japanunpaid.htm>; INSTRAW, *Measurement and Valuation of Unpaid Contribution: Accounting Through Time and Output* (Santo Domingo: 1995); INSTRAW, *Valuation of Household Production and the Satellite Accounts* (Santo Domingo: 1996); Office of National Statistics, United Kingdom, "A Household Satellite Account for the UK," by Linda Murgatroyd and Henry Neuberger, *Economic Trends* (October 1997) <www.statistics.gov.uk/hhsa/hhsa/Index.html>; Hilkka Pietilä, "The Triangle of the Human Ecology: Household-Cultivation-Industrial Production," *Ecological Economics Journal* 20 (1997); UN Development Programme, Human Development Report (New York: Oxford University Press, 1995); Wages For Housework <ourworld.compuserve.com/homepages/crossroadswomenscentre/WFH.html>

ARTICLE 1.4

September/October 2004

UNEMPLOYMENT RATE DECEPTION

BY EOGHAN STAFFORD

When June's dismal unemployment data came out (at 6.4%, the official unemployment rate hit its highest level in nine years), the administration was quick to put a positive spin on the news. "While the unemployment rate is disappointing," Labor Secretary Elaine Chao reassured us, "it can be viewed as an indication of renewed confidence in the economy with the increased labor-force participation rate." In other words, the jump in unemployment reflects renewed optimism among the jobless—or so the administration would have the country believe.

The key to understanding Secretary Chao's statement lies in the way unemployment is figured. The official unemployment rate, as calculated by the Bureau of Labor Statistics (BLS), includes only jobless people who have looked for work in the previous four weeks—the unemployed who are "in the labor force." The BLS considers people who want jobs but don't have them and who have sought work in the past year but not in the past month to be "marginally attached" to the labor force, whatever their reason for not looking. Those who give an economic reason (for example, they were previously unable to find work in their field, they feel they need more training, or they suffered discrimination in hiring) are considered "discouraged workers," a subset of the marginally attached.

Secretary Chao suggests that official unemployment increased because the labor force increased; some of the marginally attached felt optimistic enough about their prospects to take up new job searches. But this would be cause for optimism only if the increase in the labor force (up 611,000) coincided with a decline in the number of the marginally attached. In actuality, the ranks of the marginally attached increased by about 40,000 between May and June. In addition, during that same period, another 444,000 people began working part-time despite wanting full-time work.

The secretary's attempt to spin the news inadvertently points to a yet larger issue: The official unemployment rate actually understates the the extent of unemployment. A more realistic unemployment rate—one that includes the marginally attached—is shown in Table 1. Counting all marginally attached individuals (discouraged workers plus the rest of the marginally attached) as unemployed brings June's unemployment rate up to 7.3%. If those working part-time involuntarily are added (by counting them as unemployed—the BLS considers them employed), the figure climbs to 10.5%. In total, the government's official measure of unemployment disregards nearly 7 million people who are unemployed or underemployed. (The tables are based on July 2003 BLS data.)

The administration's downplaying of the scale of unemployment is matched by its silence about the effects of the economic downturn on workers of color. Although both white and black workers entered the labor force in June, white workers gained jobs overall, while black workers lost jobs (despite searching for positions in growing numbers). (See Tables 2 and 3.) Racial inequity in the job market is nothing new. Over the past decade, the unemployment rate among African Americans was always more than double that of Whites. (See Table 4.) In the boom year of 1998, African-American unemployment was worse than white unemployment in the recessionary year of 2003. Today African-American unemployment has reached crisis proportions at 10.8%—and that's just the *official* rate.

Common sense might tell you that the millions of jobless and underemployed workers, huge gaps in the employment prospects of different races, and a swelling pool of jobless, disenfranchised youth call for urgent reform. But judging by its complete silence on these issues, the administration appears not to think so—or not to care.

Resources: Bureau of Labor Statistics <www.bls.gov>; "Unemployment Rate Jumps, While Payrolls Decline," Economic Policy Institute (July 3, 2003).

TABLE 1
ALTERNATIVE UNEMPLOYMENT RATE, JULY 2003*

	Rate	Thousands**
Unemployed (official)	6.3%	9,313
+ discouraged workers	6.6%	9,788
+ other marginally attached	7.3%	10,907
+ involuntarily part-time	10.5%	16,250

*Not seasonally adjusted
**Cumulative total

TABLE 2
LABOR FORCE BY RACE (IN THOUSANDS)

	May	June	Change
White	120,420	120,881	+0.38%
African-American	16,618	16,717	+0.59%

TABLE 3
EMPLOYED PERSONS BY RACE (IN THOUSANDS)

	May	June	Change
White	113,882	114,203	+0.28%
African-American	14,819	14,746	–0.49%

TABLE 4
ANNUAL AVERAGE OF MONTHLY UNEMPLOYMENT RATES BY ETHNICITY

	1993	1998	2003*
Whites	6.1%	3.9%	5.3%
Hispanics	10.7%	7.2%	7.8%
African Americans	11.5%	8.9%	10.8%

*January through July

CHAPTER 2
Wealth and Inequality

INTRODUCTION

Wealth and inequality are both end products of today's economic growth. But while all macroeconomics textbooks investigate wealth *accumulation*, most give less attention to wealth *disparities*. The authors in this chapter fill in the gap by looking at who makes out, and who doesn't, with the accumulation of wealth.

"Inequality by the Numbers" (Article 2.1) starts the discussion by providing hard numbers on income and wealth gaps. Inequality in the United States has reached levels unseen since the Great Depression. That is true for income (how much you or your family makes in a year) and wealth (the assets you or your family own minus your debts). Today, the top 1% of households own nearly two-fifths of the nation's wealth; the richest 20 percent get one-half of our national income.

All told, greater wealth hasn't made for greater equality or social mobility. As Paul Krugman reports, it is not just left critics who say so, but the business press as well. The number of people who go from rags to riches—while always so few as to be near-mythical—has become even smaller since 1980 (Article 2.3). And, as John Miller (Article 2.2) documents, the current economic recovery has done less to improve wages than any other recovery since World War II. With economic advancement more limited than at any time in three decades, Ellen Frank (Article 2.4) argues that increasing social wealth—through improved social insurance programs like Social Security, unemployment insurance, better public education and publicly-financed higher education and health care—will do more to enrich most people than any attempt to promote private savings, for example, by creating tax-favored savings plans.

Worst of all, it didn't have to be this way. Chris Tilly debunks the myth that inequality is necessary for economic growth, showing that among both developing and industrial economies and across regions within countries, there is no correlation between higher levels of inequality and faster economic growth. He argues that greater equality does not kill off economic growth, but actually supports it by bolstering spending, promoting agricultural and industrial productivity, and lessening social conflict (Article 2.5).

DISCUSSION QUESTIONS

1) (General) The authors in this chapter believe that the distribution of wealth is as important as wealth itself, and consider greater economic equality an important macroeconomic goal. What are some arguments for and against this position? Where do you come down in the debate?

2) (Articles 2.1, 2.2, 2.3) Who benefited from the wealth accumulation of the 1990s? How did stockholders fare versus wage earners? How did the concentration of wealth holding by income group and by race change during the decade?

3) (Articles 2.1, 2.2, 2.3) "A rising tide lifts all boats," proclaimed John F. Kennedy as he lobbied for pro-business tax cuts in the early 1960s. Did the 1990s boom and the current economic recovery lift all boats? What do the changes in income, wealth, and poverty suggest?

4) (Article 2.3) The "New Economy" fed the myth that anyone can get rich quick in this country, but Paul Krugman says it just ain't so. What evidence does he present to argue that social mobility is declining? Do you find his evidence persuasive?

5) (Article 2.4) How would the improved social insurance programs that Ellen Frank advocates resolve the paradox of thrift and enhance social mobility and wealth accumulation for most people? Does Frank's approach to augmenting social wealth make good economic sense?

6) (Article 2.5) Why do conservatives argue that inequality is good for economic growth? What counterarguments does Tilly use to challenge this traditional view of the tradeoff between inequality and growth? What evidence convinces Tilly that equality is good for economic growth? Does that evidence convince you?

KEY TO COLANDER

E = Economics. M = Macroeconomics.

This chapter fits with chapters E22-E23 or M6-M7; and informs chapters E24-E26 or M8-M10. Inequality and wealth accumulation are also important topics in chapters on monetary policy (E27-E28; M11-M12), inflation, unemployment, and growth (E29; M13) and the section "Policy Issues In Depth" (E30-E31; M14-M15).

Articles 2.1, 2.2, and 2.3 fit with chapter E22 or M6, and the discussion of who benefits from the "New Economy" in chapter E29 or M13.

Article 2.4 goes well with E22 or M6 and Article 2.5 fits with any discussion of the requisites for growth, such as chapter E24 or M8.

January/February 2004, revised October 2004

WEALTH INEQUALITY BY THE NUMBERS

BY DOLLARS & SENSE AND UNITED FOR A FAIR ECONOMY

INCOME INEQUALITY IN 1970, 1980, 1990, AND 2003

Household	Mean Income (in 2003)	Share of Aggregate Income			
		1970	1980	1990	2003
Lowest Fifth	$9,996	4.1%	4.3%	3.9%	3.4%
Second Fifth	$25,678	10.8%	10.3%	9.6%	8.7%
Third Fifth	$43,588	17.4%	16.9%	15.9%	14.8%
Fourth Fifth	$68,994	24.5%	24.9%	24.0%	23.4%
Highest Fifth	$147,078	43.0%	43.7%	46.6%	49.8%
Top 5%	$253,239	16.6%	15.8%	18.6%	21.4%

Source: U.S. Bureau of the Census, Historical Tables H-1 and H-2.

THE WEALTH PIE

The wealthiest 1% of households owns almost a third of the nation's household wealth. The next tier, those in the 95th through 98th percentiles, claims another 25%. While the top 5% holds well over half of the wealth pie, the bottom 50% makes do with the crumbs—holding a meager 2.8% of total net worth.

Source: Arthur B. Kennickell, "A Rolling Tide."

INCOME INEQUALITY

Income has never been distributed equally in the United States, but over the past thirty years the gap has been widening. The top 20% now gets half of all the national income, up from 43% in 1970. The top 5% claims over a fifth. The mean income for the top fifth of households is nearly 15 times more than that of the bottom fifth.

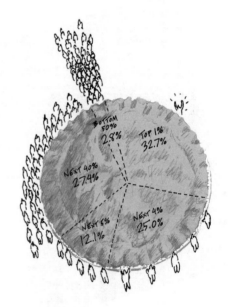

NICK THORKELSON

THE WEALTHLESS

The 1980s and 1990s were supposed to be economic good times, but the share of Americans with no wealth at all was larger in 2001 than it had been in 1983. The late-1990s economy gave a small boost to those at the bottom, but it didn't make up for the losses of the previous 15 years. The result: even after the 1990s—the most fabulous decade of economic growth in recent U.S. history—over a quarter of American households had less than $5,000 in assets.

HOUSEHOLDS WITH LITTLE OR NO NET WORTH, 1983–2001

	Percentage of households with zero or negative net worth*	Percentage of households with net worth less than $5,000*
1983	15.5%	25.4%
1989	17.9%	27.6%
1992	18.0%	27.2%
1995	18.5%	27.8%
1998	18.0%	27.7%
2001	17.6%	26.6%

* Constant 1995 dollars. Excluding the value of automobiles.

Source: Edward N. Wolff, "Changes in Household Wealth." Studies of wealth ownership define wealth differently. Because Wolff subtracts the value of automobiles, his figures show a higher percentage of the population with little or no wealth than studies that include cars as wealth.

THE SUPER-RICH

Over a 30-year period beginning in 1970, the richest 1% (as ranked by income) accrued a mounting share of the nation's private wealth. Throughout the 1990s, the top percentile held a larger concentration of total household wealth than at any time since the 1920s. Its wealth share declined somewhat during the 2001 recession, thanks to falling corporate share prices, but remained above 33%.

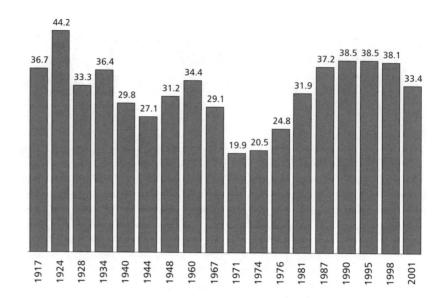

PERCENTAGE SHARE OF HOUSEHOLD WEALTH HELD BY THE TOP 1%, 1917–2001

Sources: Edward N. Wolff, *Top Heavy,* The New Press, 2002 (for 1917-1989) and Wolff, "Recent Trends in Wealth Ownership 1983-1998," Jerome Levy Economics Institute, April 2000 (for 1992-1998).

MEDIAN FINANCIAL ASSETS, NONFINANCIAL ASSETS, AND DEBT BY RACE, 2001

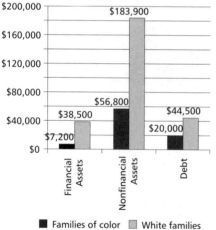

■ Families of color ▨ White families

Source: Ana M. Aizcorbe, Arthur B. Kennickell, and Kevin B. Moore, "Recent Changes in U.S. Family Finances: Evidence from the 1998 and 2001 Survey of Consumer Finances," *Federal Reserve Bulletin,* vol. 89 (January 2003). Also see "African Americans Have Less Wealth and More Debt than White Americans," <www.FairEconomy.org>.

THE RACIAL WEALTH GAP

The United States has a racial wealth gap that far exceeds its racial income gap. This wealth gap persists even during periods of economic growth. Over the course of the 1990s boom, the wealth of families of color (non-white and Latinos of all races) actually *fell.* This intransigent wealth gap is the product of a long history of discrimination in the United States, and it's perpetuated by family inheritance patterns that pass accumulated racial advantages and disadvantages from one generation to the next. The median net worth of families of color is just a fraction of that of white families'. White families not only have more financial assets (e.g. savings, bonds, stocks, pensions, etc.) and nonfinancial assets (e.g. homes and other property, vehicles, privately held businesses, etc.) than families of color, but also have an easier time securing credit through debt (e.g. mortgages, credit card balances, and other loans).

WEALTH VS. INCOME BY RACE, 1995–2001

		1995	1998	2001	$ change	% change
Median Net Worth	*Families of color*	$18,300	$17,900	$17,100	– $1,200	– 7%
	White families	$88,500	$103,400	$120,900	$32,400	3
Median Income	*Families of color*	$23,000	$25,400	$25,700	$2,700	12%
	White families	$38,200	$41,100	$45,200	$7,100	18%

Source: Ana M. Aizcorbe, Arthur B. Kennickell, and Kevin B. Moore, "Recent Changes in U.S. Family Finances: Evidence from the 1998 and 2001 Survey of Consumer Finances," *Federal Reserve Bulletin,* vol. 89 (January 2003), pp. 1-32, <www.federalreserve.gov>. Also see "African Americans Have Less Wealth and More Debt than White Americans," <www.FairEconomy.org>.

September/October 2004

SLOW WAGE GROWTH BUT SOARING PROFITS

BY JOHN MILLER

The current economic recovery has done less to raise wages and more to pump up profits than any of the eight other recoveries since World War II. No wonder inequality continues to worsen, and most people still wonder whether the economic turnaround will ever benefit them.

A recent study conducted by the Economic Policy Institute, a labor-funded think tank, reports the alarming details. Over the three-year period beginning in early 2001, when the last economic expansion peaked and the recession began, corporate profits rose 62.2%. That's more than five times the average rate of growth in profits in other postwar recoveries that lasted that long. Total labor compensation (the sum of all paychecks and employee benefits), on the other hand, grew only 2.8%, well under the historical average of 9.9%. (See Figure 1.) What's more, most of labor's gains came in the form of higher benefits payments to cover the increasing cost of health care and pensions, not higher wages. In fact, in 2003 median weekly wages corrected for inflation *declined*, for the first time since 1996.

The extreme imbalance between wage and profit growth in this recovery is hardly surprising. Corporate cost-cutting has been the hallmark of this recovery; instead of hiring new workers, bosses have squeezed more out of the old ones. Corporate restructuring, layoffs, and the global outsourcing of both white-collar and manufacturing jobs have all made new jobs scarce. This recovery is still a long way from even replacing the jobs lost since the recession officially began in March 2001. As of June 2004, some 39 months after the recession began—and 31 months after it officially ended—total employment was still down 1.2 million jobs. Every other economic recovery, even the jobless recovery of the early 1990s, had restored job losses *and* added a large number of new jobs to the economy by the 39-month mark.

Poor jobs growth has left workers in no position to push for higher wages. Only the jobless recovery of the early 1990s did as poorly as the current job-loss recovery at improving workers' wages and salaries. After adjusting for inflation, wages and salaries increased just 1.1% during the first two years of each of these two recoveries, reports economist Christian Weller of the Center for American Progress. Wages and salaries in all other postwar recoveries, on the other hand, rose an average of 12.1% in the same period, or about 11 times more quickly. (See Figure 2.)

At the same time, corporate cost-cutting measures have made for rapid increases in productivity—how much a worker can produce per hour. For instance, in 2002 and 2003, the hourly output of U.S. workers went up at a 5.3% pace, more than double the productivity growth rate during the "new economy" boom of 1996 to 2001. For the first time in a postwar recovery, productivity is growing far faster than the economy.

With little wage growth, the gains from improved productivity have gone nearly exclusively to corporate profits. But few of those profits are getting reinvested. Relative to the size of the economy, real investment at the end of 2003, some 10.3% of GDP, remained well below its pre-recession level of 12.6% of GDP at the end of 2000. Weller estimates that nonfinancial corporations are investing fewer of their resources than at any time since the 1950s. And with little investment, soaring profits have not translated into a hiring boom.

In short, corporations are exceedingly profitable and flush with cash, but nonetheless remain reluctant to invest or hire. But why?

The answer is twofold. First, U.S. companies are still saddled with excess capacity. Even in May 2004, just over three-quarters of manufacturing capacity was being put to use, well below their 30-year averages, leaving corporations with little incentive to invest in new plant and equipment.

Second, much like the rest of us, corporate America doubts that the current economic recovery is sustainable. Consumers, as Weller puts it, have been the "energizer bunnies of this recovery"—they just keep on spending. But they have relied on debt, not improving incomes. Rising interest rates are now driving up the cost of borrowing and closing off home mortgage refinancing, making for hard times for these debt-strapped consumers.

The other fuel of the recovery, government-administered economic stimulants—from tax cuts to low interest rates to military spending—are just as unsustainable. And they too have failed to activate the "multiplier effects" necessary to sustain economic growth over time. Typically, higher government spending calls forth more output. Employers in turn hire more workers. New jobs put money in workers' pockets and empower workers who already have jobs to press for higher wages. And that additional income fuels consumption. But with corporate investment still sluggish, few new jobs, and meager wage gains, that internally generated fuel is all but absent in the current upturn.

Only when labor markets genuinely tighten will workers be able to press for wage gains that match those of workers in earlier economic expansions. Until then, the benefits of this economic expansion, for as long as it can continue without the self-sustaining fuel of wage growth, will continue to go overwhelmingly to profits, exacerbating an economic inequality that is already unprecedented by postwar standards.

Sources: Economic Policy Institute, Job Watch Bulletin, July 2, 2004; Economic Policy Institute, "When do workers get their share?" Economic Snapshot, May 27, 2004; Christian Weller, "Reversing the 'Upside-Down' Economy: Faster Income Growth Necessary for Strong and Durable Growth," Center for American Progress, May 24, 2004.

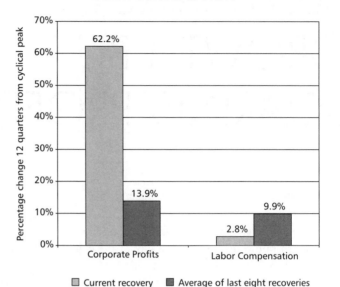

FIGURE 1
GROWTH IN CORPORATE PROFITS AND LABOR COMPENSATION

Source: Economic Policy Institute, "When do workers get their share?" Economic Snapshot, May 27, 2004. Data from the National Income and Product Accounts, Bureau of Economic Analysis, U.S. Dept. of Commerce.

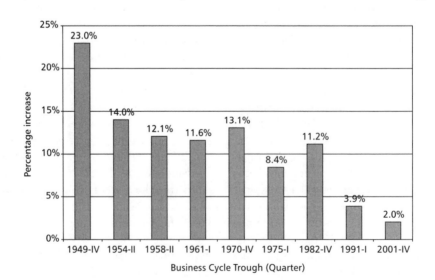

FIGURE 2
REAL WAGE GROWTH IN POSTWAR RECOVERIES
(Percent Increase over the Eight Quarters after the Start of the Recovery)

Source: Christian Weller, "Reversing the 'Upside-Down' Economy," Center for American Progress, May 24, 2004. Data from the National Income and Product Accounts, Bureau of Economic Analysis, U.S. Dept. of Commerce.

ARTICLE 2.3

THE DEATH OF HORATIO ALGER

BY PAUL KRUGMAN

The other day I found myself reading a leftist rag that made outrageous claims about America. It said that we are becoming a society in which the poor tend to stay poor, no matter how hard they work; in which sons are much more likely to inherit the socioeconomic status of their fathers than they were a generation ago.

The name of the leftist rag? *Business Week*, which published an article titled "Waking Up From the American Dream." The article summarizes recent research showing that social mobility in the United States (which was never as high as legend had it) has declined considerably over the past few decades. If you put that research together with other research that shows a drastic increase in income and wealth inequality, you reach an uncomfortable conclusion: America looks more and more like a class-ridden society.

And guess what? Our political leaders are doing everything they can to fortify class inequality, while denouncing anyone who complains—or even points out what is happening—as a practitioner of "class warfare."

Let's talk first about the facts on income distribution. Thirty years ago we were a relatively middle-class nation. It had not always been thus: Gilded Age America was a highly unequal society, and it stayed that way through the 1920s. During the 1930s and '40s, however, America experienced what the economic historians Claudia Goldin and Robert Margo have dubbed the Great Compression: a drastic narrowing of income gaps, probably as a result of New Deal policies. And the new economic order persisted for more than a generation. Strong unions, taxes on inherited wealth, corporate profits and high incomes, and close public scrutiny of corporate management all helped to keep income gaps relatively small. The economy was hardly egalitarian, but a generation ago the gross inequalities of the 1920s seemed very distant.

Now they're back. According to estimates by the economists Thomas Piketty and Emmanuel Saez—confirmed by data from the Congressional Budget Office—between 1973 and 2000 the average real income of the bottom 90 percent of American taxpayers actually fell by 7 percent. Meanwhile, the income of the top 1 percent rose by 148 percent, the income of the top 0.1 percent rose by 343 percent and the income of the top 0.01 percent rose 599 percent. (Those numbers exclude capital gains, so they're not an artifact of the stock-market bubble.) The distribution of income in the United States has gone right back to Gilded Age levels of inequality.

Never mind, say the apologists, who churn out papers with titles like that of a 2001 Heritage Foundation piece, "Income Mobility and the Fallacy of Class-Warfare Arguments." America, they say, isn't a caste society—people with high incomes this year may have low incomes next year and vice versa, and the route to wealth is open to all. That's where those commies at *Business Week* come in. As they point out (and as economists and sociologists have been pointing out for some time), America actually is more of a caste society than we like to think. And the caste lines have lately become a lot more rigid.

The myth of income mobility has always exceeded the reality. As a general rule, once they've reached their 30s, people don't move up and down the income ladder very much. Conservatives often cite studies like a 1992 report by Glenn Hubbard, a Treasury official under the elder Bush who later became chief economic adviser to the younger Bush, that purport to show large numbers of Americans moving from low-wage to high-wage jobs during their working lives. But what these studies measure, as the economist Kevin Murphy put it, is mainly "the guy who works in the college bookstore and has a real job by his early 30s." Serious studies that exclude this sort of pseudo-mobility show that inequality in average incomes over long periods isn't much smaller than inequality in annual incomes.

It is true, however, that America was once a place of substantial intergenerational mobility—sons often did much better than their fathers. A classic 1978 survey found that among adult men whose fathers were in the bottom 25 percent of the population as ranked by social and economic status, 23 percent had made it into the top 25 percent. In other words, during the first thirty years or so after World War II, the American dream of upward mobility was a real experience for many people.

Now for the shocker: The *Business Week* piece cites a new survey of today's adult men, which finds that this number has dropped to only 10 percent. That is, over the past generation upward mobility has fallen drastically. Very few children of the lower class are making their way to even moderate affluence. This goes along with other studies indicating that rags-to-riches stories have become vanishingly rare, and that the correlation between fathers' and sons' incomes has risen in recent decades. In modern America, it seems, you're quite likely to stay in the social and economic class into which you were born.

Business Week attributes this to the "Wal-Martization" of the economy, the proliferation of dead-end, low-wage jobs and the disappearance of jobs that provide entry to the middle class. That's surely part of the explanation. But public policy plays a role—and will, if present trends continue, play an even bigger role in the future.

Put it this way: Suppose that you actually liked a caste society, and you were seeking ways to use your control of the government to further entrench the advantages of the haves against the have-nots. What would you do?

One thing you would definitely do is get rid of the estate tax, so that large fortunes can be passed on to the next generation. More broadly, you would seek to reduce tax rates both on corporate profits and on unearned income such as dividends and capital gains, so that those with large accumulated or inherited wealth could more easily accumulate even more. You'd also try to create tax shelters mainly useful for the rich. And more broadly still, you'd try to reduce tax rates on people with high incomes, shifting the burden to the payroll tax and other revenue sources that bear most heavily on people with lower incomes.

Meanwhile, on the spending side, you'd cut back on healthcare for the poor, on the quality of public education and on state aid for higher education. This would make it more difficult for people with low incomes to climb out of their difficulties and acquire the education essential to upward mobility in the modern economy.

And just to close off as many routes to upward mobility as possible, you'd do everything possible to break the power of unions, and you'd privatize government functions so that well-paid civil servants could be replaced with poorly paid private employees.

It all sounds sort of familiar, doesn't it?

Where is this taking us? Thomas Piketty, whose work with Saez has transformed our understanding of income distribution, warns that current policies will eventually create "a class of rentiers in the U.S., whereby a small group of wealthy but untalented children controls vast segments of the US economy and penniless, talented children simply can't compete." If he's right—and I fear that he is—we will end up suffering not only from injustice, but from a vast waste of human potential.

Goodbye, Horatio Alger. And goodbye, American Dream.

Reprinted with permission from the January 5, 2004 issue of *The Nation*. For subscription information call 1-800-333-8536. Portions of each week's *Nation* magazine can be accessed at http://www.thenation.com.

ARTICLE 2.4

May/June 2004

NO MORE SAVINGS!

THE CASE FOR SOCIAL WEALTH

BY ELLEN FRANK

Pundits from the political left and right don't agree about war in Iraq, gay marriage, national energy policy, tax breaks, free trade, or much else. But they do agree on one thing: Americans don't save enough. The reasons are hotly disputed. Right-wingers contend that the tax code rewards spenders and punishes savers. Liberals argue that working families earn too little to save. Environmentalists complain of a work-spend rat race fueled by relentless advertising.

But the bottom line seems beyond dispute.

Data on wealth-holding reveal that few Americans possess adequate wealth to finance a comfortable retirement. Virtually none have cash sufficient to survive an extended bout of unemployment. Only a handful of very affluent households could pay for health care if their insurance lapsed, cover nursing costs if they became disabled, or see their children through college without piling up student loans. Wealth is so heavily concentrated at the very top of the income distribution that even upper-middle class households are dangerously exposed to the vagaries of life and the economy.

With low savings and inadequate personal wealth identified as the problem, the solutions seem so clear as to rally wide bipartisan support: Provide tax credits for savings. Encourage employers to establish workplace savings plans. Educate people about family budgeting and financial investing. Promote home ownership so people can build home equity. Develop tax-favored plans to pay for college, retirement, and medical needs. More leftish proposals urge the government to redistribute wealth through federally sponsored "children's development accounts" or "American stakeholder accounts," so that Americans at all income levels can, as the Demos-USA website puts it, "enjoy the security and benefits that come with owning assets."

But such policies fail to address the paradoxical role savings play in market economies. Furthermore, looking at economic security solely through the lens of personal finance deflects focus away from a better, more direct, and far more reliable way to ensure Americans' well-being: promoting social wealth.

THE PARADOX OF THRIFT

Savings is most usefully envisaged as a physical concept. Each year businesses turn out automobiles, computers, lumber, and steel. Households (or consumers) buy much, but not all, of this output. The goods and services they leave behind represent the economy's savings.

Economics students are encouraged to visualize the economy as a metaphorical plumbing system through which goods and money flow. Firms produce goods, which flow through the marketplace and are sold for money. The money flows into peoples' pockets as income, which flows back into the marketplace as demand for goods. Savings represent a leak in the economic plumbing. If other purchasers don't step up and buy the output that thrifty consumers shun, firms lay off workers and curb production, for there is no profit in making goods that people don't want to buy.

On the other hand, whatever consumers don't buy is available for businesses to purchase in order to expand their capacity. When banks buy computers or developers buy lumber and steel, then the excess goods find a market and production continues apace. Economists refer to business purchases of new plant and equipment as "investment." In the plumbing metaphor, investment is an injection—an additional flow of spending into the economy to offset the leaks caused by household saving.

During the industrial revolution, intense competition meant that whatever goods households did not buy or could not afford would be snatched up by emerging businesses, at least much of the time. By the turn of the 20th century, however, low-paid consumers had become a drag on economic growth. Small entrepreneurial businesses gave way to immense monopolistic firms like U.S. Steel and Standard Oil whose profits vastly exceeded what they could spend on expansion. Indeed expansion often looked pointless since, given the low level of household spending, the only buyers for their output were other businesses, who themselves faced the same dilemma.

As market economies matured, savings became a source of economic stagnation. Even the conspicuous consumption of Gilded Age business owners couldn't provide enough demand for the goods churned out of large industrial factories. Henry Ford was the first American corporate leader to deliberately pay his workers above-market wages, reasoning correctly that a better-paid work force would provide the only reliable market for his automobiles.

Today, thanks to democratic suffrage, labor unions, social welfare programs, and a generally more egalitarian culture, wages are far higher in industrialized economies than they were a century ago; wage and salary earners now secure nearly four-fifths of national income. And thrift seems a quaint virtue of our benighted grandparents. In the United States, the personal savings rate—the percentage of income flowing to households that they did not spend—fell to 1% in the late 1990s. Today, with a stagnant economy making consumers more cautious, the personal savings rate has risen—but only to around 4%.

Because working households consume virtually every penny they earn, goods and services produced are very likely to find buyers and continue to be produced. This is an important reason why the United States and Europe no longer experience the devastating depressions that beset industrialized countries prior to World War II.

SOCIAL SECURITY BENEFITS REPLACE, ON AVERAGE, ONLY ONE-THIRD OF PRIOR EARNINGS. IN EUROPE, PUBLIC PENSIONS REPLACE FROM 50% TO 70% OF PRIOR EARNINGS.

Yet there is a surprisingly broad consensus that these low savings are a bad thing. Americans are often chastised for their lack of thrift, their failure to provide for themselves financially, their rash and excessive borrowing. Politicians and economists constantly exhort Americans to save more and devise endless schemes to induce them to do so.

At the same time, Americans also face relentless pressure to spend. After September 11, President Bush told the public they could best serve their country by continuing to shop. In the media, economic experts bemoan declines in "consumer confidence" and applaud reports of buoyant retail or auto sales. The U.S. economy, we are told, is a consumer economy—our spendthrift ways and shop-til-you-drop culture the motor that propels it. Free-spending consumers armed with multiple credit cards keep the stores hopping, the restaurants full, and the factories humming.

Our schizophrenic outlook on saving and spending has two roots. First, the idea of saving meshes seamlessly with a conservative ideological outlook. In what author George Lakoff calls the "strict-father morality" that informs conservative Republican politics, abstinence, thrift, self-reliance, and competitive individualism are moral virtues. Institutions that discourage saving—like Social Security, unemployment insurance, government health programs, state-funded student aid—are by definition socialistic and result in an immoral reliance on others. Former Treasury Secretary Paul O'Neill bluntly expressed this idea to a reporter for the *Financial Times* in 2001. "Able-bodied adults," O'Neill opined, "should save enough on a regular basis so that they can provide for their own retirement and for that matter for their health and medical needs." Otherwise, he continued, elderly people are just "dumping their problems on the broader society."

> INDIVIDUALS AND HOUSEHOLDS FARE BETTER WHEN THEY ARE ASSURED SOME SECURE POLITICAL CLAIM ON THE ECONOMY'S OUTPUT . . . BECAUSE SOCIAL CLAIMS ON THE ECONOMY RENDER THE ECONOMY ITSELF MORE STABLE.

This ideological position, which is widely but not deeply shared among U.S. voters, receives financial and political support from the finance industry. Financial firms have funded most of the research, lobbying, and public relations for the campaign to "privatize" Social Security, replacing the current system of guaranteed, publicly-funded pensions with individual investment accounts. The finance industry and its wealthy clients also advocate "consumption taxes"—levying taxes on income spent, but not on income saved—so as to "encourage saving" and "reward thrift." Not coincidentally, the finance industry specializes in committing accumulated pools of money to the purchase of stocks, bonds and other paper assets, for which it receives generous fees and commissions.

Our entire economic system requires that people spend freely. Yet political rhetoric combined with pressure from the financial services industry urges individuals to save, or at least to try to save. This rhetoric finds a receptive audience in ordinary households anxious over their own finances and among many progressive public-interest groups alarmed by the threadbare balance sheets of so many American households.

So here is the paradox. People need protection against adversity, and an ample savings account provides such protection. But if ordinary households try to save and protect themselves against hard times, the unused factories, barren malls, and empty restaurants would bring those hard times upon them.

SOCIAL WEALTH

The only way to address the paradox is to reconcile individuals' need for economic security with the public need for a stable economy. The solution therefore lies not in personal thrift or individual wealth, but in social insurance and public wealth.

When a country promotes economic security with dependable public investments and insurance programs, individuals have less need to amass private savings. Social Security, for example, provides the elderly with a direct claim on the nation's economic output after they retire. This guarantees that retirees keep spending and reduces the incentive for working adults to save. By restraining personal savings, Social Security improves the chances that income earned will translate into income spent, making the overall economy more stable.

Of course, Americans still need to save up for old age; Social Security benefits replace, on average, only one-third of prior earnings. This argues not for more saving, however, but for more generous Social Security benefits. In Europe, public pensions replace from 50% to 70% of prior earnings.

Programs like Social Security and unemployment insurance align private motivation with the public interest in a high level of economic activity. Moreover, social insurance programs reduce people's exposure to volatile financial markets. Proponents of private asset building seem to overlook the lesson of the late 1990s stock market boom: that the personal wealth of small-scale savers is perilously vulnerable to stock market downswings, price manipulation, and fraud by corporate insiders.

It is commonplace to disparage social insurance programs as "big government" intrusions that burden the public with onerous taxes. But the case for a robust public sector is at least as much an economic as a moral one. Ordinary individuals and households fare better when they are assured some secure political claim on the economy's output, not only because of the payouts they receive as individuals, but because social claims on the economy render the economy itself more stable.

Well-funded public programs, for one thing, create reliable income streams and employment. Universal public schooling, for example, means that a sizable portion of our nation's income is devoted to building, equipping, staffing, and maintaining schools. This spending is less susceptible than private-sector spending to business cycles, price fluctuations, and job losses.

Programs that build social wealth also substantially ameliorate the sting of joblessness and minimize the broader economic fallout of unemployment when downturns do occur. Public schools, colleges, parks, libraries, hospitals, and transportation systems, as well as social insurance programs like unemployment compensation and disability coverage, all ensure that the unemployed continue to consume at least a minimal level of goods and services. Their children can still attend school and visit the playground. If there were no social supports, the unemployed would be forced to withdraw altogether from the economy, dragging wages down and setting off destabilizing depressions.

In a series of articles on the first Bush tax cut in 2001, the *New York Times* profiled Dr. Robert Cline, an Austin, Texas, surgeon whose $300,000 annual income still left him worried about financing college educations for his six children. Dr. Cline himself attended the University of Texas, at a cost of $250 per semester ($650 for medical school), but figured that "his own children's education will likely cost tens of thousands of dollars each." Dr. Cline supported the 2001 tax cut, the *Times* reported. Ironically, though, that cut contributed to an environment in which institutions like the University of Texas raise tuitions, restrict enrollments, and drive Dr. Cline and others to attempt to amass enough personal wealth to pay for their children's education.

Unlike Dr. Cline, most people will never accumulate sufficient hoards of wealth to afford expensive high-quality services like education or to indemnify themselves against the myriad risks of old age, poor health, and unemployment. Even when middle-income households do manage to stockpile savings, they have little control over the rate at which their assets can be converted to cash.

Virtually all people—certainly the 93% of U.S. households earning less than $150,000—would fare better collectively than they could individually. Programs that provide direct access to important goods and services—publicly financed education, recreation, health care, and pensions—reduce the inequities that follow inevitably from an entirely individualized economy. The vast majority of people are better off with the high probability of a secure income and guaranteed access to key services such as health care than with the low-probability prospect of becoming rich.

The next time a political candidate recommends some tax-exempt individual asset building scheme, progressively minded people should ask her these questions. If consumers indeed save more and the government thus collects less tax revenue, who will buy the goods these thrifty consumers now forgo? Who will employ the workers who used to manufacture those goods? Who will build the public assets that lower tax revenues render unaffordable? And how exactly does creating millions of little pots of gold substitute for a collective commitment to social welfare?

July/August 2004

GEESE, GOLDEN EGGS, AND TRAPS

WHY INEQUALITY IS BAD FOR THE ECONOMY

BY CHRIS TILLY

Whenever progressives propose ways to redistribute wealth from the rich to those with low and moderate incomes, conservative politicians and economists accuse them of trying to kill the goose that lays the golden egg. The advocates of unfettered capitalism proclaim that inequality is good for the economy because it promotes economic growth. Unequal incomes, they say, provide the incentives necessary to guide productive economic decisions by businesses and individuals. Try to reduce inequality, and you'll sap growth. Furthermore, the conservatives argue, growth actually promotes equality by boosting the have-nots more than the haves. So instead of fiddling with who gets how much, the best way to help those at the bottom is to pump up growth.

But these conservative prescriptions are absolutely, dangerously wrong. Instead of the goose-killer, equality turns out to be the goose. Inequality stifles growth; equality gooses it up. Moreover, economic expansion does *not* necessarily promote equality—instead, it is the types of jobs and the rules of the economic game that matter most.

INEQUALITY: GOOSE OR GOOSE-KILLER?

The conservative argument may be wrong, but it's straightforward. Inequality is good for the economy, conservatives say, because it provides the right incentives for innovation and economic growth. First of all, people will only have the motivation to work hard, innovate, and invest wisely if the economic system rewards them for good economic choices and penalizes bad ones. Robin Hood-style policies that collect from the wealthy and help those who are worse off violate this principle. They reduce the payoff to smart decisions and lessen the sting of dumb ones. The result: people and companies are bound to make less efficient decisions. "We must allow [individuals] to fail, as well as succeed, and we must replace the nanny state with a regime of self-reliance and self-respect," writes conservative lawyer Stephen Kinsella in *The Freeman: Ideas on Liberty* (not clear how the free woman fits in). To prove their point, conservatives point to the former state socialist countries, whose economies had become stagnant and inefficient by the time they fell at the end of the 1980s.

> BUT THESE CONSERVATIVE PRESCRIPTIONS ARE ABSOLUTELY, DANGEROUSLY WRONG. INSTEAD OF THE GOOSE-KILLER, EQUALITY TURNS OUT TO BE THE GOOSE. INEQUALITY STIFLES GROWTH; EQUALITY GOOSES IT UP.

If you don't buy this incentive story, there's always the well-worn trickle-down theory. To grow, the economy needs productive investments: new offices, factories, computers, and machines. To finance such investments takes a pool of savings. The rich save a larger fraction of their incomes than those less well-off. So to spur growth, give more to the well-heeled (or at least take less away from them in the form of taxes), and give less to the down-and-out. The rich will save their money and then invest it, promoting growth that's good for everyone.

Unfortunately for trickle-down, the brilliant economist John Maynard Keynes debunked the theory in his *General Theory of Employment, Interest, and Money* in 1936. Keynes, whose precepts guided liberal U.S. economic policy from the 1940s through the 1970s, agreed that investments must be financed out of savings. But he showed that most often it's changes in investment that drive savings, rather than the other way around. When businesses are optimistic about the future and invest in building and retooling, the economy booms, all of us make more money, and we put some of it in banks, 401(k)s, stocks, and so on. That is, saving grows to match investment. When companies are glum, the process runs in reverse, and savings shrink to equal investment. This leads to the "paradox of thrift": if people try to save too much, businesses will see less consumer spending, will invest less, and total savings will end up diminishing rather than growing as the economy spirals downward. A number

of Keynes's followers added the next logical step: shifting money from the high-saving rich to the high-spending rest of us, and not the other way around, will spur investment and growth.

Of the two conservative arguments in favor of inequality, the incentive argument is a little weightier. Keynes himself agreed that people needed financial consequences to steer their actions, but questioned whether the differences in payoffs needed to be so huge. Certainly state socialist countries' attempts to replace material incentives with moral exhortation have often fallen short. In 1970, the Cuban government launched the *Gran Zafra* (Great Harvest), an attempt to reap 10 million tons of sugar cane with (strongly encouraged) volunteer labor. Originally inspired by Che Guevara's ideal of the New Socialist Man (not clear how the New Socialist Woman fit in), the effort ended with Fidel Castro tearfully apologizing to the Cuban people in a nationally broadcast speech for letting wishful thinking guide economic policy.

But before conceding this point to the conservatives, let's look at the evidence about the connection between equality and growth. Economists William Easterly of New York University and Gary Fields of Cornell University have recently summarized this evidence:

- Countries, and regions within countries, with more equal incomes grow faster. (These growth figures do not include environmental destruction or improvement. If they knocked off points for environmental destruction and added points for environmental improvement, the correlation between equality and growth would be even stronger, since desperation drives poor people to adopt environmentally destructive practices such as rapid deforestation.)
- Countries with more equally distributed land grow faster.
- Somewhat disturbingly, more ethnically homogeneous countries and regions grow faster—presumably because there are fewer ethnically based inequalities.

In addition, more worker rights are associated with higher rates of economic growth, according to Josh Bivens and Christian Weller, economists at two Washington think tanks, the Economic Policy Institute and the Center for American Progress.

These patterns recommend a second look at the incentive question. In fact, more equality can actually *strengthen* incentives and opportunities to produce.

EQUALITY AS THE GOOSE

Equality can boost growth in several ways. Perhaps the simplest is that study after study has shown that farmland is more productive when cultivated in small plots. So organizations promoting more equal distribution of land, like Brazil's Landless Workers' Movement, are not just helping the landless poor—they're contributing to agricultural productivity!

Another reason for the link between equality and growth is what Easterly calls "match effects," which have been highlighted in research by Stanford's Paul Roemer and others in recent years. One example of a match effect is the fact that well-educated people are most productive when working with others who have lots of schooling. Likewise, people working with computers are more productive when many others have computers (so that, for example, e-mail communication is widespread, and know-how about computer repair and software is easy to come by). In very unequal societies, highly educated, computer-using elites are surrounded by majorities with little education and no computer access, dragging down their productivity. This decreases young people's incentive to get more education and businesses' incentive to invest in computers, since the payoff will be smaller.

Match effects can even matter at the level of a metropolitan area. Urban economist Larry Ledebur looked at income and employment growth in 85 U.S. cities and their neighboring suburbs. He found that where the income gap between those in the suburbs and those in the city was largest, income and job growth was slower for everyone.

"Pressure effects" also help explain why equality sparks growth. Policies that close off the low-road strategy of exploiting poor and working people create pressure effects, driving economic elites to search for investment opportunities that pay off by boosting productivity rather than squeezing the have-nots harder. For example, where workers have more rights, they will place greater demands on businesses. Business owners will respond by trying to increase productivity, both to remain profitable even after paying higher wages, and to find ways to produce with fewer workers. The CIO union drives in U.S. mass production industries in the 1930s and 1940s provide much of the explanation for the superb productivity growth of the 1950s and 1960s. (The absence of pressure effects may help explain why many past and present state socialist countries have seen slow growth, since they tend to offer numerous protections for workers but no right to organize independent unions.) Similarly, if a government buys out large land-holdings in order to break them up, wealthy families who simply kept their fortunes tied up in land for generations will look for new, productive investments. Industrialization in Asian "tigers" South Korea and Taiwan took off in the 1950s on the wings of funds freed up in exactly this way.

INEQUALITY, CONFLICT, AND GROWTH

Inequality hinders growth in another important way: it fuels social conflict. Stark inequality in countries such as Bolivia and Haiti has led to chronic conflict that hobbles economic growth. Moreover, inequality ties up resources in unproductive uses such as paying for large numbers of police and security guards—attempts to prevent individuals from redistributing resources through theft.

Ethnic variety is connected to slower growth because, on the average, more ethnically diverse countries are also more likely to be ethnically divided. In other words, the problem isn't ethnic variety itself, but racism and ethnic conflict that can exist among diverse populations. In nations like Guatemala, Congo, and Nigeria, ethnic strife has crippled growth—a problem alien to ethnically uniform Japan and South Korea. The reasons are similar to some of the reasons that large class divides hurt growth. Where ethnic divisions (which can take tribal, language, religious, racial, or regional forms) loom large, dominant ethnic groups seek to use government power to better themselves at the expense of other groups, rather than making broad-based investments in education and infrastructure. This can involve keeping down the underdogs—slower growth in the U.S. South for much of the country's history was linked to the Southern system of white supremacy. Or it can involve seizing the surplus of ethnic groups perceived as better off—in the extreme, Nazi Germany's expropriation and genocide of the Jews, who often held professional and commercial jobs.

Of course, the solution to such divisions is not "ethnic cleansing" so that each country has only one ethnic group—in addition to being morally abhorrent, this is simply impossible in a world with 191 countries and 5,000 ethnic groups. Rather, the solution is to diminish ethnic inequalities. Once the 1964 Civil Rights Act forced the South to drop racist laws, the New South's economic growth spurt began. Easterly reports that in countries with strong rule of law, professional bureaucracies, protection of contracts, and freedom from expropriation—all rules that make it harder for one ethnic group to economically oppress another—ethnic diversity has *no* negative impact on growth.

If more equality leads to faster growth so everybody benefits, why do the rich typically resist redistribution? Looking at the ways that equity seeds growth helps us understand why. The importance of pressure effects tells us that the wealthy often don't think about more productive ways to invest or reorganize their businesses until they are forced to. But also, if a country becomes very unequal, it can get stuck in an "inequality trap." Any redistribution involves a tradeoff for the rich. They lose by giving up part of their wealth, but they gain a share in increased economic growth. The bigger the disparity between the rich and the rest, the more the rich have to lose, and the less likely that the equal share of boosted growth they'll get will make up for their loss. Once the gap goes beyond a certain point, the wealthy have a strong incentive to restrict democracy, and to block spending on education which might lead the poor to challenge economic injustice—making reform that much harder.

DOES ECONOMIC GROWTH REDUCE INEQUALITY?

If inequality isn't actually good for the economy, what about the second part of the conservatives' argument—that growth itself promotes equality? According to the conservatives, those who care about equality should simply pursue growth and wait for equality to follow.

"A rising tide lifts all boats," President John F. Kennedy famously declared. But he said nothing about which boats will rise fastest when the economic tide comes in. Growth does typically reduce poverty, according to studies reviewed by economist Gary Fields, though some "boats"—especially families with strong barriers to participating in the labor force—stay "stuck in the mud." But inequality can increase at the same time that poverty falls, if the rich gain even faster than the poor do. True, sustained periods of low unemployment, like that in the late 1990s United States, do tend to raise wages at the bottom even faster than salaries at the top. But growth after the recessions of 1991 and 2001 began with years of "jobless recoveries"—growth with inequality.

For decades the prevailing view about growth and inequality within countries was that expressed by Simon Kuznets in his 1955 presidential address to the American Economic Association. Kuznets argued that as countries grew, inequality would first increase, then decrease. The reason is that people will gradually move from the low-income agricultural sector to higher-income industrial jobs—with inequality peaking when the workforce is equally divided between low- and high-income sectors. For mature industrial economies, Kuznets's proposition counsels focusing on growth, assuming that it will bring equity. In developing countries, it calls for enduring current inequality for the sake of future equity and prosperity.

But economic growth doesn't automatically fuel equality. In 1998, economists Klaus Deininger and Lyn Squire traced inequality and growth over time in 48 countries. Five followed the Kuznets pattern, four followed the reverse pattern (decreasing inequality followed by an increase), and the rest showed no systematic pattern. In the United States, for example:

- incomes became more equal during the 1930s through 1940s New Deal period (a time that included economic decline followed by growth)
- from the 1950s through the 1970s, income gaps lessened during booms and expanded during slumps
- from the late 1970s forward, income inequality worsened fairly consistently, whether the economy was stagnating or growing.

The reasons are not hard to guess. The New Deal introduced widespread unionization, a minimum wage, social security, unemployment insurance, and welfare. Since the late 1970s, unions have declined, the inflation-adjusted value of the minimum wage has fallen, and the social safety net has been shredded. In the United States, as elsewhere, growth only promotes equality if policies and institutions to support equity are in place.

TRAPPED?

Let's revisit the idea of an inequality trap. The notion is that as the gap between the rich and everybody else grows wider, the wealthy become more willing to give up overall growth in return for the larger share they're getting for themselves. The "haves" back policies to control the "have-nots," instead of devoting social resources to educating the poor so they'll be more productive.

Sound familiar? It should. After two decades of widening inequality, the last few years have brought us massive tax cuts that primarily benefit the wealthiest, at the expense of investment in infrastructure and the education, child care, and income supports that would help raise less well-off kids to be productive adults. Federal and state governments have cranked up expenditures on prisons, police, and "homeland security," and Republican campaign organizations have devoted major resources to keeping blacks and the poor away from the polls. If the economic patterns of the past are any indication, we're going to pay for these policies in slower growth and stagnation unless we can find our way out of this inequality trap.

CHAPTER 3
Savings and Investment

INTRODUCTION

Never a slip from the savings cup to the investment lip. That is the orderly world of classical macroeconomics, where every cent of household savings is neatly transferred to corporate investment. In the classical world, savings markets—governed by all-powerful interest rates—work seamlessly to assure that savings are matched by investments, fueling growth in the private economy, which in turn guarantees full employment. Should the flow of savings exceed the uptake of corporate investment, falling interest rates automatically solve the problem.

In the real world, macroeconomies are far messier than classical macroeconomics suggests. Keynes argued that there is no neat connection, or nexus, between savings and investment in a modern financial economy. Savings often sit, hoarded and uninvested. And interest rates, no matter how low, seldom coax balky investors to lay out their money in a weak economy. In the Keynesian world, economies regularly suffer from investment shortfalls that lead to recessions and cost workers their jobs.

In this chapter, Randy Albelda and Gretchen McClain report on one critical test of the classical and Keynesian visions, conducted by economist Steven Fazzari. In a massive study of 5,000 manufacturing firms, Fazzari rated the influence of interest rates, business cycle conditions, and firms' financial conditions on their investment in plant and equipment. He concluded that the influence of interest rates is overrated, putting him squarely in the Keynesian camp (Albelda and McClain, article 3.1). Ted Schmidt provides evidence for the Keynesian argument that declining incomes, and not lower interest rates, are drying up household savings. He shows that borrowing by the cash-strapped bottom three-fifths of households has more than offset the increase in savings by the rich. To reverse the decline in savings, he recommends redistributing income to lower-income groups (Schmidt, article 3.5).

Dean Baker and Ellen Frank challenge the mainstream claims that higher corporate profits and stock prices boost investment. Baker tracks corporate profits and investment since the 1970s, and shows that corporations have pursued a strategy of increasing profits *without* increasing investment proportionally (Baker, article 3.3). And Frank explains why there is no logical connection between rising stock prices and rising investment. Stock prices are based on traders' guesses about which stocks are likely to catch the eye of other traders—guesses that can have little to do with actual economic conditions (Frank, article 3.4). She concludes that the tremendous run-up in stock prices during the last 20 years created the illusion of wealth, not greater investment or faster economic growth (Frank, article 3.2).

DISCUSSION QUESTIONS

1) (Articles 3.1 and 3.5) Keynes argued that savings and investment were not balanced by the interest rate but by changes in the level of aggregate output. How does the essay by McClain and Albelda support Keynes's claim about investment? And how does Schmidt's essay support Keynes's claim about savings?

2) (Article 3.1) According to McClain and Albelda, how did Fazzari rate the influence of interest rates, business cycle conditions, and firms' financial conditions on corporate investment? What do his findings suggest about Keynesian and classical theories of investment? Based on his findings, what might be appropriate stabilization policies to promote investment?

3) (Article 3.2) How does Frank make the case that the enormous paper wealth "created" by the stock never existed, except as a mass delusion? What were the signs that the stock wealth of the last decade was illusory?

4) (Article 3.3) While economist Dean Baker agrees that most corporate investment comes from profits, he maintains that the notion that "profits equal investment" is a scam. What evidence convinces him that corporate profits rose without adding to investment during the 1980s and early 1990s? Why did this disconnect go unrecognized by other economists?

5) (Article 3.4) During the 1930s, Keynes compared the stock market to a newspaper beauty contest that asked readers to pick the photo of the contestant that other readers would pick as the prettiest. Frank suggests that Keynes's analogy still holds for today's stock market. How does Frank's explanation of stock prices compare with those in your textbook? Do you find it convincing?

KEY TO COLANDER

E = Economics.   M = Macroeconomics.

This chapter takes up topics in chapters E24-E26 or M8-M10; and prefigures the policy debates in chapters E28 and E34, or M12 and M19.

Articles 3.1 and 3.3 discuss investment, the subject of chapter E24 or M8; the macro models in chapters E25-E26 or M9-M10; and the effectiveness of lowering interest rates to encourage investment, the topic of chapter E29 or M13.

Articles 3.2 and 3.4 fit with the discussion of growth in chapter E24 or M8, and the box on the stock boom in chapter E34 or M19.

Article 3.5 fits with chapters E24-E26 or M8-M10, which rely on an understanding of household savings.

July 1993, revised April 2001

BOOSTING INVESTMENT

THE OVERRATED INFLUENCE OF INTEREST RATES

BY GRETCHEN McCLAIN AND RANDY ALBELDA

Few economists or politicians would disagree that an economy's prospects for long-term growth depend on the productive capacity of its people and its physical equipment. But what to invest in—and how to get the appropriate economic actors to invest—is a matter of much debate.

All economies face a choice between using their productive resources to produce goods and services to be consumed now, and forsaking today's consumption to produce more goods for the future. While catering to consumption today may be more satisfying for wealthier countries and absolutely vital for poor countries, it fails to provide for future growth.

Investing in new plant and equipment can stimulate growth over time, as it provides the physical capacity for new production. Moreover, new plant and equipment tend to be better designed than the existing capital stock, and the improvement usually helps to boost output per worker. If this new productivity translates into higher wages, investment can also increase a country's standard of living and improve employment possibilities. In turn, improving human productive capacity—through training and education—can lead to growth and increased productivity in the long run.

Investment, and the consequent increase in productivity, is critical for international economic success. The more efficiently a country can produce a product, the more competitive that country will be in the world market. Since international markets provide an avenue of demand for our goods, the more domestically produced products and services we can sell abroad, the more jobs we can support here.

Investment can also help stimulate the economy in the short run. During an economic downturn, increased investment will yield more jobs and income for workers who would otherwise be unemployed. They will then return their income to the market when they purchase goods and services, which will boost demand for those products.

Economists call this the "multiplier effect." The increase in demand in turn encourages firms to invest more so that they can meet that demand—known to economists as the "accelerator effect." All in all, such a cycle creates more jobs, income, and spending.

While few economists dispute the importance of investment, many disagree on what type is needed, which sectors of the economy are best able to provide it, and what are the best ways to encourage investment. Typically, these debates have revolved around the government's role in encouraging private investment in new plant and equipment. But the role that public investment in infrastructure and education plays in promoting not only our economic well-being and growth, but also in encouraging private investment, could and should widen the terms of the debate.

THE BACKDROP

The traditional economic argument about investment—and the prevailing conservative line espoused by elected officials at the federal and state levels—has been that the most important fiscal policies to encourage privately owned firms to invest are those which boost profits. If the government helps provide the conditions for profitability, the argument goes, firms will be encouraged to make the right types of investment.

Government tax-and-spend policies during the 1980s and 1990s have often tried to promote investment by reducing corporate taxes, in order to boost profits and stimulate savings. Such measures were supposed to leave firms with a bigger bottom line, in the hope that they would turn profits into new plant and equipment. Cuts in personal income tax rates—especially for the wealthiest—were intended to leave people with more after-tax income that they could save. Higher savings, according to this logic, translates into lower interest rates which in turn lead to more investment. While such policies have been very effective in redistributing money from the poor to the wealthy, they did not do much for investment. For example, the amount of new fixed investment (i.e., new plant and equipment) relative to the total amount of plant and equipment actually sank to its lowest post-World War II mark between 1989 and 1991.

Merely providing the conditions for profit-making does not mean that private firms will plow those profits back into new plant and equipment. Speculation on real-estate markets, the value of foreign currencies, or the price of silver and gold could easily eat up new profits. Much of the money generated for investment in the 1980s financed mergers and acquisitions, which generally resulted in less employment and little new physical productive capacity. And, perhaps even more important, new investment by U.S. firms may not take place in the United States. Investing abroad has been the trend since the 1970s. Finally, even if there is domestic investment and it increases productivity, unless workers share in those gains it may not promote robust growth or increase the standard of living of the country as a whole.

In the face of the failure of the 1980s policies to promote investment, conservatives came up with a new explanation of why the economy was so sluggish: the deficit. Ironically, the conservative policies mentioned above were largely responsible for the public debt, but nonetheless Republicans, along with many Democrats galvanized by billionaire Ross Perot, latched onto deficit reduction as the most important fiscal policy of the 1990s.

The deficit, they argued, kept long-term interest rates high because it created competition for precious funds. The result was that federal borrowing, necessitated by debt-financed government spending and tax cuts, "crowded out" private investment. The best solution, they said, was to reduce the deficit and bring down long-term interest rates so that private investment would thrive.

IDENTIFYING INFLUENCE

Economist Steven Fazzari tackled these assumptions in a study of the influence of the federal government's taxing and spending policies on private investment. Using a large data base from Standard and Poor on over 5,000 manufacturing firms from 1971 to 1990, Fazzari tested three different factors for their effects on levels of investment in plant and equipment: interest rates, the business cycle, and the financial conditions of the firms.

According to Fazzari, these three "channels of influence" shape patterns of investment. First, he takes on the traditionalists, by addressing the costs associated with investment: the price of borrowing money (i.e., interest rates), depreciation (how fast the new piece of equipment or building will lose its value), and taxes affecting both corporate profits and dividends. To measure this channel, Fazzari employs the interest rate on one type of corporate bond.

Next, he considers the influence of the business cycle by looking at sales growth. Traditional economic theory tends to assume a ready market, but Fazzari suggests instead that firms make investment decisions based on their perception of their ability to sell their products. The more robust current sales are and are expected to be, the more likely firms will be willing to risk new investment—regardless of the interest rate. Since the general condition of the economy influences sales levels, it also has an impact on investment.

In Fazzari's examination of the third channel of influ-

ence—the financial condition of firms—he again questions conventional wisdom, this time about the supply and demand for loans. Most economists assume that if the expected return on an investment exceeds the interest rate, then the project is profitable and will be undertaken. This is most likely to be true when the firm in question has enough cash on hand from prior profits to make the investment without asking a bank for a loan. Many firms, though, need to borrow money, and some are unable to persuade banks to loan it to them. Banks often refuse loan applications from new businesses with few assets, or charge them prohibitively high interest rates. Even if a young firm finds a potentially profitable investment, severe constraints on raising capital may prevent the firm from pursuing it. A firm's financial condition—not the projected rate of return on the new investment—can thus end up determining whether or not investment takes place.

PERFECTING POLICY

After looking at the importance of interest rates, the business cycle, and the financial conditions of firms in determining investment, Fazzari found that interest rates exert the weakest influence of the three factors. He concludes that there is no evidence that interest rates significantly affect investment for the fastest growing firms in his sample. Based on these findings, Fazzari claims that "it would be speculative to base policy on the assumption that interest rates drive investment to an important extent, especially for growing firms."

CONCERNS ABOUT INVESTMENT SHOULD NOT STAND IN THE WAY OF POLICY INITIATIVES THAT ARE IMPORTANT FOR SOCIETY.

So, what kinds of fiscal policies should we adopt? If we believe Fazzari's results, we should be looking for those that attend to the financial conditions of firms and stimulate demand for products.

A tax cut targeted not at the very rich but at the "middle class" would probably give investment at least a temporary boost by generating increased consumption. Increased sales from a temporary tax cut create the illusion of a permanent increase in demand, and the multiplier and accelerator effects discussed earlier come into play. In order to meet what firms believe is a permanent increase in demand for their goods, they make investments in more equipment, more factories, and more employees.

Another means of encouraging investment that Fazzari evaluates is cutting corporate income taxes. Such cuts increase firms' after-tax profits, leaving them with a larger pool of funds to invest if they so choose. Since there is no guarantee that they will invest the savings from reduced taxes, though, Fazzari prefers investment tax credits (ITCs) to cuts in taxes for all firms. Only if firms invested would they be able to reduce their corporate tax bills. In Fazzari's view, ITCs will effectively encourage investment whether it is sensitive to interest rates or not.

The most important lesson from Fazzari's analysis is that concerns about investment should not stand in the way of policy initiatives that are important for society, such as spending on education and job training, simply because they may increase the federal budget deficit and cause interest rates to rise. Government investments in public works and education will likely increase productivity in the long run, and this can only be good for investment. Moreover, if investment is not sensitive to interest rates, then the much-discussed "crowding out" effect of deficit spending on private business is bound to be very small. And as Faz-

zari points out, when unemployment is high, the stimulative effects of deficit spending on sales may far outweigh the impacts of increased interest rates.

The focus on balanced budgets should be tempered by a thorough analysis of what this policy implies for society's immediate and long-term welfare. When we underinvest in the economy during a recession by eliminating educational and social investments, the foregone technical innovation resulting from this underinvestment may lead to less efficient workers, and lower productivity, for many years.

Fazzari's results not only repudiate the traditional answer to lagging investment—tax cuts for the wealthy and the lowering of interest rates. Instead, the government should be trying to stimulate the economy through improved physical and social infrastructure, which will boost not only sales but investment and incomes.

ARTICLE 3.2   *November/December 2002*

THE GREAT STOCK ILLUSION

BY ELLEN FRANK

During the 1980s and 1990s, the Dow Jones and Standard & Poor's indices of stock prices soared ten-fold. The NASDAQ index had, by the year 2000, skyrocketed to 25 times its 1980 level. Before the bubble burst, bullish expectations reached a feverish crescendo. Three separate books—*Dow 36,000, Dow 40,000* and *Dow 100,000*—appeared in 1999 forecasting further boundless growth in stock prices. Bullish Wall Street gurus like Goldman's Abby Cohen and Salomon's Jack Grubman were quoted everywhere, insisting that prices could go nowhere but up.

But as early as 1996, skeptics were warning that it couldn't last. Fed chair Alan Greenspan fretted aloud about "irrational exuberance." Yale finance professor Robert Shiller, in his 2001 book titled *Irrational Exuberance*, insisted that U.S. equities prices were being driven up by wishful thinking and self-fulfilling market sentiment, nourished by a culture that championed wealth and lionized the wealthy. Dean Baker and Marc Weisbrot of the Washington-based Center for Economic and Policy Research contended in 1999 that the U.S. stock market looked like a classic specu-

lative bubble—as evidence they cited the rapidly diverging relationship between stock prices and corporate earnings and reckoned that, to justify the prices at which stocks were selling, profits would have to grow at rates that were frankly impossible.

In 1999 alone, the market value of U.S. equities swelled by an astounding $4 trillion. During that same year, U.S. output, on which stocks represent a claim, rose by a mere $500 billion. What would have happened if stockholders in 1999 had all tried to sell their stock and convert their $4 trillion into actual goods and services? The answer is that most would have failed. In a scramble to turn $4 trillion of paper gains into $500 billion worth of real goods and services, the paper wealth was bound to dissolve, because it never existed, save as a kind of mass delusion.

THE ILLUSION OF WEALTH CREATION

Throughout the 1990s, each new record set by the Dow or NASDAQ elicited grateful cheers for CEOs who were hailed for "creating wealth." American workers, whose retirement savings were largely invested in stocks, were encouraged to buy more stock—even to bet their Social Security funds in the market—and assured that stocks always paid off "in the long run," that a "buy-and-hold" strategy couldn't lose. Neither the financial media nor America's politicians bothered to warn the public about the gaping disparity between the inflated claims on economic output that stocks represented and the actual production of the economy. But by the end of the decade, insiders saw the writing on the wall. They rushed to the exits, trying to realize stock gains before the contradictions inherent in the market overwhelmed them. Prices tumbled, wiping out trillions in illusory money.

The case of Enron Corp. is the most notorious, but it is unfortunately not unique. When Enron filed for bankruptcy protection in November of 2001 its stock, which had traded as high as $90 per share a year before, plummeted to less than $1. *New York Times* reporter Jeffrey Seglin writes that the elevators in Enron's Houston headquarters sported TV sets tuned to CNBC, constantly tracking the firm's stock price and acclaiming the bull market generally. As Enron stock climbed in the late 1990s, these daily market updates made employees—whose retirement accounts were largely invested in company shares—feel quite wealthy, though most Enron workers were not in fact free to sell these shares. Enron's contributions of company stock to employee retirement accounts didn't vest until workers reached age 50. For years, Enron had hawked its stock to employees, to pension fund managers, and to the world as a surefire investment. Many employees used their own 401(k) funds, over and above the firm's matching contributions, to purchase additional shares. But as the firm disintegrated amid accusations of accounting fraud, plan managers froze employee accounts, so that workers were unable to unload even the stock they owned outright. With employee accounts frozen, Enron executives and board members are estimated to have dumped their own stock and options, netting $1.2 billion cash—almost exactly the amount employees lost from retirement accounts.

Soon after Enron's collapse, telecommunications giant Global Crossing imploded amid accusations of accounting irregularities. Global Crossing's stock, which had traded at nearly $100 per share, became virtually worthless, but not before CEO Gary Winnick exercised his own options and walked away with $734 million. Qwest Communications director Phil Anschutz cashed in $1.6 billion in the two years before the firm stumbled under a crushing debt load; the stock subsequently lost 96% of its value. The three top officers of telecom equipment maker JDS Uniphase collectively raked in $1.1 billion between 1999 and 2001. The stock is now trading at $2 per share. An investigation by the *Wall Street Journal* and Thompson Financial analysts estimates that top telecommunications executives captured a staggering $14.2 billion in stock gains between 1997 and 2001. The industry is now reeling, with 60 firms bankrupt and 500,000 jobs lost. The *Journal* reports that, as of August 2002, insiders at 38 telecom companies had walked away with gains greater than the current market value of their firms. "All told, it is one of the greatest transfers of wealth from investors—big and small—in American history," reporter Dennis Berman writes. "Telecom executives … made hundreds of millions of dollars, while many investors took huge, unprecedented losses."

Executives in the energy and telecom sectors were not the only ones to rake in impressive gains. Michael Eisner of Disney Corp. set an early record for CEO pay in 1998, netting $575 million, most in option sales. Disney stock has since fallen by two-thirds. Lawrence Ellison, CEO of Oracle Corp., made $706 million when he sold 29 million shares of Oracle stock in January 2001. Ellison's sales flooded the market for Oracle shares and contributed, along with reports of declining profits, to the stock's losing two-thirds of its value over the next few months. Between 1999 and 2001, Dennis Kozlowski of Tyco International sold $258 million of Tyco stock back to the company, on top of a salary and other compensation valued near $30 million. Kozlowski defended this windfall with the claim that his leadership had "created $37 billion in shareholder wealth." By the time Kozlowski quit Tyco under indictment for sales tax fraud in 2002, $80 billion of Tyco's shareholder wealth had evaporated.

Analyzing companies whose stock had fallen by at least 75%, *Fortune* magazine discovered that "executives and directors of the 1,035 companies that met our criteria took out, by our estimate, roughly $66 billion."

THE ILLUSION OF RETIREMENT SECURITY

During the bull market, hundreds of U.S. corporations were also stuffing employee savings accounts with corporate equity, creating a class of captive and friendly shareholders who were in many cases enjoined from selling the stock. Studies by the Employee Benefit Research Council found that, while federal law restricts holdings of company stock to 10% of assets in regulated, defined-benefit pension plans, 401(k)-type plans hold an average 19% of assets in company stock. This fraction rises to 32% when companies match employee contributions with stock and to 53% where companies have influence over plan investments. Pfizer Corporation, by all accounts the worst offender, ties up 81% of employee 401(k)s in company stock, but Coca-Cola runs a close second with 76% of plan assets in stock. Before the firm went bankrupt, WorldCom employees had 40% of their 401(k)s in the firm's shares. Such stock contributions cost firms virtually nothing in the short run and, since employees usually aren't permitted to sell the stock for years, companies needn't worry about diluting the value of equity held by important shareholders—or by their executive option-holders. Commenting on recent business lobbying efforts to gut legislation that would restrict stock contributions to retirement plans, Marc Machiz, formerly of the Labor Department's retirement division, told the *Wall Street Journal*, "business loves having people in employer stock and lobbied very hard to kill this stuff."

Until recently, most employees were untroubled by these trends. The market after all was setting new records daily. Quarterly 401(k) statements recorded fantastic returns year after year. Financial advisers assured the public that stocks were and always would be good investments.

But corporate insiders proved far less willing to bank on illusory stock wealth when securing their own retirements.

Pearl Meyer and Partners, an executive compensation research firm, estimates that corporate executives eschew 401(k) plans for themselves and instead negotiate sizable cash pensions—the average senior executive is covered by a defined-benefit plan promising 60% of salary after 30 years of service. Under pressure from the board, CEO Richard McGinn quit Lucent at age 52 with $12 million in severance and a cash pension paying $870,000 annually. Lucent's employees, on the other hand, receive a 401(k) plan with 17% of its assets invested in Lucent stock. The stock plunged from $77 to $10 after McGinn's departure. Today it trades at around $1.00. Forty-two thousand Lucent workers lost their jobs as the firm sank.

IF STOCKS AND PROFITS ARE ROUTINELY BESTING THE ECONOMY, THEN EITHER WAGE-EARNERS ARE LAGGING BEHIND OR SOMEBODY IS COOKING THE BOOKS.

When Louis Gerstner left IBM in 2002, after receiving $14 million in pay and an estimated $400 million in stock options, he negotiated a retirement package that promises "to cover car, office and club membership expenses for 10 years." IBM's employees, in contrast, have been agitating since 1999 over the firm's decision to replace its defined benefit pension with a 401(k)-type pension plan that, employee representatives estimate, will reduce pensions by one-third to one-half and save the firm $200 million annually. Economist Paul Krugman reports in the *New York Times* that Halliburton Corp. eliminated its employee pensions; first, though, the company "took an $8.5 million charge against earnings to reflect the cost of its parting gift" to CEO Dick Cheney. *Business Week*, surveying the impact of 401(k)s on employee retirement security, concludes that "CEOs deftly phased out rich defined-benefit plans and moved workers into you're-on-your-own 401(k)s, shredding a major safety net even as they locked in lifetime benefits for themselves."

Since 401(k)s were introduced in the early 1980s their use has grown explosively, and they have largely supplanted traditional defined-benefit pensions. In 2002, three of every four dollars contributed to retirement accounts went into 401(k)s. It is thanks to 401(k)s and other retirement savings plans that middle-income Americans became stock-owners in the 1980s and 1990s. It is probably also thanks to 401(k)s, and the huge demand for stocks they generated, that stock prices rose continuously in the 1990s. And it will almost certainly be thanks to 401(k)s that the problems inherent in using the stock market as a vehicle to distribute income will become glaringly apparent once the baby-boom generation begins to retire and liquidate its stock.

If stocks begin again to rise at historical averages—something financial advisors routinely project and prospective retirees are counting on—the discrepancy between what the stock market promises and what the economy delivers will widen dramatically. Something will have to give. Stocks cannot rise faster than the economy grows, not if people are actually to live off the proceeds.

Or rather, stock prices can't rise that fast unless corporate profits—on which stocks represent a legal claim—also surpass GDP gains. But if corporate earnings outpace economic growth, wages will have to stagnate or decline.

Pension economist Douglas Orr believes it is no accident that 401(k)s proliferated in a period of declining earnings and intense economic insecurity for most U.S. wage-earners. From 1980 until the latter half of the 1990s, the position of the typical American employee deteriorated noticeably. Wages fell, unemployment rose, benefits were slashed, stress levels and work hours climbed as U.S. firms "downsized" and "restructured" to cut costs and satiate investor hunger for higher profits. Firms like General Electric cut tens of thousands of jobs and made remaining jobs far less secure in order to generate earnings growth averaging 15% each year. Welch's ruthless union-busting and cost-cutting earned him the nickname "Neutron Jack" among rank-and-file employees. GE's attitude towards its employees was summed up by union negotiator Steve Tormey: "No matter how many records are broken in productivity or profits, it's always 'what have you done for me lately?' The workers are considered lemons and they are squeezed dry." Welch was championed as a hero on Wall Street, his management techniques widely emulated by firms across the nation. During his tenure, GE's stock price soared as the firm slashed employment by nearly 50%.

The Institute for Policy Studies, in a recent study, found that rising stock prices and soaring CEO pay packages are commonly associated with layoffs. CEOs of firms that "announced layoffs of 1,000 or more workers in 2000 earned about 80 percent more, on average, than the executives of the 365 firms surveyed by *Business Week*."

Throughout the 1980s and 1990s, workers whose jobs were disappearing and wages collapsing consoled themselves by watching the paper value of their 401(k)s swell. With labor weak and labor incomes falling, wage and salary earners chose to cast their lot with capital. In betting on the stock market, though, workers are in reality betting that wage incomes will stagnate and trying to offset this by grabbing a slice from the profit pie. This has already proved a losing strategy for most.

Even at the peak of the 1990s bull market, the net wealth—assets minus debts—of the typical household fell from $55,000 to $50,000, as families borrowed heavily to protect their living standards in the face of stagnant wages. Until or unless the nation's capital stock is equitably distributed, there will always be a clash of interests between owners of capital and their employees. If stocks and profits are routinely besting the economy, then either wage-earners are lagging behind or somebody is cooking the books.

Yet surveys show that Americans like 401(k)s. In part, this is because savings accounts are portable, an important consideration in a world where workers can expect to change jobs several times over their working lives. But partly it is because savings plans provide the illusion of self-sufficiency and independence. When retirees spend down their savings, it feels as if they are "paying their own way." They do not feel like dependents, consuming the fruits of other people's labor. Yet they are. It is the nature of retirement that retirees opt out of production and rely on the young to keep the economy rolling. Pensions are always a claim on the real economy—they represent a transfer of goods and services from working adults to non-working retirees, who no longer contribute to economic output. The shift from defined-benefit pensions to 401(k)s and other savings plans in no way changes the fact that pensions transfer resources, but it does change the rules that will govern how those transfers take place—who pays and who benefits.

Private defined-benefit pensions impose a direct claim on corporate profits. In promising a fixed payment over a number of years, corporations commit to transfer a portion of future earnings to retirees. Under these plans, employers promise an annual lifetime benefit at retirement, the amount determined by an employee's prior earnings and years of service in the company. How the benefit will be paid, where the funds will come from, whether there are enough funds to last through a worker's life—this is the

company's concern. Longevity risk—the risk that a worker will outlive the money put aside for her retirement—falls on the employer. Retirees benefit, but at a cost to shareholders. Similarly, public pension programs, whether through Social Security or through the civil service, entail a promise to retirees at the expense of the taxpaying public.

Today, the vast majority of workers, if they have pension coverage at all, participate in "defined contribution" plans, in which they and their employer contribute a fixed monthly sum and invest the proceeds with a money management firm. At retirement, the employee owns whatever funds have accrued in the account and must make the money last until she dies. Defined-contribution plans are a claim on nothing. Workers are given a shot at capturing some of the cash floating around Wall Street, but no promise that they will succeed. 401(k)s will add a huge element of chance to the American retirement experience. Some will sell high, some will not. Some will realize gains. Some will not.

Pearl Meyer and Partners estimate that outstanding, unexercised executive stock options and employee stock incentives today amount to some $2 trillion. Any effort to cash in this amount, in addition to the stock held in retirement accounts, would have a dramatic impact on stock prices. American workers and retirees, in assessing their chances for coming out ahead in the competition to liquidate stock, might ponder this question: If, as employees in private negotiations with their corporate employers, they have been unable to protect their incomes or jobs or health or retirement benefits, how likely is it that they will instead be able to wrest gains from Wall Street where corporate insiders are firmly in control of information and access to deals?

September/October 1995

THE "PROFITS = INVESTMENT" SCAM

BY DEAN BAKER

Corporate profits have been rising rapidly in the United States—and much of the reason is that both wages and corporate taxes have been falling. Many political and business leaders claim that these losses to workers and the public sector are worthwhile, because higher profits yield more investment. And investment is the engine that drives growth in output, which then benefits everyone as employees and consumers.

But recent evidence does not support the claim that growing profits yield widespread prosperity—because the growth rate of investment has fallen drastically since the 1970s. Without investment, higher profits are an unmitigated loss for the vast majority of people.

The real wages of most workers have declined over the last 20 years, with the median wage falling by 7.5% between 1973 and 1993. (The median means that half of workers got a higher wage, and half a lower one.) This has occurred even though the Gross Domestic Product (GDP) per employee has been rising steadily.

Part of the decline in median wages is due to growing wage inequality, as workers at the top end of the income distribution have made substantial gains during this period. Another reason is the rapid rise in health care costs, which have drained a portion of workers' compensation away from wages and into benefits.

But part of the explanation for declining wages is rising profits. As a result of changes in the economy and the political system in recent decades, income that would have gone to workers as wages is now going to investors in the form of profits, dividends, and interest.

During the recent recovery, even while many companies have shown record growth and profits, they have given meager wage increases. They have also eliminated workers in droves, sub-contracting the jobs to firms that pay far less. American Airlines, for example, laid off hundreds of ticket agents, who made up to $19 an hour, replacing them with workers from a contracting firm that pays $7 to $9 an hour. Mobil Oil, despite $1.7 billion in profits during 1994, is planning a similar move with its clerical and support staff.

Another reason profits rose in recent years was a fall in the tax rate on capital. With lower federal tax revenues, the increase in profitability has thus contributed to the deficit. So both falling real wages and threats to government support for programs such as Medicare, Medicaid, food stamps, and Aid to Families with Dependent Children (welfare) are directly connected to the rise in corporate profits.

A PUZZLE: PROFIT SHARES AND RATES

Many analysts have overlooked the increase in corporate profitability because they have examined profit *shares*, the percentage of output going to owners of capital, rather than profit *rates*, the ratio of annual profits to the total amount invested over time. The share of corporate output that ends up as capital income, either as profits or interest, has changed little over the last 20 years, hovering around 14%. (The corporate sector accounts for over 90% of private business in the United States. The rest of the business sector is mainly family-run businesses where the distinction between wages and profits is often unclear.)

Profit rates, however, have followed a very different pattern during this period. Since they fluctuate greatly depending on whether the economy is in a recession or a recovery, it is common to average profit rates over a business cycle. In the cycle that ran from 1974 to 1979, the rate averaged 2.4%. This means that firms received 2.4 cents, after taxes, in interest or profit for each dollar's worth of physical capital (factories, machinery, land, or inventories) they owned. This rose to 4.1% in the business cycle from 1980 to 1989, and to 5.8% in the most recent cycle from 1990 to the present. So in the 1990s firms have been getting more than twice as much back in profit as they did in the 1970s.

How can profit rates rise when profit shares stay the same? There are two reasons. First, if firms invest less, relative to the size of the economy, while profit shares stay the same, then profit rates will rise (profit rate = profits/investment). This is exactly what has happened in the last 15 years. The percentage of output going to new investment in plant and equipment fell throughout the 1980s, and hit record lows in the early 1990s. New investment was just 0.9% of output in 1992, compared with a high of 4.7% in 1979. But due to the rise in the profit rate, the profit share of total output remained unchanged. This is comparable to a situation where workers received the same annual pay, even though they worked two months less each year. The profit rate can be thought of as the hourly pay rate for capital, and in the last 15 years, it more than doubled.

The second factor driving up profit rates has been lower taxes on corporate earnings. Even though before-tax corporate profits have not changed much over the last 20 years, after-tax profit shares have risen significantly. Since the early 1970s, corporate taxes have dropped from over 40% to about 30% of the profits and interest earned by the corporate sector. This lower tax rate on capital income raises corporate profits and the national deficit by about $50 billion annually—a total cost to the government of $700 billion during the past 15 years. If we view this as an addition to the national debt, the interest on this debt, together with the annual loss of tax revenue, is nearly $100 billion, or more than half of the yearly budget deficit at present.

Corporate taxes fell for two reasons. First, the federal government deliberately cut the tax rates on corporate income in a series of tax code changes. Second, firms have become more effective at avoiding taxes. For example, money that firms pay as dividends to shareholders is counted as profits and, therefore, is subject to the corporate income tax. But money that firms pay as interest to bondholders is not counted as profits, so no corporate income taxes are paid on the interest. The share of interest in capital income has risen from less than 12% in the early 1970s to nearly 30% in recent years.

If part of the rise in profit rates comes at the expense of government tax revenue, the other part comes out of wage income. If profit rates and the tax rates on corporate income had remained at their mid-70s levels, the amount of income going to workers would be approximately $300 billion higher each year, a 7% increase. Clearly, the fact that corporations have kept the same share of output as profits, even though they have invested far less, explains much of the decline in wages experienced by many.

Declining wages are due to several factors that have undermined the bargaining position of workers. These include increased international competition, declining unionization rates, decreased government protection for workers' rights, and the Federal Reserve Board's insistence on maintaining high unemployment rates in order to fight inflation.

Such factors have enabled firms to experience large increases in profits without sharing their gains with workers.

Of course profits are not bad in and of themselves. Most investment is financed by corporate profits, and there would be no investment at all if corporations didn't anticipate making a profit. But the enormous rise in profitability over the last 15 years has not paid off in terms of higher investment rates. Instead the profits have simply enhanced the living standards of the small number of people who have great wealth.

Resources: Sam Bowles, David Gordon, and Thomas Weisskopf, *After the Wasteland*, 1990.

ARTICLE 3.4   *May/June 2002*

WHO DECIDES STOCK PRICES?

BY ELLEN FRANK

Dear Dr. Dollar:

During the course of a single day, a stock can go up and down frequently. These changes supposedly reflect the changing demand for that stock (and its potential resale value) or changing expectations of a company's profitability. But this seems too vague to me. How can these factors be so volatile? Who actually decides, or what is the mechanism for deciding, when a stock price should go up or down and by how much?

—*Joseph Balszak,*
Muskegon, Michigan

Let's start with your last question first—how are stock prices determined? Shares in most large established corporations are listed on organized exchanges like the New York or American Stock Exchanges. Shares in most smaller or newer firms are listed on the NASDAQ—an electronic system that tracks stock prices.

Every time a stock is sold, the exchange records the price at which it changes hands. If, a few seconds or minutes later, another trade takes place, the price at which that trade is made becomes the new market price, and so on. Organized exchanges like the New York Stock Exchange will occasionally suspend trading in a stock if the price is excessively volatile, if there is a severe mismatch between supply and demand (many people wanting to sell, no one wanting to buy) or if they suspect that insiders are deliberately manipulating a stock's price. But in normal circumstances, there is no official arbiter of stock prices, no person or institution that "decides" a price. The market price of a stock is simply the price at which a willing buyer and seller agree to trade.

Why then do prices fluctuate so much? The vast bulk of stock trades are made by professional traders who buy and sell shares all day long, hoping to profit from small changes in share prices. Since these traders do not hold stocks over the long haul, they are not terribly interested in such long-term considerations as a company's profitability or the value of its assets. Or rather, they are interested in such factors mostly insofar as news that would affect a company's long-term prospects might cause *other traders* to buy the stock, causing its price to rise. If a trader believes that others will buy shares (in the expectation that prices will rise), then she will buy as well, hoping to sell when the price rises. If others believe the same thing, then the wave of buying pressure will, in fact, *cause* the price to rise.

Back in the 1930s, economist John Maynard Keynes compared the stock market to a contest then popular in British tabloids, in which contestants had to look at photos and choose the faces that *other contestants* would pick as the prettiest. Each contestant had to look for photos "likeliest to catch the fancy of the other competitors, all of whom are looking at the problem from the same point of view." Similarly, stock traders try to guess which stocks other traders will buy. The successful trader is the one who anticipates and outfoxes the market, buying before a stock's price rises and selling before it falls.

Financial firms employ thousands of market strategists and technical analysts who spend hours poring over historical stock data, trying to divine the logic behind these price changes. If they could unlock the secret of stock prices, they could arm their traders with the ability to always buy low and sell high. So far, no one has found this particular holy grail. And so traders continue to guess and gamble and, in doing so, send prices gyrating.

For small investors, who do hold stock for the long term and will need to cash in their stocks at some point to finance their retirements, the volatility of the market can be a source of constant anxiety. Every time a share in, say, General Electric is traded, the new price is used to revalue *all* outstanding shares—just as the value of your home appreciates when the house down the block sells for more than a similar house sold last week. But the value of your home wouldn't be so high if every house on your block were suddenly put up for sale. Similarly, if all ten billion outstanding shares of General Electric—or even a small fraction of them—were put up for sale, they wouldn't fetch anywhere near the current market price. Small investors need to keep in mind that the gains and losses on their 401(k) statements are just hypothetical paper gains and losses. You won't know the true value of your stocks until you actually try to sell them.

—*Ellen Frank*

January/February 1997

WHY HAVE SAVINGS FALLEN?

RISING INEQUALITY DESERVES THE BLAME

BY TED SCHMIDT

Beginning in the mid-1970s the share of their incomes which U.S. households save steadily declined, and this drop accelerated in the 1980s. According to household surveys, the savings rate averaged 13.8% of income during 1981 to 1983, but fell sharply to 10% during 1987 to 1991.

Most orthodox economists, and many policymakers, believe this decline is a critical economic problem. Why? First, since they view saving as the source of capital for business investment, lower savings will mean higher interest rates, resulting in less investment and slower economic growth. Second, higher interest rates will harm consumers by making it more difficult to finance home mortgages, car loans and other purchases. Third, the current generation, by not saving enough, will face greater hardships in retirement.

While economists and policymakers of many political stripes agree that we should be deeply troubled about this situation, they don't agree on why the rate fell, or what to do about it.

One political viewpoint, that of "supply side" economics, became prominent in part due to concerns during the 1980s about the falling savings rate. Among other things, supply-siders argue for redistributing income toward corporations and the wealthy, on the theory that these sectors save at higher rates. But while such a redistribution *has* taken place during the past 15 years, overall savings have continued to fall.

Evidence from recent decades shows that while the rich are saving more, this increase has been outweighed by dramatically lower savings from all other income groups. And the reason is that widening inequality has so harmed the incomes of moderate- and low-income households that they are unable to save, and in fact are living on borrowed money (dissaving).

While many orthodox economists have focused on ways to redress this "crisis" in U.S. household savings, their models of savings behavior offer no explanation for the decline. Since they don't understand the causes of the problem, these economists' remedies are likely to be misguided.

One problem with orthodox models is that they assume all households, regardless of their income or wealth, make consumption decisions in similar ways. All families, the models assume, balance their current consumption needs versus the need to save for retirement, and all have reliable estimates of their future income. These assumptions are suspect for several reasons.

First, only households that have relatively stable sources of income can make long-term decisions concerning future consumption in retirement. But a large and growing number of households face great uncertainty concerning their jobs and income. Second, many households, even if they would like to save for retirement, cannot do so, because they don't have enough income to cover their current consumption needs.

IT'S ALL RELATIVE

Orthodox models also fail by assuming that households adjust their behavior similarly whether incomes rise or fall—when they rise, households consume more, and when they fall, households consume proportionally less. But the "Relative Income Hypothesis" (RIH), suggested in 1949 by economist James Duesenberry, argues that when incomes decline (such as in a recession), households resist giving up the consumption patterns they have become accustomed to.

To maintain their previous living standards, households will either reduce their savings rates, consume out of previous savings, increase their use of debt, or raise household income by having another household member enter the labor market. Although the RIH is more realistic than orthodox theories, mainstream economists have neglected it because it does not fit into their neat mathematical models.

Duesenberry's RIH is valuable for analyzing the effects of a recession, or of a long-term decline in income for all of society. But understanding the past two decades of U.S. history requires a recognition that households' consumption decisions are based not only on their own incomes, but also on their economic standing relative to other households.

In recent years, for example, moderate- and low-income people have seen their actual incomes stagnate, while falling relative to the wealthy. In this situation, those with lower incomes may resist cutting their consumption, as they observe the affluent lifestyles of others around them.

In addition, how fast and to what extent income changes affect consumption depends on whether the income is derived from wages or from ownership of property. In fact, the consumption behavior of rich households probably depends more on changes in their wealth than in their incomes. A stock market boom or crash, for example, will affect the wealthy's consumption decisions more so than any change in their salaries.

We can conclude that savings rates depend on both changes in average income per person and changes in the distribution of income and wealth among households. A recent study by economist David Bunting provides evidence in support of this conclusion. Bunting analyzed data from the Bureau of Labor Statistics' 1972 and 1991 Consumer Expenditure Surveys, ranking households by income level. He then divided them into five equally sized groups, or fifths.

Income shares and saving rates for each fifth are shown in the table. The first column for each year shows the percentage of total U.S. income received by that fifth. In 1981 to 1983, for example, the poorest fifth received 3.9% of total household income while the richest fifth received 44.4%. Column two shows the savings rate of each fifth, meaning the fraction of their incomes which they saved, on average. The poorest two fifths had *negative* savings rates— meaning that they were spending more than the income they received, by living on borrowed money.

Given the shift in income toward the wealthy during the 1980s, what caused the decline in savings rates from 1981-83 to 1987-91? It was not a lack of savings by the richest Americans, but rather by everyone else. The *dissavings* rates of the lowest two fifths rose, while the savings rates for the third and fourth fifths (perhaps approximating the middle class) fell greatly.

In 1981-83 the lowest two fifths dissaved at rates of -108% and -15% respectively, while in 1987-91 their negative saving rates grew to -122% and -28%. In addition, the third fifth went from net savers to dissavers, while the savings of the fourth fifth fell from 18% to 12% of their incomes.

The savings rate of the wealthiest fifth of households also worsened slightly. But this was more than offset by their increased share of national income. As a result, this was the only income group that increased its total savings (from a 13.9 to a 14.4 percentage point contribution toward the overall savings rate, as shown in column three of the table).

Many analysts expected the overall U.S. savings rate to rise as wealthier households, with higher savings propensities, gained a greater share of the total income. And supply-side theorists continue to recommend shifting income toward the wealthy as a means of raising total savings in the United States.

But the evidence demonstrates the opposite—higher savings by the rich did not make up for the severely reduced savings of the remaining 80% of households. As economist Robert Pollin has argued, the bottom three fifths found it necessary to increase their *dissaving* in order to maintain living standards in the face of stagnating real incomes and rising costs of living, especially for housing, since the early 1970s.

This conclusion can only be reached by recognizing that lower-income groups must make their consumption decisions in a different fashion than the rich, a distinction that mainstream theorists are reluctant to make. The clear policy implication directly contradicts the course advocated by supply-side theories: In order to reverse the decline in savings, income must be redistributed *not* to the wealthy, but away from them, to the middle and working classes, and to the poor.

Resources: David Bunting, "Saving and the Distribution of Income," *Journal of Post-Keynesian Economics*, Fall 1991; Christopher D. Carroll and Lawrence H. Summers, "Why Is U.S. National Saving So Low?," *Brookings Papers on Economic Activity*, No. 2, 1987; Robert N. Pollin, "Deeper in Debt: The Changing Financial Conditions of U.S. Households," Economic Policy Institute, September 1990.

INCOME AND SAVINGS BY INCOME QUINTILES (FIFTHS)

income quintile (fifth)	share of total income (I)	fraction of income saved (savings rate, or S)	contribution to overall saving rate (I times S)
		1981 TO 1983 AVERAGE	
lowest	3.9%	-108.2%	-4.2%
second	10.1%	-15.4%	-1.6%
third	16.7%	6.3%	1.1%
fourth	24.8%	18.4%	4.6%
highest	44.4%	31.3%	13.9%
overall savings rate (1981-83)			**13.7%**
		1987 TO 1991 AVERAGE	
lowest	3.8%	-122.6%	-4.7%
second	9.3%	-28.1%	-2.6%
third	15.8%	-0.9%	-0.1%
fourth	24.3%	12.2%	3.0%
highest	46.9%	30.6%	14.4%
overall savings rate (1987-91)			**9.9%**

Source: Bureau of Labor Statistics, U.S. Department of Labor, *Consumer Expenditure Surveys.*

CHAPTER 4
Fiscal Policy, Deficits, and Debt

INTRODUCTION

Most textbooks depict a macroeconomy stabilized by government intervention. Reflecting the influence of Keynes, they look at ways that the government can use fiscal policy—government spending and taxation—to bolster a flagging economy. Despite its recent pick up in economic growth, the U.S. economy is still reeling from the collapse of the high-tech sector, a soggy stock market, and the job losses of the last four years (see Article 1.1). What is the role of fiscal policy in this context? How is the federal government, under an administration committed to shrinking the size of government, using fiscal tools?

Articles 4.1–4.3 look at the Bush Administration's reversal of fiscal fortune. The Bush team turned unprecedented projected budget surpluses into deficits likely to persist until 2013. The cause of those deficits, as John Miller shows in Article 4.1, was the Bush tax cuts and military buildup, not a boom in social spending, as the *Wall Street Journal* alleges. In Article 4.2, Ellen Frank explains the reasons that Republicans who once decried deficit spending are now spearheading it—and argues that their newfound love of deficits has little to do with the progressive tradition of Keynes. In Article 4.3, Adria Scharf documents the devastating fiscal effects of the Bush tax cuts. Making those tax cuts permanent, as Scharf demonstrates, would cost more than the money necessary to keep Social Security solvent in the decades ahead.

The hallmark of Bush's tax policy has been tax cuts for the rich. John Miller responds to the Bush administration's claim that the rich are "double-taxed," noting that *all* taxpayers face double taxation (Article 4.4). While the administration argues that the well-to-do pay more than their fair share of taxes, Ellen Frank shows that U.S. tax policy actually does little to redistribute income (Article 4.5). Finally, Miller explains just why the Bush tax cut is ill-designed and ill-timed to turn the economy around in the short term (Article 4.6).

One of the key debates in policy circles today is whether to privatize programs that have long been the responsibility of the government. In Article 4.7, Ann Markusen takes a close look at today's military spending, especially the Pentagon's large-scale effort to outsource its operation to private corporations. Markusen argues that there is little evidence that the privatization of military contracts has generated efficiencies. Rather, without close monitoring, the Pentagon has awarded lucrative contracts to corporations with a history of cost overruns, such as Halliburton subsidiary Kellogg Brown & Root.

Unlike the military, Social Security has not enjoyed an influx of funds. How will it fare as baby boomers retire? Ellen Frank answers that question, putting to rest much of the talk about a Social Security crisis (Article 4.8). Next, Elise Gould shows that the 2003 Medicare Modernization Act fails to provide seniors with the universal health care insurance and prescription drug coverage promised by the Bush Administration (Article 4.9). Finally, Frank challenges proposals to privatize Social Security by toting up the higher costs and added risks that would come with private accounts (Article 4.10).

Of course, macroeconomics textbooks examine not only the ups and downs of the business cycle, but also trade-offs in economies whose resources are fully employed. Many present the famed trade-off between "guns" and "butter." Economists use a *production possibilities curve* to demonstrate the *opportunity cost* of devoting economic resources to certain kinds of production. For example, the opportunity cost of producing arms ("guns") is the set of social goods ("butter") that society must forego. That trade-off is being made today in the United States, and Alejandro Reuss presents a vivid depiction of its staggering social cost, as well as its global political significance (Article 4.11).

KEY TO COLANDER

E = Economics. M = Macroeconomics.

Articles 4.1, 4.2, and 4.3 address topics from E31 or M15. Articles 4.4, 4.5, and 4.6 go with chapters E25-E26 or M9-M10, or the macro policy discussions in E30, E31, and E34, or M14, M15, and M19. Article 4.7 also illustrates macroeconmic policy issues in chapters E30, E31, and E 34, or M14, M15, and M19. Articles 4.8, 4.9, and 4.10 add to the discussion of Social Security and social spending in E31 or M15.

DISCUSSION QUESTIONS

1) (Article 4.1) How have Bush administration policies affected non-defense discretionary spending?
2) (Article 4.2) Are budget deficits a macroeconomic problem? Are they a political and social policy problem? Explain your answers.
3) (Article 4.3) What is the cost of making the Bush tax cuts permanent? What would be the likely impact on social spending if this were to happen?
4) (Article 4.4) Why does Miller argue that taxing dividends is fair? Why doesn't he think that eliminating the dividends tax will lead to faster economic growth?
5) (Article 4.5) According to Frank, how significantly does the U.S. tax code redistribute income? What evidence does she consider that the Heritage Foundation does not, and how does it influence her conclusion?

6) (Article 4.6) The *Wall Street Journal* maintains that the tax burden has reached unprecedented levels and that the government has grown too large. How does Miller respond to these charges?

7) (Article 4.7 and 4.11) What evidence does Markusen present to call into question the claim that privatizing military spending will create competition that spurs on efficiency and improves military services? How Reuss calculate the real cost of the military buildup?

8) (Article 4.8) Where is the money in the Social Security trust fund, and what is it doing?

9) (Article 4.9) According to Gould, what are the "three strikes" against the Bush Administration's health care reform proposals? Do you agree with Gould's alternative proposal to provide health care insurance?

10) (Article 4.10) How would private accounts affect the administrative costs for Social Security and the economic security of workers?

ARTICLE 4.1

November/December 2003

WHAT SPENDING BOOM?

BY JOHN MILLER

THE SPENDING BOOM

If our politicians are shedding more than crocodile tears about the deficit, we have a suggestion. They could always slow the growth of their own spending. CBO points out that in fiscal 2003 non-defense discretionary spending will … increase to 3.9% [of GDP], 'its highest level since 1985.' Anyone who argues that the war on terror is crowding out domestic spending should be laughed out of the room.

The CBO report makes another useful point: Its deficit estimates … do not include the monumental increases in federal outlays that are certain to follow the passage of a new Medicare entitlement for prescription drugs for seniors. If someone wants to guarantee deficits as far as the eye can see, just pass that huge expansion of the entitlement state.

— *The Wall Street Journal*, Aug. 27, 2003

Next year's federal deficit will reach $480 billion, the federal government will not balance its budget again before fiscal year 2013, and the deficit could get yet worse in the decade ahead. Those are the projections the Congressional Budget Office (CBO) made in its August *Budget and Economic Outlook* update.

Bad news for the Bush administration and its tax-cutting agenda, right? Not so, say the editors of *The Wall Street Journal*. In an editorial the day after the CBO update was released, they blamed the budget deficit not on the Bush administration but on a congressional "spending boom." That might come as a surprise to anyone who's been watching with alarm as vital government programs, from environmental protection to job training, get slashed. The surprise is warranted. As it turns out, while the *Journal*'s editorial may quote the CBO numbers accurately, its analysis is grossly misleading and plainly illogical.

First, the title. There is no "spending boom." According to the CBO report, post-9/11 spending has merely arrested the shrinking of the federal government that Reagan initiated and Clinton carried out so effectively. Relative to the size of the economy, today's federal government is no larger than in the past. At 20.2% of GDP, federal budget outlays in 2003 are no greater than the average from 1962 to 2001, and lower than federal outlays relative to GDP in every year during the 1980s and the first half of the 1990s. They're particularly low for a period of high unemployment: In 1991 and 1992, during the last recession, federal government outlays averaged a considerably higher 22.3% of GDP.

Second, the Bush administration's war on terror has in fact crowded out much-needed domestic spending. True enough: in 2003 "non-defense discretionary spending" (more or less everything outside of Social Security, Medicare, and the military) will reach its highest levels since 1985, some 3.9% of GDP. But that number is deceptive. To begin with, it is well below the 5.2% of GDP that went to these expenditures in 1980, before the Reagan administration began gutting social spending. Beyond that, the 3.9% figure includes not only domestic but also international spending, primarily foreign military assistance. Subtracting that out leaves domestic non-defense discretionary spending at just 3.5% of GDP.

That 3.5% represents more domestic spending than when Bush took office. But when the *Journal*'s editors claim that growing non-defense spending means that the war on terror is not crowding out domestic spending, they're just flat-out wrong—the bulk of the new spending is *for* the war on terror. Over three-quarters of the new domestic discretionary spending from January 2001 to April 2003 that the *Journal* complains about went to homeland security (49.2%), New York City relief and recovery (22.5%), and airline relief (4.4%). The rest of the additional spending went to fund educational initiatives (although Head Start and even the president's No Child Left Behind Act were never fully funded), to double the National Institutes of Health budget, to pay for voting reform, and to provide medical care for veterans.

THERE IS NO "SPENDING BOOM." RELATIVE TO THE SIZE OF THE ECONOMY, TODAY'S FEDERAL GOVERNMENT IS NO LARGER THAN IN THE PAST.

Domestic discretionary spending in all other areas declined by $11 billion. Among the programs suffering deep budget cuts were housing assistance (down $2.9 billion or 9.1%), spending on the environment and natural resources (down $1.3 billion or 4.3%), and job training and employment services (down $675 million or 11.5%).

Third, the gaping budget deficits that the CBO forecasts are not the result of congressional overspending. Bush's pro-rich tax cuts, which will siphon off about $275 billion in 2004 alone, along with slower economic growth, have constricted the flow of revenues to the federal government, holding them well below historic levels. Government revenues will amount to just 17.9% of GDP in 2004, according to the report, the lowest figure in a decade. Those lost revenues have saddled the federal government with a whopping deficit, some 4.2% of GDP in 2003, more than twice the size of the average deficit from 1962 to 2001.

Finally, what about the *Journal*'s clincher: that additional entitlement spending, not the war on terror, threatens to create a genuine and sustained budget crisis? Even if Congress passes a new prescription drug benefit for seniors under Medicare, it will not push federal outlays beyond historic levels. For instance, according to budget analyst Richard Kogan with the Center on Budget and Policy Priorities, spending $700 billion over ten years, enough to cover half of the prescription drug costs of the entire Medicare population and far more than Congress is likely to allocate, would still leave government outlays in 2012 at 20.1% of GDP—no higher than today.

If the *Wall Street Journal* editors were really worried about policies likely "to guarantee deficits as far as the eye can see," then they would drop their demand that the Bush tax cuts be made permanent, a staple of their editorial page. Permanently enacting Bush's 2001 and 2002 tax cuts, including the repeal of the estate tax, would drain over $1 trillion from federal revenues, according to the CBO update. Using the more realistic spending and taxing assumptions hidden in the footnotes of the CBO report, the federal government would be left with a $1.1 trillion deficit in fiscal year 2013.

But then isn't that the goal of the Bush administration's anti-public sector agenda: to starve the government of tax revenues and open up large, sustained deficits that will make further entitlement spending—so loathed by the *Journal*'s editors—impossible?

Resources: "The Spending Boom," *The Wall Street Journal*, 8/27/03; "The Budget and Economic Outlook: An Update," Congressional Budget Office, August, 2003; "Bush's $10 Trillion Borrowing Binge," Citizens For Tax Justice, 9/11/03; "What Has Caused Growth in Discretionary Spending," Democratic Staff, Senate Budget Committee, 5/5/03; Isaac Shapiro and Richard Kogan, "OMB Figures Show Revenues—Due to Tax Cuts—At Exceptionally Low Levels, While Spending Levels Are Not Especially High," Center on Budget and Policy Priorities, 7/23/03; Richard Kogan, "Costs of the Tax Cut and a Medicare Prescription Drug Benefit," Center on Budget and Policy Priorities, 6/14/02.

ARE REPUBLICANS THE NEW "SPENDOCRATS"?

BY ELLEN FRANK

Dear Dr. Dollar:

Bush's budget has the federal government running huge deficits for years to come. Democrats say this will cause high interest rates and low growth. Republicans argue that deficits don't matter at all. Isn't this the exact opposite of what the two parties usually claim? Is my memory shot or am I missing something here?
—*Joan Williamson, Sewanee, Tennessee*

Welcome to the topsy-turvy world of deficit politics, where nothing is what it seems! Your memory is fine, just too long for a career in politics. Republicans did oppose federal budget deficits as recently as a year or two ago. And once upon a time, Democrats were staunch advocates of Keynesian stimulus policies—running big deficits during a slump to stabilize the economy and promote employment. But Republicans have changed their minds.

When the government spends more than it collects in taxes, it finances the gap by borrowing on the bond market. Government bonds are virtually risk-free. They are as safe as cash but unlike cash, bonds pay interest.

When Bill Clinton was in office, conventional wisdom held that corporate executives loathed deficits because in their view, deficits forced private firms to compete with the government for borrowed funds. Given a choice between risk-free federal bonds and more risky corporate bonds, investors would opt to lend to the government. Economists worried this might drive up interest charges to private borrowers, "crowding them out" of the financial markets and reducing private investment in new facilities and technologies. This is how Federal Reserve chairman Alan Greenspan explained the "facts" of economic life to Clinton in 1992. A chastened Clinton set about putting the government's books in order.

We now know that life is more complicated. Corporate leaders do indeed detest budget deficits, but only when they are run by Democratic administrations.

Democrats favor policies that redistribute wealth downward—at least some of the time. Clinton, for example, raised the top tax rate on very high incomes from 31% to 39.6%. His administration increased aid to higher education and financial transfers to the working poor. He proposed, but failed to pass, a plan (admittedly badly designed) to provide universal health coverage. Conservatives believe, not without reason, that if Democrats are able to command greater public resources—whether from borrowing or taxing—they will use them to expand public services and social spending. So conservative pundits assailed Clinton for running deficits and, when he closed the deficit, for raising taxes and, when the budget was in surplus, for stealing taxpayers' hard-earned money.

Republican policies, however, generally redistribute wealth upward. Republicans cut taxes on the wealthy and increase spending on things beneficial to their corporate interests—military hardware, homeland security, agricultural subsidies. Then the Treasury borrows from the wealthy to cover the resulting budgetary shortfall. So the rich receive interest on the loans that cover the debt that their tax breaks and subsidies create.

Congress meanwhile erupts in wrath over "out-of-control entitlements" and proposes "painful but essential" cuts in public services and social insurance programs. In March, the Republican-led House passed Bush's latest tax cut as part of a budget promising deep cuts in everything but defense and homeland security. The wealthy do not fund candidates promising them tax cuts simply to see their wealth redistributed through the back door via deficit-financed social programs. Cuts in social programs are the whole point.

The problem for conservatives is how to reconcile current budget plans with their erstwhile opposition to deficits.

Milton Friedman, guru of free-market economics and an ardent foe of deficit spending, recently laid out the new conservative "theory" of deficits in a *Wall Street Journal* editorial. "Deficits," he writes, are probably "the only effective restraint on the spending propensities of the executive branch and the legislature." Former deficit hawk Rep. Sue Myrick (R-N.C.) concurred, telling the *New York Times*, "Anything that will help us stop spending money, I'm in favor of. And if there's a deficit, that may help us."

So the Republican agenda is to cut taxes and use the resulting deficits to force cuts in spending. What spending? Look at their budget and the party platform: Medicare, Medicaid, Food Stamps and Social Security are all targeted for cuts, privatization or eventual elimination. Of course, if you're a Republican politician, you can't stand up in the hometown coffee shop and brag that the deficits you've wracked up are actually good because they're enabling you to cut Medicaid. But neither can you adhere to the Republican tradition of denouncing deficits. So for now, the party line is simply that deficits don't matter.

As for the Democrats, they made a strategic decision under Clinton to embrace the morality of fiscal discipline. Despite the fact that the typical American household borrows to finance everything from homes to cars to college to washing machines, ancient moral enjoinders against borrowing weigh heavily on the popular conscience. Republicans in the past proved adept at tapping into these moral anxieties. The Democratic leadership is apparently employing this tactic now to fight Bush's tax cuts.

Such is the sorry state of U.S. political discourse that the really important questions—what the government does with its resources and who, ultimately, foots the bill—have become mired in these exasperating and exhausting debates about deficits.

March/April 2004

TAX CUT TIME BOMB

BY ADRIA SCHARF

President George W. Bush and Congress planted a time bomb in the federal budget, and they're about to light the fuse. The largest parts of the tax cuts passed in 2001 and 2003 didn't activate immediately, but were designed to kick in later this decade. If they go forward, the cuts will likely cripple or destroy the social programs that form the cornerstone of the federal welfare state. Even worse, the Bush administration is now pushing to make permanent virtually all of the 2001 and 2003 tax cuts, which were originally set to expire by 2010.

In 2001, Bush sought and won the largest income tax rollback in two decades—it reduced tax rates on the top four income brackets and gave advance refunds of $300 to $600 to 94 million taxpayers. In 2003, despite the growing budget deficit, the administration secured a second tax cut—the third largest in U.S. history. The 2003 package shrank dividend and capital gains taxes and accelerated the 2001 rate cut for top income brackets. Combined, the 2001 and 2003 tax cuts will cost at least $824.1 billion between 2001 and 2010, even if Republicans don't succeed in renewing the provisions scheduled to expire, or "sunset," according to Citizens for Tax Justice (CTJ). If the cuts are extended, CTJ estimates they will cost more than $1 trillion between 2004 and 2014, with over 80% of the revenue loss hitting after 2009. (See figure 1.)

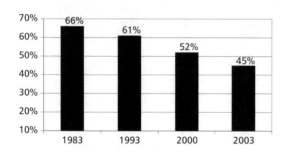

FIGURE 1
DELAYED EFFECT:
COST OF ADMINISTRATION PLAN TO MAKE THE 2001-2003 TAX CUTS PERMANENT

Source: Citizens for Tax Justice, February 3, 2004.
From the administration's fiscal 2005 budget proposal.

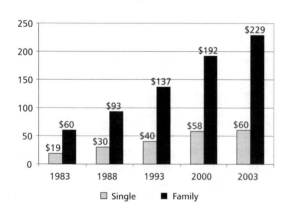

FIGURE 2
SHARE OF THE 2001-2003 BUSH TAX CUTS BY YEAR*

☐ Single ■ Family

*with sunsets

Source: Citizens for Tax Justice, December 17, 2003.

FIGURE 3
AVERAGE TAX CUTS UNDER THE 2001-2003 BUSH TAX CUTS BY CALENDAR YEAR*

	2001	*2005*	*2010*
Top 1%	$3,221	$41,264	$85,002
Next 4%	$1,015	$3,913	$2,780
Next 15%	$742	$2,015	$1,225
Fourth 20%	$572	$971	$1,081
Middle 20%	$403	$563	$791
Second 20%	$266	$371	$508
Lowest 20%	$57	$77	$98

*with sunsets

Source: Citizens for Tax Justice, December 17, 2003.

Aside from their sheer size, the 2001 and 2003 packages were notable for a couple of reasons: First, their major provisions were deliberately scheduled to hit later in the decade. Republican congressional leaders delayed the largest cuts to protect the bills from filibuster and deflect attention from their long-term effects on the budget and inequality. Second, they were frontloaded with tiny morsels for the middle class and backloaded with enormous benefits for the top 1%. (See figures 2 and 3, which are conservative in that they assume expiring provisions will in fact "sunset.")

Over the next 75 years, the cost of extending the 2001 and 2003 tax cuts would amount to $5.9 trillion, or 1.1% of gross domestic product (GDP), according to William G. Gale and Peter R. Orszag of the Brookings Institution. To put that figure into perspective, the expected costs of funding Social Security during that same period are just $3.8 trillion (or 0.7% of GDP). Gale and Orszag warn the new Bush budget plan will necessitate one of the following changes, or a "change of a similar magnitude," within the decade, and argue that even deeper cuts may be required:

- A 29% cut in Social Security benefits;
- A 70% cut in federal Medicaid benefits;
- A 49% cut in all domestic discretionary spending, or
- A 21% increase in payroll taxes.

Resources: William G. Gale and Peter R. Orszag, "Should the President's Tax Cuts be Made Permanent?" Brookings, Washington, D.C., February 24, 2004; "The Bush Tax Cuts: The Most Recent CTJ Data," Citizens for Tax Justice, December 17, 2003, <www.ctj.org>; "Details of the Administration's Budget Proposals," Citizens for Tax Justice, February 3, 2004, <www.ctj.org>.

ARTICLE 4.4   *March/April 2003*

DOUBLE TAXATION DOUBLE SPEAK

WHY REPEALING DIVIDEND TAXES IS UNFAIR

BY JOHN MILLER

Concerned that the most well off in our society might be suffering a bout of the post-holiday blues, the *Wall Street Journal*'s day-after-Christmas editorial urged the Bush Administration to end the "double taxation" of dividends—payments of corporate profits to stockholders. Nothing lifts the spirits of the wealthy like yet another tax giveaway.

But for the editors of the *Journal*, making dividends tax exempt is not just psychotherapy for stock investors. It's a matter of economic justice and sound economic policy. (See excerpts.) In their hands, however, notions of a fair and effective policy response to today's stagnant economy become "double taxation" doublespeak. Let's try to set the record straight.

> **"The equity argument [for ending the dividend tax] is that it is unfair to tax anything twice, even at the highest levels of income. Americans will favor repealing the double tax on dividends because it offends their sense of fair play."***

The "double taxation" of dividends is the heart of their argument. But there is nothing about double taxation that ought to offend Americans' sense of fair play. True enough, the government collects income taxes on dividends paid out of the profits of corporations that have already been taxed. But being taxed more than once on the same income is a fact of life for every taxpayer, not just dividends collectors. Most workers, for instance, pay Social Security payroll taxes and income taxes on their wages, and then sales taxes when they spend what remains of their paycheck.

Beyond that, the claim that dividends are "double" taxed is an exaggeration. To begin with, in the year 2000 more than half of corporate dividends went to tax-exempt pension funds, individual retirement accounts, and non-profit foundations or to individuals who owed no income tax. In addition, corporate *income* is hardly taxed the first time around. Relative to GDP, U.S. corporate income taxes are no more than half those of other wealthy industrial (OECD) countries. By our own historical standards, corporate income taxes have fallen from 4.1% of GDP in 1960 to just 1.7% of GDP in 2001. In addition, the average rate of taxation on corporate profits currently stands at 15%, far below the top corporate tax rate of 35%. Worse yet, in 1998, twenty-four highly profitable major corpora-

*All quotations are from the editorial "Ending Double Tax Trouble," *Wall Street Journal*, December 26, 2002.

tions, including Pfizer, PepsiCo, MCI Worldcom, General Motors, and Texaco, paid no corporate income taxes—and received a tax rebate. Robert McIntyre, director of Citizens for Tax Justice, estimates that "barely more than half of corporate profits are subject to tax at any level."

More importantly when it comes to fairness, the issue is not *how often* we pay taxes, but *how much* we pay in taxes. By that standard, eliminating taxes on dividends would surely violate most people's sense of fair play. As even the *Wall Street Journal* allows, the beneficiaries would be those "at the highest levels of income." Some 42% of the benefits from repealing taxes on dividends would go to the richest 1% of taxpayers, and three-quarters of the tax benefits would go the richest 10%, reports the Tax Policy Center of the Urban Institute and the Brookings Institution. The top 1% of taxpayers, those with yearly incomes greater than $373,000, also benefited most from the economic growth of the last two decades. After adjusting for inflation, their real average before-tax income more than doubled (a 138% increase) from 1979 and 1997, according to the Congressional Budget Office, while their tax burden, much like that of large corporations, has declined. By 1997, the richest 1% of U.S. families paid out about 1/3 of their income in all federal taxes, far less than the 2/5 they paid in 1977. These figures will only get worse due to the 2001 Bush tax cut or the elimination of dividends taxation.

> "[Taxing dividends] creates huge distortions in both corporate and investor behavior.... [O]n the corporate side, taxation creates incentives for companies to finance themselves via debt (interest on debt is tax deductible, dividend payouts are not). Increased debt can of course result in increased financial fragility for the company and risk for investors."

The *Journal* editors argue that repealing the taxation of dividends might reduce corporations' reliance on debt financing. Interest payments are currently tax-exempt. By putting the taxation of interest payments and dividends on an equal footing, the government would take away the incentive for corporations to finance themselves through borrowing. But so too would several other changes in the tax code that would not result in a tax windfall for the super-wealthy. For instance, to eliminate the tax bias in favor of "growth stocks" (which benefit investors by increasing in price), we could just remove the 20% cap on income taxes on capital gains (the sale of stocks and other assets). But the editors of the *Wall Street Journal* are loathe to consider any proposal that would boost government revenues and arrest the decline in the tax burden of the rich or large corporations.

> "The tax penalty also prompts companies to retain earnings ... rather than paying profits to investors. This can freeze capital—rather than allowing investors to reinvest cash in other businesses where rates of return might be higher, thus permitting capital to flow to more productive uses."

Cutting taxes on dividends is surprisingly less than popular with corporate managers. Both Carter and Reagan administration proposals to reduce or eliminate the double taxation found little support among business elites. Joel Slemrod, a former Reagan administration White House aide and tax economist, told the *Wall Street Journal* that business executives dismissed the Reagan proposal to cut dividend taxes as "just for shareholders," saying that they preferred tax relief that comes directly to corporations. While the *Wall Street Journal* editorial touts dividend paying corporations as a good investment in today's bear market, some economists are not convinced. Economist Alan Auerbach argues, for instance, that with lower dividend taxes, investors would expect corporations to pay out more of their earnings in the form of dividends, reducing the cash available for new corporate investments.

Finally, repealing the tax on dividends is unlikely to provide the stimulus necessary to counteract today's economic stagnation. As Slemrod's comments suggest, business investment is unlikely to pick up in response to cutting dividend taxes, especially in face of the overcapacity in today's economy. Even if shareholders do pour new money into stocks paying dividends, that will do little to spark new corporate investment. The vast majority of stock sales are not new issues, but resales of existing stock from one stock investor to another, which do not provide corporations with new funds for investment. During the 1990s stock boom, economists Robert Pollin, Dean Baker, and Marc Schaberg put the ratio of stock resales to new stock sales at 113.8 to 1.

If fairness and effectiveness are the issues, then a cut in the Social Security payroll taxes will do more to spread widely the benefit of cutting taxes and do far more to get the economy going again than eliminating dividend taxes. Today, three quarters of taxpayers pay more in payroll taxes than income taxes. In addition, we can count on those middle- and low-income households, many of them strapped for cash with the economic slowdown, to spend more of their income than the super-rich who would make out with the repeal of taxes on dividends.

A one-year payroll-tax holiday on the first $10,000 of wages would give workers a tax cut of up to $765, with much of the benefit going to middle- and low-income taxpayers. The AFL-CIO, the Business Round-table, and the Economic Policy Institute all support proposals similar to this one. The Tax Policy Center estimates that 45.4% of the benefits of a Social Security payroll-tax holiday would go to the bottom 60%, as opposed to 4.7% of the benefits from repealing dividend taxation.

A payroll tax holiday would do as much to lift the spirits of most people as repealing dividends taxation would do to buck up the super-rich. It's the right thing to do. Don't let all the double taxation doublespeak make you doubt that for one minute.

DON'T THE RICH PAY A LOT OF TAXES?

BY ELLEN FRANK

Dear Dr. Dollar:

The Heritage Foundation, a conservative think tank, has a website that purports to present evidence that the wealthiest group of Americans historically pay more taxes than middle- or low-income folks. Their sources include the U.S. Treasury Department, the Office of Management and Budget, and the Census Bureau. The wealthiest 1% paid over a third of taxes, while those in the lower 50% paid only 4% of income taxes in 1999. How do those of us who criticize the tax system as inherently unfair to middle- and lower-income folks respond to this apparently progressive tax system?

—*Bruce Boccardy, Allston, Massachusetts*

The most comprehensive source of information on "tax incidence"—who actually pays how much in taxes—is the Congressional Budget Office (CBO), which compiles data from the Internal Revenue Service every couple of years. The CBO's most recent report, entitled *Effective Tax Rates*, was released in October 2001 and is available online at <www.cbo.gov>. (The effective tax rate is the percentage of income actually paid in taxes—as opposed to the tax bracket—after deductions and exemptions and loopholes and all the rest.)

The CBO divides families into five "quintiles"—from the lowest earning one-fifth of taxpayers (incomes ranging from $0 to $13,000 in 1997) to the highest paid fifth (incomes of $50,800 and up)—and further breaks down the top fifth into the top 10%, 5%, and 1%.

As the table shows, the top income groups do in fact pay income taxes at a greater rate than they earn. The poorest quintile gets 4% of income but pays -2% of federal income taxes—negative because most qualify for the Earned Income Tax Credit.

The top fifth garners 53% of income but shells out 80% of the income tax. And the richest 1% of taxpayers (average income of $1,016,000) receives about 16% of income but pays one-third of federal income taxes. After those taxes are collected, the wealthiest income groups end up with a slightly smaller share of the economic pie than they started out with, while the poorer groups end up with slightly more. So the folks at Heritage are not wrong. The federal income tax is indisputably progressive; it is intended to redistribute income, and that is what it does.

But the redistributive impact is mild—and it's milder still since last year's tax reform. The top quintile starts out with slightly more than half of all pre-tax income generated by the U.S. economy, and ends up with just under half of all after-tax income. The poorest fifth begins the game with just 4% of income and ends up with less than 5%. The folks at Heritage, of course, oppose government redistribution schemes on principle. But redistributing income is the whole point of a progressive tax, and advocates of progressive taxation should not shy away from defending this. If

---

DISTRIBUTION OF INCOME AND TAXES BY INCOME GROUPS, 1997

Income Group	1	2	3	4	5	6
Lowest 20%	$11,400	4.0%	–2.0%	4.8%	0.9%	12.4%
Second 20%	$28,600	9.0%	1.1%	10.1%	5.2%	10.3%
Third 20%	$45,500	13.9%	6.4%	14.9%	10.4%	9.4%
Fourth 20%	$65,600	20.2%	14.5%	20.8%	18.1%	8.6%
Top 20%	$167,500	53.2%	80.0%	49.7%	65.4%	7.0%
Top 10%	$240,700	38.7%	65.4%	35.3%	50.4%	n.a.
Top 5%	$355,800	28.9%	53.8%	25.8%	39.4%	n.a.
Top 1%	$1,016,000	15.8%	33.6%	13.7%	23.1%	5.8%

1 = Average Household Income; 2 = Share of Pre-Tax Income; 3 = Share of Federal Income Taxes; 4 = Share of After-Tax Income; 5 = Share of All Federal Taxes; 6 = Effective State and Local Tax Rate (1995)

Sources: Congressional Budget Office, *Effective Tax Rates, 1979-1997*; Citizens for Tax Justice, *Who Pays? A Distributional Analysis of the Tax Systems in All 50 States*, 1995 (last column).

one believes that Ken Lay deserved no less than the $100 million he collected from Enron last year, while the burger-flippers and office cleaners of America deserve no more that the $6.50 an hour they collect, then a progressive tax would seem immoral. But if one believes that incomes are determined by race, gender, connections, power, luck and (occasionally) fraud, then redistribution through the tax system is a moral imperative.

The Heritage study also conveniently overlooks the impact of levies other than the federal income tax. Social Security taxes, excise levies, tariffs, and other duties are regressive—their effective rates decline as income goes up. When these other federal taxes are added in, the tax burden on lower-income groups increases significantly. Social Security taxes take an especially large bite out of low-income workers' paychecks; the bite is even larger when we include payroll taxes paid by the employer. (Labor economists believe that the employer share of the Social Security tax functions, in practice, as a levy on wages, since employers reduce wages to compensate for the tax instead of paying for it out of profits). Further, because state and local governments collect regressive sales, excise, and property taxes, the lower four quintiles pay a larger share of their income in state and local taxes than the top quintile. If we were to add all of these taxes together, we would almost certainly find that the U.S. tax system, as a whole, is not progressive at all.

ARTICLE 4.6

March/April 2001

STILL A BAD IDEA

THE BUSH TAX CUT

BY JOHN MILLER

We said we didn't want it. Most people didn't even vote for it. In survey after survey, public opinion polls rank a large tax cut as one of the least desirable uses of the federal budget surplus. And Republican and Democratic leaders alike have warned the President-select that his tax cut package will never emerge whole from Congress.

But all to no avail. George W. Bush has yet to back off from the monstrous, surplus-draining tax cut proposal that was the cornerstone of his campaign. Now he's even telling us that it's for our own good: His tax cut will cure our softening economy and stave off the threat of recession by "encouraging capital formation, economic growth, and job creation." Even Alan Greenspan, chair of the Federal Reserve Board and a debt-reduction hawk, is prepared to accommodate the Bush plan.

At least one group is happy to swallow the Bush tax cut medicine—"the haves and the haves-more," as Bush referred to his supporters during a fundraiser last year. After all, it is their taxes he will cut. Together, lower income tax rates (with the biggest drop at the top) and the repeal of the estate tax account for nearly three-quarters of the Bush tax cut. Nearly three-fifths of the total benefits of the tax cut package will go to the richest 10% of all taxpayers, and some 43% will go just to the top 1%, those who make more than $319,000 a year and showed average income of $915,000 in 1999.

But no matter what Bush says, his tax giveaway to the wealthy will not inoculate us against recession. Nor are well-to-do taxpayers suffering from over-taxation, as the Bush team insists. One thing is sure. If the Bush tax cut goes through, social programs that have already been neglected for more than two decades will continue to suffer.

DEFENDING THE INDEFENSIBLE

The editors of the *Wall Street Journal* never met a pro-rich tax cut they didn't like. And the Bush tax cut is much to their liking. Last December, they argued the case for a massive tax cut on three grounds:

• "Taxes are too high. Last year [1999], federal tax revenue as a percentage of the economy reached an historic peak—20.4% of GDP."

• "For the past couple of years, our tax overpayments have put the federal budget in surplus. And Congress, incited by this surplus, has exceeded its own budget caps and increased its spending beyond the rate of inflation. And they've just done it again, passing a humongous budget."

• "The economy is beginning to wobble. Economic forecasters are sniffing a recession; they are busily lowering growth projections for next year. And for good reason; some of the data are starting to look scary."

On closer inspection, none of these arguments holds up. First, let's look at what the *Journal* editors had to say about government being too large and taxes too high.

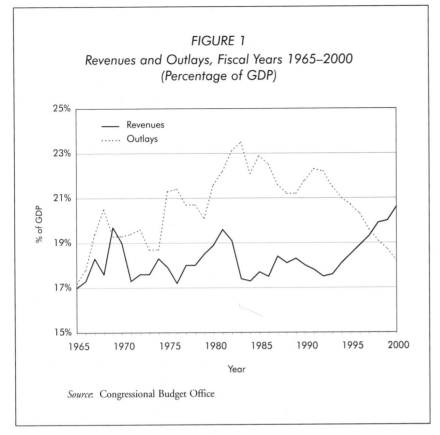

FIGURE 1
Revenues and Outlays, Fiscal Years 1965–2000
(Percentage of GDP)

Source: Congressional Budget Office

Federal tax revenues—as a percentage of Gross Domestic Product (GDP), or national output—are currently, as the editors suggest, at their highest levels since World War II. But that is not because government got bigger during the 1990s or because today's federal budget is "humongous" in historical terms.

The economic boom of the 1990s—faster economic growth and a skyrocketing stock market—did enlarge the tax base and allow the federal government to collect more tax *revenues*. Those added tax dollars closed a $300 billion deficit in the federal budget and then generated the current surplus. But that surplus hasn't translated into bigger government, as the *Journal* editors claim. During the 1990s, federal *spending* as a share of GDP actually got smaller, not bigger, slipping below 20%. In 2000, it reached just 18.2%, the lowest mark in 35 years. (See Figure 1.)

Even some conservatives, if not the *Journal*'s editorial writers, noticed the drop. "The good news of the Clinton presidency," says Stephen Moore of the Cato Institute, a libertarian think tank, is that "the federal government is getting smaller, at least relative to the size of the economy."

So much for the government being too big by historical standards. But what about the beef about "over-taxation"? It misses the mark as well.

The *Journal* editors are fond of pointing out, in their paeans to the "New Economy," that any serious assessment of the 1990s should take into account the wealth amassed through the stock market boom and other investments. But

tax revenue as a share of GDP is a misleading measure of the decade's tax burden precisely because it fails to do this.

Here's how. According to economists Alan Auerbach and William Gale, about one-third of the surge in tax revenues during the 1990s came from taxes on the capital gains realized when stockholders and other investors cashed in their holdings. The calculation of taxes as a share of GDP counts capital gains tax revenues but ignores gains in wealth that have not been cashed in. From 1989 to 1999, the total wealth or net worth of households (their total assets minus debt) more than doubled. Had all of that new wealth been included in the *Journal*'s calculation, then taxes as a share of economic activity would have shown a decline.

Economists have long argued that, for tax purposes, changes in net worth should be counted as income. Even conservative economists agree. For instance, Bruce Bartlett, former Reagan administration Treasury official, says that today most people regard increases in net worth as "the equivalent of increases in income," even before they realize their investments. When Bartlett calculated taxes as a share of economic activity, he adjusted his measure for changes in net worth and found that the tax share declined during the 1990s. In 1990, tax revenues measured 18.3% of the sum of GDP plus year-to-year changes in household net worth, but were just 15.1% in 1998. (See Figure 2.)

For Bartlett, that downward trend goes a long way toward explaining why "tax cuts have fallen sharply as an issue of concern to voters" and why "the tax revolt went into hibernation." When the Heritage Foundation, the Washington-based conservative think tank, published Bartlett's study in 1999, they distributed it to journalists with a cover letter instructing "conservatives who favor tax cuts" to "wake up and smell the apathy."

The *Journal* editors weren't listening. Rather than face up to the implications of an intellectually honest analysis of federal taxes by a fellow conservative, they prefer to spend their time spinning data in a desperate attempt to awaken the tax revolt from its slumber.

NO RECESSION FIGHTER

Crying recession is the *Journal* editors' and the Bush team's latest attempt to resuscitate the tax revolt. The threat of recession is genuine enough. Slower economic growth abroad, higher oil prices, stagnating stock prices, and jacked-up interest rates have already damped down U.S.

economic growth and surely could bring the current expansion to an end. Still, that is no reason to give in to the chicanery that we must bribe the rich with a tax cut if we want to forestall a recession.

The Bush tax cut is no recession fighter. First off, it will do little to combat slower growth in a timely way. Even if Congress passes the proposal intact, none of the cuts would be enacted before 2002. In truth, much of the Bush proposal would be slowly phased in over ten years, with just 11% of the tax cut coming in the first three years. Worse yet, the later and larger tax cuts would take place regardless of economic conditions—and in all likelihood well after the end of the next recession.

Aside from its poor timing, the Bush tax cut is ill-designed to jumpstart the economy. The immediate effect of lower taxes comes from increasing consumer spending. But by targeting the rich, who consume less of their income than others, the Bush tax will offer little of this stimulus. That holds for both the repeal of the estate tax—whose benefits will go exclusively to the richest 2% of the population—and the across-the-board cut in income tax rates, which is weighted heavily in favor of the wealthiest taxpayers.

Nor are repealing the estate tax and cutting income taxes likely to provide the long-term stimulus to capital formation and job creation that Bush promises. Tax-cut backers can't point to a single credible economic study showing that eliminating the estate tax will boost investment. The track record of cutting income taxes is problematic as well. The Reagan administration reduced income tax rates across the board and lowered capital gains taxes—cuts that supply-side economists claimed would encourage people to work, save, and invest. But when mainstream economists, such as Barry Bosworth and Gary Burtless of the Brookings Institution, checked out the effects of the '80s tax cut, they found quite different results. Male workers put in about the same number of hours after the tax cut as before it, and while women did work more hours, their earnings failed to improve. Not only that, relative to the size of the economy, savings plummeted and net investment declined. That hardly fits with the claims of the Bush team.

Finally, if slower growth is now the justification for cutting taxes, then the budgetary implications of the Bush tax cut are even more alarming than when it was originally proposed. In January, the Congressional Budget Office (CBO) projected that the federal budget (except for Social Security) will run a surplus of $3.1 trillion over the period 2002 to 2011. The CBO projection assumes brisk economic growth averaging 3.1% over those ten years (comparable to that of the 1990s), no recession this year, a continuation of the rapid productivity gains of the last five years, and a hot stock market. But deteriorating economic conditions, let alone a prolonged recession, could compromise each of those assumptions and leave a surplus far smaller than the amount of the Bush tax cut, pushing the budget back into deficit.

Even if the CBO projections hold up, financing the Bush tax cut out of the surplus will be difficult. A recent study by the Center on Budget and Policy Priorities (CBPP), a liberal think tank, found that much of the surplus was unavailable for a tax cut. Some $400 billion of the projected surplus comes from the Medicare Hospital Insurance Fund, and there is overwhelming bipartisan consensus that those funds, along with the Social Security surpluses, should be set aside, not used for tax initiatives. Another $600 billion of the projected surplus disappears if current spending policies are maintained; the bulk of that would go to adjust discretionary spending for inflation and changes in the U.S. population. That still leaves about $2 trillion unallocated. But at least $500 billion, according to the

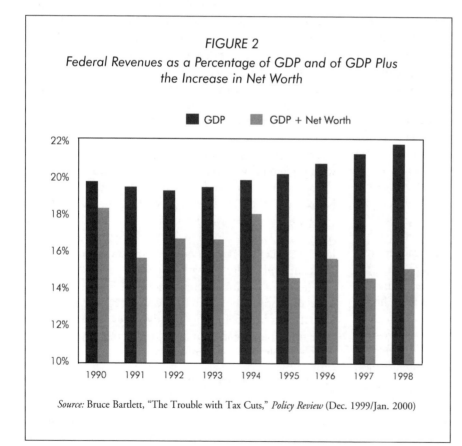

FIGURE 2

Federal Revenues as a Percentage of GDP and of GDP Plus the Increase in Net Worth

Source: Bruce Bartlett, "The Trouble with Tax Cuts," *Policy Review* (Dec. 1999/Jan. 2000)

CBPP, would be needed to help restore the long-term solvency of Social Security and Medicare, if Bush intends to keep that campaign promise.

Finally, an honest accounting of the cost of the Bush tax cut reveals that it will drain at least $1.9 trillion from the projected surplus, not $1.3 trillion, as his campaign claimed. According to Citizens for Tax Justice director Robert McIntyre, the Bush figure is based on nine years, not ten, because it starts its projection in 2001, a year before the tax cut would go into effect. On top of that, the government would have to borrow money to finance the Bush tax cut in its first years (before the larger surpluses kick in), but the Bush calculation doesn't include the cost of the interest on that borrowing. Those interest payments will be even larger if the economy slows, drying up projected tax revenues. Not only that, McIntyre now estimates that the total cost of the tax cut could be as high as $2.5 trillion, due to a quicker phase-in of the proposed cuts, new CBO revenue projections, and a likely reduction in the 26% minimum tax that upper-income taxpayers are now required to pay on their taxable income.

WE CAN DO BETTER

How might we make better use of the projected surpluses in the federal budget? On that score, the Democrats are not much help. In reaction to the extremism of the Bush tax cuts for the wealthy, they are offering up a warmed-over Eisenhower-moderate-Republican proposal from the 1950s—use the surplus to pay down the debt.

But devoting the surplus to retiring government debt is unlikely to produce a more robust economy. Reduced government borrowing is intended to lower interest rates and thus juice up capital investment, which accelerates economic growth. In practice, however, government borrowing and interest rates are not closely correlated, and lower interest rates are seldom by themselves sufficient to coax balky investors to part with their money. But if lower interest rates are the goal, the Federal Reserve can bring them down without expending the surplus. In fact, the Fed furiously lowered interest rates in the first two months of this year. Fed action makes sense, since it's the Fed's numerous hikes of the interest rate during 1999 and 2000 that helped to jeopardize the current economic expansion in the first place.

It's not hard to enumerate better uses of the budget surplus. To begin with, if a tax cut is needed to bolster the economy, then why not use the surplus to pay for a cut in the payroll taxes paid by wage workers? The majority of taxpayers now pay more in payroll taxes—deductions from paychecks to fund Social Security and Medicare—than in income taxes. Reducing payroll taxes would have a greater impact on most families than an income tax cut of the same size, while disproportionately favoring low-income earners. Also, by targeting wage workers, who are often strapped for cash, a payroll tax cut—in effect an across-the-board raise—would immediately boost consumer spending. A 10% reduction in Social Security and Medicare tax rates would cost about $60 billion in fiscal year 2001, according to the CBO, and could be funded from the projected budget surplus (leaving much of the surplus to meet other demands).

But what we really ought to do with the projected surplus is dedicate it to pressing social needs. In the United States today, 32.3 million people are living below the official poverty line, 44 million go without health insurance, and perhaps as many as seven million have no place to live. Our public schools are deteriorating, the state of public transportation is abysmal, and decent, affordable housing is practically impossible to find.

Even if we simply maintained current spending levels, adjusted for inflation and population growth, we could inject badly-needed funds into a large swath of government activities, including education, environmental protection, food and safety inspection, the National Park Service, and Head Start. While we're at it, we could shore up the Medicare trust fund. That would still leave vast resources to provide universal health care coverage, combat childhood poverty, renew public investment, and support numerous other social programs that the federal government has ignored. Even if the entire $3.1 trillion projected surplus were used for public spending, federal outlays in fiscal year 2011, according to the CBO, would be just 18.4% of GDP—smaller than at any point during the 1970s, 1980s, or 1990s.

With budget surpluses now projected for the rest of the decade, these proposals are hardly beyond our means. It's just a matter of political will. In the last 20 years, social programs have been slashed almost beyond recognition. Squandering the surplus on a tax giveaway for the wealthy, while continuing to turn our backs on those in need, would be a criminal act.

Resources: Alan Auerbach and William Gale, *Does the Budget Surplus Justify Big Tax Cuts? Updates and Extensions* (The Brookings Institution, 1999); Bruce Bartlett, "The Trouble With Tax Cuts," *Policy Review* (December 1999/January 2000); Barry Bosworth and Gary Burtless, "The Effects of Tax Reform on Labor Supply, Investment, and Savings," *Journal of Economic Perspectives* (Winter 1992); "The Bush Tax Cut," *Wall Street Journal*, 19 December 2000; Congressional Budget Office, *The Budget and Economic Outlook: An Update*, 18 July 2000; James Horney, Isaac Shapiro, and Robert Greenstein, "How Should the Surplus Be Used?" (Center on Budget and Policy Priorities, September 2000).

THE CASE AGAINST PRIVATIZING NATIONAL SECURITY

BY ANN MARKUSEN

In the past 20 years, this country has undergone a transformation in the way it prepares for, conducts, and mops up after war. The Pentagon has overseen a large-scale effort to outsource all aspects of its operations to private corporations. But despite the claims of privatization proponents, there's scant evidence that private firms perform better or at lower cost than public-sector agencies. More troubling, as corporations cash in on lucrative contracts, they encroach on the political process, driving up military spending and influencing military and foreign policy.

THE GROWING "SHADOW PENTAGON"

National defense is one of the most heavily outsourced activities in the U.S. federal government. From 1972 to 2000, private contractors' share of all defense-related jobs climbed from 36% to 50%. While the country's public-sector defense workforce remains large—about 2.2 million in 2000—its "shadow workforce," the true number of people supported by federal government spending and mandates, is far larger. (See Figure 1.)

Of the dozens of major military contract firms in the United States today, Lockheed Martin, Boeing, and Northrop Grumman are the largest three—they divvied up $50 billion of the $209 billion the Pentagon awarded in prime contracts in 2003, according to defense analyst William Hartung—but lesser-known info-tech and engineering companies like Computer Sciences Corporation, BDM International, and Science Applications International Corporation are emerging as major Department of Defense (DOD) suppliers, each with billions of dollars in defense business annually.

Despite the popular image of a defense contract as a contract for building large weapons systems like aircraft, missiles, or tanks, contracts for services are actually more typical. Service workers—not production workers—accounted for nearly three out of four contract-created jobs in 1996, up more than 50% since 1984. A growing legion of contracted employees install, maintain, trouble-shoot, operate, and integrate military hardware. Similarly, research and development work is increasingly farmed out. (Navy technical centers outsourced 50% of research, development, test, and evaluation work by 1996, up from 30% in 1970.) And other, lower-skill, service contract firms perform a panoply of other functions, from base maintenance and catering and support, to security detail and military training. (See "Privatized Military Training and Operations," p. 60.)

ECONOMIC EXPECTATIONS

According to economic theory, it's competition, not privatization per se, that is expected to produce cost savings and performance improvements. Competition is key because private contractors are profit-seeking firms whose first loyalties are to their shareholders. Without competition, and in the absence of close monitoring, the corporations have every incentive to raise prices and hide information about their products and services. Defense economists suggest competition should generate efficiencies, but only under certain conditions: four or more firms competing for a given job, ongoing competition over time, clarity by the government buyer about task and performance requirements, and active, sustained government monitoring.

That's the theory. In the real world of military contracting, these conditions are rarely met. Most contracts that are opened to competing bids have fewer than three bidders. Once signed, contracts last for long periods, insulating firms from ongoing competitive pressures. The bidding process itself may be distorted in that firms "low-ball" bids, knowing they can negotiate add-ons later. And with the dramatic consolidation of the industry in the mid-1990s, and the shrinking number of large prime contractors, collusion among firms is a recurrent problem.

Several Pentagon contracts are "cost-plus," meaning the companies recoup their costs, including a portion of overhead, and are guaranteed a percentage of the costs as profit—a recipe for cost inflation. For example, Halliburton subsidiary Kellogg Brown & Root was given a 10-year multibillion dollar contract to provide logistical support services to U.S. troops overseas. The contract guarantees the firm will receive 1% of total costs as profit. In addition, KBR is eligible for a bonus payment of up to 2%. The firm has a long record of cost overruns in Kosovo, and its performance to date in Iraq has been weak. KBR admitted to overcharging the government by $61 million for gasoline, and its own internal audit of its Iraq operations reveals serious problems including a failure to control subcontractor costs and widespread loss of supplies and equipment, according to the *Wall Street Journal*.

THE EVIDENCE ON EXPECTED GAINS FROM PRIVATIZATION

Given the colossal sum of government dollars doled out in defense contracts, you'd think Congress and the Pentagon would carefully track cost and performance outcomes. But Pentagon records are sketchy and largely hidden from public view. Even the U.S. General Accounting Office (GAO), the investigative arm of Congress, has had difficulty prying data from the Pentagon. What's more, the few assessments that do exist focus on competitions between public and private bidders (where a government agency bids for work in competition with a private entity), and not private-private competitions, or the 50% of DOD purchases that are sole-sourced, simply given to a contractor with no competitive bidding process at all.

Some have estimated that the DOD saves 20% to 30% from public-private competitions, but those approximations are based on savings estimates at the initial bidding stage. In other words, they look at the promise of savings, not actual savings over time—a poor measure, since cost overruns are common and contracts are often renegotiated or otherwise changed after they're awarded.

The few existing studies of longer-term outcomes—conducted mainly by the Center for Naval Analysis (CNA), a federally funded research and development center, and the GAO—offer mixed results.

A CNA study of surface ships found that readiness was about the same whether the work was done in a public Navy yard or a private yard; a study of Navy maintenance work over time found that for a period of around two years, the contractors' performance was worse than that of the Navy in-house team, but that overall, the contractors performed better than the Navy team.

CNA insists that public-private competitions do generate bids and plans which would, if implemented, save the Pentagon money. But CNA analyses are emphatic that "competition produces the savings and not outsourcing per se." Its simulations suggest that 65% of total savings should in theory be achieved simply by the exercise of competing, even if no private firm receives a contract.

GAO is less sanguine about the potential for cost savings. The agency investigated some of the Pentagon's savings estimates and concluded that they were overstated because "DOD has not fully calculated either the investment costs associated with undertaking these competitions or the personnel separation costs likely to be associated with implementing them." DOD had assumed it would cost just $2,000 per position to conduct a competition, but in actuality the costs run from $7,000 to $9,000. In a later review of the Pentagon's claim that it had saved $290 million through public-private competition in 1999, the GAO concluded that it was difficult to determine how much had actually been saved. A large part of the problem, again, is that the DOD does not systematically track or update its savings estimates once contracts are underway.

GAO also cautions that savings from outsourcing come chiefly from cuts in personnel costs. We cannot know whether these cuts normally take the form of wage and benefit reductions, the use of temporary workers, cuts to the full-time workforce, or some combination, because private-sector firms refuse to share personnel information, calling it proprietary.

The large role of labor-cost savings in Pentagon outsourcing should give policymakers pause. It's troubling that the Pentagon does not monitor the pay and working condi-

FIGURE 1
ESTIMATED FULL-TIME EQUIVALENT FEDERAL CIVIL SERVICE, CONTRACT, AND GRANT JOBS BY CATEGORY, 1996

Federal Agency	Civil Service Jobs	Contract Jobs	Grant Jobs*	Ratio of Civil Service to Contract + Grant Jobs
Defense	778,900	3,634,000	53,000	1:4.7
Energy	19,100	633,000	40,200	1:37
NASA	20,100	350,600	26,900	1:19
Total Defense-Related	818,100	4,617,600	120,100	1:5.8
All Other Federal	**1,073,900**	**1,017,400**	**2,292,900**	**1:3.1**

*Jobs created by money given as a grant rather than a contract for performance of services. The grant category includes research grants to universities.

Source: Paul Light, *The True Size of Government*, Washington, DC: Brookings Institution Press, 1999.

PRIVATIZED MILITARY TRAINING AND OPERATIONS

Military training and operations is perhaps the smallest, but in many ways the most troubling, arena in which privatization is taking place.

Around the world, including Guantanamo Bay, Cuba; Colombia; Afghanistan; and Iraq, new private-sector teams of skilled former military personnel are offering their services to a range of clients, including governments, the United Nations, nongovernmental organizations, warlords, and drug kings.

In Iraq, private firms represent the second largest contributor of forces to the war effort, according to the *Guardian*. Numbering about 10,000, private contractor employees are believed to exceed the number of British troops on the ground. They provide training and operations, food catering, engineering, consulting, and security. Many are armed.

Blackwater Security Consulting, whose four employees were killed and mutilated by an angry crowd in Fallujah in March, is a North Carolina-based company headed by former U.S. Navy SEALs. The four employees were guarding a convoy delivering U.S. government food. Blackwater is one of over a dozen security companies hired by the Pentagon to guard key installations, protect the Coalition Provisional Authority, and train the Iraqi army and police. Other security firms in Iraq include Virginia-based Custer Battles; the British companies Erinys and Global Risk; and DynCorp of Reston, Virginia. The United States awarded DynCorp, now owned by the multibillion dollar Computer Sciences Corporation, a contract for as much as $250 million to provide up to 1,000 civilian advisors to organize civilian law enforcement in post-war Iraq.

The presence of contractors in Iraq is unprecedented in its scale, but their involvement tions of its "shadow employees." If private prison administrators are required to share employment data with evaluators, why shouldn't Pentagon contractors face the same requirement?

In sum, the jury's still out on whether outsourcing military work produces efficiencies, and little is known about how savings that are achieved may result from cutting wages. Furthermore, no study has included the cost of competent oversight in the outsourcing calculus, or looked systematically at performance outcomes.

CORRUPTION AND POLICY INFLUENCE

Beyond efficiency and performance concerns, the increasing reliance on for-profit firms for national defense creates deeper political and institutional problems—namely, the capture of public decision-making by private military interests.

Through lobbying, advertising, and heavy campaign contributions, the private defense sector calls for weapons systems and defense initiatives that generate lucrative contracts. Since the end of the Cold War, private military contractors have formed a powerful lobby to protect obsolete Cold War weapons systems. For example, during the Reagan years, strenuous lobbying overcame even the highly mobilized and scientifically well-informed opposition to the B-1 bomber and the Star Wars program, two of the most costly weapons programs in the postwar period. In the 1990s, lobbyists undermined important initiatives to control the export of conventional arms, and recently the aerospace industry—led by Lockheed Martin—pushed hard to bring Poland, Hungary, and the Czech Republic into NATO in the expectation that these countries would then upgrade their militaries with costly new hardware. In general, the defense industry's leverage in Congress makes it difficult for the nation to shift resources toward peacekeeping missions, negotiated settlements, and the use of economic development in place of regional warfare.

As John Donahue summarizes in *The Privatization Decision*:

> In any contractual relationship between government and private business, a key question becomes who is representing the broader public interests. Unless there are sturdy provisions to prevent it—and even if all parties are immune to corruption—the natural outcome is an alliance between private-sector suppliers and government officials at the taxpayers' expense.

Less visible than the congressional lobbyists and trade groups, but just as significant, contractors employ their superior technical expertise to sell Pentagon procurement managers and top military leaders on pricey and risky new projects. Sitting on Pentagon advisory committees helps, as does the firms' insulation from public scrutiny. The quickening pace of privatization in research and development has left the government without the expertise to assess and monitor contractors' proposals.

WHAT'S DRIVING DEFENSE PRIVATIZATION?

The political, intellectual, and financial impetus for government privatization began in the 1970s and received its major political boost from the Reagan administration, which shrank government even as it increased defense expenditures by 50% in real terms. The Clinton administration's reversal of the Carter-Reagan military buildup had the unintended consequence of unleashing a hungry pro-privatization lobby onto the political scene—the mid-1990s reduction of the defense budget sent private contractors scrambling for new markets. At the same time, a raft of mergers consolidated the industry into a powerful handful of giant firms, all focused on developing new streams of government revenue. Their efforts on Capitol Hill dovetailed with and drew life from the 20-year ideological assault on public-sector provision of goods and services. During the Clinton years, insiders also adopted and capitalized on the "reinventing government" agenda spearheaded by Vice President Al Gore at the federal level.

Since the 1990s, private business groups, DOD advisory boards and key managers, and both the Clinton and Bush administrations have heightened calls to privatize national-security activity. For Pentagon managers, privatization offers a means of coping with a "go it alone" defense doctrine that deploys U.S. armed forces around the world with little international support.

Advocacy groups heavily populated by large defense contractors issue a stream of pronouncements and publications urging privatization. They recommend outsourcing functions outright rather than relying on public-private competitions (which give public agencies a chance to bid for projects), and back the wholesale privatization of complex business areas that currently involve large numbers of government employees.

One such task force, the Defense Science Board Task Force on Outsourcing and Privatization, issued studies in 1996 claiming that $10 billion to $30 billion could be saved through privatizing DOD's support and maintenance services.

Needless to say, they offered inadequate evidence to support these multibillion-dollar savings estimates. The panel that released the first study was headed by the CEO of military contractor BDM International.

At about the same time, Business Executives for National Security (BENS), a group founded in 1982 as a watchdog organization to monitor the Pentagon on weapons costs and nuclear, chemical, and biological warfare, transformed itself into an outspoken advocate of outsourcing. In 1996, BENS launched a high-profile commission to "promote outsourcing and privatization, closing unneeded military bases and implementing acquisition reform" with a self-described membership of "business leaders, former government officials and retired military officers." The commission published op-eds and position papers claim-

reflects a long-term trend. Over 9,000 contract employees worked in the Persian Gulf War theatre in 1990, and 1,400 went to Bosnia as part of U.S. peacekeeping forces in 1997. In the late 1990s, the United States and United Kingdom hired DynCorp to oversee withdrawal of Serb forces from Kosovo.

The pitfalls of privatized training of foreign military forces are illustrated in Deborah Avant's research on Military Professional Resources Inc. (MPRI) in Croatia. MPRI is a northern Virginia firm founded in 1986 by several high-ranking retired American military officers. By the late 1990s, it employed 350 people full time and could call upon a database of over 7,000 potential employees, all with significant experience in the U.S. armed forces. In 1994, Croatia hired MPRI to educate its military leaders in western-style civilian-military relations. The Pentagon vetted the operation, granting the firm an export license and extensively briefing MPRI personnel before their departure to Croatia. This way, the United States was able to remain formally neutral while influencing and monitoring events on the ground. Observers believe that the firm's training activities and support enabled the Croatians to launch a bloody ethnic cleansing offensive in Slovenia and the Krajina region that resulted in the displacement of more than 150,000 Serbs.

All this raises important questions: How will such firms be held accountable to civilian and democratic goals? What happens when the firm's interest diverges from the home government's interest? Because sending contractors instead of military personnel into conflict zones is more politically palatable, and often invisible to the public, will it give the national security apparatus a way to get around the constraints of Congress? These dilemmas should spark a public debate on the advisability of selling advanced western military training on the private market.

ing the Pentagon civilian workforce is bloated. It decried what it misleadingly described as the bleeding away of private-sector defense jobs. (BENS used 1988 as its baseline; the year was an anomaly that included a spike in Reagan-era defense contracts.) It also claimed the Pentagon lags behind private corporations in outsourcing, and that the United States lags behind Europeans in privatization. Neither assertion is borne out by the evidence.

Under Clinton, Secretary of Defense William Cohen and other top DOD officials echoed BENS' calls for a "Revolution in Military Business Affairs." Dr. Jacques Gansler, President Clinton's undersecretary of defense for acquisition and technology, frequently spoke out in favor of outsourcing and a business approach:

> To meet the challenge of modernization, the Department of Defense ... must do business more like private business.... My top priority, as Under Secretary of Defense, is to make the Pentagon look much more like a dynamic, restructured, reengineered, world-class commercial sector business.

In February 2001, just after George W. Bush took office, a defense reform conference organized by the Aerospace Industries Association of America and Boeing, Lockheed Martin, Northrop Grumman, Raytheon, TRW, Inc., and BAE Systems met to set the agenda for the new administration. It attracted 500 participants and drew up a "Blueprint for Action" to slash bureaucracies, reduce "cycle times" and restore operational and financial strength to the defense industrial base. Also in February 2001, a BENS initiative, "Improving the Business End of the Military," identified activities the DOD can discontinue and "replace with world class business models," turning entire functions (housing, communications, power utilities, logistics systems) over to the private sector.

Since George W. Bush took office, the military budget has grown from $300 billion to $400 billion, not counting the $200 billion in supplemental expenditures for Iraq and Afghanistan. The spending hike has set off a feeding frenzy among contractors, some of which have seen double-digit growth in profits.

The Bush administration is intensifying efforts to transfer work from inside the Pentagon to private contractors. The DOD is expected to put 225,000 jobs up for competition between public employee groups and private companies by the end of Bush's first term. Many more jobs have been displaced through direct outsourcing. The Bush push appears to be driven by a combination of ideology and political calculation, reinforced by defense-sector campaign contributions and the accelerating revolving door between the Pentagon and private contractors.

But this strategy poses serious risks and may threaten the possibility of society exercising democratic control over the evolution and use of military force. George Washington University political scientist Deborah Avant stresses that privatizing security "almost inevitably redistributes power over the control of violence both within governments and between states and non-state actors." In the United States, the private delivery of services has strengthened the executive branch, diminished the control of Congress, and reduced transparency. And, she warns, the process is cumulative—as private security companies are integrated into military efforts, the companies gain greater influence over foreign and military policy-making.

Resources: Deborah Avant, *The Market for Force: Private Security and Political Change,* manuscript under review, 2004; "The Revolution in Business Affairs: Realizing the Potential," Conference Summary, CNA Corporation, Alexandra, VA: 1998; John Donahue, *The Privatization Decision: Public Ends, Private Means,* New York: Basic Books, 1989; William D. Hartung, "Making Money on Terrorism," *The Nation,* February 5, 2004; Paul Light, *The True Size of Government,* Washington, DC: Brookings Institution Press, 1999.

This article was adapted from a longer article published in the journal *Governance,* Vol. 16, No. 4 (October, 2003).

November/December 2001

SOCIAL SECURITY Q&A

BY ELLEN FRANK

Q. Is there or is there not an actual Social Security trust fund?
A. Since the mid-1980s, the Social Security Administration (SSA) has been collecting more in payroll taxes each year than it pays out in pension, survivor, and disability benefits. The difference between receipts and payments grew significantly in the 1990s, and now amounts to some $160 billion each year. The Social Security system is expected to continue running annual surpluses at least through 2025.

Each year, SSA turns over any surplus funds to the U.S. Treasury, which spends the funds. In return, SSA receives special-issue, non-negotiable U.S. Treasury securities, which represent an implicit promise by the U.S. government to repay Social Security when and if additional money is needed to cover benefits. These bonds are what we call the "trust fund." In 2000, the trust fund contained bonds valued at $1.2 trillion; by 2025, the accumulated surpluses should top $3 trillion.

These, of course, are projections—the surpluses (and thus the trust fund) could be larger or smaller than anticipated, depending on wage growth, population changes, the overall state of the economy, and so on. Under the SSA's "low-cost" (or best-case) scenario, the Social Security trust fund will grow continuously until late in the 21st century.

So, yes, there is a trust fund, representing the excess of payroll taxes over benefit claims, and it is "invested" in promissory notes issued by the government.

Q. Is there actually money in the Social Security trust fund? And if not, where is it?
A. There is not actually "money" in the trust fund, any more than there is actually "money" in your bank account. When you open a bank account, the bank lends your money out. You exchange money for a promise from the bank to repay you, subject to whatever limitations and provisions you may have agreed to in advance. Your money is replaced with a piece of paper laying out those terms and obligations—a bank statement, passbook, quarterly notice, whatever. Your money has become a claim on a financial firm and is as good as the stability of that financial firm.

Similarly, the surplus revenues flowing into Social Secu-
rity over the years have all been lent to the Treasury and spent—all, that is, except this year's $160 billion surplus. Before the attacks in September, Congress was still arguing over this money. By December, the surplus is almost certain to have disappeared in any case.

Some critics of Social Security use alarmist rhetoric in discussing the trust fund: The SSA is bankrupt, our hard-earned money is gone, the government has blown it all. They're right that there's no money in the trust fund. But there's nothing duplicitous in this. All money gets lent or spent and replaced with other kinds of paper claims. Banks and other financial firms don't keep money lying around either.

Q. Then why do I keep hearing about a "crisis" in Social Security?
A. The problems with Social Security are not really financial in nature. They stem from the fact that, over the last 30 years or so, birth rates have declined in the United States, while life expectancies have increased. If these trends continue (and there's no reason to suppose they will not), the ratio of retirees to workers will rise. Unless the economy grows faster than the SSA predicts—unless those future workers are more productive than the SSA projects, or the workforce grows faster than expected due to immigration—the cost of supporting all these retirees will exceed the revenues that would accrue from current tax rate of 12.4% on payroll.

According to SSA's none-too-optimistic projections, the Social Security system will have enough revenue from payroll taxes alone to cover benefits at their current levels (adjusted for inflation) up until 2016. For seven years after that, there will be enough revenue from payroll taxes and interest on the bonds held by the trust fund to cover benefits at current levels. Then, in 2023, SSA will need to begin redeeming the bonds. When that happens, the system will have enough revenue—from payroll taxes, interest, and bond redemption combined—to cover legislated benefits for another 15 years or so.

The problem is this. Once we reach a point where payroll tax receipts fall below projected benefit payments—once the SSA actually needs the interest and principle from the bonds to meet its obligations—the U.S. Treasury will have to find resources to pay the SSA, just like it has to find resources to pay back any other creditor. They can do this by raising taxes, cutting spending on other federal programs, or borrowing from the private financial markets.

Q. But if the government has to raise money to pay the SSA in the future anyway, then what's the point of collecting these surpluses today?

A. Good question. From a purely economic perspective, there is no point. The federal government is collecting surplus payroll taxes and then spending them, and will have to raise revenue somehow in the future to pay Social Security benefits. The bonds in the trust fund do nothing to alter this.

Realize that the bonds are non-negotiable, and SSA cannot redeem them for cash unless Congresses allocate money for this purpose. But if future Congresses choose not to repay Social Security, they can simply raise payroll taxes or cut benefits and avoid altogether the need to redeem the bonds. Understanding this, some Democrats have insisted in recent years that Social Security surpluses be used exclusively to repay debts that the government currently owes to the financial markets. This is the idea behind the so-called Social Security "lockbox."

THERE IS NO ACTUAL "MONEY" IN THE TRUST FUND, ANY MORE THAN THERE IS ACTUAL "MONEY" IN YOUR BANK ACCOUNT.

In fact, it makes absolutely no difference to the trust fund whether the surpluses are used to repay public debt, cut taxes, or pay for expanded federal programs, any more than you, as a depositor, need concern yourself with where a bank lends your deposits. But the defenders of the trust fund apparently feel that using the surpluses to repay debt will harden the federal government's commitment to the security of future retirees. If the money has purportedly been "saved" in a rhetorical "lockbox," the reasoning goes, it will be pretty hard for opponents of Social Security to turn around 10 or 20 years from now and argue that benefits need to be cut.

Now look at this from the perspective of anti-government Republicans. They oppose higher taxes, have little faith in the ability of government to cut spending (and plenty of ideas on how to raise spending for defense and corporate subsidies), and object to the government borrowing cash from the financial markets. They are also none too keen on the idea of workers retiring into extended periods of idleness. Back in the 1930s, when Social Security was established, conservative business groups vehemently opposed it.

They gave their support grudgingly, and only when then-President Roosevelt assured them that the system would be funded entirely by payroll taxes on working stiffs. General tax revenues, which are paid largely by upper-income groups, were never to be tapped for Social Security.

But if governments of the future are to honor the commitment implicit in the trust fund, then general revenues will have to be tapped. Real resources will need to be transferred to retirees, above and beyond the 12.4% payroll tax, so that retirees can survive without a paycheck. The amount needed is not that large, but it's large enough to worry those corporate and wealthy taxpayers who neither need nor want Social Security and who are likely to be asked to foot the bill.

This is why proponents of privatization are claiming that the Social Security trust fund is on the verge of collapse. The trust fund was designed to solve a potential economic problem—transferring resources to seniors in the future so that American workers can continue to enjoy retirement—with a political accounting device. Privatization boosters are today exploiting the contradictions inherent in that accounting device to attack Social Security and to justify regressive policies such as raising current payroll taxes or cutting current benefits.

Q. But there will be a shortfall in Social Security at some point in the future. What can we do about that?

A. It's difficult to say for sure whether the projected shortfalls will materialize. But they may. And if they do, privatization is definitely not the answer. The economic problem of caring for a large number of retirees in the future cannot be solved with private accounts. Even if they worked as their boosters claim (and they won't—see Article 4.10, "The Hidden Costs of Private Accounts"), private stock accounts are just another sort of accounting device. Eventually, all those private account holders are going to retire and try to sell their stock for the cash needed to buy real resources—food, shelter, health care. If the economy has not grown sufficiently to provide the resources, the stocks will rapidly become worthless.

The only real investment we can make today to strengthen Social Security is in economic growth and enhanced economic well-being. Next time your Congressional representative talks about Social Security, ask her what she's doing today to ensure that America's future workers will be healthy enough, happy enough, secure enough, and skilled enough to care for their aging parents. That's the only security we can count on.

May/June 2004

BUSH STRIKES OUT ON HEALTH CARE

BY ELISE GOULD

In his State of the Union address in January 2004, President Bush claimed to be addressing the twin crises of rising health care costs and declining access. He touted the Medicare bill Congress passed late last year for adding a prescription drug benefit for seniors, creating tax-free health savings accounts, and generally "strengthening Medicare." He then made some new proposals, including a tax credit to help uninsured people buy health insurance and a tax deduction to encourage people to buy catastrophic (or high-deductible) health insurance policies.

Dollars & Sense asked Economic Policy Institute economist Elise Gould to explain what these programs are—or are not—likely to accomplish.

PRIVATE INSURERS AND PRESCRIPTION DRUGS: STRIKE ONE

The 2003 Medicare Modernization Act is an inadequate, poorly-devised excuse for Medicare expansion. Its key provisions include new money for private insurers involved with Medicare, a prescription drug benefit, and tax-advantaged Health Savings Accounts. Originally scored at $395 billion, now estimated to cost $534 billion, the bill makes big payments to private insurance and pharmaceutical companies, but provides little bang for the buck for Medicare beneficiaries.

One aspect of the new law has received almost no attention: it raises payments to private insurers to entice them into the business of providing insurance for the Medicare population. Actually, Medicare is already partially privatized. For a number of years, the government has contracted with private insurance companies to offer their own Medicare plans to seniors. As it turned out, many of these companies, unable to turn a profit, ended up dropping their Medicare plans. (Meantime, traditional Medicare has rolled right along, with an excellent track record of beneficiary satisfaction and a super-low overhead cost under 4%.) The new, higher payments included in the 2003 law are designed to attract private companies back into the Medicare business. Proponents argue that private industry is more efficient than government and that privatization will lower Medicare's costs. But if private insurance companies are so efficient, why do they need higher reimbursement rates?

In one respect, private insurers may prove to be cheaper—but not because they're more efficient. Private insurers can tailor their plans—what's covered, what's not, whether patients have a choice of specialists, and so forth—to attract the healthiest of the Medicare population and discourage sicker elders from signing on. Of course, the healthiest are also the least expensive to insure. Splitting the Medicare pool in this way decreases the viability of the system in the long run.

What about the prescription drug benefit? It's full of holes—literally. There's the so-called donut hole in the coverage: for seniors who spend between $2,250 and $5,100 annually on prescription drugs, the amount they spend above $2,250 is entirely out-of-pocket.

Then there are the rate increases. The premiums and deductibles for the new drug coverage are expected to rise at average annual rates of 7.5% and 8.6%, respectively, from 2006 to 2013. This far exceeds the annual cost-of-living adjustments Social Security recipients get, which have averaged just 2.4% over the past 10 years. Medicare Part B (the section that provides coverage for doctor visits) has built-in protections that keep out-of-pocket expenses from rising faster than seniors' Social Security checks; the prescription drug benefit, however, includes no such protection. Even with the new benefit, then, drug costs will eat up a growing share of Medicare beneficiaries' incomes over time.

The new law also fails to treat "dual eligibles"—that is, low-income seniors eligible for both Medicare and Medicaid—fairly. The law prohibits the use of federal Medicaid dollars to pay for prescription drugs not covered by the new Medicare drug plan. This means that individuals currently on Medicaid can actually lose some of their existing coverage.

If the prescription drug benefit is offering less-than-meets-the-eye to seniors, then who does benefit from the massive new expenditure? Primarily, the pharmaceutical companies. The new law specifically prohibits the government from negotiating lower prices with drug companies. The Medicare population accounts for about half the prescription drug market. If the government were allowed to negotiate over prices—the same type of negotiation that goes on between private insurers and providers already—costs of the program would go down substantially.

Private insurers also stand to gain. The new prescription drug benefit will not be administered as part of traditional Medicare. Instead, seniors who want the benefit will have to choose a private drug plan; the plans will in turn be paid by Medicare. It's no surprise that the drug benefit is structured so as to accelerate the privatization of Medicare.

Instead of an inadequate program that wastes billions of dollars subsidizing private insurers and pharmaceutical companies, the government should offer a drug benefit that helps people who most need the care and cannot afford it.

HEALTH SAVINGS ACCOUNTS: STRIKE TWO

The new law also provides for health savings accounts (HSAs). HSAs provide tax benefits for individuals and families who buy eligible high-deductible health insurance plans—those with an annual deductible of at least $1,000 (for individuals, or $2,000 for a family). If you purchase such a plan, which typically has relatively low premiums, you can contribute to an HSA up to a set maximum. HSA contributions are fully tax deductible. Nor do you pay any tax—even on accrued interest—when you withdraw funds from the account to pay medical expenses.

HSAs were billed as a health cost-containment vehicle and a savings mechanism designed to help people prepare for future medical expenses. Their most likely primary use, however, will be as a generous tax shelter for the upper-income set. Consider two people with HSAs, a higher-income person in the 35% tax bracket and a lower-income person in the 10% bracket. The lower-income person pays 90 cents for every dollar she puts in her HSA then withdraws for medical bills, while the higher-income person pays only 65 cents. (Assuming that the lower-income person has any extra money to contribute to the HSA in the first place!) Clearly, higher-income families have much more to gain from these accounts than middle- or low-income families. And unlike many tax deductions, there is no phase-out range or maximum income limit. Further, wealthy people who have exhausted their other tax-advantaged savings vehicles or who have income too high to qualify for traditional IRAs will be most likely to participate. Since people over 65 can withdraw money from their accounts tax-free for any reason— not only for medical expenses—with no penalty, HSAs subsidize the retirement savings of wealthy people at the expense of lost tax revenue.

Because the benefits of an HSA come through a tax deduction, they are of no use to the many Americans who do not file taxes or who have little tax liability. A married couple with two children would receive no tax benefit whatsoever from contributing to an HSA unless their income was

> **IF PRIVATE INSURANCE COMPANIES ARE SO EFFICIENT, WHY DO THEY NEED HIGHER REIMBURSEMENT RATES?**

at least $40,200—more than twice the poverty level.

HSAs are not an effective means of cost containment as they create conflicting incentives. It's true that moving people to high-deductible plans ought to induce lower spending on health care. But by giving people a tax break when they spend money on health care, this plan reduces the cost-containment advantage of high-deductible insurance.

Nor is encouraging people to move to high-deductible plans good for the health insurance system as a whole. High-deductible plans have lower premiums and are a good deal for healthy people who don't need much care. When the healthy are siphoned off into these plans, risk pools become unbalanced and costs rise for everyone else. The result: it gets harder and harder for the less healthy to afford adequate coverage.

TAX PROPOSALS: STRIKE THREE

New Bush administration proposals for improving health care access suffer from the same problems. The president proposes an income tax deduction for high-deductible health insurance premiums. Only families with income tax liability gain from the proposal; it will do little to reduce the number of uninsured, about half of whom are from households with income too low to benefit from the deduction at all.

The Health Insurance Tax Credit (HITC), another administration proposal introduced in the Senate this March, is intended to help the uninsured obtain coverage. The HITC would provide low-income Americans with a tax credit of up to $1,000 for individuals and $500 per child to assist them in buying private health insurance. Individuals with incomes up to $30,000 and families with incomes up to $60,000 who have no job-based or government health insurance are eligible for the credit, which is refundable— in other words, those with little or no income tax liability will receive the amount of the credit as a direct payment from the government.

The HITC has three major problems as a vehicle for widening health insurance access: it doesn't help the sick, it isn't age adjusted, and it simply isn't generous enough. The HITC applies only to the purchase of individual or non-group health coverage. People who are already sick have an extremely difficult time getting insurance in the individual market. When they are not turned down outright, the premiums are prohibitively high, and insurers often add riders that disallow coverage on pre-existing conditions and reserve the right not to renew. The benefit isn't age adjusted, but premiums are. So the HITC disproportionately benefits younger people, the least in need of health insurance.

Non-group insurance is expensive: premiums and deductibles are higher and overall plan benefits are less generous than for group plans. In one market, premiums for non-group family plans average $13,214 a year. Even with the maximum $3,000 per family credit, eligible families would still have to pay over $10,000 a year for coverage—

far beyond the means of most low- and moderate-income families. And while non-group health plans are a poor substitute for employer-provided health insurance, tax preferences for these plans may give companies an excuse to stop offering insurance to their employees.

A WHOLE NEW BALLGAME

If the administration really wants to lower the number of uninsured, there are better ways than through the tax system. For the estimated cost of $95 billion in the first five years, researchers estimate the HITC and the new tax deduction for high-deductible plan premiums *combined* will insure an additional 1.3 million people—barely a dent in the estimated 43 million uninsured Americans. Why not expand Medicaid to cover more people, encourage the creation of risk pools to cover the sick, provide an affordable safety net for the unemployed—or dare to think about a single-payer system?

Sources: U.S. Congressional Budget Office, "Estimating the Cost of the Medicare Modernization Act," testimony before the House Ways and Means Committee, 3/24/04; U.S. Treasury Dept., "General Explanations of the Administration's Fiscal Year 2005 Revenue Proposals," February 2004; Kaiser Family Foundation, *Employer Health Benefits 2003 Annual Survey;* Kaiser Family Foundation, "Coverage and Cost Impacts of the President's Health Insurance Tax Credit and Tax Deduction Proposals," March 2004; Massachusetts Blue Cross and Blue Shield; U.S. Census Bureau, "Health Insurance Coverage in the United States: 2002," September 2003.

November/December 2001

THE HIDDEN COSTS OF PRIVATE ACCOUNTS

BY ELLEN FRANK

As Bush's handpicked commission on Social Security grapples with the details of diverting Social Security revenue into private accounts, it will almost certainly confront a knotty little logistical problem—an issue that so stumped privatization boosters in the past that most either finessed the problem or threw up their hands entirely. The problem is how to actually manage the 150 million plus personal accounts even a partially privatized system would require.

When privatization was initially floated several years back, advocates had in mind something along the lines of the current employer-sponsored 401(k) programs. In a 401(k) plan, employers contract with a fund manager to invest employee contributions. To minimize paperwork and oversight costs, they limit the number of available investment options, generally to around 10 funds, though sometimes to as few as three or four, so that workers are not wholly free to actively manage their own portfolios.

Even so, tracking this money is neither easy or cost-free. Employers need to set up accounting and compliance systems, select investment options, and monitor fund performance. The U.S. Department of Labor estimates that administrative costs run somewhere between $100 and $200 per year for each person enrolled in a plan. On top of that, fund managers rake off fees—usually 1 to 2% of the balance—to cover costs and leave some profit. And the system doesn't work seamlessly. Contributions get lost, delayed, misdirected; sometimes willfully, sometimes by accident.

Consider, then, how a national 401(k)-type program, funded out of payroll taxes and covering every single worker in the United States, would operate. Each and every employer in the country would need to set up a monitoring system and contract with financial firms to manage the accounts of even part-time, transient workers. The plan Bush put forth during his presidential campaign would divert two percentage points of the 12.4% payroll tax to personal investment accounts. Presumably, the law would require employers to offer some minimum array of investing options. Let's say they would have to offer five options, and let's imagine further that the typical employee would choose to allocate her savings equally among the five funds.

Consider, as an example, the local donut franchise with several part-time employees, typically working 20 hours each week at $7.50 an hour. Currently, the business owner sends $18.60 per worker to the Social Security Administration (SSA)—the combined employee and employer share of payroll taxes. Now, though, the donut shop will need to send out two checks—$15.60 to the government, and $3 to the financial contractor managing the employee's investment accounts. That's 60 cents in each of the five funds. The cost to the donut shop owner of setting up and monitoring these accounts could add up to thousands of dollars each year.

Now, imagine that our representative fast food worker quits after 10 weeks and takes a job with the pizza shop down the road. Does she shift her $30 in accumulated savings to the pizza maker's plan? Must the pizza shop owner offer the same five investment options as the donut franchiser? If not, who will arrange for the transfer of her funds from one financial contractor to another?

Or can the worker simply leave her miniscule balances—$6 in each of five funds—where they are, opening new funds with new financial firms as she shifts from part-time job to part-time job in the low-wage sector of the economy? If so, who will pay the administrative costs of maintaining all these accounts? The donut shop? The pizza store? The worker herself? Will the typical U.S. teenager complete high school with perhaps 20 different accounts, each containing a few dollars apiece, and those few dollars destined to be eaten away by annual management fees and administrative costs? And what happens if funds are lost, or deliberately withheld, or sent to the wrong fund manager? Would the federal government oversee this? Would the grocer, the baker, and the pizza maker pay for independent oversight? Would the mutual fund industry want this headache? Would anyone?

Chewing over this logistical nightmare, earlier advocates of privatization proposed to streamline the process. To ease the burden on small businesses, employers would instead send all payroll tax money to the SSA, as they do now, and the SSA would place two percentage points in privately managed accounts, nominally owned by the covered workers. Acting like a centralized human resources office for the entire U.S. labor force, the SSA could offer a wider array of investment choices and set up a system, similar to those offered today by a number of large employers, that would allow workers to actively manage their savings.

This is undoubtedly much simpler. But it is not cheap. The SSA would now be responsible for two major administrative functions—managing the flow of funds to current pensioners, and handling the mutual fund monitoring and record-keeping for 150 million private accounts. Economists estimate that this would at least double the administrative costs of running Social Security, raising the annual cost of administration from nearly 1% to just under 2% of payroll taxes. Will these costs be paid by workers? If so, nearly half of the projected returns from private accounts will be lost to administrative costs—and this is before we even talk about fees charged by the finance industry.

Or will Social Security's extra costs be paid by the Treasury out of general tax revenues? In this case, the government could save itself the trouble. If general revenues amounting to an additional 1% of payroll taxes were shifted to the SSA, that would go a long way towards solving Social Security's long-range financing problems, adding a number of years to the life of the trust fund.

Then there's another question. If all the money targeted for private accounts must, in any case, flow through the SSA, why bother with private accounts in the first place? Why not let the SSA invest the same share of its own revenues in private assets, manage its own portfolio, and use the presumably higher returns to fund higher benefits, or close future operating deficits?

"Absolutely not!" say privatization boosters. Allowing a federal agency to manage billions in private assets in its own name on behalf of 150 million taxpayers is socialism. Allowing the same agency to contract with financial firms to manage those same stocks in the name of said taxpayers is free-market capitalism. So does ideology trump common sense in the Social Security debate.

Last year, the conservative Federalist Society invited me to debate Charles Rounds, Suffolk University law professor and supporter of private accounts. The audience questioned Rounds closely on how the accounts would operate. Would workers actually own their own savings? If so, could they withdraw funds and spend them as they chose? Or invest them in anything at all—say, Florida real estate or an internet start-up? And what would happen if their investments went sour or they spent down their savings before retiring?

These are the sorts of questions privatization boosters prefer not to address. A libertarian and Cato Institute researcher, Rounds criticized Social Security as a big-government welfare scheme which, disguised as a pension plan, coerces American workers to support retirees. Yet he conceded that a privatized system would itself necessitate quite a lot of federal coercion—workers would be required to save, to place their savings in a few pre-selected stock funds, and to keep them there until retirement. He also acknowledged that Congress might need to saddle the SSA with yet another task—administering a supplementary welfare program for those who outlived their savings.

That is the dirty little secret of privatization. A system of private accounts would be so expensive to set up and monitor, and would expose workers to so much risk and so many fees, that the federal government would almost certainly have to manage the whole mess, from choosing investment options and monitoring accounts, to establishing a parallel welfare system for those whose investments prove unprofitable.

So the push for privatization is not about freedom and individual choice after all. It's about diverting the money now going to SSA into the coffers of Wall Street.

RULING THE EMPIRE

BY ALEJANDRO REUSS

Every few years, the President issues a document called the "National Security Strategy of the United States." Always eagerly awaited, the document is often described as the administration's "blueprint" for U.S. foreign policy. But it's really more like a press release, designed to give the U.S. government's global aims a noble-sounding spin.

The Bush administration's most recent "National Security Strategy," issued September 2002, abounds with pious lip service: On the subject of democracy, it applauds the "elected leaders replac[ing] generals in Latin America" without mentioning who put the generals in power in the first place. On the environment, it calls for "global efforts to stabilize greenhouse gas concentrations" without mentioning that the U.S. government had scuttled the Kyoto Protocol. On the global economy, it decries as "neither just nor stable" a state of affairs "where some live in comfort and plenty, while half of the human race lives on less than $2 a day," yet it offers no solution other than more "free markets and free trade."

The document's crowning hypocrisy, however, is its repeated use of the buzz-phrase "a balance of power that favors freedom," as if that were what the U.S. government was really after. You get the distinct feeling that the drafters don't believe in it for a minute. By its final and most important section, on the country's "National Security Institutions," the document abandons all pretext. The "unparalleled strength of the United States armed forces, and their forward presence, have maintained the peace," it declares. The United States must "reaffirm the essential role of American military strength" and "build and maintain our defenses beyond challenge." It must maintain forces "strong enough to dissuade potential adversaries" from

the dream of ever "surpassing, or equaling, the power of the United States."

Well, if those are the real aims of U.S. ruling elites, they're off to a good start. In 2001, U.S. military spending—the highest, by far, of any country in the world—exceeded the combined spending of the next eight countries—Russia, France, Japan, the United Kingdom, Germany, Chi-

GRAPH 1
2001 MILITARY SPENDING

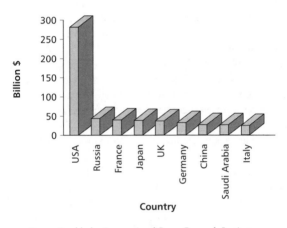

Source: Stockholm International Peace Research Institute, SIPRI Yearbook 2002.

GRAPH 2
2001 FEDERAL FUNDS BUDGET
(Excludes Social Security)

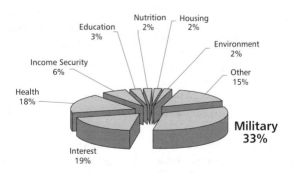

Source: National Priorities Project. Includes only the federal funds portion of the federal budget. Military includes veterans' benefits and the military share of interest on the national debt.

na, Saudi Arabia, and Italy (see Graph 1). In fact, U.S. military spending represented over one third of the total of the *entire world*. This grotesquely overgrown war machine comes at no little cost. In 2001, total federal military spending (including interest payments on past military spending and benefits for former military personnel) devoured about one third of the federal funds portion of the budget (not including trust fund items like Social Security), as much as spending on health, income security, education, nutrition, and housing *combined* (see Graph 2).

In light of these realities, the "balance of power" rhetoric isn't really fooling anybody. Writing in the mainstream *Christian Science Monitor*, Gail Russell Chaddock argues that the document "asserts American dominance as the lone superpower—a status no rival power will be allowed to challenge." It is a vision, she says, of a "Pax Americana" (the modern-day equivalent of Roman imperial power). Even the senior defense policy analyst at the right-wing Cato Institute, Charles V. Peña, writes that "although it's all dressed up with the rationale of extending liberty, democracy, and freedom around the globe (except, of course, in Saudi Arabia and Pakistan)" the document really envisions a "Pax Americana enforced by dominant military power and … U.S. forces deployed around the globe."

None of this is exactly news. The United States, after all, has been a major imperial power in the Western Hemisphere for over a century. And it has been the single dominant capitalist power for more than half that period. The truth, however, should be clearer than ever. As the title of Peña's article puts it: "The New National Security Strategy Is American Empire."

CHAPTER 5

Monetary Policy and Financial Markets

INTRODUCTION

Alan Greenspan, the man behind the curtain of the Federal Reserve Board, must possess some wizard-like qualities. Despite overseeing the high-tech wreck, a stock market that went South, a shrinking manufacturing base, and an economic recovery that has lost more than two million jobs, Greenspan's boss (President Bush) renewed his contract.

Somebody must think Greenspan's doing something right. The Fed is charged with using monetary policy to keep inflation in check and provide liquidity to keep the economy going, or bolster a flagging economy. The Fed is supposed to use its three tools—the reserve requirement, the discount rate and federal funds rates, and open market operations—to manipulate banking activity, control the money supply, and direct the economy to everyone's benefit.

It all sounds value-free. But what Greenspan is really doing "right" is serving those who hold financial assets. And that is just what's wrong with Fed monetary policy. When it comes to making monetary policy, the Fed puts the interests of bondholders first, well before those of job-seekers and workers. Investors look to the Fed to protect the value of their stocks and bonds by keeping inflation low—and if that means keeping a cap on employment growth, so be it.

That is why monetary policy is not just a matter for financial market junkies, but for anyone concerned with the social policies it holds hostage. As Doug Orr and Ellen Frank argue in this chapter, "Whenever any policy is proposed, be it in health care, housing or transportation, the first question politicians ask is, 'What will the bond market think about it?'" (Article 5.3). Frank goes on to show just how monetary policy under Greenspan has worked against most of us. The Fed hiked interest rates during the late 1990s to insure against the inflation associated with rapid growth and higher wages. As Frank argues, this actually helped push the economy into its current slowdown (Article 5.4).

Other articles in this chapter look closely at diverse aspects of Fed policy-making. Doug Orr Explains in everyday language what money is and how the Fed attempts to control the money supply (Article 5.1). Arthur MacEwan compares monetary and fiscal policy, highlighting the greater powers of fiscal policy to counteract recessions (Article 5.5). Frank describes how changes in the interest rate the Fed charges on loans to commercial banks affect those banks' financial positions, as well as market-wide interest rates (Article 5.6).

Several articles address the context in which the Fed operates. In Article 5.2, James K. Galbraith explains how the value of the dollar, the world's reserve currency, depends on the willingness of foreign central banks and international investors to hold U.S. assets, and how that willingness is being eroded by the deteriorating U.S. trade position. Banking expert Jim Campen (Article 5.7) gives a close-up view of the "new world of banking" in which the Fed now conducts monetary policy—a world dominated by giant financial holding companies. Finally, Nomi Prins (Article 5.8) shows that the much touted 2003 Wall Street settlement is unlikely to undo that domination.

DISCUSSION QUESTIONS

1) (Article 5.1) What are the mechanisms the Fed uses to "control" the creation of money by the banking system. Why, according to Orr, is the Fed's control over the creation of money "limited"?
2) (Article 5.2) According to Galbraith, how has the United States becoming a debtor nation threatened the status of the dollar as the world's reserve currency? How serious a threat is this for the U.S. economy?
3) (Article 5.3) According to Orr and Frank, monetary policy serves the interests of bondholders at the expense of people seeking work, and everyone who benefits from social spending. What evidence do they provide to show that Fed policy has this class character? Do you find it convincing?
4) (Article 5.5) What advantage is there in using monetary policy to slow down the economy? Why might fiscal policy be a more effective tool for lifting the economy out of a recession?
5) (Articles 5.7 and 5.8) How do the financial holding companies, made possible by the bank reform of 1999, differ from traditional banks and securities forms? Why, according to Prins, is the 2003 Wall Street settlement unlikely to change the dominance of these financial holding companies?

KEY TO COLANDER

E = Economics M = Macroeconomics.

These readings complement E27, E28, and E34, or M11, M12, and M19.

Articles 5.1, 5.3, 5.4, 5.5 and 5.6 look at the working of monetary policy, who it serves, the differences between monetary and fiscal policy, and Greenspan's record at the Fed. They fit with chapter E28 or M12. Article 5.2 takes up a complication of conducting monetary policy in an international economy, and fits with chapter E34 or M19. Article 5.7 describes the new deregulated world of mega-banks that monetary policy must engage, the subject of chapter E27 or M11.

November/December 1993

WHAT IS MONEY?

BY DOUG ORR

We all use money every day. Yet many people do not know what money actually is. There are many myths about money, including the idea that the government "prints" all of it and that it has some intrinsic value. But actually, money is less a matter of value, and more a matter of faith.

Money is sometimes called the universal commodity, because it can be traded for all other commodities. But for this to happen, everyone in society must believe that money will be accepted. If people stop believing that it will be accepted, the existing money ceases to be money. Recently in Poland, people stopped accepting the zloty, and used vodka as money instead.

In addition to facilitating exchanges, money allows us to "store" value from one point in time to another. If you sell your car today for $4,000, you probably won't buy that amount of other products today. Rather, you store the value as money, probably in a bank, until you want to use it.

The "things" that get used as money have changed over time, and "modern" people often chuckle when they hear about some of them. The Romans used salt (from which we get the word "salary"), South Sea Islanders used shark's teeth, and several societies actually used cows. The "Three Wise Men" brought gold, frankincense and myrrh, each of which was money in different regions at the time.

If money does not exist, or is in short supply, it will be created. In POW camps, where guards specifically outlaw its existence, prisoners use cigarettes instead. In the American colonies, the British attempted to limit the supply of British pounds, because they knew that by limiting the supply of money, they could hamper the development of independent markets in the colonies. Today, the United States uses a similar policy, through the International Monetary Fund, in dealing with Latin America.

To overcome this problem, the colonists began to use tobacco leaves as money. This helped the colonies to develop, but it also allowed the holders of large plots of land to grow their own money! When the colonies gained independence, the new government decreed gold to be money, rather than tobacco, much to the dismay of Southern plantation owners. Now, rather than growing money, farmers had to find or buy it.

To aid the use of gold as money, banks would test its purity, put it in storage, and give the depositor paper certificates of ownership. These certificates, "paper money," could then be used in place of the gold itself. Since any bank could store gold and issue certificates, by the beginning of the Civil War, over 7,000 different types of "paper money" were in circulation in the United States, none of it printed by the government.

While paper money is easier to use than gold, it is still risky to carry around large amounts of cash. It is safer to store the paper in a bank and simply sign over its ownership to make a purchase. We sign over the ownership of our money by writing a check. Checking account money became popular when the government outlawed the printing of paper money by private banks in 1864.

HOW BANKS CREATE MONEY

Banks are central to understanding money, because in addition to storing it, they help to create it. Bankers realize that not everyone will withdraw their money at the same time, so they loan out much of the money that has been deposited. It is from the interest on these loans that banks get their profits, and through these loans the banking system creates new money.

If you deposit $100 cash in your checking account at Chase Manhattan Bank, you still have $100 in money to use, because checks are also accepted as money. Chase must set aside some of this cash as "reserves," in case you or other depositors decide to withdraw money as cash. Current regulations issued by the Federal Reserve Bank (the Fed) require banks to set aside three cents out of each dollar. So Chase can make a loan of $97, based on your deposit. Chase does not make loans by handing out cash but instead by putting $97 in the checking account of the person, say Emily, taking out the loan. So from your initial deposit of $100 in cash, the economy now has $197 in checking account money.

The borrower, Emily, pays $97 for some product or service by check, and the seller, say Ace Computers, deposits the money in its checking account. The total amount of checking account money is still $197, but its location and ownership have changed. If Ace Computer's account is at Citibank, $97 in cash is transferred from Chase to Citibank. This leaves just $3 in cash reserves at Chase to cover your original deposit. However, Citibank now has $97 in "new" cash on hand, so it sets aside three cents on the dollar ($2.91) and loans out the rest, $94.09, as new checking account money. Through this process, every dollar of "reserves" yields many dollars in total money.

If you think this is just a shell game and there is only $100 in "real" money, you still don't understand money. Anything that is accepted as payment for a transaction is "real" money. Cash is no more real than checking account money. In fact, most car rental companies will not accept cash as payment for a car, so for them, cash is not money!

Today, there is $292 billion of U.S. currency, i.e. "paper money," in existence. However, somewhere between 50% to 70% of it is held outside the United States by foreign banks and individuals. The vast majority of all money actually in use in the United States is not cash, but rather checking account money. This type of money, $726 billion, was created by private banks, and was not "printed" by anyone. In fact, this money exists only as electronic "bits" in banks' computers. (The less "modern" South Sea Islanders could have quite a chuckle about that!)

The amount of money that banks can create is limited by the total amount of reserves, and by the fraction of each deposit that must be held as reserves. Prior to 1914, bankers themselves decided what fraction of deposits to hold as reserves. Since then, this fraction has been set by the main banking regulator, the Fed.

Until 1934, gold was held as reserves, but the supply of gold was unstable, growing rapidly during the California and Alaska "gold rushes," and very slowly at other times. As a result, at times more money was created than the economy needed, and at other times not enough money could be created. Starting in 1934, the U.S. government decided that gold would no longer be used as reserves. Cash, now printed by the Fed, could no longer be redeemed for gold, and cash itself became the reserve asset.

Banks, fearing robberies, do not hold all of their cash reserves in their own vaults. Rather, they store it in an ac-count at a regional Fed bank. These accounts count as reserves. What banks do hold in their vaults is their other assets, such as Treasury bonds and corporate bonds.

THE FED AND BANK RESERVES

The only role of the government in creating money is through the Fed. If the Fed wants to expand the money supply, it must increase bank reserves. To do this, the Fed buys Treasury bonds from a bank, and pays with a check drawn on the Fed itself. By depositing the check in its reserve account at the Fed, the bank now has more reserves, so the bank can now make more loans and create new checking account money.

By controlling the amount of reserves, the Fed attempts to control the size of the money supply. But as recent history has shown, this control is limited. During the recent recession, the Fed created reserves, but many banks were afraid to make loans, so little new money was created. During the late 1970s, the Fed tried to limit the amount of money banks could create by reducing reserves, but banks simply created new forms of money, just like the POW camp prisoners. In 1979, there was only one form of checking account money. Today, there are many, with odd names such as NOWs, ATSs, repos, and money market deposit accounts.

These amorphous forms of money function only because we believe they will function, which is why the continued stability of the banking system is so critical. Banks do not have cash reserves to cover all checking account money. If, through a replay of the savings & loan debacle, we lose faith in the commercial banking system and all try to take out our "money" as cash, the banks will become insolvent (fail), and the money they have created will simply disappear. This would create a real crisis, since no market economy can function without its money.

ARTICLE 5.2   *May/June 2003*

THE DECLINE OF THE DOLLAR SYSTEM

BY JAMES K. GALBRAITH

Today, the U.S. dollar is the world's reserve currency. Nations around the world invest most of their foreign exchange reserves in dollar assets. The international economic position of the United States depends on this.

So long as foreign central banks and international investors are willing to take and hold U.S. assets (including stocks, bonds, and cash) this system works—and shamefully to the interest of Americans. Their demand keeps the value of the dollar high. This means that we have been able to consume comfortably, and in exchange for very little effort, the products of hard labor by poor people. (As the supplier of liquidity to the world system, our situation is akin to that of, say, Australia in the late 19th century when gold fields were discovered, except that, in our case, no actual effort is required to extract the gold.) And meanwhile (thanks to am-

ple cheap imports), we are not obliged to invest unduly in maintaining our own industrial base, which has substantially eroded since the 1970s. We could afford to splurge on new technologies and telecommunications systems whose benefits were, to a very great extent, figments of the imagination. And even when the bubble burst in those sectors, life went on, for most Americans, substantially undisturbed—at least for now.

But for how long can this system endure? There can be no definitive answer; the few economists who have worried about this issue are far from being in agreement. On one side, it is argued that the dominant currency holds a "lock-in advantage"; that is, there are economies (reduced transaction costs and reduced risk) associated with keeping all reserves in one basket. The United States in particular is in a strong position to pressure foreign central banks—notably Japan's—to absorb the dollars that private parties may not wish to hold, at least within limits.

Furthermore, oil is bought and sold in dollars. As a result, oil importers must buy dollars in order to buy oil, and oil exporters accumulate dollars as they sell oil. To some extent this arrangement further strengthens the dollar—though it is not obvious why it requires anyone to hold dollars for very long, once they start falling in value.

Against this, the question remains: As the U.S. trade position continues to erode, will foreigners be willing to add to their holdings of dollar assets by enough to allow the United States to return to full employment? The amount to be absorbed at present—the trade deficit at full employment—is in the range of half a trillion dollars per year. This was easily handled when dollar asset prices were rising. But now that these prices are falling, they are not as attractive as they once were. If foreigners are not willing to absorb all the dollars we need to place, and if asset prices do not quickly fall to the point where U.S. stocks appear cheap to investors, dollar dumping is, sooner or later, inevitable.

To keep the dollar's fall from getting out of hand, the United States will be strongly tempted to slow the rate at which new U.S. assets reach the world system, by restricting its imports. Having renounced the traditional tools of trade protectionism, it can only do this by raising interest rates, holding down economic growth, and keeping incomes, and therefore imports, well below the full-employment level. In that situation—which may actually already have arrived—the United States joins Brazil and other developing nations as a country effectively constrained by its debts. Indeed, the world prognosis from that point forward becomes grim, since high levels of American demand have been just about the only motor of growth and development (outside, perhaps, of China and India) in recent years.

THE UNITED STATES AS A DEBTOR NATION

There are economists who advocate dollar devaluation, believing that the richer countries of the world would quickly rally to purchase increasing quantities of made-in-America

exports, thus reversing the manufacturing decline of the past 20 years. But this is very unlikely. Exports to the rich regions may not be very price-sensitive.

And exports to the developing regions are very sensitive to income and credit conditions, which would get worse. At least in the short and medium term, there is no foolproof adjustment process to be had by these means. Where a high dollar provides U.S. consumers with cheap imports and capital inflows to finance domestic activity, a falling dollar would have opposite effects. A falling dollar would raise the price of imports into the United States, especially from the richer countries. Meanwhile, a declining dollar would hit at the value of developing countries' reserves and their access to credit, and so it would diminish their demand for our exports. (It would help, in some cases, on their debts.) The most likely outcome from dollar devaluation is a general deepening of the world slump, combined with pressure on American banks and markets as global investors seek safer havens in Europe.

This specter of financial vulnerability means that for the United States, the combination of falling internal demand, falling asset prices, and a falling dollar represents a threat that can best be described as millennial. (My colleague Randall Wray has called it the "perfect fiscal storm.") The consequences at home would include deepening unemployment. There would be little recovery of privately financed investment, amid a continued unraveling of plans—both corporate and personal—that had been based on the delirious stock market valuations of the late 1990s. The center of the world banking industry would move, presumably to continental Europe. Over time, the United States could lose both its position as the principal beneficiary of the world financial order and its margin of maneuver on the domestic scene. This would be not unlike what happened to the United Kingdom from 1914 to 1950.

It is not obvious that senior financial policymakers in the United States have yet grasped this threat, or that there is any serious planning under way to cope with it—apart from a simpleminded view among certain strategic thinkers about the financial advantages of the control of oil. Instead it appears that the responsible officials are confining themselves to a very narrow range of Third-World debt management proposals, whose premises minimize the gravity of the issue and whose purpose is to keep the existing bonds of debt peonage in place as long as possible.

The alternative? It would involve rebuilding a multilateral monetary system, demolished for the benefit of the private commercial banks in 1973. The way forward would probably entail new regional systems of financial stabilization and capital control, such as the Asian Monetary Fund proposed by Japan in 1997. Such a course would be unpalatable to current American leadership. But we may find, down the road, that for the sake of our own prosperity, let alone that of the rest of the world, there is no other way.

FOCUS ON THE FED

THE BOND MARKET VERSUS THE REST OF US

BY DOUG ORR AND ELLEN FRANK

Why should anyone involved in environmental issues, or education reform efforts, or efforts to house the homeless, or anyone else, care about monetary policy? After all, it only affects the financial markets, right? *Wrong*. Monetary policy is holding all other social policy hostage, and is part of the cause of the rapid increase in income inequality in the United States. Whenever any policy change is proposed, be it in health care, housing or transportation, the first question politicians ask is, "What will the bond market think about this?"

"The bond market" is a euphemism for the financial sector of the U.S. economy and the Federal Reserve Bank (the Fed), which regulates that sector. The Fed is the central bank of the U.S. government. It controls monetary policy, and has been using its power to help the banking industry and the holders of financial assets, while thwarting government attempts to deal with pressing social problems.

Since 1979, the Fed has had an unprecedented degree of independence from government control. This independence had put it in a position to veto any progressive fiscal policy that the Congress might propose. To understand how this situation developed, we must understand the function of banks, the structure of the Fed, and the role of monetary policy.

BANKS AND INSTABILITY

Government regulates the banking industry because private sector, profit-driven banking is inherently unstable. Banks do more than just store money—they help create it. If you deposit a dollar in the bank, you still have that dollar. Commercial banks will set aside three cents as "reserves" to "cover" your deposit, and the remaining 97 cents is loaned out to someone else who now has "new money." By making loans, banks create new money and generate profit. The drive to maximize profits often leads banks to become overextended: making too many loans and holding too few reserves. This drive for profits can undermine a bank's stability.

If depositors think the bank is holding too few reserves, or is making overly speculative loans, they might try to withdraw their money as cash. Large numbers of depositors withdrawing cash from a bank at the same time is called a "run on the bank." Since banks only hold 3% of their deposit liabilities as cash, even a moderate-sized "run" would be enough to drain the bank of its cash reserves. If a bank has no reserves, it is insolvent and is forced to close. At that point, all remaining deposits in the bank cease to exist, and depositors lose their money.

The failure of a bank affects more than just that bank's depositors. One bank's excesses tend to shake people's faith in other banks. If the run spreads, "bank panics" can occur. During the 1800s, such panics erupted every 10 to 15 years, bankrupting between 10% and 25% of the banks in the United States and creating a recession each time.

THE CREATION OF THE FED

The panic of 1907 bankrupted some of the largest banks and led to demands for bank reforms that would stabilize the system. Reform proposals ranged from doing almost nothing to nationalizing the entire banking industry. As a compromise, the Federal Reserve was created in 1913. The U.S. government saw the Fed as a way for bankers to regulate themselves, and structured the Federal Reserve System so that it could be responsive to its main constituents: banks and other financial-sector businesses that are now called, euphemistically, "the bond market." While ideally it should serve the interests of the general public when it conducts monetary policy, in reality the Fed balances two, occasionally conflicting goals: maintaining the stability of "the bond market" and maximizing financial-sector profits. Over time, Congress and the President have varied the degree of independence that they have given to the Fed to choose between these goals.

Initially, the Fed enjoyed a high degree of independence. Unfortunately, it was more successful in aiding bank profits than in stabilizing the system. During the 1920s, the Fed allowed member banks to engage in highly speculative activities, including using depositor's money to play the stock market. While many banks were very profitable, speculative excesses caused almost 20% of the banks in existence in 1920 to fail during the following decade. With the onset of the Great Depression, between 1929 and 1933, more than 9,000 banks, 38% of the total, failed. Since the Fed had not achieved its first goal, in 1935 Congress responded with laws that put many new regulations on banks, and reduced the Fed's independence.

FED INDEPENDENCE LOST

Under the new regulations, commercial banks were restricted to taking deposits and making commercial loans. Thus, the only opportunity for making a profit was to maintain a "spread" between the interest rate paid on deposits and that charged on loans. Loans are made for relatively long terms, and deposits are not. If the short-term interest rate on deposits varies widely, the spread will grow and shrink, which makes bank profits unstable. In order to stabilize bank profits, during the 30 years after 1935, the Treasury mandated that the Fed keep this rate approximately constant.

Under this arrangement, Congress indirectly controlled monetary policy. If Congress wanted to stimulate the economy it could increase government spending or cut taxes. Both led to an increase in spending and an increase in the demand for money. To keep interest rates, which are the price of money, from rising, the Fed must increase the supply of money. Thus, the Fed "accommodated" fiscal policy decisions made by Congress and the President.

During most of this period, growth was moderate and prices were stable. The Fed went along because this arrangement did not threaten bank profits. Starting in the mid-1960s, however, stimulative fiscal policy started to push up the inflation rate, which did threaten bank profits. A confrontation over Fed independence ensued and grew in intensity throughout the 1970s.

INFLATION'S IMPACT

Contrary to the view commonly propagated by the media, inflation does not affect everyone equally. In fact, there are very clear winners and losers. Inflation is an increase in the average level of prices, but some prices rise faster than average and some rise slower. If the price of something you are selling is rising faster than average, you win. Otherwise, you lose. Inflation redistributes income, but in an arbitrary manner. This uncertainty makes inflation unpopular, even to the winners. However, one industry always loses from unexpected inflation, and that industry is finance.

Banks make loans today that will be repaid, with interest, in the future. If inflation reduces the value of those future payments, the banks' profits will be reduced. So bankers are interested in the "real interest rate," that is, the actual (nominal) interest rate on the loan minus the rate of inflation. If the interest rate on commercial bank loans is 7% and the rate of inflation is 3%, the real rate of interest is 4%. In the early postwar period, real interest rates were relatively stable at about 2%.

From 1965 on, unexpected increases in inflation reduced the real interest rate. This cheap credit was a boon to home buyers, farmers, and manufacturers, but it greatly reduced bank profits. Banks wanted inflation cut. The Keynesian view of monetary policy offered a simple but unpopular solution: raise interest rates enough to cause a re-

cession. High unemployment and falling incomes would take the steam out of inflation.

Putting people out of work to help bankers would be a hard sell. The Fed needed a different story to justify shifting its policy from stabilizing interest rates to fighting inflation. That story was monetarism, a theory that claims that changes in the money supply affect prices, but nothing else in the economy.

THE MONETARIST EXPERIMENT

On October 6, 1979, Fed Chair Paul Volcker, using monetarist theory as a justification, announced that the Fed would no longer try to keep interest rates at targeted levels. He argued that Fed policy should concentrate on controlling inflation, and to do so he would now focus on limiting the money supply growth rate. Since neither Congress nor the President attempted to overrule Volcker, this change ushered in an era of unprecedented independence for Fed monetary policy.

During the next three years, the Fed reduced the rate of growth in the money supply, but this experiment did not yield the results predicted by the monetarists. Instead of a swift reduction in the rate of inflation, the most immediate outcome was a rapid rise in the real interest rate and the start of the worst recession since the Great Depression.

As the Keynesian view predicted, the recession occurred because high interest rates slowed economic growth and increased unemployment. In 1979, the unemployment rate was 5.8%. By 1982 it had reached 10.7%, the first double-digit rate since the Depression. With fewer people working and buying products, the inflation rate, which had been 8.7% in 1979, finally started to slow in 1981 and was approaching 4% by the end of 1982. Tight money policies by the Fed kept nominal interest rates from falling as fast as inflation. This raised real interest rates (nominal rates minus inflation) on commercial loans from 0.5% in 1979 to 10% in 1982.

The Fed's fight against inflation had a severe impact on the entire economy. All businesses, especially farming and manufacturing, run on credit. The rise in interest rates, combined with lower prices, squeezed the profits of farmers and manufacturers.

Both of these industries rely heavily on exports, and so were also hurt by the negative effect of high interest rates on the competitiveness of U.S. exports. Real interest rates in the United States were the highest in the world, thereby attracting financial investment from abroad. In order for foreigners to buy financial assets in the United States, they first had to buy dollars. This demand for dollars drove up their value in international markets. While a "strong" dollar means imports are relatively cheap, it also means that U.S. exports are expensive. Foreign countries could not afford to buy our "costly" agricultural and manufactured exports. As a result, during this period, bankruptcy rates in these two industries were massive, higher than during the 1930s.

Despite its high cost to the rest of the economy, the monetarist experiment did not benefit many banks. Initially, the high real interest rates appeared to help bank profits. Regulations capped the interest rates banks could pay on deposits, but rates charged on loans were not regulated. This increased the profit on loans. Many investors, however, started moving their deposits to less regulated financial intermediaries, such as mutual funds, that could pay higher rates on deposits. In addition, the recession forced many borrowers to declare bankruptcy and default on their loans. Both of these factors pushed banks toward insolvency.

REVERSING COURSE

It was bank losses, rather than the pain in the rest of the economy, that led Volcker to announce in September 1982 that he was abandoning monetarism. His new policy aimed to provide enough reserves to keep most banks solvent and to allow a *slow* recovery from the recession. Unemployment remained high for the next five years, so inflation continued to slow. Real interest rates stayed near 8% through 1986, so interest-sensitive industries, such as farming and manufacturing, did not take part in the recovery.

IN 1995 THE WEALTHIEST 10% OF HOUSEHOLDS OWNED 89.8% OF ALL BONDS, 88.4% OF ALL STOCKS, 88.5% OF FINANCIAL TRUSTS, AND 91% OF OTHER BUSINESS EQUITY.

Volcker made his allegiance to the banking industry very clear during a meeting, in February 1985, with a delegation of state legislators, laborers, and farmers who were demanding easier money and lower interest rates. He told them, "Look, your constituents are unhappy, mine aren't."

Yet by 1985, the crisis in the savings and loan industry was spreading into commercial banking. To provide cash ("liquidity") to the banks, Volcker allowed the money supply to grow by 12% during 1985 and by 17% in 1986. Monetarists raised the specter of a return to double-digit inflation. Instead, the rate of inflation continued to slow, demonstrating that a simple link between the money supply and inflation does not exist.

THE VETO

Despite the failure and subsequent abandonment of monetarist policies, the Fed still uses monetarist *theory* to justify its continued focus on "fighting inflation." The myth that monetary policy only affects inflation provides a convenient "cover" that allows the Fed to serve its narrow constituency: "the bond market." During 1998, nominal interest rates appeared low, but because inflation is so low, real interest rates on commercial loans were 6.8%—3.2 times the post-World War II average. Real interest rates remain high because "the bond market" worries about any possible increase in future inflation.

Fighting inflation benefits the bond market. However, despite the near-depression that monetarism caused in the 1980s and the extremely slow rate of economic growth that has occurred in the 1990s, the Fed continues to claim that fighting inflation serves the interests of the entire country. The public's widespread belief in this myth denies progressives in Congress the support they need to force the Fed back into accommodating fiscal policy. It also provides support for those in Congress that want to block any expansion of social programs.

If Congress decides to spend more for environmental clean-up, housing the homeless, or education, "the bond market" will raise the specter of renewed inflation. The Fed will then raise interest rates, as it did in June 1999, as a "pre-emptive strike" to prevent inflation. The increase in interest rates, if large enough, will slow the economy, increase unemployment, reduce government revenues, and return the federal budget to a deficit. Since Congress is aware of this probable outcome, and knows it will be incorrectly blamed for it, Congress won't pass any legislation "the bond market" doesn't like. This is how the bond market holds Congress hostage. As long as Congress and the President allow the Fed to follow an inflation-fighting policy, the Fed can maintain a veto threat over the elected government.

The Fed has also played a large role in the rapid increase in income and wealth inequality that started in the 1980s and has accelerated in the 1990s. The two decades following World War II are often called the "golden age" of the U.S. economy. On average, Gross Domestic Product (GDP) grew 4.2% each year, unemployment averaged 4.6%, and real commercial interest rates averaged 2.1%. Average real wages, that is, wages adjusted for inflation, grew at an annual rate of 2.1%, rising from $8.34 an hour in 1950 to $12.75 in 1970 (both measured in 1998 dollars). This period saw the creation of a true middle class in the United States.

In the two decades since 1980, GDP growth has averaged 2.6% each year, unemployment has averaged 6.6%, and real interest rates have averaged 5.9%. Average real wages *declined* every year from 1980 to 1996. In fact, the real wage in 1996 was exactly the same as in 1968. If wages had continued to grow at 2.1%, the average wage today would be almost twice what it is. Without the slow growth policies of the Fed and the anti-labor policies started under Reagan, the average income of the majority of the people in the United States would be twice as large. Instead, we've seen a hollowing out of the middle class, and a rapid transfer of wealth and income to those already wealthy.

By focusing on inflation rather than interest rates, the media deflect attention from a critical social issue—how high interest rates transfer income from the indebted middle class to the very rich. The social consequences of high interest rates can be gauged by looking at the share of interest income in total U.S. personal income. Between 1980 and 1989, real interest rates rose from 1.8% to 6.1%. The share of income received as interest rose from 11% to 15.2%. As rates came back down slightly in the mid-1990s, so did the share of income going to interest.

WHERE DO INTEREST PAYMENTS GO?

If ownership of financial assets was evenly distributed among households, the growth in interest income would not be of much importance. When increases in interest rates outstripped wage and salary gains, the typical household would simply gain on the asset side what they were losing on the liability side. An increase in the size of their mortgage payment would be matched by an increase in their interest income.

But ownership of financial assets is heavily concentrated. A mere 7% of families with incomes of $100,000 or more control nearly half of total household net worth. Yet this number understates the concentration of financial wealth. Almost 80% of families in the United States have almost no assets, outside the equity in their homes and vehicles. As a result, despite the massive increase in financial asset values during the 1990s, median net worth was no higher in 1995 than it was in 1989. Almost all of the growth in net worth accrued to the few owners of financial assets.

Detailed studies of wealth data collected by the Fed report that in 1995 the wealthiest 10% of households owned 89.8% of all bonds, 88.4% of all stocks, 88.5% of financial trusts, and 91% of other business equity. Despite the media hype about the "democratization" of the stock market, between 1989 and 1995 the concentration of stock ownership increased. In 1995 only 15.3% of households held stocks directly and only 12% owned shares in mutual funds outside of their retirement accounts.

The "poorest" nine-tenths of the U.S. population—that is, most of us—have virtually no financial assets. Such families gain little from rising interest rates. But the higher mortgage, credit card, and auto payments that result take a real toll on living standards. Each uptick in the real interest rate entails a transfer of income from the lowest 90% of the population to the highest 10%. And most of that income goes to the very, very wealthy who are yet another part of "the bond market" served by the Fed.

Economist James Galbraith has called today's high interest rates a form of taxation without representation. The term is apt. Tax increases are passed by Congress, which has at least some public oversight. Interest rate hikes are decided by the Fed, an institution over which the President, Congress and the public have virtually no control.

Like taxes, rising interest rates are a drain on the resources and income of the vast majority of U.S. households. But unlike tax revenues that can be used to provide education, environmental clean-up, homeless shelters, roads, airports, and other infrastructure, interest payments flow into the pockets of the very rich, who become ever so much richer.

Resources: Arthur B. Kennickell, Martha Starr-McCluer, and Annika E. Sunden, "Family Finances in the U.S.: Recent Evidence from the Survey of Consumer Finances," *Federal Reserve Bulletin* (Jan. 1997); Lawrence Mishel, Jared Bernstein, and John Schmitt, *The State of Working America 1998-99*, 1999.

SAINT GREENSPAN?

BY ELLEN FRANK

In April 2003, President Bush reappointed Alan Greenspan chair of the Federal Reserve. The appointment zipped through the Senate and was met in the media with reverential awe. At the time, one might almost have thought that Greenspan had been nominated for sainthood rather than a fifth term as chair of the Federal Reserve. In the U.S. business press, the very name Greenspan was synonymous with wise and masterly control of economic affairs. Criticism of his tenure as Fed chair was so rare as to border on heresy.

Yet in 2003, the economy remained stalled after the recession of 2001. Unemployment was high, wages stagnant, consumer debt loads rising at unprecedented rates and Wall Street still embroiled in scandal. What responsibility does Alan Greenspan and the Fed bear for the economy's precarious state? Quite a bit actually.

According to law, the Fed's mandate is to promote "full employment, balanced growth and … reasonable price stability." Since Greenspan became chair in 1987, the Fed has mostly ignored the first part of this mandate, indicating repeatedly that its overriding goal is to prevent inflation even when that means promoting relatively high unemployment. Not only has Greenspan's Fed willfully ignored its legal responsibility for full employment, it has quietly pushed for legislation to eliminate altogether the Fed's statutory obligation to workers.

When Clinton reappointed Greenspan in 1995, media retrospectives cited Greenspan for wisely cutting interest rates during the recession of 1991. They failed to note that the Fed's tight money and high interest rates had sunk the economy in the first place. Former president George H. W. Bush still blames Greenspan for the recession that scuttled his reelection bid.

The recession in 1991 set off waves of bank failures, which forced the Fed to cut interest rates in 1992 and 1993. No sooner had the large banks recovered, though, than the Fed raised interest rates once more, doubling short-term rates over the course of 1994. Soon real (inflation adjusted) interest rates reached historic highs. Higher mortgage and debt service payments sent national income flowing to the finance sector—by mid-decade, New York had the most unequal income distribution of all the 50 states—and set the stage for nearly four years of declining wages and stagnant family incomes.

How quickly we seem to have forgotten that it was Greenspan who, during much of the 1990s, insisted that an unemployment rate of 6% was "natural," Greenspan who threatened to hike interest rates each time an unemployed worker got a job. Only in the late 1990s did Greenspan's Fed ease off the brakes. In his book *Maestro: Alan Greenspan and the American Economy*, journalist Bob Woodward notes that Greenspan became convinced, by the late 1990s, that the unemployment rate could fall below 6% without sparking inflation:

> The old belief held that with a low unemployment rate, workers would have the upper hand and demand higher wages. Yet the data showed that wages weren't rising that much. … Greenspan hypothesized at one point to colleagues within the Fed about the 'traumatized worker'—someone who felt job insecurity in the changing economy and so was accepting smaller wage increases. He had talked to business leaders who said that their workers were not agitating and were fearful that their skills might not be marketable if they were forced to change jobs.

More than a decade of relatively high interest rates and high unemployment, engineered in part by the Fed's own policies, so devastated the confidence of ordinary working Americans that they were unable to press for higher wages even at the peak of the late 1990s boom. By the time the Fed began cutting interest rates it was too late. The high-tech stock bubble—fed by financial deregulation and volatile interest rates, thanks to the Fed—burst and the economy sank.

In response to the recession and then to 9/11, Greenspan cut the overnight bank lending rate to 1%. Again, he was heralded for his masterful use of monetary policy. But with unemployment still high in 2004, the Fed once more began raising interest rates in order to "pre-empt" inflation. Though 5.4% unemployment leaves millions without jobs, it is apparently not low enough to keep workers sufficiently "traumatized."

The reverence afforded Greenspan is truly disturbing in a democratic society. By sanctifying Greenspan, the media are effectively ceding to the Fed the right to answer the most momentous question of national economic policy—what level of unemployment should a civilized society tolerate and who should suffer when war, or price shocks, or shortages, or economic distress create conflict over the distribution of income?

> NOT ONLY WAS GREENSPAN *NOT* RESPONSIBLE FOR RECENT U.S. PROSPERITY, MUCH OF WHAT IS WRONG IN THE WORLD ECONOMY TODAY CAN BE TRACED TO THE FED'S DOOR.

HOW DO FISCAL AND MONETARY POLICY COMPARE?

BY ARTHUR MacEWAN

The Federal Reserve influences the economy through monetary policy—the actions the Fed takes to affect the cost and availability of credit. For example, in March of this year, the Fed, led by its chairman Alan Greenspan, decided that it was time to slow economic growth. So it induced banks and other lenders to raise their interest rates. Higher interest rates mean fewer businesses and individuals will take out loans and spend the borrowed money. Lower spending means slower economic growth.

The federal government can also influence economic growth and the demand for goods and services through fiscal policy—the way it taxes and spends. If the government wants to slow down the economy, for example, it can raise taxes and reduce its own spending. Less money ends up in people's hands if the government hires fewer construction workers to build roads, or if it cuts back on education programs.

One problem with fiscal policy is that changing the budget takes time—except for programs whose spending levels change automatically when the economy does, like unemployment compensation. To slow down the economy, Congress has to pass new laws raising taxes—certainly a "no no" these days—or cutting spending. Then the President has to accept Congress's new law, which might require negotiations, or more legislative action. All this is to say that the political process involves considerable delays and might result in no action at all.

Monetary policy is different because the Fed does not have to bother with this messy political process that we call democracy. It is "independent" since its members, appointed by the President, serve long terms. They decide whether to ease or tighten the availability of credit, without any role for Congress or the President. To be sure, the "independence" of the Fed is not enshrined in the Constitution. Yet

> THE FED DOES NOT HAVE TO BOTHER WITH THIS MESSY POLITICAL PROCESS THAT WE CALL DEMOCRACY.

for Congress and the President to pass new laws which directed or restricted the Fed's action would be a serious disruption of well-established policy.

The law governing the Fed says that it should pursue both stable prices (low inflation) and full employment. In fact, the Fed focuses almost exclusively on the goal of stable prices. If unemployment has to rise to meet this goal, well, too bad. It is easy to see why the Fed does its work best when it doesn't have to worry about getting democratic approval.

Fiscal policy is somewhat more constrained by democratic processes than is monetary policy. For example, conservative attacks on Medicare and Social Security have not gotten very far because these programs are very popular.

But the recent mania to balance the budget makes it difficult to use fiscal policy to stimulate economic expansion by increasing spending. This may present some serious problems during economic downturns. The monetary policy of the Fed, it turns out, is not nearly so effective in stimulating economic expansion during a recession as it is in slowing growth during relatively good times. In a recession, the Fed can induce commercial banks to lower their interest rates. But if the recession leads investors to worry that demand for products and services will fall, the lower interest rates might not reignite economic growth. What's the point, for example, in building a new office building when it doesn't look like it will be possible to rent out the space in existing buildings for quite a while?

In a recession, then, trying to use monetary policy to get the economy going can be like pushing on a string. It simply won't do any good. Fiscal policy, however, might directly create demand, present businesses with the reality of a new expansion, and generate a new period of investment and growth.

THE DISCOUNT RATE

BY ELLEN FRANK

Dear Dr. Dollar:

The Federal Reserve keeps fussing with the "discount rate" and everybody thinks it's important. This is, if I understand it right, the rate banks charge each other for overnight loans. Now presumably someone makes money on the interest that's charged and someone loses money (or makes less) when the rate is lowered. But no one screams. Why not? If it's because the charges among banks just cancel one another out, then why does the rate even matter? Or is it that the Federal Reserve itself charges this interest, in which case the taxpayers lose when the rate it lowered?   —*Peter Marcuse, New York*

To answer your question, it helps to understand how the U.S. Federal Reserve system works. The quasi-public Federal Reserve has two parts, neither of which is actually part of the federal government. First, there are the district banks—12 Federal Reserve Banks scattered across the country, charged with regulating and overseeing the commercial banks in their region and each wholly owned by those banks. Then there is the Board of Governors, a seven-member board with a vast research staff, based in Washington, D.C., and chaired by Alan Greenspan.

Every six weeks, the board and the presidents of the regional banks meet together as the so-called *Federal Open Market Committee* (FOMC), where they set targets for the *fed funds rate*—a rate that commercial banks charge one another for overnight loans. After the fed funds target is announced, the district banks will generally raise or lower the *discount rate*—the rate that commercial banks pay when they borrow from their local Fed—so that the two rates stay roughly equal.

In order to reduce the fed funds rate, the FOMC directs traders at the New York Federal Reserve Bank to buy U.S. Treasury bills on the financial markets. The Fed creates new money—quite literally, since paper printed by the Fed *is* money—to pay for these bills. When this new money enters the economy, it tends to be deposited in banks that, suddenly awash in cash, must find borrowers for it if they are to earn a profit. (To raise interest rates the FOMC does the opposite, selling U.S. Treasury bills and taking cash out of circulation.)

Since the district banks are owned not by the federal government but by the commercial banks, reductions in the discount rate do not affect the public treasury. And since commercial banks are both borrowers and the lenders in the fed funds market, gains and losses for the banks do tend, as you suspect, to cancel out. The point of reducing the fed funds rate, though, is to drive down other interest rates. If the financial markets are swimming in cheap cash, then competition for borrowers ought to push down rates on auto loans, business loans, mortgages, rates on bonds, and so forth.

Financial firms earn money by charging interest. In general, they prefer high interest rates to low. But they prefer low interest rates to watching their business dry up and their clients default on loans. Banks recognize that in a recession, lower interest rates may be necessary to spur growth and prevent bankruptcies. They accept the Fed's authority to reduce rates and print new money when circumstances warrant it. And they also know that the Fed, traditionally, has been their advocate—if not their mouthpiece—in Washington.

The district banks are owned outright by the finance industry and appointees to the Board of Governors nearly always have close industry ties. Greenspan himself has a well-established record as an "inflation hawk" who tends to err on the side of high interest rates. Moreover, in his nearly 12 years as Fed chair, Greenspan has presided over the slow erosion of the Fed's policy authority, so that a lower fed funds rate often does not translate into lower interest rates for businesses and consumers. Over the past year, for example, the FOMC cut its target fed funds rate from 6.0% to 1.75%, yet rates on home mortgages have fallen by only one percentage point. If the Fed really wanted to bring down long-term interest rates (like mortgage rates), it could sell not only short-term Treasury bills but also long-term bonds. The Fed could use a variety of other means to lower interest rates set in other markets (like the bond market), but such policies could eat into the finance industry's earnings. Instead, the Fed's recent interest rate reductions have meant that banks pay lower rates on deposits, while earning fairly high rates on loans to consumers and businesses.

If the recession persists and competition for credit-worthy customers intensifies, however, lending rates will fall and banks will feel the pinch of the Fed's cheap credit policy. But don't expect to see Citigroup lambasting the Fed on the *New York Times* editorial page or lobbying Congress to oust Greenspan. The banks have a more direct avenue for airing their complaints. Every six weeks, on the day before the FOMC meets to set interest rate policy, the Board meets with the Federal Advisory Council—a group of private bankers from each of the 12 Fed districts—to hear their advice on how high interest rates should be.

Economist Edwin Dickens from Drew University, who has done extensive archival research on the Fed, notes that banks often "are adamant that they can't take the hit in in-come" if the Fed cuts rates. Records show that they have of-ten thwarted rate cuts, even in recessions. So if lowered rates begin to squeeze financial earnings, the finance indus-try won't scream. Who needs to scream when you can whisper?

ARTICLE 5.7

February 2000

THE NEW WORLD OF BANKING

BY JIM CAMPEN

Ever since Jimmy Carter was president in the late 1970s, the halls of Congress have echoed with passionate speeches about the need to modernize the nation's banking laws. These laws, most importantly the Glass-Steagall Act of 1933 and the Bank Holding Company Act of 1956, pro-hibited banks, insurance companies, and securities firms from entering each other's businesses. Now all that is changed.

For more than 20 years, Congress was gridlocked as dif-ferent types of financial firms fought over who would gain the most from rewriting the laws. Last year, however, things were different. On November 12, shortly after Congress approved a compromise acceptable to all three industries, Bill Clinton signed into law the Gramm-Leach-Bliley Act of 1999 (named by and for the chairmen of the three Con-gressional committees that shaped the legislation). The key provisions of the act make possible a new kind of corpora-tion—called a *financial holding company*—that allows any number of banks, insurance companies, and securities firms to be brought together under the same corporate um-brella. The result is likely to be another wave of financial megamergers, as the largest firms in each of the three indus-tries begin buying each other. A preview of what is to come was provided by the 1998 deal that joined Citibank, Trav-elers Insurance, and the Wall Street firm Solomon Smith Barney into Citigroup, the country's largest financial firm with over $700 billion in assets. This merger, technically il-legal at the time, is now fully legal; without the change in the law, Citigroup would have had to break apart in a few years. In fact, pressure from Citigroup helped ensure that the long-delayed legislation actually passed.

THE "ONGOING REVOLUTION"

Some observers hail the new law as the most important fi-nancial legislation in over 60 years. In their view, the repeal of the Glass-Steagall Act is a long-overdue piece of "finan-cial modernization" that allows U.S. financial companies to of-fer financial services more cheaply and conveniently and to better compete in the global economy. In their mind, the law allows the creation of "fi-nancial supermarkets" where customers—both businesses and consumers—can engage in "one-stop" shopping for all of their financial needs.

This view is greatly exaggerated. Rather than being a dramatic break from the past, the Gramm-Leach-Bliley Act is best seen as one symbolically important milestone in what former Federal Reserve Board Chair Arthur Burns, writing in 1987, described as "the ongoing revolution in American banking."

During the three decades following World War II, the U.S. financial system, operating under a set of laws and reg-ulations established during the Great Depression of the 1930s, changed very little. These laws compartmentalized the financial system both by type of product and by geogra-phy. But for at least the last 25 years, these barriers have steadily eroded as high-paid lawyers found loopholes in the existing laws and regulators relaxed their interpretations of the rules under pressure from banks which were feeling the heat from increased competition and computerization.

Years before last fall's new law, it was possible to buy in-surance or invest in mutual funds at many banks, to get checking accounts from investment companies, or to invest in the stock and bond markets through insurance compa-nies. All this was supposedly illegal under Depression-era laws. By 1997, barriers barring banks from expanding both within and between states had disappeared, and now one bank—BankAmerica—has over 2,500 branches ranging from Alaska to Florida. Even the heart of the Glass-Steagall Act, the wall separating commercial banks—which offered checking accounts and business loans—from investment banks—which helped corporations raise money by selling stocks and bonds—was already seriously breached.

Thus, the new law is best regarded as tidying up and consolidating the dramatic set of changes in the financial system that had been going on for many years. Nevertheless, its passage provides a good opportunity to consider the significance and impact of these changes.

ASSESSING "FINANCIAL DEFORM"

As always, it is useful to ask who wins and who loses as a result of a new law. Although the President, Congressional leaders, and bank spokespeople all claimed the new law would benefit consumers, consumer advocates themselves strongly disagreed. Not long before the law passed, 41 national organizations—including consumer, civil rights, labor, affordable housing, human services, and environmental groups—had sent a joint letter to Congress urging lawmakers to vote against the measure. Consumer advocate Ralph Nader concluded that under the new law consumers would face "fewer choices, higher prices, and greater risks for taxpayers." That the real winners are the country's largest financial corporations can be seen in the upward surge of their stock prices in mid-October when it finally became clear that the new law would go through.

To better assess the impact of the new banking law, we need to consider the relationship between the financial system and the rest of the economy. The banks and other financial companies are not particularly important in themselves. For example, the banking industry employs less than 1.2% of the nation's workers. What does matter is the financial system's crucial role shaping investment in the "real," productive sectors of the economy. Banks and other financial companies channel funds from investors and savers who have more money than they will spend to borrowers who want to spend more than they currently have. Almost every major expenditure—whether by a business building a new factory, a family buying a new home, or a local government upgrading school facilities—involves borrowing money either by issuing stock in their company, taking out a loan, or selling bonds to be paid back later.

To evaluate the functioning of financial systems, we should consider first whether its mode of operation contributes to the *stability* in the economy. Lawmakers designed the system of banking laws and regulations in the 1930s primarily with this criterion in mind, in the well-founded belief that speculation and collapse in financial markets and widespread bank failures played a crucial role in bringing about the Great Depression.

Second, we should consider whether the financial system promotes economic *efficiency* by channeling funds to those who will make the most productive use of them. Third, does the operation of the financial system promote *fairness* by providing capital, credit, and financial services in a nondiscriminatory and nonexploitative manner that enables all citizens to participate equitably in economic life?

Unfortunately, in important ways Gramm-Leach-Bliley Act will make things worse according to all three criteria. That's why Hubert Von Tol, of the Wisconsin Rural Development Center, rather than referring to the changes as "financial reform," characterizes them as "financial deform" instead.

THE BIGGER THEY ARE, THE HARDER THEY FALL

As banking institutions get bigger and bigger, there is growing danger that the failure of a single company could destabilize the entire financial structure and send the real economy into a tailspin. This is exactly the fear of Federal Reserve Board Chair Alan Greenspan, who has warned that the megabanks are becoming "complex entities that create the potential for unusually large systemic risks in the national and international economy should they fail." Senator Paul Wellstone, the Democrat from Minnesota, used more expressive language: "Today's quest for giantism has swept aside the voices of prudence."

Now that more types of financial activities are under one roof, there's a greater chance that one of the new financial conglomerates will fail since their top managers probably have neither the expertise nor the brute brain capacity to effectively monitor and control it all. Even worse, although the 1999 law allowed the conglomeration of companies, it did not unify the regulatory oversight of these companies. Financial regulation remains fragmented under the new law, which divides oversight responsibility among the Fed, three other bank regulators, the Securities and Exchange Commission, and other agencies, none of which wanted to lose power in the restructuring. Furthermore, even though insurance companies can now affiliate with federally insured banks in the newly authorized financial holding companies, Congress decided to leave regulation of the insurance industry exclusively to the states, where regulatory agencies are generally understaffed, underfunded, and no match for the insurance companies that they are supposed to supervise. As a result there is growing danger that some risky activity will fall between the cracks and not be noticed by any of the regulators.

MONOPOLY POWER AND INEFFICIENCY

One of the basic assumptions of mainstream economics is that producers and customers, each seeking their own advantage in competitive markets, will generally bring about efficient (though not just) use of resources. On the other hand, mainstream economic theory also recognizes that unregulated markets don't always work properly and that in these cases of "market failure," the government needs to intervene to bring about efficient outcomes.

As financial companies become ever larger, their economic and political power increases, increasing the possibility of "market failure." In the marketplace, concentrated economic power becomes monopoly power allowing large financial companies to set prices (such as checking account fees) higher than they would be able to in a competitive market where many banks vie for business. At the same time, the concentrations of economic power contribute to concentrations of political power, as megacompanies prevent the government from adopting policies aimed at curbing their monopoly power.

In addition, as banks get bigger and bigger their decision-making power is concentrated in headquarters located hundreds or even thousands of miles from the communities where their customers live. Megabanks may be able to mass-produce standardized loan products at relatively low cost, but they lose touch with the details of local economic life needed to actually direct financial resources to their most productive use. For example, minority-owned small businesses that are well-adapted to neighborhood conditions may not do well in the new automated "credit-scoring" typically used by the big lenders, and may therefore end up being denied the credit they need to survive and expand.

FADING FAIRNESS

Fairness suffers under the new law not because of what it contains, but because of what it omits. Congress enacted the Community Reinvestment Act (CRA) in 1977 because banks were unfairly neglecting inner city neighborhoods when it came time to lend money. Over the years, and especially in the 1990s, the CRA—which requires banks to loan money in all of the neighborhoods where they do business—has contributed greatly to economic fairness by forcing banks to meet the credit needs of lower-income and minority borrowers and neighborhoods that had previously been underserved.

However, when the Gramm-Leach-Bliley Act "modernized" the financial system by allowing different kinds of financial companies to expand into each other's businesses, it failed to simultaneously "modernize" and expand the reach of the CRA. The CRA only oversees bank loans. It does not demand fairness to low-income communities from other types of financial institutions and other forms of credit. The new bank law should have expanded CRA's reach to include the other kinds of financial companies that compete with banks in making loans and by imposing similar obligations on insurance companies and investment firms. As the relative importance of these other financial companies steadily grows, this failure to "modernize" the CRA means that it "will apply to an ever shrinking share of the financial services world," according to Debby Goldberg of the Center for Community Change in Washington, D.C.

Some members of the House Banking Committee, including Maxine Waters, the California Democrat, and Mike Capuano, the Massachusetts Democrat, introduced and fought for amendments that would have extended and expanded the CRA. The amendments also would have increased fairness in other ways, such as requiring companies to offer cheap "lifeline" bank accounts to people currently shut out of the mainstream financial system. In the end, however, it took a determined and united stand by Congressional Democrats, backed up by the consistent threat of a presidential veto, simply to stop Congress from seriously cutting the CRA back. The Republican assault on the law was led by Senate Banking Committee Chair—and former economics professor—Phil Gramm of Texas. The *New York Times* quoted Gramm as saying that the existing CRA rules were "an evil like slavery in the pre-Civil War era."

The new law makes the financial system even more unfair because it fails to deal with the new, growing threats to consumer privacy. One reason banks and other kinds of financial companies are eager to merge is so they can assemble vast databases of information on customers across companies to use in marketing and decision-making. This trend will worsen under the new structure of financial holding companies OK'd by Congress. All the companies sharing a legal umbrella can consolidate information about a person's spending (from checking and credit card records), investing (from brokerage and mutual fund records), and even medical conditions (from insurance records).

ALTHOUGH THE GRAMM-LEACH-BLILEY ACT ALLOWED THE CONGLOMERATION OF FINANCIAL COMPANIES, IT DID NOT UNIFY THE REGULATORY OVERSIGHT OF THESE COMPANIES.

The law imposes absolutely no limits on the ability of financial holding companies to share all of this information among the various affiliated companies operating under the same corporate umbrella. It only weakly limits sharing the information with outside companies. Even conservative senator Richard Shelby of Alabama, the second-ranking Republican on the Senate Banking Committee, called the privacy protections in the new law "a sham." He joined colleagues from both Houses and both parties in organizing a Congressional Privacy Caucus to push for more meaningful protection of people's confidential financial information.

Advocates of greater privacy rights and of expanding the CRA promise to wage a grass-roots campaign that will persuade Congress to redress its failures in the Gramm-Leach-Bliley Act of 1999. Their demands for a minimum level of financial fairness offer one more reason to see this law as just one important development in an on-going process of change in the financial system, rather than as the end of the story.

THE NEW OLD WALL STREET SETTLEMENT

BY NOMI PRINS

You may have experienced a sense of déjà vu soaking in the media fanfare surrounding the recent Wall Street settlement, a $1.4 billion wrist-slap levied on the investment banking industry in the name of reform. That's because the headlines that accompanied the finalization of the "global" agreement were recycled versions of the ones that came out in December 2002, when the settlement was first publicized.

On April 28, 2003, the Securities and Exchange Commission (SEC), the New York Stock Exchange (NYSE), the National Association of Securities Dealers (NASD), and New York State Attorney General Eliot Spitzer settled "enforcement actions" with 10 top Wall Street banks and two star 1990s research analysts. The banks—including Citigroup-Salomon Brothers, JPM Chase, Goldman Sachs, Merrill Lynch, and Morgan Stanley—were charged with deliberately misleading investors with biased stock research that exaggerated the virtues of key client corporations.

The process leading up to the settlement started in late 2001 when Spitzer's office began investigating conflicts of interest on Wall Street. In April 2002, regulators at the SEC hopped on board with a joint investigation into the "undue influence of investment banking interest on securities research at brokerage firms."

The settlement makes three main changes to banking practices. First, it is supposed to insulate (or "firewall") research analysts from the influence of investment bankers by demanding that analyst pay be set with no input from the investment-banking department. Second, it requires that investment banks and brokerage firms provide independent research purchased from external sources to their clients (but only until 2008—not exactly a permanent fix) and it makes analyst opinions public 90 days after they have been issued privately. Third, it bans firms from practicing hot IPO "spinning," or doling out initial public offering stock to the senior executives of client companies.

According to Spitzer's statement, the settlement "implements far-reaching reforms that will radically change behavior on Wall Street." But nothing in the settlement poses a serious threat to the status quo.

It's quite telling that no Wall Street firm has complained about the settlement. That's because it doesn't impact how they do business.

Here are the top 10 reasons this settlement is a smokescreen:

#1 The fines are tiny. If you remove the $513 million thrown in for spurious investor research and education activities—banks will distribute research from independent firms *that they select*—you're left with less than a billion bucks in fines. Putting that into perspective, the top 10 Wall Street firms made $62 billion in fees alone over the four years in which their activities are in question. The fines amount to just 1.5% of fee revenue. And that's not to mention the $1 trillion in other revenues these banks garnered over the same period. The settlement fines are so miniscule they are unlikely to deter future wrongdoing.

#2 Individual investors will see little of the settlement money. Spurred by class-action lawyers, Spitzer et al. established 10 different distribution funds for customers whose claims are "deemed appropriate" by the federal court at some future date. About $387.5 million of the $1.4 billion will go to the funds. But with thousands misled by brokers (*brokers*, not just analysts), it will take years to divvy up that cash.

#3 It is not a global settlement even though it was spun as such. It's a U.S. settlement, and about as global as the World Series. Even the original 2002 SEC press release put the word "global" in quotes. Though most of the named firms are international, their practices outside the United States don't fall under SEC jurisdiction. And foreigners who bought stock under misleading information won't receive compensation.

#4 No bank admitted any wrongdoing. This is, unfortunately and consistently, par for the course with all SEC corporate corruption settlements. There is never an admission of any culpability.

#5 Acting contrite is no substitute for being held to account. And banks are not even managing to act contrite. At an investor conference held days after the settlement announcement, the *New York Times* reported Morgan Stanley CEO Philip Purcell saying, "I don't see anything in the settlement that will concern the retail investor about Morgan Stanley. Not one thing." (He's right, but that's because the settlement doesn't say anything meaningful at all, not because Morgan Stanley was above the fray.) SEC chairman

William Donaldson shot off an irate response, concerned that those remarks were "evidence [of] a troubling lack of contrition." It is totally hypocritical for Donaldson to accuse Purcell of not acting sorrier. If that's the best our new SEC head can do, we're in trouble. Plus, back to #4, why should he be sorry if he didn't admit any wrongdoing to begin with?

#6 The hardship of being prohibited from spinning hot IPOs, in a dead stock market environment when nothing's hot anyway, is a non-starter. There is no such thing as a hot IPO right now. And, when IPOs become hot again, there are myriad simple ways to get around the ban. Just wait and see. As a ban, this IPO ruling is as robust as, well, a Wall Street firewall.

#7 The increased insulation, or "firewalls," mandated by the settlement—like prohibiting investment bankers and analysts from joint business trips with clients or ensuring a few extra lawyers are present at potentially questionable internal meetings—are cosmetic changes.

Many top analysts are now switching to jobs as investment bankers or salespeople. As a result, they'll be able to say anything to customers, anyway. It just won't be *called* research. Wall Street firms are not about to physically relocate their analyst staffs to separate buildings. (And even that wouldn't be sufficient.) If you're on the same e-mail system, share the same limos home and get your food from the same cafeteria, you're connected.

#8 This settlement does nothing to change the deeply institutionalized incentive systems (and cultures) within financial firms. As a managing director at one of the fine-paying firms put it, "Hey, it's not like junior analysts in training are now being told they'll get penalized for bringing in deals." Without a deeper revision of the system, there will always be someone at a high level who will find ways to ensure someone lower doesn't publicize negative views on a company with whom the firm is about to do a large deal.

#9 The settlement scapegoats analysts while leaving senior executives and investment bankers unscathed. The central problem with Wall Street and conflicts of interest is not former Citigroup-Salomon Brothers' star telecom analyst, Jack Grubman, and is even less Merrill Lynch's Internet analyst Henry Blodget (paying $15 million and $4 million in fines respectively). These people were tools who played their roles in the whole system exceedingly well, while the media promulgated their cheerleading.

The settlement criminalizes analysts for extolling the virtues of their top client corporations, but does nothing to reform the more troublesome—and clandestine—behavior of senior executives and investment bankers who created the deals and issued the stock that analysts were paid to market.

Instead of penalizing analysts who don't even *close* investment-banking deals, the priority should be to pry apart and isolate corporate executives and investment bankers, and their corporate customers, starting at the top—with the board. Citigroup CEO Sandy Weill was on AT&T's board when Citigroup-Salomon's chief telecom analyst Grubman inflated AT&T's rating. AT&T CEO Michael Armstrong was also on Citigroup's board at the time (and still is). E-mails uncovered by Spitzer suggest that Weill had asked Grubman to upgrade AT&T's rating as a personal favor. Grubman upped AT&T's rating just before Citigroup bagged the deal to do an IPO for AT&T's wireless division. Citigroup reaped profits from doing and distributing the AT&T IPO, all the while duping investors.

Yet while Grubman was banned from ever working as an analyst again, and has to pay a multimillion dollar fine, Weill remains at Citigroup's helm, his wallet untouched by the settlement.

#10 There has been no mention of bringing back the Glass-Steagall Act, which prohibited commercial banks from owning brokerages. The repeal of Glass-Steagall in November 1999 unleashed a spate of bank mergers that resulted in many firms combining investment, broker activities, and commercial banking under the same roof.

The New Deal-era act was passed in 1933 to resolve the rampant conflicts of interest and fraud in the 1920s that led to the 1929 crash. Though hacked at for years since, Glass-Steagall was the one piece of legislation that kept the same banks that merged companies, issued debt, and created stock IPOs from touting them to the public via retail brokerage arms and commercial bank accounts.

Real reform would reinstitute strong, Glass-Steagall-type separation between investment and commercial banking activities. And it would regulate conflicted senior investment banking and corporate relationships. Key to any real reform would be regulation of the widespread practice of loan-tying, or giving cheap credit to corporate clients in exchange for profitable banking business (like IPOs and mergers). Loan-tying is a practice made easier by Glass-Steagall repeal. Citigroup became the largest issuer of Ford debt after Citigroup director and former Treasury secretary Robert Rubin joined Ford's board of directors. Because of Rubin's relationship with Ford, Citigroup gave the company preferential terms, offering to issue debt (in the form of bonds) for Ford more cheaply than other banks would. The net result was that Ford issued more debt because it was so cheap. Yet, under all that debt weight, Ford's stock price and ratings plummeted this past year, taking along jobs and pensions with them.

Of course, there's a good reason points eight, nine, and ten haven't been brought to light—they are remedies that would actually make a difference.

CHAPTER 6
Unemployment and Inflation

INTRODUCTION

During the current economic recovery corporate profits have gone up more, while wages have risen less, than they have during any of the eight previous recoveries since World War II. Although the stock market has rebounded, to the delight of investors on Wall Street, wage-earners on Main Street may wonder if they if they will also benefit from the economic turnaround.

While extreme, the imbalance between wage and profit growth in this recovery is hardly surprising. The explanation comes down to the tradeoff between inflation and unemployment. Standard macroeconomic textbooks depict that tradeoff as a "Phillips curve" in which rising employment (or falling unemployment rates) push up prices (or interest rates).

Why does this textbook tradeoff affect corporate profits and the stock market? The answer, as Robert Pollin points out, is that it is "all about class conflict." Wall Street investors—out to protect the value of their assets and the corporate profits in which they invest—are hyper-concerned with price stability, and this pits them against workers on Main Street who are out for employment and wage growth. Higher unemployment rates and fewer jobs eat away at the bargaining power of workers, keeping wage growth and inflation in check, and corporate profit margins wide.

This is exactly what happened in the current recovery, where over two million jobs were lost. The flip side of a jobless recovery is rapid productivity growth and lower labor costs: workers produce as much output as before in fewer hours. The combination of rapid productivity gains and meager wage growth widened corporate profit margins. In this way, Wall Street's positive fundamentals—rising productivity, declining unit labor costs, improved competitiveness, and low inflation rates—meant fewer rehires, continued layoffs, and deteriorating real wages. Pollin captures that dynamic in "The 'Natural Rate' of Unemployment." Why did the unemployment rate consistent with price stability, the so-called "natural rate," decline dramatically in the 1990s? Pollin's answer is that workers' economic power eroded during that decade (Article 6.1).

Arthur MacEwan shows that we need not sacrifice wage gains for price stability (Article 6.2). In Article 6.3, Chris Tilly attributes the long-term decline in pay, benefits, and working conditions for U.S. workers to slower economic growth, the business offensive against workers' protections, such as unions and the minimum wage, and businesses pushing more risks onto workers in the form of temporary work, mass layoffs, and reduced benefits.

In Article 6.4, Miller returns to the conflict between workers' wages and corporate profits to explain why it was no surprise that the stock market rallied on the day the Bureau of Labor Statistics announced that the April 2003 unemployment rate had jumped to six percent—after the economy had lost a half million jobs over the previous three months.

Finally, Bryan Snyder takes a careful look at the real costs of inflation. He argues that while higher inflation erodes the value of financial assets held by Wall Street investors, there is little evidence that inflation actually slows the investment and economic growth that make for a better life on Main Street (Article 6.5).

DISCUSSION QUESTIONS

1) (Article 6.1) What is the concept of the NAIRU, or natural rate of unemployment? Is there a natural rate? What is it?
2) (Article 6.1) Given the class conflict inherent in the tradeoff between inflation and unemployment, what policies might lead to an improved standard of living in today's economy?
3) (Article 6.2) Under what conditions do employers not pass wage hikes on to consumers by raising prices?
4) (Article 6.3) What forces have led to a raw deal for workers over the long run?
5) (Article 6.3) How have the Paradox of Corporate Thrift, the Neoliberal Paradox, and the Arkansas Paradox, complicated the task of winning a fair deal for workers?
6) (Article 6.4) Explain to stockbroker and NPR business analyst Dave Johnson why the stock market sometimes rallies when the economy loses jobs and the unemployment rate worsens. What factors in the current recovery have especially put employment conditions on Main Street at odds with stock market conditions on Wall Street?
7) (Article 6.5) What are the costs of higher inflation? And according to Snyder's evidence, what is the relationship between inflation and growth?

KEY TO COLANDER

E = Economics. M = Macroeconomics.

This entire chapter is keyed to chapter E29 or M13. Articles 6.1, 6.3, and 6.4 expose the class conflict that underlies the tradeoff between inflation and unemployment, the topic of chapter E29 or M13. Articles 6.2 and 6.5 fit squarely with the discussion of inflation and unemployment in chapter E29 or M13 and can also be used with chapter E22 or M6.

September/October 1998

THE "NATURAL RATE" OF UNEMPLOYMENT

IT'S ALL ABOUT CLASS CONFLICT

BY ROBERT POLLIN

In 1997, the official U.S. unemployment rate fell to a 27-year low of 4.9%. Most orthodox economists had long predicted that a rate this low would lead to uncontrollable inflation. So they argued that maintaining a higher unemployment rate—perhaps as high as 6%—was crucial for keeping the economy stable. But there is a hitch: last year the inflation rate was 2.3%, the lowest figure in a decade and the second lowest in 32 years. What then are we to make of these economists' theories, much less their policy proposals?

Nobel prize-winning economist Milton Friedman gets credit for originating the argument that low rates of unemployment would lead to accelerating inflation. His 1968 theory of the so-called "natural rate of unemployment" was subsequently developed by many mainstream economists under the term "Non-Accelerating Inflation Rate of Unemployment," or NAIRU, a remarkably clumsy term for expressing the simple concept of a threshold unemployment rate below which inflation begins to rise.

According to both Friedman and expositors of NAIRU, inflation should accelerate at low rates of unemployment because low unemployment gives workers excessive bargaining power. This allows the workers to demand higher wages. Capitalists then try to pass along these increased wage costs by raising prices on the products they sell. An inflationary spiral thus ensues as long as unemployment remains below its "natural rate."

Based on this theory, Friedman and others have long argued that governments should never actively intervene in the economy to promote full employment or better jobs for workers, since it will be a futile exercise, whose end result will only be higher inflation and no improvement in job opportunities. Over the past generation, this conclusion has had far-reaching influence throughout the world. In the United States

and Western Europe, it has provided a stamp of scientific respectability to a whole range of policies through which governments abandoned even modest commitments to full employment and workers' rights.

This emerged most sharply through the Reaganite and Thatcherite programs in the United States and United Kingdom in the 1980s. But even into the 1990s, as the Democrats took power in the United States, the Labour Party won office in Britain, and Social Democrats won elections throughout Europe, governments remained committed to stringent fiscal and monetary policies, whose primary goal is to prevent inflation. In Western Europe this produced an average unemployment rate of over 10% from 1990-97. In the United States, unemployment rates have fallen sharply in the 1990s, but as an alternative symptom of stringent fiscal and monetary policies, real wages for U.S. workers also declined dramatically over the past generation. As of 1997, the average real wage for nonsupervisory workers in the United States was 14% below its peak in 1973, even though average worker productivity rose between 1973 and 1997 by 34%.

Why have governments in the United States and Europe remained committed to the idea of fiscal and monetary stringency, if the natural rate theory on which such policies are based is so obviously flawed? The explanation is that the natural rate theory is really not just about predicting a precise unemployment rate figure below which inflation must inexorably accelerate, even though many mainstream economists have presented the natural rate theory in this way. At a deeper level, the natural rate theory is bound up with the inherent conflicts between workers and capitalists over jobs, wages, and working conditions. As such, the natural rate theory actually contains a legitimate foundation in truth amid a welter of sloppy and even silly predictions.

THE "NATURAL RATE" THEORY IS ABOUT CLASS CONFLICT

In his 1967 American Economic Association presidential address in which he introduced the natural rate theory, Milton Friedman made clear that there was really nothing "natural" about the theory. Friedman rather emphasized that: "by using the term 'natural' rate of unemployment, I do not mean to suggest that it is immutable and unchangeable. On the contrary, many of the market characteristics that determine its level are man-made and policy-made. In the United States, for example, legal minimum wage rates…and the strength of labor unions all make the natural rate of unemployment higher than it would otherwise be."

In other words, according to Friedman, what he terms the "natural rate" is really a social phenomenon measuring the class strength of working people, as indicated by their ability to organize effective unions and establish a livable minimum wage.

Friedman's perspective is supported in a widely-read 1997 paper by Robert Gordon of Northwestern University on what he terms the "time-varying NAIRU." What makes the NAIRU vary over time? Gordon explains that, since the early 1960s, "The two especially large changes in the NAIRU… are the increase between the early and late 1960s and the decrease in the 1990s. The late 1960s were a time of labor militancy, relatively strong unions, a relatively high minimum wage and a marked increase in labor's share in national income. The 1990s have been a time of labor peace, relatively weak unions, a relatively low minimum wage and a slight decline in labor's income share."

In short, class conflict is the spectre haunting the analysis of the natural rate and NAIRU: this is the consistent message stretching from Milton Friedman in the 1960s to Robert Gordon in the 1990s.

Stated in this way, the "Natural Rate" idea does, ironically, bear a close family resemblance to the ideas of two of the greatest economic thinkers of the left, Karl Marx and Michal Kalecki, on a parallel concept—the so-called "Reserve Army of Unemployed." In his justly famous Chapter 25 of Volume I of *Capital*, "The General Law of Capitalist Accumulation," Marx argued forcefully that unemployment serves an important function in capitalist economies. That is, when a capitalist economy is growing rapidly enough so that the reserve army of unemployed is depleted, workers will then utilize their increased bargaining power to raise wages. Profits are correspondingly squeezed as workers get a larger share of the country's total income. As a result, capitalists anticipate further declines in profitability and they therefore reduce their investment spending. This then leads to a fall in job creation, higher unemployment, and a replenishment of the reserve army. In other words, the reserve army of the unemployed is the instrument capitalists use to prevent significant wage increases and thereby maintain profitability.

Kalecki, a Polish economist of the Great Depression era, makes parallel though distinct arguments in his also justly famous essay, "The Political Aspects of Full Employment." Kalecki wrote in 1943, shortly after the 1930s Depression had ended and governments had begun planning a postwar world in which they would deploy aggressive policies to avoid another calamity of mass unemployment. Kalecki held, contrary to Marx, that full employment can be beneficial to the profitability of businesses. True, capitalists may get a smaller share of the total economic pie as workers gain bargaining power to win higher wages. But capitalists can still benefit because the size of the pie is growing far more rapidly, since more goods and services can be produced when everyone is working, as opposed to some significant share of workers being left idle.

But capitalists still won't support full employment, in Kalecki's view, because it will threaten their control over the workplace, the pace and direction of economic activity, and even political institutions. Kalecki thus concluded that full employment could be sustainable under capitalism, but only if these challenges to capitalists' social and political power could be contained. This is why he held that fascist social and political institutions, such as those that existed in Nazi Germany when he was writing, could well provide one "solution" to capitalism's unemployment problem, precisely because they were so brutal. Workers would have jobs, but they would never be permitted to exercise the political and economic power that would otherwise accrue to them in a full-employment economy.

Broadly speaking, Marx and Kalecki do then share a common conclusion with natural rate proponents, in that they would all agree that positive unemployment rates are the outgrowth of class conflict over the distribution of income and political power. Of course, Friedman and other mainstream economists reach this conclusion via analytic and political perspectives that are diametrically opposite to those of Marx and Kalecki. To put it in a nutshell, in the Friedmanite view mass unemployment results when workers demand more than they deserve, while for Marx and Kalecki, capitalists use the weapon of unemployment to prevent workers from getting their just due.

FROM NATURAL RATE TO EGALITARIAN POLICY

Once the analysis of unemployment in capitalist economies is properly understood within the framework of class conflict, several important issues in our contemporary economic situation become much more clear. Let me raise just a few:

1 Mainstream economists have long studied how workers' wage demands cause inflation as unemployment falls. However, such wage demands never directly cause inflation, since inflation refers to a general rise in prices of goods and services sold in the market, not a rise in wages. Workers, by definition, do not have the power to raise prices. Capitalists raise prices on the products they sell. At low unemployment, inflation occurs when capitalists respond to workers' increasingly successful wage demands by raising prices so that they can maintain profitability. If workers were simply to receive a higher share of national income, then lower unemployment and higher wages need not cause inflation at all.

2 There is little mystery as to why, at present, the so-called "time-varying" NAIRU has diminished to a near

vanishing point, with unemployment at a 25-year low while inflation remains dormant. The main explanation is the one stated by Robert Gordon—that workers' economic power has been eroding dramatically through the 1990s. Workers have been almost completely unable to win wage increases over the course of the economic expansion that by now is seven years old.

3 This experience over the past seven years, with unemployment falling but workers showing almost no income gains, demonstrates dramatically the crucial point that full employment can never stand alone as an adequate measure of workers' well-being. This was conveyed vividly to me when I was working in Bolivia in 1990 as part of an economic advising team led by Keith Griffin of the University of California-Riverside. Professor Griffin asked me to examine employment policies.

I began by paying a visit to the economists at the Ministry of Planning. When I requested that we discuss the country's employment problems, they explained, to my surprise, that the country *had no employment problems.* When I suggested we consider the situation of the people begging, shining shoes, or hawking batteries and Chiclets in the street just below the window where we stood, their response was that these people *were* employed. And of course they were, in that they were actively trying to scratch out a living. It was clear that I had to specify the problem at hand far more precisely. Similarly, in the United States today, we have to be much more specific as to what workers should be getting in a fair economy: jobs, of course, but also living wages, benefits, reasonable job security, and a healthy work environment.

4 In our current low-unemployment economy, should workers, at long last, succeed in winning higher wages and better benefits, some inflationary pressures are likely to emerge. But if inflation does not accelerate after wage increases are won, this would mean that businesses are not able to pass along their higher wage costs to their customers. Profits would therefore be squeezed. In any case, in response to *either* inflationary pressures or a squeeze in profitability, we should expect that many, if not most, segments of the business community will welcome a Federal Reserve policy that would slow the economy and raise the unemployment rate.

Does this mean that, as long as we live in a capitalist society, the control by capitalists over the reserve army of labor must remain the dominant force establishing the limits of workers' strivings for jobs, security, and living wages? The challenge for the progressive movement in the United States today is to think through a set of policy ideas through which full employment at living wages can be achieved and sustained.

Especially given the dismal trajectory of real wage decline over the past generation, workers should of course continue to push for wage increases. But it will also be cru-

cial to advance these demands within a broader framework of proposals. One important component of a broader package would be policies through which labor and capital bargain openly over growth of wages and profits after full employment is achieved. Without such an open bargaining environment, workers, with reason, will push for higher wages once full employment is achieved, but capitalists will then respond by either raising prices or favoring high unemployment. Such open bargaining policies were conducted with considerable success in Sweden and other Nordic countries from the 1950s to the 1980s, and as a result, wages there continued to rise at full employment, while both accelerating inflation and a return to high unemployment were prevented.

Such policies obviously represent a form of class compromise. This is intrinsically neither good nor bad. The question is the terms under which the compromise is achieved. Wages have fallen dramatically over the past generation, so workers deserve substantial raises as a matter of simple fairness. But workers should also be willing to link their wage increases to improvements in productivity growth, i.e., the rate at which workers produce new goods and services. After all, if the average wage had just risen at exactly the rate of productivity growth since 1973 and not a penny more, the average hourly wage today for nonsupervisory workers would be $19.07 rather than $12.24.

But linking wages to improvements in productivity then also raises the question of who controls the decisions that determine the rate of productivity growth. In fact, substantial productivity gains are attainable through operating a less hierarchical workplace and building strong democratic unions through which workers can defend their rights on the job. Less hierarchy and increased workplace democracy creates higher morale on the job, which in turn increases workers' effort and opportunities to be inventive, while decreasing turnover and absenteeism. The late David Gordon of the New School for Social Research was among the leading analysts demonstrating how economies could operate more productively through greater workplace democracy.

But improvements in productivity also result from both the public and private sector investing in new and better machines that workers put to use every day, with the additional benefit that it means more jobs for people who produce those machines. A pro-worker economic policy will therefore also have to be concerned with increasing investments to improve the stock of machines that workers have at their disposal on the job.

In proposing such a policy approach, have I forgotten the lesson that Marx and Kalecki taught us, that unemployment serves a purpose in capitalism? Given that this lesson has become part of the standard mode of thinking among mainstream economists ranging from Milton Friedman to Robert Gordon, I would hope that I haven't let it slip from view. My point nevertheless is that through changing power relationships at the workplace and the decision-making process through which investment decisions get made, labor and the left can then also achieve a more egalitarian economy, one in which capitalists' power to brandish the weapon of unemployment is greatly circumscribed. If the labor movement and the left neglect issues of control over investment and the workplace, we will continue to live amid a Bolivian solution to the unemployment problem, where full employment is the by-product of workers' vulnerability, not their strength.

Resources: A longer version of this article appears as "The 'Reserve Army of Labor' and the 'Natural Rate of Unemployment': Can Marx, Kalecki, Friedman, and Wall Street All Be Wrong?," *Review of Radical Political Economics*, Fall 1998. Both articles derive from a paper originally presented as the David Gordon Memorial Lecture at the 1997 Summer Conference of the Union for Radical Political Economics. See also Robert Pollin and Stephanie Luce, *The Living Wage: Building A Fair Economy*, 1998; David Gordon, *Fat and Mean*, 1997; David Gordon, "Generating Affluence: Productivity Gains Require Worker Support," *Real World Macro*, 15th ed., 1998.

ARTICLE 6.2   *May/June 1999*

WHEN WAGE HIKES DON'T MEAN PRICE HIKES

BY ARTHUR MacEWAN

Dear Dr. Dollar:

It's conventional wisdom that when wages go up, as in the case of a union campaign or minimum wage increase, prices go up. My guess is that if the owners could have raised the prices, they would have already. What is the right answer?

— Jeffrey Trivers, New Orleans

This "conventional wisdom" has a long and dishonorable history. In the 19th century, some defenders of the status quo developed theories of why workers could never improve their position. Perhaps the most vulgar expression of this position was Thomas Malthus' argument that if workers got more wages, they would simply have more children, increasing the supply of labor and forcing wages back down. Others argued a wage increase would simply get passed on as a price increase, leading to no real wage gain and no improvement in workers' buying power.

Although some economists continually resurrect this argument, it has no foundation in history or theory. Historically, over the last 150 years workers in the United States and many other countries achieved real gains in their incomes, gains that outstripped price increases. This is true in spite of the decline in workers' real wages since the mid-1970s.

The realm of theory also challenges the "conventional wisdom." When workers of a single employer win wage increases, through union action, for example, the owner is likely to try to recoup the higher costs by raising prices, not by dipping into profits. However, as the question points out ("if the owners could have raised the prices, they would have already"), the owners are constrained by the market. When they raise the price, they cannot sell as much, by the basic "law" of economics that demand falls when prices rise. Owners would lose more profits from sales dropping than they would gain from a price increase, forcing them to bear some of the costs of the wage hike. In general, the more an enterprise holds monopoly power, the more it can pass along the cost of the wage increase to consumers.

Different principles apply to the economy in general than to individual companies. If workers across the economy obtain a wage increase, their rising wages boost consumer demand (since workers are also consumers). With workers' greater buying power, it might seem employers could charge them higher prices and thereby recoup the cost of wage hikes. Yet workers are not the only buyers in the economy. Companies and their owners are also buyers, accounting for a substantial portion of overall demand; any wage increase lowers their profits and thus their buying power. So overall demand does not increase enough to allow price hikes that would wipe out the original wage gains of workers. Owners are still constrained by the market.

Also, the actions of the government's monetary authorities, minimum wage policies, and the strength of labor unions all affect employers' power to raise prices to pay for wage increases. Ultimately, these are matters that depend on the relative political strength of workers and employers.

September/October 1998

RAW DEAL FOR WORKERS

BY CHRIS TILLY

Few people have seen the inside of a "secondary meat processor"—a factory where large cuts of beef are turned into hamburger patties, roast beef, and other beef products. The workers who process beef do not have it easy. Many stand for long hours on wet floors. They are in constant contact with raw meat. In a typical plant the temperature ranges from 50° down to 3°F. Some workers rake 30-pound beef slabs from a huge bin onto a scale. Others heave giant roasts from one transmission belt to another. The work is repetitive and boring, but at the same time requires extreme attention to detail because of the potential for injury as well as food safety regulations. At one typical plant, entry-level pay is $7.75 an hour, or $16,000 a year—a poverty-level wage. There is no question that meat processors are getting a raw deal.

But the raw deal for workers is not limited to those workers who deal with raw meat. Pay, opportunities, and job quality have gotten worse for most workers in the United States over the past 30 years, across most sectors of the economy.

Obviously, the 2001 recession and the current jobless recovery have meant two-plus years of severe job shortages (see "Recession and Jobless Recovery," p. 92). But the deterioration of U.S. labor market conditions is a longer-term phenomenon. The spread of second-class jobs in the past three decades relates to fundamental changes in the economy and society, including sluggish productivity growth and employer assaults on workers' rights and protections.

The strongest evidence for the raw deal comes from looking at how workers were doing at the peak of the 1990s boom, three years ago. It was the longest boom in recorded U.S. history (lasting from March 1991 to March 2001). The expansion drove unemployment down to its lowest level in 30 years and spurred talk about a "new economy" that would turn productivity growth into endless prosperity. It should have been the best of times. But as a glance at the numbers reveals (see "Best of times?" p. 93), it was not the best of times for working people.

WHY THE RAW DEAL?

Why are workers getting such a raw deal? First, the economic pie is growing more slowly. Productivity growth during the "new economy" 1990s was only two-thirds as fast as in the "old economy" 1960s. That reflects the fact that companies have not invested as much in upgrading their equipment and training their workers as they once did—although the numbers are up compared to the 1980s, when productivity growth was even slower.

Why are these investments down? Businesses make an investment when they expect a payoff. But total global demand for goods and services grew only about half as fast in the 1980s and 1990s as it did in the 1960s and 1970s, and the increasing globalization of trade and investment meant that businesses were much more likely to face new competitors.

Second, over the last 20 years, businesses have aggressively attacked the protections that workers had built up for themselves. They have busted and blocked unions, shredded the unspoken agreements that governed many non-union workplaces, and lobbied to weaken pro-worker legislation. One consequence of these efforts: private sector workers are now less than one-third as likely to belong to a union now as they were in the mid-1950s. The minimum wage is only worth about two-thirds as much as it was at its high point in the late 1960s (after taking inflation into account). Because the low-wage workforce includes disproportionate numbers of women and people of color, the minimum wage and unions particularly benefit these groups.

Republican presidents have joined in the attacks on these protections. Every Republican administration since Ronald Reagan has doggedly opposed minimum wage increases. When Reagan fired striking air traffic controllers in 1981, he set a precedent for the permanent replacement of strikers. George W. Bush out-did Reagan in 2002 when he demanded that the Department of Homeland Security not have civil service protections and announced plans to privatize half of the federal workforce. Republicans in the White House have also stacked the National Labor Relations Board (NLRB), other federal agencies, and the courts with anti-labor appointees. As a result, these agencies offer at best weak enforcement of labor protections. To provide two recent examples: the NLRB recently ruled that unions have no right to hand out leaflets in company parking lots, and the Supreme Court ruled in 2002 that if a company terminates an undocumented worker, it need not pay the worker his or her back pay. Further, under-funding of the Occupational Safety and Health Administration (OSHA) has reduced inspections in hazardous workplaces—like meat processors. Self-styled New Democrats have backed many of these changes in the name of aiding business.

Of course, at the same time as corporations have attacked rank-and-file workers' protections, they have increased the rewards to top executives and stockholders. CEO pay kept growing through 2001, even while profits and stock values declined.

The third reason for the raw deal is that businesses have pushed more and more risk onto workers. The most extreme example of this is the growth of temporary work, which has expanded more than twenty-fold since the late 1960s. (Temporary work has been shrinking for the last two years—which of course is exactly the point: you hire temporary workers so you can dump them when the economy goes south.) But beyond the temps themselves, the frequency of mass layoffs (see boxes) highlights the fact that really, almost all jobs are temporary today.

Benefits are another area where workers bear more and more risk. Twenty-five years ago, most workers with pensions had "defined benefit" plans which specified the amount they would be paid upon retirement. Today, fewer than half of all workers are covered by any retirement plan, and fewer than one in five has a defined-benefit pension plan. Businesses prefer to offer defined-contribution plans like 401(k)s which require employee contributions and tie retirement income to market returns. In the last two years,

we saw the results for those who had invested their 401(k) savings in Wall Street. Similarly, employers who offer health insurance have made workers take on more and more of the cost of health benefits—with the result that a growing number of workers decide they can't afford their health plan and go without coverage.

BECAUSE THEY CAN

Why are businesses attacking worker protections and demanding that workers bear more risk? The first answer that many people give is "globalization"—and the increased competition that comes with it. Globalization has certainly had an important impact, but it does not offer an adequate explanation for business's newly combative stance. After all, it is the National Restaurant Association—representing an industry that experiences absolutely no global competition—that has fought hardest to keep the minimum wage low. To a large extent, businesses have gone on the offensive not because they *must*, but because they *can*.

Of course, businesses have always had the ability to lobby against the minimum wage, to cut health benefits, and to run anti-union campaigns. What has changed is the social acceptability of such actions. Princeton economist Paul Krugman recently argued that this is what accounts for the stratospheric rise of CEO pay: businesses have torn up the old social contract that placed important restraints on corporate self-seeking. Once a few large companies did this, the pressure mounted for other companies to go along or else face a competitive disadvantage, both in the stock market and in the market for goods and services. And as the social contract got rewritten, the government stopped enforcing the old rules. Cases in point are recent changes by the Supreme Court, the NLRB, and OSHA, mentioned earlier.

What can be done about this raw deal? It's tempting to think about the Arnold Schwarzenegger solution. In the 1986 movie *Raw Deal* ("They gave him a raw deal. *Nobody* gives him a raw deal."), Schwarzenegger used fists, guns, and explosives to wipe out the Chicago mob. But leveling the playing field for workers is no Hollywood action film. Complicating the task of winning a fairer share are three paradoxes.

THREE PARADOXES

The first is the *paradox of corporate thrift*. Again, businesses are spending less on investments in equipment and training, and are also doing their best to keep wages and benefits low, all because the demand for the goods and services they sell is not growing very fast. For any business individually, this kind of thrift makes sense. But the paradox is that for businesses taken as a whole, it's counterproductive. Because if businesses are keeping down their own spending, and giving workers as little as possible, the overall result is to keep down the demand for goods and services. It's a vicious circle.

Handing another million dollars to a CEO is not a good way to stimulate the economy. True, some CEOs, like Ty-

---

RECESSION AND JOBLESS RECOVERY

Officially, the recession is over. It ended in early 2002, and we are well into the "jobless recovery." Looking at changes over the last couple of years tells us the cost of the economic downturn:

- The average annual family income fell by $1,000 between 2000 and 2001.

- The number of people without health insurance rose by 1.4 million, and the number of people in poverty rose by nearly as many from 2000 to 2001.

- There were mass layoffs of 2.5 million people in 2001 and 2.2 million in 2002.

- Unemployment continues to dance with 6%, about what it was during the recession, which means over 8 million people have been out of work in each of the last 12 months. The unemployment rate for black workers is twice as high. And a larger proportion of the unemployed than in previous recessions have been out of work for six months or more.

- The stock market's swoon wiped out at least $678 billion in retiree savings in the last three years.

co's Dennis Kozlowski, found creative ways to spend the money—on art, furniture, boats, and travel. But in general, rich people save most of their income. If you took a million dollars of executive pay and divided it among 1,000 poor families, you would get a lot more economic impact.

The second paradox is what University of Massachusetts economist James Crotty calls the *neoliberal paradox*. With slow global growth and increased global competition, it's become harder for most businesses to keep profits up. But at the same time, changes in the stock market mean that investors now demand consistently high profits. The growth of large institutional investors and the invention of the hostile takeover have made it possible for investors to threaten companies with takeover or destruction unless they generate high returns. Crotty points out that profit for nonfinancial corporations actually peaked in 1997. But corporations knew what would happen if they told their shareholders this bad news. In this context, the pressures for accounting games and even fraud became irresistible.

These first two paradoxes point out that the economy is far too important to let businesses run it. But when we think about how to take more control away from businesses, we run into the third paradox, the *Arkansas Traveler paradox*, named for an old song in which a traveler comes upon a man whose roof is leaking in a rainstorm. When the traveler asks him why he doesn't fix the roof, he says, "I can't fix it when it's raining." Asked why he doesn't then repair the roof when it's sunny, he replies, "When it's sunny, there's no need to fix it."

Similarly, when the economy is booming, workers have more economic leverage. Businesses run up against labor shortages, so they're more willing to make concessions to in order to ensure they can get the workers they need. It's a good time to organize a union, push for a higher minimum wage, or demand that employers provide a training program. Governments have the money to enforce regulations or to help pay for -training.

But when the economy is booming, many workers don't see as much need to band together to defend their interests. Why form a union or lobby for a higher minimum wage when you can hop to a better paying job? Why push for a training program when even unskilled workers are getting jobs? The 1990s may not have amounted to a workers' paradise, but employment rates and wages were relatively edenic compared to the two decades that came before.

On the other hand, when the economy crashes, all of a sudden even the corporate media and mainstream politicians begin to focus on all the ways that business falls short. But when businesses are struggling for survival, they will fight desperately against any attempt to give workers a bigger share. The large numbers of unemployed job seekers put a damper on any attempts to organize unions or boost minimum wages. Governments face budget shortfalls, so they are not inclined to take on new activities.

The only way out of this box is not economic, but polit-

BEST OF TIMES?

The boom to end all booms did not undo long-term deterioration in job quality in the United States, or end the yawning gap between rich and poor.

- As of 2000, the average hourly wage (corrected for inflation) was still 8% below its level in 1973, 27 years earlier. The wage level did grow over the 1990s, but it grew slowly, and it had been beaten down so far that workers ended up below the 1973 wage level.
- While it is stunning to learn that 2.5 million workers lost their jobs from mass layoffs in the 2001 recession, it is perhaps even more stunning to realize than in 2000, at the peak of the boom, nearly *2 million* workers were laid off in mass layoffs.
- In boom year 2000, 40 million Americans had no health insurance.
- Meanwhile, the rich were getting much, much richer. In 1970, the average household in the richest 5% earned 16 times as much as average household in the bottom one-fifth; they earned 25 times as much in 2000. Between 1970 and 1999, average CEO pay went from 39 times average worker's pay to 1,000 times average worker's pay. Something was seriously wrong even during the so-called good times.

ical. We have to build a movement that sees beyond the current situation in any given year. In the boom years, we have to remember all the problems of a business-dominated economy and use our economic leverage to strengthen institutions and business practices that help workers. In the bust years, like now, we have to keep in mind that economic resources will soon enough be growing again, and put in place rules that will more equitably distribute and effectively use them. We know what rules make a difference: the most important are strong wage floors and collective bargaining protections. By making businesses work under a better set of rules, we can actually help grow those resources by steering the economy out of the paradox of thrift and the neoliberal paradox.

If the problem is a raw deal, the solution is a new New Deal. The New Deal of the 1930s and 1940s saved U.S. capitalism from itself. It looks like we're going to have to do it again.

BAD NEWS ON MAIN STREET IS GOOD NEWS ON WALL STREET. WHAT'S SO CONFUSING?

BY JOHN MILLER

On May 2, the Bureau of Labor Statistics announced that the U.S. economy lost 48,000 jobs in April, pushing the unemployment rate up to 6% and matching the eight-year high. The stock market promptly rallied. The Dow Jones Industrial Average of blue-chip stocks shot up 158 points to close at 8,582, its highest level in months. And the battered Nasdaq average of high-tech stocks gained 30 points, breaking the 1,500 barrier for the first time since June, 2002.

This uptick in the stock market in reaction to what he called "miserable" economic news left David Johnson, a Dallas stockbroker and commentator on National Public Radio's business program "Marketplace," perplexed.

"A lot of times you look at the market reactions," Johnson confessed to his radio listeners, "and it looks like the market always tries to do whatever it can to confound the greatest number of people." Johnson's reaction was typical of mainstream and business reporters, who commonly express surprise when the unemployment rate and the Dow rise in tandem.

Indeed, it might seem like a contradiction that stock prices can go up when the unemployment rate is rising. After all, a soft labor market suggests slower economic growth and dimmer prospects for corporate profits—what investors are buying shares of in the stock markets. During severe economic downturns—for example, the Great Depression—rising unemployment and a collapsing stock market do go hand in hand. But it's really no puzzler: bad news for workers on Main Street can often add up to good news for investors on Wall Street.

It's all about class conflict. Low unemployment gives workers greater bargaining power to press for higher wages and benefits. Businesses can either absorb these higher labor costs by cutting profits or pass them along by raising prices. Either way, investors lose out. If corporate profits decline, the value of investors' stock holdings is diminished. If prices rise, greater inflation cuts into the value of their assets. On the other hand, higher unemployment eats away at the bargaining power of workers, keeping their wage growth in check. And with labor costs under control, inflation remains low and corporate profit margins wide.

A closer look at current economic numbers bolsters this view. April's rising unemployment rate confirmed that the current, jobless economic recovery is doing little to empower workers, push up wages, or threaten corporate profits. In fact, since the recession officially began in March 2001, the economy has shed some 2.7 million jobs. An economic recovery that continues to destroy jobs two years after the onset of the recession is jobless in the extreme. Were this a typical post-World War II recovery, the economy would have been gaining jobs for nearly a year by now and would already have added back three-quarters of the jobs lost during the recession.

Continued job losses have put the kibosh on wages. Real weekly earnings have fallen in each of the past four quarters for the median full-time worker 25 years of age or older—the longest continuous decline in this group's real earnings since 1990.

The flip side of this jobless recovery is rapid productivity growth. Corporate restructuring, layoffs, and little rehiring have produced rapid increases in productivity—the economy's output per hour of labor. Since the fourth quarter of 2001, the hourly output of U.S. workers has gone up at a 4.2% annual rate, exceeding the "new economy" productivity growth rate of 2.4% from 1995 to 2001. And for the first time in a postwar recovery, productivity is growing faster than the economy. Rapid productivity gains have allowed companies to expand production without hiring new workers. For example, despite improving factory orders, manufacturers laid off 95,000 workers in April. That marked the 33rd consecutive month of declines in factory jobs, the longest string of manufacturing layoffs since the Great Depression.

In this way, what financial analysts call positive fundamentals—rising productivity and declining unit labor costs, improved competitiveness, and low inflation rates—have meant fewer rehires, continued layoffs, and deteriorating real wages on Main Street. For those pounding the pavement in search of work or forced to produce more in fewer hours with little or no improvement in pay, this is all bad news.

But that is not how Wall Street sees it. Higher unemployment rates boost stock prices. That should not really be surprising. For Wall Street remains, as Woody Guthrie once put it, "the street that keeps the rest of us off Easy Street."

Sources Jared Bernstein & Lawrence Mishel, "Jobless Recovery Catches Up with Wages, Stifles Growth," Economic Policy Institute Issue Brief #193, May 2003; "Marketplace," Minnesota Public Radio/PRI, May 2, 2003, transcript at <www.marketplace.org>.

July/August 1994, revised and excerpted February 1999

WHAT ARE THE REAL COSTS OF INFLATION —AND TO WHOM?

BY BRYAN SNYDER

As the American economy rolls along in a continuing boom, almost weekly the media speculate on when Federal Reserve Bank Chairman Alan Greenspan will decide to cool things down in order to stave off even a hint of rising inflation. Although workers are benefiting from low unemployment and the first real wage increases in two and a half decades, the Federal Reserve views these gains as a danger sign.

A powerful array of moneyed interests lurks behind Greenspan's attitudes. Financiers with large investments see the specter of inflation as a threat to their interests and to the economy as a whole. Because inflation erodes the value of financial assets, they argue that it discourages the investment that is needed for stable long-term economic growth. They prefer a modest growth rate of 3% or less maintained over time, which would achieve a "safe" level of wage gains and unemployment.

But is controlling inflation worth the high costs to workers of suffering from lower wages and more job insecurity? The evidence shows that price increases are not the enemy of long-term growth that financiers would have us believe. What's more, according to research by Thomas Michl of Colgate University, the other costs of moderate inflation are either avoidable or bearable. For most people, the treatment prescribed by the Fed for inflation is much more painful than the malady itself.

COUNTING THE COSTS OF INFLATION

Michl analyzed the costs of inflation by first determining which costs are avoidable and which are not. Falling real incomes are a cost of inflation that the right policies can rectify. If an economy has a moderate rate of inflation, such as 7% to 10% annually, someone living on fixed Social Security benefits would watch the actual buying power of his or her fixed income erode in direct proportion to that rate of inflation. To compensate for this, the government has built a COLA (Cost of Living Adjustment) into the Social Security benefit structure to keep real incomes constant or close to it. Likewise, employers can often anticipate moderate levels of inflation and float their pay scales accordingly.

In the area of taxation, rising wages could potentially push individuals into higher income tax brackets. This "bracket creep" could reduce workers' after-tax real wages (wages adjusted for inflation). Indexing the tax structure to the rate of inflation can take care of this problem. The 1986 Tax Reform Act does this for personal exemptions.

There is also concern that inflation depresses the housing market. Historically, banks were reluctant to give mortgage loans when the interest on their loans might be wiped out by inflation. But banks have learned to compensate for the possibility of future inflation by using variable-rate mortgages. Banks could also avoid this impact of inflation by having mortgage payments that rise gradually over time, along with expected inflation. In addition, elements of the tax code, such as deductions for mortgage interest payments, facilitate first-time mortgages.

According to Michl, some costs are less easy to offset, but that doesn't necessarily mean they're significant. A particularly good example of this is inflation's "shoe leather" costs.

Shoe leather costs result from the fact that high levels of inflation make it expensive for capitalists to keep a lot of cash on hand to cover transactions. Rather than let their cash grow less valuable, when there's high inflation they will keep their money in bank accounts that offer interest rates at least equal to the inflation rate. This keeps the value of their money constant.

The story goes that this "parking" of working funds in bank accounts leads to increased expenses (transaction costs), due to the extra time spent running to and from the bank making withdrawals and deposits, which wears down "shoe leather." This is an unavoidable cost of inflation, but it's relatively small. Michl reports that, when annual inflation is 10%, shoe leather costs would amount to $7.28 billion or 0.13% of a $5.5 trillion Gross National Product. Innovation and technological change within the banking system, including electronic fund transfers, have made these costs all but evaporate in recent years, as banks now offer firms instantly accessible interest-bearing accounts and decentralized service.

THE GROWTH QUESTION

A larger concern is whether or not inflation retards economic growth. Does inflation create uncertainty about future inflation, making capitalists reduce their level of investment and slowing economic growth in the long run? The conventional wisdom of mainstream economics answers a nervous *yes*.

Yet as Michl argues, the evidence shows that inflation and growth tend to go together in industrial societies. Between 1955 and 1973, countries such as Japan, Korea, Israel, Brazil, and Turkey had rapid rates of growth as well as relatively high inflation.

Economist Ross Levine tried to determine whether there is a correlation between rates of inflation and rates of investment and growth. Using data from 119 countries from 1969 through 1989, Levine and his colleagues found that "...inflation is not significantly negatively correlated with long-run growth.... Given the uncharacteristically unified view among economists and policy analysts that countries with high inflation rates should adopt policies to lower inflation in order to promote prosperity, the inability to find simple cross-country regressions supporting this contention is both surprising and troubling."

> INFLATION CAN SHIFT REAL INCOMES FROM CREDITORS TO DEBTORS, BY ALLOWING DEBTORS TO PAY OFF DEBTS IN LESS VALUABLE CURRENCY, ERODING THE RATE OF RETURN LENDERS CAN REALIZE FROM LOANS.

Wall Street's argument that inflation will hurt long-term investment runs like this: Inflation reduces the incentive to save money, because if you're locked into a bank account or fixed-rate investment that yields interest at a lower rate than inflation, the value of your money will deteriorate. It also reduces the incentive to lend money, as the debt will be repaid in the future when money is less valuable. To compensate for these disincentives, financial institutions raise interest rates to the level of inflation or above. Because this rise in interest rates raises the cost of borrowing money, some argue that it hurts long-term investment.

That would be true if interest rates largely determined investment. But other factors, such as sales growth and how much cash a firm has on hand, are more powerful determinants of investment than interest rates. For example, while the East Asian economies grew rapidly during the 1980s and early 1990s, their interest rates remained high, but still were below profit rates, and did not significantly stunt economic growth.

In the case of the bond market, in which bond buyers lend the government money, fears of inflation can cause a drop in bond prices and a rise in interest rates. Inflation erodes the value of bonds, as it allows the government to pay off its debt in cheaper dollars in the future. Falling bond prices in turn have prompted a hike in interest rates to appease skittish buyers. It's not surprising, then, that the bond market has put so much political pressure on the federal government to ward off inflation.

SOCIAL WELFARE, WEALTH, AND INFLATION

If they see it coming, policymakers can compensate for inflation in order to maintain real incomes. But when inflation is not anticipated and mechanisms are not in place to keep the value of assets and liabilities constant, then inflation will alter the distribution of income within society.

Specifically, inflation can shift real incomes from creditors (lenders) to debtors (borrowers). Unanticipated inflation allows debtors (such as the U.S. government, in the case of bonds) to pay off debts in less valuable currency, while eroding the rate of return lenders can realize from loans. For instance, if a bank Certificate of Deposit (CD) offers a fixed annual interest rate of 7%, and suddenly the rate of inflation rises to 7% that year, the investor would make no money since the CD's value eroded at the same rate that the interest accumulated. This cost of inflation falls on the wealthiest households, who derive the bulk of their incomes from returns on investments rather than from their labor.

A 1979 study by Joseph Minarik analyzed the effects of inflation on the distribution of incomes in the 1970s. Households with the lowest incomes actually gained slightly due to windfalls on fixed home mortgages. However, the richest 20% of households suffered a substantial loss. In fact, the study found that for those making between $200,000 and $500,000 a year, a modest 2% increase in inflation caused a 17% reduction in real income.

Because of this disproportionate impact of inflation on the wealthiest members of society, there is a consensus among the country's elite that the government should declare it to be Public Enemy Number One. Tom Michl puts it this way: "To the extent that the wealthiest citizens, who depend on interest and capital income substantially more than the average citizen, are also disproportionately represented in the political process (and who would seriously dispute that), this creates a very strong bias toward disinflationary economic policies."

The vast majority of Americans can live with moderate levels of inflation, when properly COLA-ed or indexed, and would prosper with high rates of economic growth. For them, the therapy for inflation—a sustained regimen of tight money, slow economic growth, and wages which fall or grow only slightly even during boom times—is the real burden.

Resources: Thomas Michl, "Assessing the Costs of Inflation and Unemployment," discussion paper, 1994; Ross Levine and David Renelt, "A Sensitivity Analysis of Cross Country Growth Regressions," *American Economic Review* 82 (4 September 1992); Ross Levin and Sara Zervos, "What Have We Learned about Policy and Growth from Cross Country Regressions?" *American Economic Review* 83 (2 May 1993).

CHAPTER 7

Perspectives on Macroeconomic Policy

INTRODUCTION

A few years back, political economist Bob Sutcliffe developed a sure-fire economic indicator that he called the Marx/Keynes ratio—the ratio of references to Karl Marx to references to John Maynard Keynes in Paul Samuelson's *Economics*, the best-selling introductory economics textbook during the decades following World War II. In a recession or a period of sluggish economic growth, the Marx/Keynes ratio would climb, as social commentators and even economists fretted over the future of capitalism. In economic booms, however, Marx's predictions of the collapse of capitalism disappeared from the pages of Samuelson's textbook, while the paeans to Keynesian demand-management policies multiplied.

Today Sutcliffe's ratio wouldn't work very well. Marx has been pushed off the pages of most introductory macroeconomics textbooks altogether, and even Keynes has been given a minor role. Mainstream textbooks now favor the "New Classical" economics, which depicts the private economy as inherently stable and self-regulating, and dismisses Keynesian demand-management policies as ineffectual or counterproductive. Our authors disagree. In this chapter, they reintroduce schools of thought that have been removed from economics textbooks in recent decades and critically assess New Classical economics.

John Miller and Gina Neff start with a down-to-earth ac-

count of New Classical "rational expectations" models, in which markets clear instantaneously and bungling government bureaucrats always make a mess of things. Drawing on the writings of Keynesian and New Keynesian economists, Miller and Neff argue that rational expectations models are contradicted by the historical record, which shows that bigger government has brought milder, not more severe, business fluctuations (Article 7.1).

Robert Pollin (Article 7.2) attacks the underpinnings of the neoliberal policy prescription for the global economy. As he sees it, the unfettered globalization of free markets will be unable to resolve three basic problems: an ever-larger reserve army of the unemployed that reduces the bargaining power of workers in all countries (the Marx problem); the inherent instability and volatility of investment and financial markets (the Keynes problem); and the erosion of the protections of the welfare state from full employment to social insurance (the Polanyi problem).

Ellen Frank explains the development of Keynesian economic institutions in the United States from the 1930s to the 1970s, and their subsequent dismantling under the Clinton administration. She also introduces the radical insight of Keynes—"that real wealth lies in the people, resources, and productive apparatus of a society and that citizens can, through the collective power of government, harness those resources for internal development." (Article 7.3)

Alejandro Reuss provides a primer on Marxist economics. Marx rejected the idea of a self-equilibrating economy, and argued that capitalism was inherently dynamic and unstable. Reuss describes some of Marx's key ideas, including the nature of capitalist exploitation, the necessity (for capitalists) of maintaining a "reserve army of the unemployed," and what Marx saw as two ingredients of an eventual crisis of capitalism: overproduction and the falling rate of profit (Article 7.4).

Arthur MacEwan explores the justifications for private property in a capitalist economy. He shows that the arguments for private property are instrumental—private property is necessary to make the system work—and that property rights are not eternal or fixed: they have changed over time as social movements, such as the environmental movement, have demanded greater social accountability from property owners (Article 7.5).

Finally, Randy Albelda offers a feminist analysis of poverty and gender. Feminist economists have illuminated the ways in which having and caring for children alters the economic status of women—including those who are not mothers but are still relegated to poorly-paid care-giving jobs. Feminist economists, argues Albelda, provide the best understanding of the obstacles low-income families face and the options that might improve their position in today's economy (Article 7.6).

KEY TO COLANDER

E = Economics. M = Macroeconomics.

These articles fit with chapters E25-E26 and E22, or M9-M10 and M6.

Article 7.1 complements chapter E25 or M9, especially its presentation of the classical range of the aggregate supply/aggregate demand model.

Article 7.2 works well with any of these chapters.

Article 7.3 works with chapters E25-E26 or M9-M10, or the discussion of debt and deficits in E31 or M15.

Articles 7.4 and 7.6 can be introduced with the Appendix to chapter E22 or M6, "Nonmainstream Approaches of Macroeconomics." They can also go with any discussion of the instabilities and inequalities of the modern macroeconomy.

Article 7.5 fits well with any discussion of the philosophical foundations of capitalism in the early chapters, as well as with the Appendix to chapter E22 or M6.

DISCUSSION QUESTIONS

1) (Article 7.1) How do classical economists argue that macro-economies are inherently stable, and that government intervention is ineffective or counterproductive? Are their arguments convincing?

2) (Article 7.1) Why are Keynesians convinced that markets don't clear instantaneously, and that government intervention can and must stabilize market economies? Evaluate the evidence for their position.

3) (Article 7.2) Summarize the Marx, Keynes, and Polanyi problems. Why does Pollin think that neoliberal globalization policies will be unable to resolve them?

4) (Article 7.3) What do the terms "fiscal policy," "automatic stabilizer," "cyclical deficit," "federal deficit" mean? How do they relate to Keynesian policy-making?

5) (Article 7.3) How did the Democrats bring down Keynes?

5) (Article 7.3) What would a macroeconomic policy that captured Keynes's radical insights look like?

6) (Article 7.4) In Marxist theory, how is a dynamic capitalist economy felled by instability? What roles do a "falling rate of profit," a "reserve army of the unemployed," and "overproduction" play in Marx's theory of how capitalism will fall into a crisis? Do you think today's macroeconomy displays any of those tendencies?

7) (Article 7.5) As MacEwan tells it, what is the usual justification for private property rights in a capitalist economy? What does the fact that the rights of property owners have changed over time suggest about the power of social movements?

8) (Article 7.6) How does feminist economics' focus on gender challenge other theories of poverty? How are feminist theories of poverty different from Keynesian, Marxist, Institutionalist, and neoclassical analyses?

ARTICLE 7.1   *May/June 1996, revised April 2002*

THE REVENGE OF THE CLASSICS

BY JOHN MILLER AND GINA NEFF

Nineteen ninety-five was not a good year for the welfare state. A Gingrich-led Congress attempted to pull the plug on universal entitlements for the poor, from welfare to Medicaid. And the Royal Swedish Academy of Science awarded the Nobel Prize in economics to Robert Lucas, a 58-year-old University of Chicago economist, for his "insights into the difficulties of using economic policy to control the economy."

Using sophisticated mathematics and economic models, Lucas has persuaded much of the economics profession that the economic policies John Maynard Keynes developed to combat the Great Depression—the economic underpinnings of the welfare state and the mixed economy—are ineffective.

What would Lucas do instead? Forsake those policies, dismantle the welfare state, and embrace the market. That was a job that, back in the mid-1990s, Gingrich and his crowd seemed only too happy to take up. They were glad to join forces with a Federal Reserve Board (the "Fed") already

under the influence of the conservative counterrevolution in macroeconomics, led initially by Milton Friedman, another University of Chicago monetary theorist, and then by Lucas.

The Fed has accepted the futility of using monetary policy to promote long-run employment, leaving inflation alone as the ultimate target of its policies. In addition, the Fed's practice of making early announcements of changes in monetary policy, which is probably a good thing, can be directly attributed to Lucas. He has argued that unannounced changes provoke instability in the private sector instead of muting it.

Lucas and his school of followers call themselves New Classical economists. Like the classical economists who predated Keynes, these modern conservatives believe the economy possesses powerful self-correcting forces that guarantee full employment. Their vision of a stable market economy rests on three building blocks: rational expectations, market clearing, and imperfect information.

Let's look first at rational expectations, a notion which does seem rational enough. After all, every one of our economic actions is directed toward the future. Using whatever economic information we can get our hands on about prices, growth, and other economic activity, we predict our economic future. And usually we are good at it. When fellow workers are getting laid off at the company we are employed in, for instance, chances are that buying an expensive house is not at the top of our to-do list.

When we do get things wrong, we reevaluate our predictions. And, says Lucas, we keep up this process of prediction and evaluation until there is no way to improve those predictions, ensuring that we won't consistently make the same forecasting mistakes. In that way we form what Lucas calls "rational expectations." As he sees it, people act much like experienced bettors at the track. They get good at picking horses, but are never able to pick the winning horse every time.

Lucas has made a career out of expressing these ideas in mathematical terms. He argues that predictions about the rates of interest, unemployment, and inflation shape how consumers, workers, and business people decide their economic future. From consumers buying a new home to workers looking for a new job to bosses hiring or laying off employees, rational expectations theory seeks to describe what motivates economic actors.

ADAM SMITH RETURNS

But Lucas does not stop there—with merely a theory of how people make economic decisions. New Classical economic theory also assumes that markets "clear" instantaneously. In the bat of an eye, prices adjust so that how much sellers bring to market just matches whatever buyers take away. For instance, in a labor market, wages (the price of labor) fall quickly enough to guarantee that every worker willing to work (or sell their labor) at the going wage finds a job with an employer (or buyer of labor). For New Classical economists that constitutes full employment. Only workers unwilling to work at the market clearing wage are out of a job. Those workers are voluntarily unemployed—they chose not to work and brought unemployment upon themselves.

The point here is simple: Market capitalism is stable. "Price flexibility" and "market clearing" guarantee a booming full-employment economy—one that does not need economic policymaking to stabilize it. In fact, in Lucas's framework, government attempts to fine tune the economy actually backfire.

Here's why. If people expect the government to change economic policy, they too change their economic actions. That is rational expectations at work. And when prices and wages adjust instantaneously as people scramble to match their economic actions to their new expectations, those adjustments nullify the government's actions.

For instance, suppose the Fed tries to reduce unemployment by increasing the money supply, in the hope of raising spending and putting people to work. Lucas's rational workers anticipate that more spending and hiring will bring not only higher wages but also instantaneously higher prices, leaving their purchasing power unchanged. In this world people are not forced to work to avoid starving, but rather choose to offer their services only when their in-

flation-adjusted wages are sufficiently high. So no rational worker is lured into the market. The Fed's actions fail to lower unemployment, and succeed only in driving up prices.

As far-fetched as this theory might seem, the stagflation (simultaneous stagnation and inflation) of the 1970s lent these ideas plausibility. New Classical economics gathered adherents as Keynesian policies seemed increasingly ineffectual.

In New Classical economics, meddlesome government is not only ineffective, it is the enemy. Why does Lucas's inherently stable capitalism suffer through the ups and downs of the business cycle? His answer: Washington types trying to fine tune the economy. This is where imperfect information, the third building block of Lucas' theory, enters the model. Even Lucas's rational actors in this market-clearing world possess only limited information and can be fooled by bungling bureaucrats and re-election minded politicians who launch surprise (unannounced) changes in government policy.

> WHILE KEYNESIANS MAY ACCEPT THE IDEA OF RATIONALLY FORMED EXPECTATIONS, THEY FIND THE IDEAS OF FLEXIBLE PRICES AND CLEARING MARKETS PREPOSTEROUS.

People know the economy around them—their own wages or profits, the prices of the products they sell and those that they buy—better than what is going on across the economy. So if the Federal Reserve, without announcing it, increases the money supply in order to beef up spending and lower unemployment, even people with rational expectations can be confounded. They see their prices or wages go up, but don't anticipate prices going up elsewhere in the economy.

And that causes a problem. Corporate managers, for instance, hike up production, thinking that a higher price must signal a soaring demand for their products. Output rises across the economy. But soon inventories pile up, because the price increases were due to general inflation rather than greater demand. Corporate managers realize that the higher production levels were unwarranted, and they order a cutback—below even the initial output. The economy contracts, causing a recession.

What can return stability to the economy? Forsaking government intervention into the economy. In Lucas's world, unannounced changes in government policy cause the ups and downs of the business cycle. And announced changes in government policies are fully anticipated and therefore ineffective. For Lucas, the only rational course of action is to turn our backs on active government attempts to soften the blows of the market economy.

KEYNESIAN CRITICS

Not all economists are convinced by Lucas's arguments or support the draconian policy implications of New Classical economics. The proponents of Keynesian economic policy have been among the most vocal critics. While Keynesians may accept the idea of rationally formed expectations, they find the ideas of flexible prices and clearing markets preposterous. One Nobel laureate, James Tobin, called these ideas a "great myth"—powerful in its effect on how we see the economy, but nonetheless a myth.

Another Keynesian Nobel winner, Franco Modigliani, railed that it is as if "what happened in the United States in the 1930s was a severe attack of contagious laziness." For these dyed-in-the-wool Keynesians, the private economy will not necessarily be driven toward full employment even in the long run and Keynes's fundamental message still holds: "a modern monetized economy needs to be stabilized, can be stabilized, and should be stabilized" by government intervention.

More recently, "New Keynesian" economists have fashioned a different critique of New Classical economics. These modern Keynesians accept not only the idea that people form rational expectations about what will happen in the economy, but also the idea that in the long run the private economy tends toward full employment. Still, they argue that for good economic reasons, wages and prices are "sticky" and much slower to adjust than Lucas suggests. For instance, given the high cost of negotiating a wage settlement, most labor contracts are long term. In the United States, nearly 80% of union contracts are for three years and only about two-fifths of them contain cost-of-living adjustments. Corporations also often rely on long-term pricing agreements to afford them the price stability necessary to bid on contracts.

Thus, while the economy might eventually reach the full employment outcome Lucas's model predicts, the wait is likely to be intolerably long. What's needed is active government intervention designed for the workable policy time frame of three to five years, for as Keynes once wrote, "in the long run we are all dead."

More fundamentally, Lucas's way of thinking exaggerates the amount of power people really have over their economic lives. Economist E. Ray Canterbery writes mockingly that in the New Classical school, "The marginal blue collar worker on his way to the factory anticipates an increase in the money supply then fully anticipates the inflation within his monetarist model ... and a fall in the real interest rates and a fall in real wages. The worker does a U-turn, drives home, and voluntarily disemploys himself." In New Classical economics bosses raise their workers' wages when the economy is doing well rather than pocketing the extra profits. And workers have the power to choose whether or not to work, to ask for higher wages when they expect inflation to go up, or to move into a different industry when they fear the worst for their own job. This is indeed a great myth.

Perhaps the most mythical aspect of New Classical economics is its claim that capitalism is stable—that if only policy makers would cease their interventions, economic stability would be assured and full employment guaranteed. But the instability of capitalism has been with us since long before Keynesian economic policy, which after all was a response to the Great Depression of the 1930s.

And that instability will worsen if New Classical economics is able to undo what Keynesian policy makers have done to mitigate the instability of capitalism since World War II. Current economic anxiety will heighten as workers struggle with real-life adjustments like stagnant wages and rising layoffs. At the same time, Lucas and his New Classical followers will continue to construct mathematical paeans to the rationality of these adjustments and the inherent stability of capitalism, even if that stability is evident only in their seminar rooms and the the Royal Swedish Academy of Science.

Resources: Robert J. Gordon, *Macroeconomics*, 6th ed., 1994; Robert Lucas, *Studies in Business Cycle Theory*, 1989; N. Gregory Mankiw, "A Quick Refresher Course in Macroeconomics," *Journal of Economic Literature*, December 1990; James Tobin, *Asset Accumulation and Economic Activity*, 1980; *The End of Economic Man*, reviewed by E. Ray Canterbery in *Challenge*, Nov./Dec. 1995.

WHAT'S WRONG WITH NEOLIBERALISM?

THE MARX, KEYNES, AND POLANYI PROBLEMS

BY ROBERT POLLIN

During the years of the Clinton administration, the term "Washington Consensus" began circulating to designate the common policy positions of the U.S. administration along with the International Monetary Fund (IMF) and World Bank. These positions, implemented in the United States and abroad, included free trade, a smaller government share of the economy, and the deregulation of financial markets. This policy approach has also become widely known as *neoliberalism*, a term which draws upon the classical meaning of the word *liberalism*.

Classical liberalism is the political philosophy that embraces the virtues of free-market capitalism and the corresponding minimal role for government interventions, especially as regards measures to promote economic equality within capitalist societies. Thus, a classical liberal would favor minimal levels of government spending and taxation, and minimal levels of government regulation over the economy, including financial and labor markets. According to the classical liberal view, businesses should be free to operate as they wish, and to succeed or fail as such in a competitive marketplace. Meanwhile, consumers rather than government should be responsible for deciding which businesses produce goods and services that are of sufficient quality as well as reasonably priced. Businesses that provide overexpensive or low-quality products will then be outcompeted in the marketplace regardless of the regulatory standards established by governments. Similarly, if businesses offer workers a wage below what the worker is worth, then a competitor firm will offer this worker a higher wage. The firm unwilling to offer fair wages would not survive over time in the competitive marketplace.

This same reasoning also carries over to the international level. Classical liberals favor free trade between countries rather than countries operating with tariffs or other barriers to the free flow of goods and services between countries. They argue that restrictions on the free movement of products and money between countries only protects uncompetitive firms from market competition, and thus holds back the economic development of countries that choose to erect such barriers.

Neoliberalism and the Washington Consensus are contemporary variants of this longstanding political and economic philosophy. The major difference between classical liberalism as a philosophy and contemporary neoliberalism as a set of policy measures is with implementation. Washington Consensus policy makers are committed to free-market policies when they support the interests of big business, as, for example, with lowering regulations at the workplace. But these same policy makers become far less insistent on free-market principles when invoking such principles might damage big business interests. Federal Reserve and IMF interventions to bail out wealthy asset holders during the frequent global financial crises in the 1990s are obvious violations of free-market precepts.

Broadly speaking, the effects of neoliberalism in the less developed countries over the 1990s reflected the experience of the Clinton years in the United States. A high proportion of less developed countries were successful, just in the manner of the United States under Clinton, in reducing inflation and government budget deficits, and creating a more welcoming climate for foreign trade, multinational corporations, and financial market investors. At the same time, most of Latin America, Africa, and Asia—with China being the one major exception—experienced deepening problems of poverty and inequality in the 1990s, along with slower growth and frequent financial market crises, which in turn produced still more poverty and inequality.

If free-market capitalism is a powerful mechanism for creating wealth, why does a neoliberal policy approach, whether pursued by Clinton, Bush, or the IMF, produce severe difficulties in terms of inequality and financial instability, which in turn diminish the market mechanism's ability to even promote economic growth? It will be helpful to consider this in terms of three fundamental problems that result from a free-market system, which I term "the Marx

Problem," "the Keynes problem," and "the Polanyi problem." Let us take these up in turn.

THE MARX PROBLEM

Does someone in your family have a job and, if so, how much does it pay? For the majority of the world's population, how one answers these two questions determines, more than anything else, what one's standard of living will be. But how is it decided whether a person has a job and what their pay will be? Getting down to the most immediate level of decision-making, this occurs through various types of bargaining in labor markets between workers and employers. Karl Marx argued that, in a free-market economy generally, workers have less power than employers in this bargaining process because workers cannot fall back on other means of staying alive if they fail to get hired into a job. Capitalists gain higher profits through having this relatively stronger bargaining position. But Marx also stressed that workers' bargaining power diminishes further when unemployment and underemployment are high, since that means that employed workers can be more readily replaced by what Marx called "the reserve army" of the unemployed outside the office, mine, or factory gates.

Neoliberalism has brought increasing integration of the world's labor markets through reducing barriers to international trade and investment by multinationals. For workers in high-wage countries such as the United States, this effectively means that the reserve army of workers willing to accept jobs at lower pay than U.S. workers expands to include workers in less developed countries. It isn't the case that businesses will always move to less developed countries or that domestically produced goods will necessarily be supplanted by imports from low-wage countries. The point is that U.S. workers face an increased *credible* threat that they can be supplanted. If everything else were to remain the same in the U.S. labor market, this would then mean that global integration would erode the bargaining power of U.S. workers and thus tend to bring lower wages.

But even if this is true for workers in the United States and other rich countries, shouldn't it also mean that workers in poor countries have greater job opportunities and better bargaining positions? In fact, there are areas where workers in poor countries are gaining enhanced job opportunities through international trade and multinational investments. But these gains are generally quite limited. This is because a long-term transition out of agriculture in poor countries continues to expand the reserve army of unemployed and underemployed workers in these countries as well. Moreover, when neoliberal governments in poor countries reduce their support for agriculture—through cuts in both tariffs on imported food products and subsidies for domestic farmers—this makes it more difficult for poor farmers to compete with multinational agribusiness firms. This is especially so when the rich countries maintain or increase their own agricultural supports, as has been done in the United States under Bush. In addition, much of the growth in the recently developed export-oriented manufacturing sectors of poor countries has failed to significantly increase jobs even in this sector. This is because the new export-oriented production sites frequently do not represent net additions to the country's total supply of manufacturing firms. They rather replace older firms that were focused on supplying goods to domestic markets. The net result is that the number of people looking for jobs in the developing countries grows faster than the employers seeking new workers. Here again, workers' bargaining power diminishes.

This does not mean that global integration of labor markets must necessarily bring weakened bargaining power and lower wages for workers. But it does mean that unless some non-market forces in the economy, such as government regulations or effective labor unions, are able to counteract these market processes, workers will indeed continue to experience weakened bargaining strength and eroding living standards.

THE KEYNES PROBLEM

In a free-market economy, investment spending by businesses is the main driving force that produces economic growth, innovation, and jobs. But as John Maynard Keynes stressed, private investment decisions are also unavoidably risky ventures. Businesses have to put up money without knowing whether they will produce any profits in the future. As such, investment spending by business is likely to fluctuate far more than, say, decisions by households as to how much they will spend per week on groceries.

But investment fluctuations will also affect overall spending in the economy, including that of households. When investment spending declines, this means that businesses will hire fewer workers. Unemployment rises as a result, and this in turn will lead to cuts in household spending. Declines in business investment spending can therefore set off a vicious cycle: the investment decline leads to employment declines, then to cuts in household spending and corresponding increases in household financial problems, which then brings still more cuts in business investment and financial difficulties for the business sector. This is how capitalist economies produce mass unemployment, financial crises, and recessions.

Keynes also described a second major source of instability associated with private investment activity. Precisely because private investments are highly risky propositions, financial markets have evolved to make this risk more manageable for any given investor. Through financial markets, investors can sell off their investments if they need or want to, converting their office buildings, factories, and stock of machinery into cash much more readily than they could if they always had to find buyers on their own. But Keynes warned that when financial markets convert long-term assets into short-term commitments for investors, this also fosters a speculative mentality in the markets. What becomes central for investors is not whether a company's products will produce profits over a long term, but rather whether the short-term financial market investors *think* a company's fortunes will be strong enough in the present and immediate future to drive the stock price up. Or, to be more precise, what really matters for a speculative investor is not what they think about a given company's prospects per se, but rather what they think *other investors are thinking*, since that will be what determines where the stock price goes in the short term.

Because of this, the financial markets are highly susceptible to rumors, fads, and all sorts of deceptive accounting practices, since all of these can help drive the stock price up in the present, regardless of what they accomplish in the longer term. Thus, if U.S. stock traders are convinced that Alan Greenspan is a *maestro*, and if there is news that he is about to intervene with some kind of policy shift, then the rumor of Greenspan's policy shift can itself drive prices up, as the more nimble speculators try to keep one step ahead of the herd of Greenspan-philes.

Still, as with the Marx problem, it does not follow that the inherent instability of private investment and speculation in financial markets are uncontrollable, leading inevitably to persistent problems of mass unemployment and recession. But these social pathologies will become increasingly common through a neoliberal policy approach committed to minimizing government interventions to stabilize investment.

THE POLANYI PROBLEM
Karl Polanyi wrote his classic book *The Great Transformation* in the context of the 1930s depression, World War II, and the developing worldwide competition with Communist governments. He was also reflecting on the 1920s, dominated, as with our current epoch, by a free-market ethos. Polanyi wrote of the 1920s that "economic liberalism made a supreme bid to restore the self-regulation of the system by eliminating all interventionist policies which interfered with the freedom of markets."

Considering all of these experiences, Polanyi argued that for market economies to function with some modicum of fairness, they must be embedded in social norms and institutions that effectively promote broadly accepted notions of the common good. Otherwise, acquisitiveness and competition—the two driving forces of market economies—achieve overwhelming dominance as cultural forces, rendering life under capitalism a Hobbesian "war of all against all." This same idea is also central for Adam Smith. Smith showed how the invisible hand of self-interest and competition will yield higher levels of individual effort that increases the wealth of nations, but that it will also produce the corruption of our moral sentiments unless the market is itself governed at a fundamental level by norms of solidarity.

In the post-World War II period, various social demo-cratic movements within the advanced capitalist economies adapted the Polanyi perspective. They argued in favor of government interventions to achieve three basic ends: stabilizing overall demand in the economy at a level that will provide for full employment; creating a financial market environment that is stable and conducive to the effective allocation of investment funds; and distributing equitably the rewards from high employment and a stable investment process. There were two basic means of achieving equitable distribution: relatively rapid wage growth, promoted by labor laws that were supportive of unions, minimum wage standards, and similar interventions in labor markets; and welfare state policies, including progressive taxation and redistributive programs such as Social Security. The political ascendancy of these ideas was the basis for a dramatic increase in the role of government in the post-World War II capitalist economies. As one indicator of this, total government expenditures in the United States rose from 8% of GDP in 1913, to 21% in 1950, then to 38% by 1992. The International Monetary Fund and World Bank were also formed in the mid-1940s to advance such policy ideas throughout the world—that is, to implement policies virtually the opposite of those they presently favor. John Maynard Keynes himself was a leading intellectual force contributing to the initial design of the International Monetary Fund and World Bank.

FROM SOCIAL DEMOCRACY TO NEOLIBERALISM
But the implementation of a social democratic capitalism, guided by a commitment to full employment and the welfare state, did also face serious and persistent difficulties, and we need to recognize them as part of a consideration of the Marx, Keynes, and Polanyi problems. In particular, many sectors of business opposed efforts to sustain full employment because, following the logic of the Marx problem, full employment provides greater bargaining power for workers in labor markets, even if it also increases the economy's total production of goods and services. Greater worker bargaining power can also create inflationary pressures because businesses will try to absorb their higher wage costs by raising prices. In addition, market-inhibiting financial regulations limit the capacity of financial market players to diversify their risk and speculate.

Corporations in the United States and Western Europe were experiencing some combination of these problems associated with social democratic capitalism. In particular, they were faced with rising labor costs associated with low unemployment rates, which then led to either inflation, when corporations had the ability to pass on their higher labor costs to consumers, or to a squeeze on profits, when competitive pressures prevented corporations from raising their prices in response to the rising labor costs. These pressures were compounded by the two oil price "shocks" initiated by the Oil Producing Exporting Countries (OPEC)—an initial fourfold increase in the world price of oil in 1973, then a second four-fold price spike in 1979.

These were the conditions that by the end of the 1970s led to the decline of social democratic approaches to policymaking and the ascendancy of neoliberalism. The two leading signposts of this historic transition were the election in 1979 of Margaret Thatcher as Prime Minister of the United Kingdom and in 1980 of Ronald Reagan as the President of the United States. Indeed, it was at this point that Mrs. Thatcher made her famous pronouncement that "there is no alternative" to neoliberalism.

This brings us to the contemporary era of smaller government, fiscal stringency and deregulation, i.e., to neoliberalism under Clinton, Bush, and throughout the less-developed world. The issue is not a simple juxtaposition between either regulating or deregulating markets. Rather it is that markets have become deregulated to support the interests of business and financial markets, even as these same groups still benefit greatly from many forms of government support, including investment subsidies, tax concessions, and rescue operations when financial crises get out of hand. At the same time, the deregulation of markets that favors business and finance is correspondingly the most powerful regulatory mechanism limiting the demands of workers, in that deregulation has been congruent with the worldwide expansion of the reserve army of labor and the declining capacity of national governments to implement full-employment and macroeconomic policies. In other words, deregulation has exacerbated both the Marx and Keynes problems.

Given the ways in which neoliberalism worsens the Marx, Keynes, and Polanyi problems, we should not be surprised by the wreckage that it has wrought since the late 1970s, when it became the ascendant policy model. Over the past generation, with neoliberals in the saddle almost everywhere in the world, the results have been straightforward: worsening inequality and poverty, along with slower economic growth and far more unstable financial markets. While Margaret Thatcher famously declared that "there is no alternative" to neoliberalism, there are in fact alternatives. The experience over the past generation demonstrates how important it is to develop them in the most workable and coherent ways possible.

February 2000, revised May 2001

LIFE AFTER KEYNES

BY ELLEN FRANK

Current conventional wisdom has it that business cycles are obsolete; promarket policies have swept recessions into history's proverbial dustbin. The generation of policymakers nurtured on notions of government economic management after World War II is retiring or dying off, replaced by "new economy" enthusiasts like Bill Clinton, who famously declared in 1996 that "the age of big government is over."

But what happens if the economy slips?

The old-fashioned big-government programs that pulled the United States through many an economic downturn have, in the last decade, been mostly dismantled. Many presume that the government will pick its recession-fighting tactics up again, should the economy falter—priming the economic pump by cutting taxes and raising spending, as Reagan did in the 1980s and Bush in the 1991 recession. Indeed, Treasury Secretary Larry Summers defended the Clinton administration's plan to pay off the federal debt by contending that Clinton was merely "reloading the fiscal cannon": saving against the bad times when heavy federal spending and borrowing might really be needed.

But the tools of macroeconomic management are not so easily discarded and taken up again; not, at least, in the U.S. political environment. From the 1930s, efforts to push through programs to ameliorate recessions and relieve unemployment in this country have been fraught with controversy and fiercely contested.

During the 1930s President Franklin Roosevelt's "New Deal" attempted to implement the "Keynesian Revolution"—the programs proposed by British economist John Maynard Keynes to end depressions, such as public works programs financed through deficit spending. Roosevelt, to be sure, pressed throughout the 1930s to expand federal jobs programs, but did not actually succeed until the Second World War. After the war, it took years of careful and deliberate effort to craft the political and intellectual infrastructure for continued Keynesian policy in the United States. That infrastructure is now largely gone. Putting it back together again will not be easy.

THE KEYNESIAN CONSENSUS

When Richard Nixon declared in 1972 that "we are all Keynesians now," it seemed that the consensus for active, government management of the economy in the manner of

Keynes was unshakable. Just a few years after Nixon's speech, Congress passed the Humphrey-Hawkins Act which committed the federal government to use its virtually unlimited taxing and spending powers to avert economic downturns and promote full employment.

In fact, though, the Keynesian consensus was already shattering. In 1967, the influential American Economic Association elected arch-conservative and Keynesian nemesis Milton Friedman as its president. In 1969, the prestigious *American Economic Review* published a paper by Robert Lucas outlining the new theory of rational expectations which purported to "prove" that government macroeconomic policy was useless.

Keynes had taught that the cycle of economic boom and bust could be eliminated with judicious government spending to create demand for goods and workers. By running deficits, governments could fuel economic growth, borrowing idle funds (or printing new money) to pay the employees that private businesses put to work. Known as fiscal stabilization policy or expansionary macroeconomic policy, these tools proved highly effective in combating business cycles. Even those initially hostile to Keynesian ideas in the 1930s could not deny the evidence of World War II when, thanks to massive government spending, the U.S. economy went from deep depression to rapid boom virtually overnight.

But support forged during the war for federal involvement in taming the business cycle and creating full employment proved hard to sustain once the war ended. The American version of Keynesianism, though tepid and watered-down compared to European programs or to Keynes' own proposals, was sufficiently left-wing to galvanize unending hostility in the deeply conservative pro-business arena of U.S. politics. Continued government spending after the war faced determined opposition from businesses who decried swollen government budgets as "creeping socialism" and complained that government programs amounted to "unfair competition" with the private sector. In 1954, one radical economist pronounced Keynesianism in the United States "deader than the dodo."

To be sure, business leaders supported the federal highway program, cold war military build-up of weapons, and the Korean and Vietnam wars. But they did not support the deficit financing of these ventures, nor did they back using federal programs as tools of macroeconomic management. By the early 1960s, even moderate gestures toward fiscal stabilization had become a hard sell in Congress. Keynesian economists worried openly about "implementation lags"—the yawning gap between the onset of a recession and the time it might take Congress to do something.

FULL-EMPLOYMENT BUDGETING

Throughout the 1960s and 1970s, coalitions of liberals and moderates tried to stem the backlash, quietly constructing a macroeconomic policy infrastructure that would weave some basic fiscal stabilization into the fabric of federal law.

Under the Johnson and Nixon administrations, federal entitlement programs—Social Security, Medicaid, Medicare, Food Stamps, and the plethora of welfare programs—were enacted or vastly expanded. Economists called these automatic stabilizers, because, as enacted, eligible applicants could not be denied benefits for lack of funding. Thus government's mandated spending levels would rise and fall predictably with the unemployment rate. Entitlements legally committed the government to increase spending during economic downturns, regardless of, or despite, sentiment in Congress for Keynesian fiscal policies. Thus the government would automatically send money into the economy via these social programs during downturns.

These programs were neither massive nor generous—especially compared with their European counterparts—but taken together they provided a bedrock level of federal spending in lean years as well as a minimal guaranteed income to prevent wages from plummeting in a recession.

With the sole exception of Reagan's tax cut and military build-up in the early 1980s, automatic increases in entitlement spending have been the only significant source of fiscal stimulus in the United States since 1973. During the recession of 1991, for example, virtually all of the $47 billion increase in the federal deficit came about because of increased welfare and Social Security spending.

THE CENTRAL INSIGHT OF KEYNESIAN THOUGHT WAS THAT REAL WEALTH LIES IN THE PEOPLE, RESOURCES, AND PRODUCTIVE APPARATUS OF A SOCIETY.

Furthermore, Keynesian-trained economists insisted that the budget deficits that resulted when recessions suddenly swelled welfare and Social Security rolls should not really count as deficits at all. In annual economic reports, the president's economic advisors carefully distinguished between a structural deficit—in which the government's budget was out of balance even with a booming economy—and a cyclical deficit—where the deficit soared unavoidably due to rising entitlements and falling tax collections. Full-employment budgeting—the position that balancing the federal budget should take a back seat to expanded financing of entitlements during a recession—sustained Keynesian fiscal policy even during the Reagan-Bush years.

THE END OF MACROECONOMIC POLICY

Though Reagan is credited with killing Keynesian economics, neither the Bush nor Reagan administrations were able to dismantle the policy apparatus inherited from the

1970s. Despite substantial cuts in the average benefit for many welfare programs, for example, total spending on entitlement programs rose throughout the 1980s, contributing (along with tax cuts and a military build-up) to the largest peacetime deficits ever run by the U.S. government. AFDC, Food Stamps, WIC and other programs, though perhaps stingier than before, enlarged their spending with each downward shift in the economy during the 1980s. Deficits ballooned and a Democratic House resisted major changes in entitlements.

Reagan's budget director, David Stockman, contended in 1984 that Reagan's huge deficits were a deliberate strategy to discredit Keynesian policy and part of a larger plan to undermine Congressional support for further expansions of federal spending. While this may well have been Reagan's intention, Keynesian economics was not finished, politically, until Bill Clinton's watch.

Upon attaining a legislative majority in 1994, conservatives in Congress singlemindedly set about dismantling the key legislative vestiges of Keynesian economic policy in the United States. Welfare reform, their most important victory, is instructive. When the Personal Responsibility Act passed in 1996, much was made of the five-year lifetime limit on welfare benefits, the work requirements, and so forth. Rarely noted was the fact that the legislation transformed the fiscal nature of most federal welfare programs. Welfare benefits are no longer an entitlement. Annual spending levels are now capped and will not rise with the unemployment rate unless Congress specifically allocates new funds. It was this provision of the legislation that led official Peter Edelman to resign from the Department of Health and Human Services in protest when Clinton signed the legislation.

The Food Stamp and Medicaid programs remain entitlements in theory, still available to all comers. But in enacting the 1996 reforms, Congress turned responsibility for managing these programs over to local officials who have been known to turn away applicants not already receiving welfare. Meanwhile, conservatives lobby intensely to privatize and effectively dismantle Social Security—the largest of all federal entitlement programs—though so far without success.

Republican leadership had hoped to bury Keynesian stabilization policy altogether by passing a constitutional amendment requiring an annually balanced federal budget, which would put an end once and for all to full-employment budgeting. The amendment failed by one vote to pass the Senate, but conservatives scored a partial victory with the Balanced Budget Agreement of 1997, committing Congress and the administration to balance the budget each year for the next decade, regardless of the state of the economy. Whether the agreement survives an economic downturn remains to be seen, but the strident antideficit rhetoric of the last decade will certainly make stabilization policies a tough, if not an impossible, sell.

Under Clinton, the outlook for macroeconomic policy grew bleak indeed. Clinton attributed the economic boom to tough spending caps and fiscal restraint and made a fetish of further fiscal austerity. White House press releases conceived the future exclusively in terms, not simply of budgetary balance, but of burgeoning surpluses and massive debt repayment. Rather than fight recessions or expand jobs programs, $3.5 trillion of tax revenue would buy back federal bonds from financial institutions. Clinton's millennial State of the Union address laid out the goal of Clintonomics: "Make America debt-free for the first time since 1835." Candidate Al Gore assured voters that he planned to reduce the debt "even if the economy slows." Sounding uncannily like the ghost of Herbert Hoover or Calvin Coolidge, Gore maintained that a recession would provide "an opportunity" to cut government spending "just like a corporation has to cut expenses if revenues fall." When Bill Bradley floated a modest proposal to use surplus funds for health care, Gore attacked the idea as "fiscally irresponsible," and warned it might plunge the U.S. economy in recession. Hillary Clinton, running for the Senate from New York, declared that most problems facing the country "cannot be solved by government" and staunchly supported running budget surpluses to pay off the national debt. When Democrats are hawking debt reduction and warning that deficits cause recessions, Keynesian policy has truly drawn its last gasp.

It is no good thinking these statements can be unsaid, conveniently forgotten when the next recession revives talk of an active, proemployment government. The political programs that buttressed American Keynesianism are gone. The intellectual backing and public rhetoric that sustained Keynesian ideas no longer exist or are dwarfed by the editorial pages of the *Wall Street Journal*. College economics textbooks, through which hundreds of thousands of voters and policymakers learn the rudiments of macroeconomics, barely bother with Keynes these days—or with recessions for that matter. The hottest new text by Gregory Mankiw (for which Prentice-Hall paid an unprecedented $1.4 million advance) does not even mention economic downturns until a few pages at the very end.

LIFE AFTER KEYNES

So what if the "new economy" turns out to be the same old economy? The last U.S. recession officially ended in 1991. In the eight years since, GDP has grown steadily and unemployment rates have fallen. If this is just the start of an endless millennial boom, there is no reason to worry. But what if the United States is on the brink of a Y2K recession? This is not the first time in history that Americans have lived through a prolonged boom—the economy grew for eight years straight in the 1960s—but it is the first time since the Depression that politicians and policymakers have rested their hopes so utterly on the boom's continuing.

Many on the left, of course, do not mourn Keynes' passing. Keynes, after all, despised the British Labor party and proudly proclaimed his allegiance to "the educated bourgeoisie." Socialists have long argued that Keynesian programs were meant not to help workers or humanize the economy, but to placate and defuse a potentially powerful workers' movements awakened by the Depression. Environmentalists too criticize Keynesian thinking for its mindless worship of economic growth, its predilection to solve all economic problems with more production, more work, more growth, more stuff.

But Keynes' understanding of capitalist economies was, nevertheless, profoundly radical. Any effort to construct a new kind of economic policy in the future will need to build on and attend to his fundamental insights. Keynes understood that the matters of debt and budget deficits, of interest payments and paper wealth that so obsess private business people and financial interests are, ultimately, irrelevant to all but the wealthy elite. The central insight of Keynesian thought was that real wealth lies in the people, resources, and productive apparatus of a society and that citizens can, through the collective power of government, harness those resources for internal development.

In the early years of the New Deal, government jobs programs funded public art works, community theaters, oral history projects, and the creation of hiking trails in national forests—programs that would warm the hearts of environmentalists and radicals alike. The government disbanded the efforts in the face of business opposition. In the end, Americans got a timid version of Keynesianism, complete with probusiness tilt and antigovernment bias, that flexed the collective muscle of government weakly indeed and only at the federal level. The most U.S. Keynesians managed to accomplish was to secure a minimal living standard for the very poor and very old, and to provide a fair number of makeshift defense jobs for the otherwise unemployed.

Should the boom prove not to be eternal, it is inevitable that many voices will call to reestablish the dismantled and discredited programs of postwar American Keynesianism. It will be wasted breath. The real challenge for the new millennium will be to forge a post-Keynesian economic policy. This will entail thinking about how citizens can harness their collective power to produce more leisure rather than more jobs, more equity rather than more income, more conservation rather than more production, more satisfaction rather than more consumption, more quality rather than more quantity.

February 2000

OPENING PANDORA'S BOX

THE BASICS OF MARXIST ECONOMICS

BY ALEJANDRO REUSS

In most universities, what is taught as "economics" is a particular brand of orthodox economic theory. The hallmark of this school is a belief in the optimal efficiency (and, it goes without saying, the equity) of "free markets."

The orthodox macroeconomists—who had denied the possibility of general economic slumps—were thrown for a loop by the Great Depression of the 1930s, and by the challenge to their system of thought by John Maynard Keynes and others. Even so, the orthodox system retains at its heart a view of capitalist society in which individuals, each equal to all others, undertake mutually beneficial transactions tending to a socially optimal equilibrium. There is no power and no conflict. The model is a perfectly bloodless abstraction, without all the clash and clamor of real life.

KARL MARX AND THE CRITIQUE OF CAPITALIST SOCIETY

One way to pry open and criticize the orthodox model of economics is by returning to the idiosyncrasies of the real world. That's the approach of most of the articles in this book, which describe real-world phenomena that the orthodox model ignores or excludes. These efforts may explain particular facts better than the orthodoxy, while not necessarily offering an alternative general system of analysis. They punch holes in the orthodox lines but, ultimately, leave the orthodox model in possession of the field.

This suggests the need for a different conceptual system that can supplant orthodox economics as a whole. Starting in the 1850s and continuing until his death in 1883, the German philosopher and revolutionary Karl Marx dedicated himself to developing a conceptual system for explaining the workings of capitalism. The system which Marx developed and which bears his name emerged from his criticism of the classical political economy developed by Adam Smith and David Ricardo. While Marx admired Smith and Ricardo, and borrowed many of their concepts, he approached economics (or "political economy") from a very different standpoint. He had developed a powerful criticism of capitalist society before undertaking his study of the economy. This criticism was inspired by French socialist ideas and focused on the oppression of the working class. Marx argued that wage workers—those working for a paycheck—were "free" only in the sense that they were not beholden to a single lord or master, as serfs had been under feudalism. But they did not own property, nor were they craftspeople working for themselves, so they were compelled to sell themselves for a wage to one capitalist or another. Having surrendered their freedom to the employer's authority, they were forced to work in the way the employer told them while the latter pocketed the profit produced by their labor.

MARX'S DISCUSSIONS OF CAPITALISM'S IRRESISTIBLE EXPANSIVE IMPULSE SEEM AS APT TODAY AS THEY DID 150 YEARS AGO.

Marx believed, however, that by creating this oppressed and exploited class of workers, capitalism was creating the seeds of its own destruction. Conflict between the workers and the owners was an essential part of capitalism. But in Marx's view of history, the workers could eventually overthrow the capitalist class, just as the capitalist class, or "bourgeoisie," had grown strong under feudalism, only to supplant the feudal aristocracy. The workers, however, would not simply substitute a new form of private property and class exploitation, as the bourgeoisie had done. Rather, they would bring about the organization of production on a cooperative basis, and an end to the domination of one class over another.

This line of thinking was strongly influenced by the ideas of the day in German philosophy, which held that any new order grows in the womb of the old, and eventually bursts forth to replace it. Marx believed that the creation of the working class, or proletariat, in the heart of capitalism was one of the system's main contradictions. Marx studied capitalist economics in order to explain the conditions under which it would be possible for the proletariat to overthrow capitalism and create a classless society. The orthodox view depicts capitalism as tending towards equilibrium (without dynamism or crises), serving everyone's best interests, and lasting forever. Marx saw capitalism as crisis-ridden, full of conflict, operating to the advantage of some but not others, and far from eternal.

CLASS AND EXPLOITATION

Marx studied history closely. Looked at historically, he saw capitalism as only the latest in a succession of societies based on exploitation. When people are only able to produce the bare minimum needed to live, he wrote, there is no room for a class of people to take a portion of society's production without contributing to it. But as soon as productivity exceeds this subsistence level, it becomes possible for a class of people who do not contribute to production to live by appropriating the surplus for themselves. These are the masters in slave societies, the lords in feudal societies, and the property owners in capitalist society.

Marx believed that the owners of businesses and property—the capitalists—take part of the wealth produced by the workers, but that this appropriation is hidden by the appearance of an equal exchange, or "a fair day's work for a fair day's pay."

Those who live from the ownership of property—businesses, stocks, land, etc—were then a small minority and now are less than 5% of the population in countries like the United States (Marx wrote before the rise of massive corporations and bureaucracies, and did not classify managers and administrators who don't own their own businesses as part of the bourgeoisie.) The exploited class, meanwhile, is the vast majority who lived by earning a wage or salary—not just the "blue collar" or industrial workers but other workers as well.

Marx's view of how exploitation happened in capitalist society depended on an idea, which he borrowed from Smith and Ricardo, called the Labor Theory of Value. The premise of this theory, which is neither easily proved nor easily rejected, is that labor alone creates the value which is embodied in commodities and which creates profit for owners who sell the goods. The workers do not receive the full value created by their labor and so they are exploited.

Students are likely to hear in economics classes that profits are a reward for the "abstinence" or "risk" of a businessperson—implying that profits are their just desserts. Marx would argue that profits are a reward obtained through the exercise of power—the power owners have over those who own little but their ability to work and so must sell this ability for a wage. That power, and the tribute it allows owners of capital to extract from workers, is no more legitimate in Marx's analysis than the power of a slaveowner over a slave. A slaveowner may exhibit thrift and take risks, after all, but is the wealth of the slaveowner the just reward for these virtues, or a pure and simple theft from the slave?

As Joan Robinson, an important 20th-century critic and

admirer of Marx, argues, "What is important is that owning capital is not a productive activity. The academic economists, by treating capital as productive, used to insinuate the suggestion that capitalists deserve well by society and are fully justified in drawing income from their property."

THE FALLING RATE OF PROFIT

Marx believed that his theory had major implications for the crises that engulf capitalist economies. In Marx's system, the value of the raw materials and machinery used in the manufacture of a product does not create the extra value that allows the businessman to profit from its production. That additional value is created by labor alone.

Marx recognized that owners could directly extract more value out of workers in three ways: cutting their wages, lengthening their working day, or increasing the intensity of their labor. This need not be done by a direct assault on the workers. Capitalists can achieve the same goal by employing more easily exploited groups or by moving their operations where labor is not as powerful. Both of these trends can be seen in capitalism today, and can be understood as part of capital's intrinsic thirst for more value and increased exploitation.

With the mechanization of large-scale production under capitalism, machines and other inanimate elements of production form a larger and larger share of the inputs to production. Marx believed this would result in a long-term trend of the rate of profit to fall as less of production depended on the enriching contribution of human labor. This, he believed, would make capitalism increasingly vulnerable to economic crises.

This chain of reasoning, of course, depends on the Labor Theory of Value (seeing workers as the source of the surplus value created in the production process) and can be avoided by rejecting this theory outright. Orthodox economics has not only rejected the Labor Theory of Value, but abandoned the issue of "value" altogether. After lying fallow for many years, value analysis was revived during the 1960s by a number of unorthodox economists including the Italian economist Piero Sraffa. Marx was not the last word on the subject.

UNEMPLOYMENT, PART I: THE "RESERVE ARMY OF THE UNEMPLOYED"

Marx is often raked over the coals for arguing that workers, under capitalism, were destined to be ground into ever more desperate poverty. That living standards improved in rich capitalist countries is offered as proof that his system is fatally flawed. While Marx was not optimistic about the prospect of workers raising their standard of living very far under capitalism, he was critical of proponents of the "iron law of wages," such as Malthus, who held that any increase in wages above the minimum necessary for survival would simply provoke population growth and a decline in wages back to subsistence level.

Marx emphasized that political and historical factors influencing the relative power of the major social classes, rather than simple demographics, determined the distribution of income.

One economic factor to which Marx attributed great importance in the class struggle was the size of the "reserve army of the unemployed." Marx identified unemployment as the major factor pushing wages down—the larger the "reserve" of unemployed workers clamoring for jobs, the greater the downward pressure on wages. This was an influence, Marx believed, that the workers would never be able to fully escape under capitalism. If the workers' bargaining power rose enough to raise wages and eat into profits, he argued, capitalists would merely substitute labor-saving technology for living labor, recreating the "reserve army" and reasserting the downward pressure on wages.

Though this has not, perhaps, retarded long-term wage growth to the degree that Marx expected, his basic analysis was visionary at a time when the Malthusian (population) theory of wages was the prevailing view. Anyone reading the business press these days—which is constantly worrying that workers might gain some bargaining power in a "tight" (low unemployment) labor market, and that their wage demands will provoke inflation—will recognize its basic insight.

> AS AESTHETICALLY APPEALING AS THE CLOCKWORK HARMONY OF THE ORTHODOX MODEL MAY BE, THIS IS PRECISELY ITS FAILING.

UNEMPLOYMENT, PART II: THE CRISIS OF OVERPRODUCTION

Marx never developed one definitive version of his theory of economic crises (recessions) under capitalism. Nonetheless, his thinking on this issue is some of his most visionary. Marx was the first major economic thinker to break with the orthodoxy of "Say's Law." Named after the French philosopher Jean-Baptiste Say, this theory held that each industry generated income equal to the output it created. In other words, "supply creates its own demand." Say's conclusion, in which he was followed by Smith, Ricardo, and orthodox economists up through the Great Depression, was that while a particular industry such as the car industry could overproduce, no generalized overproduction was possible. In this respect, orthodox economics flew in the face of all the evidence. In his analysis of overproduction, Marx focused on what he considered the basic contradiction of capitalism—and, in microcosm, of the commodity itself—the contradiction between "use value" and "exchange value." The idea is that a commodity both satisfies a specific need (it has "use value") and can be exchanged for other articles (it has "exchange value"). This distinction was not invented by Marx; it can be found in the work of Smith. Unlike Smith, however, Marx emphasized the way exchange value—what something is worth in the market—overwhelms the use value of a commodity. Unless a commodity can be sold, the portion of society's useful labor embodied in it is wasted (and the product is useless to those in need). Vast real needs remain unsatisfied for the majority of people, doubly so when—during crises of overproduction—vast quantities of goods remain unsold because there is not enough "effective demand."

It is during these crises that capitalism's unlimited drive to develop society's productive capacity clashes most sharply with the constraints it places on the real incomes of the majority to buy the goods they need. Marx developed this notion of a demand crisis over 75 years before the so-called "Keynesian revolution" in economic thought (whose key insights were actually developed before Keynes by the Polish economist Michal Kalecki on the foundations of Marx's analysis).

Marx expected that these crises of overproduction and demand would worsen as capitalism developed, and that the crises would slow down more and more the development of society's productive capacities (what Marx called the "forces of production"). Ultimately, he believed, these crises would be capitalism's undoing. He also pointed to them as evidence of the basic depravity of capitalism. "In these crises," Marx writes in the *Communist Manifesto*,

> there breaks out an epidemic that, in all earlier epochs would have seemed an absurdity, the epidemic of overproduction. Society suddenly finds itself put back into a state of momentary barbarism; it appears as if a famine, a universal war of devastation had cut off the supply of every means of subsistence; industry and commerce seem to be destroyed; and why? Because there is too much civilization, too much means of subsistence, too much industry, too much commerce...
>
> And how does the bourgeoisie get over these crises? On the one hand by enforced destruction of productive force; on the other hand, by the conquest of new markets, and by the more thorough exploitation of old ones.

This kind of crisis came so close to bringing down capitalism during the Great Depression that preventing them became a central aim of government policy. While government intervention has managed to smooth out the business cycle, especially in the wealthiest countries, capitalism has hardly become crisis-free.

While the reigning complacency about a new, crisis-free capitalism is much easier to sustain here than in, say, East Asia, capitalism clearly has not yet run up against any absolute barrier to its development. In fact, Marx's discussions (in the *Communist Manifesto* and elsewhere) of capitalism's irresistible expansive impulse—capital breaking down all barriers, expanding into every crevice, always "thirsting for surplus value" and new fields of exploitation—seem as apt today as they did 150 years ago.

MARX AS PROPHET

Marx got a great deal about capitalism just right—its incessant, shark-like forward movement; its internal chaos, bursting forth periodically in crisis; its concentration of economic power in ever fewer hands. Judged on these core insights, the Marxist system can easily stand toe-to-toe with the orthodox model. Which comes closer to reality? The capitalism that incessantly bursts forth over new horizons, or the one that constantly gravitates towards comfortable equilibrium? The one where crisis is impossible, or the one that lurches from boom to bust to boom again? The one where perfect competition reigns, or the one where a handful of giants towers over every industry?

In all these respects, Marx's system captures the thundering dynamics of capitalism much better than the orthodox system does. As aesthetically appealing as the clockwork harmony of the orthodox model may be, this is precisely its failing. Capitalism is anything but harmonious.

There was also a lot that Marx, like any other complex thinker, predicted incorrectly, or did not foresee. In this respect, he was not a prophet. His work should be read critically, and not, as it has been by some, as divine revelation. Marx, rather, was the prophet of a radical approach to reality. In an age when the "free market" rides high, and its apologists claim smugly that "there is no alternative," Joan Robinson's praise of Marx is apt: "[T]he nightmare quality of Marx's thought gives it … an air of greater reality than the gentle complacency of the orthodox academics. Yet he, at the same time, is more encouraging than they, for he releases hope as well as terror from Pandora's box, while they preach only the gloomy doctrine that all is for the best in the best of all *possible* worlds."

Resources: Joan Robinson, *An Essay on Marxian Economics* (Macmillan, 1952); "Manifesto of the Community Party," and "Crisis Theory (from Theories of Surplus Value)," in Robert C. Tucker, ed., *The Marx-Engels Reader* (W.W. Norton, 1978); Roman Rosdolsky, *The Making of Marx's 'Capital'* (Pluto Press, 1989); Ernest Mandel, "Karl Heinrich Marx"; Luigi L. Pasinetti, "Joan Violet Robinson"; and John Eatwell and Carlo Panico, "Piero Sraffa"; in John Eatwell, Murray Milgate, and Peter Newman, eds., *The New Palgrave: A Dictionary of Economics* (Macmillan, 1987).

September/October 2002

PROPERTY

WHO HAS A RIGHT TO WHAT AND WHY?

BY ARTHUR MACEWAN

In 1948, siblings Joseph and Agnes Waschak purchased a home in Taylor, Pennsylvania, in the midst of coal mining country. Within a few years, hydrogen sulfide fumes and other gases from the nearby mines and mine waste turned the Waschaks' white house black and stained all the internal fixtures yellowish-brown or black. The Waschaks filed suit for damages. According to evidence presented in the subsequent court case, the Waschaks and other area residents who were forced to breathe the gases "suffered from headaches, throat irritation, inability to sleep, coughing, light-headedness, nausea and stomach ailments."

Eric Freyfogle describes the *Waschak v. Moffat* case in his book *The Land We Share: Private Property and the Common Good* as an illustration of how changing concepts of property relate to the preservation of the natural environment. Eventually, the case worked its way up to the Pennsylvania Supreme Court. *Waschak v. Moffat* was not simply an instance of citizens challenging property owners, but of one set of property owners positioned against another. On one side were the Waschaks and others who claimed that the actions of the coal companies constituted a nuisance that prevented them from fully using their property; on the other side were the coal companies who wanted to use their mines as they saw fit. The court had to decide not *whether* property rights would prevail, but *which* set of property rights had priority.

In 1954, the court ruled that a nuisance existed only when the actions involved were intentional or the result of negligence. The coal companies, the court maintained, intended no harm and were not negligent because they were following standard practices in the mining industry. The Waschaks lost.

Four decades later, concepts of property rights and priorities had changed, as illustrated by a 1998 case in Iowa, *Borman v. Board of Supervisors,* also described by Freyfogle. In this case, the landowning plaintiffs wanted to prevent another landowner from developing a "Confined Animal Feeding Operation" (CAFO) that would involve thousands of animals generating large amounts of waste, odors, and other damage to the surrounding properties. Again, the dispute was between the conflicting rights of two sets of property owners.

The Iowa Supreme Court ruled in favor of the plaintiffs, agreeing that the nuisance that would be created by the CAFO would be an illegitimate interference with their property rights. The court did not deny that its ruling limited the property rights of the CAFO planners, but it gave priority to the rights of the plaintiffs. Moreover, the court ruled that the CAFO planners were not due any compensation by the state, even though it was preventing them from using their land as they chose and thereby reducing the value of that property.

What changed between 1954 and 1998? Many things were different, of course, including the fact that the earlier case was in one state and the later case in another. But the most important difference was that society's views on environmental issues had changed, evolving along with the development of a broad social movement to protect the environment. As a result, concepts regarding property rights changed. What had earlier been seen as legitimate action by a property owner was, by the end of century, viewed as an illegitimate degradation of the environment.

Property rights, it turns out, are not fixed. They change. They are a product of society and of social decisions. As society changes, so too do property rights. And the changes in property rights are contested, subject to political power and social struggle.

WHY DO WE PROTECT PRIVATE PROPERTY?

Although we often take property rights for granted, as though they are based on some absolute standard, in reality they are both changing and ambiguous. Moreover, many widely accepted ideas about property rights start to fall apart when we ask: Why do we protect private property?

For example, suppose a family has a deed on a particular field. Why do we as a society say that another family cannot come along, take part of that field, and sow and reap their own crops? Does it make any difference if the family with the deed has never used the field for any productive purpose, but has simply let it sit idle?

Or, for another example, suppose a pharmaceutical company develops a new antibiotic. Why do we allow that company the right to take out a patent and then prevent other firms or individuals from producing and selling that same antibiotic? Does it make any difference if the antibiotic is one that would save the lives of many people were it more readily available—that is, available at a lower price than the company charges?

Or, for still another example, what if a man owns a large house in the suburbs, an extensive apartment in the city, a ski lodge in the mountains, a beach house at the shore, two or three other homes at convenient sites, three yachts, a jet plane, and seven cars? Why do we prevent a poor man who has nothing—no home, no car, and certainly no yacht or jet plane—from occupying one of these many homes?

Perhaps the most common argument in favor of our protection of private property is the claim: We protect private property because it works to do so. That is, secure property rights are viewed as a basis for a stable and prosperous society. If people do not know that their accumulated wealth—held in the form of cash, land, houses, or factories—will be protected by society, they will see little point in trying to accumulate. According to the argument, if the pharmaceutical company cannot be assured of the profit from its patent, it will have no incentive to finance the research that leads to the drug's development. And if the state did not protect people's wealth, society could be in a continual state of instability and conflict.

> IF WE DETERMINE THAT THE LARGER GOOD OF SOCIETY DICTATES A CHANGE IN PROPERTY RIGHTS, THEN THE IT-WORKS-TO-DO-SO ARGUMENT PROVIDES NO DEFENSE.

As a defense of private property rights, however, this it-works-to-do-so argument is incomplete, as the *Waschak* and *Borman* cases illustrate, because it does not tell us what to do when property rights come into conflict with one another. This defense of property rights is also flawed because it is too vague, failing to provide a sufficiently clear statement of what things can legitimately be held as private property. Can air or water or people be held as private property? Can a patent be held forever?

What's more, the argument puts defenders of property rights in a precarious position because it implicitly concedes that private property rights exist in order to serve the larger good of society. If we determine that the larger good of society dictates a change in property rights—new restrictions on the use of property, for example—then the it-works-to-do-so argument provides no defense.

In many instances, property owners have claimed that environmental regulations infringe on their property rights. Property owners who are prevented from establishing a CAFO as in the Borman case, from filling wet-lands, from building along fragile coast lines, or from destroying the habitat of an endangered species argue that government regulation is, in effect, taking away their property because it is reducing the value of that property. And they demand payment for this "taking." Such a claim loses its ideological and legal force, however, in a world where property rights change, where they are a creation of society, and where the larger good of society is the ultimate justification for protecting private property.

While questions about property rights are surrounded by ideology, legal complications, and arguments about the larger good of society, at the core of these questions lie fundamental disputes about the distribution of wealth. Who gets to use a field, the extent of a pharmaceutical company's patent rights, the preservation of a rich man's houses—each of these examples illustrates a conflict over the distribution of wealth as much as it illustrates a complication of how we define and protect property rights. Property rights are the rules of the game by which society's wealth gets divided up, and how we shape those rules is very much connected to how we define the larger good of society.

PATENTS VERSUS LIFE

The relationship between property rights and the larger good of society has come to a head in recent years in the dispute over patent rights and AIDS drugs. It has become increasingly apparent that, when it comes to protecting the property rights of the pharmaceutical companies that hold patents on these life-saving drugs, it-*doesn't*-work-to-do-so.

In low-income countries, multinational pharmaceutical companies have attempted to enforce their patents on life-saving AIDS drugs and prevent the provision of these drugs at affordable prices. The matter has been especially important in several African countries where governments, ignoring the companies' patents, have taken steps to allow local production or importation of low-cost generic forms of the drugs. Large pharmaceutical corporations such as Glaxo, Merck, and Roche have fought back, and their resistance has received extensive support from the U.S. government. In 1998, for example, the South African government of Nelson Mandela passed a law allowing local firms to produce low-cost versions of the AIDS drugs on which U.S. pharmaceutical firms hold patents. The Clinton administration responded on behalf of the firms, accusing the South Africans of "unfair trade practices" and threatening the country with trade sanctions if it implemented the law. The drug companies have since backed off, seeking compromises that would allow access to the drugs in particular cases but that would avoid precedents undermining their property rights in the patents.

The conflict between patent rights and the availability of AIDS drugs, however, has continued and spread. In Thailand, for example, the Government Pharmaceutical Organization (GPO) sought permission from the country's Commerce Department to produce a drug, didanosine, for which Bristol-Myers Squibb holds the patent. In spite of the fact that the locally produced drug would allow treatment of close to a million HIV-positive people in Thailand who would otherwise be unable to afford the didanosine, the permission was rejected because the Thai Commerce Department feared trade retaliation from the United States. Instead, the GPO was only allowed to produce a form of the drug that has greater side effects. Early in 2004, however, Bristol-Myers Squibb ceded the issue. Fearing public outcry and damaging precedents in the courts, the company surrendered in Thailand its exclusive patent rights to manufacture and sell the drug.

These conflicts have not been confined to the particular case of AIDS drugs, but have also been major issues in World Trade Organization (WTO) negotiations on the international extension of patent rights in general. Popular pressure and government actions in several low-income regions of the world have forced compromises from the companies and at the WTO.

But the dispute is far from over, and it is not just about formal issues of property rights and patents. At its core, it is a dispute over whether medical advances will be directed toward the larger good of society or toward greater profits for the pharmaceutical companies and their shareholders. It is a dispute over the distribution of wealth and income.

"FREE THE MOUSE!"

Patents and, similarly, copyrights are a form of property (known as "intellectual property") that is quite clearly a creation of society, and the way society handles patents and copyrights does a great deal to shape the distribution of wealth and income. Acting through the state (the Department of Commerce in the United States), society gives the creator of a new product exclusive rights—in effect, monopoly control—to make, use, or sell the item, based on the general rationale that doing so will encourage the creation of more products (machines, books, music, pharmaceuticals, etc.).

The general rationale for these property rights, however, does not tell us very much about their nature. How long should patents and copyrights last? What can and what cannot be patented? What, exactly, constitutes an infringement of the copyright holder's property rights? And what if the rationale is wrong in the first place? What if patent and copyright protections are not necessary to promote creative activity? The answer to each of these questions is contested terrain, changing time and again as a consequence of larger political and social changes.

Beyond the issue of AIDS drugs, there are several other patent or copyright-related conflicts that illustrate how these rights change through conflict and the exercise of political power. One case is the Napster phenomenon, where people have shared music files over the Internet and generated outcry and lawsuits from music companies. This

battle over property rights, inconceivable a generation ago, is now the subject of intense conflict in the courts.

An especially interesting case where rights have been altered by the effective use of political power has been the Mickey Mouse matter. In 1998, Congress passed the Sonny Bono Copyright Term Extension Act, extending copyright protection 20 years beyond what existing regulations provided for. One of the prime beneficiaries of—and one of the strongest lobbyists for—this act was the Disney company; the act assures Disney's control over Mickey Mouse until 2023—and Pluto, Goofy, and Donald Duck until 2025, 2027, and 2029, respectively.

Not surprisingly, the Copyright Extension Act aroused opposition, campaigning under the banner "Free the Mouse!" Along with popular efforts, the act was challenged in the courts. While the challenge had particular legal nuances, it was based on the seemingly reasonable argument that the Copyright Extension Act, which protects creative activity retroactively, could have no impact now on the efforts of authors and composers who created their works in the first half of the 20th century. The Supreme Court, apparently deciding that its view of the law trumped this reasonable argument, upheld the act. Congress and the Court provided a valuable handout to Disney and other firms, but it is hard to see how a 20-year extension of copyright protection will have any significant impact on creative efforts now or in the future.

> WILL MEDICAL ADVANCES BE DIRECTED TOWARD THE LARGER GOOD OF SOCIETY OR TOWARD GREATER PROFITS FOR THE PHARMACEUTICAL COMPANIES AND THEIR SHAREHOLDERS?

"COULD YOU PATENT THE SUN?"

Indeed, in a recent paper issued by the Federal Reserve Bank of Minneapolis, economists Michele Boldrin and David K. Levine suggest that the government's granting of protection through patents and copyrights may not be necessary to encourage innovation. When government does grant these protections, it is granting a form of monopoly. Boldrin and Levine argue that when "new ideas are built on old ideas," the monopoly position embodied in patents and copyrights may stifle rather than encourage creativity. Microsoft, a firm that has prospered by building new ideas on old ideas and then protecting itself with patents and copyrights, provides a good example, for it is also a firm that has attempted to control new innovations and limit the options of competitors who might bring further advances. (Microsoft, dependent as it is on microprocessors developed in federal research programs and on the government-sponsored emergence of the Internet, is also a good example of the way property is often brought into being by public, government actions and then appropriated by private interests. But that is another story.)

Boldrin and Levine also point out that historically there have been many periods of thriving innovation in the absence of patents and copyrights. The economic historian David Landes relates how medieval Europe was "one of the most inventive societies that history has known." Landes describes, as examples, the development of the water wheel (by the early 11th century), eyeglasses (by the early 14th century), and the mechanical clock (by the late 13th century). Also, first invented by the Chinese in the ninth century, printing rapidly developed in Europe by the middle of the 15th century with the important addition of movable type. Yet the first patent statute was not enacted until 1474, in Venice, and the system of patents spread widely only with the rise of the Industrial Revolution. (There had been earlier ad hoc patents granted by state authorities, but these had limited force.)

Even in the current era, experience calls into question the necessity of patents and copyrights to spur innovations. The tremendous expansion of creativity on the Internet and the associated advances of open-access software, in spite of Microsoft's best efforts to limit potential competitors, illustrate the point.

The most famous inventor in U.S. history, Benjamin Franklin, declined to obtain patents for his various devices, offering the following principle in his autobiography: "That as we enjoy great Advantages from the Inventions of Others, we should be glad of an Opportunity to serve others by any Invention of ours, and this we should do freely and generously." Probably the most outstanding example of successful research and scientific advance without the motivation of patents and consequent financial rewards is the development of the polio vaccine. Jonas Salk, the principal creator of the polio vaccine, like Franklin, did not seek patents for his invention, one that has saved and improved countless lives around the world. Salk was once asked who would control the new drug. He replied: "Well, the people, I would say. There is no patent. Could you patent the sun?"

*   *   *   *

It turns out, then, that there is no simple answer to the question: "Why do we protect private property?" because the meaning of private property rights is not fixed but is a continually changing product of social transformation, social conflict, and political power. The courts are often the venue in which property rights are defined, but, as illustrated by the Pennsylvania and Iowa cases, the definitions provided by the courts change along with society.

The scourge of AIDS combined with the advent of the current wave of globalization have established a new arena for conflict over patent laws governing pharmaceuticals, and an international social movement has arisen to contest property laws in this area. The advances of information technology have likewise generated a new round of legal changes, and the interests, demands, and actions of a vast array of music listeners will be a major factor affecting those changes. With the emergence of the environmental movement and widespread concern for the protection of the natural environment, traditional views of how owners can use their land are coming into question. When society begins to question property rights, it is also questioning the distribution of wealth and income, and it is questioning the distribution of power.

Few realms of property rights can be taken for granted for very long. Whether we are talking about property in the most tangible form as land or property in the intangible form of patents and copyrights, the substance of property rights—who has a right to what and why—is continually changing.

September/October 2002

UNDER THE MARGINS

FEMINIST ECONOMISTS LOOK AT GENDER AND POVERTY

BY RANDY ALBELDA

For all the hype about welfare-to-work, most former welfare recipients are still living in poverty. It is true that, since the advent of 1990s-style "welfare reform," families no longer on welfare are earning more, on average, than those still on welfare. But more often than not, the jobs that former welfare mothers find don't provide employer-sponsored health insurance, vacation time, sick leave, or wages sufficient to support their families. In fact, the percentage of families who are "desperately" poor (with incomes at or below 50% of the official poverty line) has gone up since the mid-1990s, and so has the percentage of former welfare recipients who report hardships such as difficulty feeding their families or paying bills. And remember: All of this occurred during a so-called economic boom.

So why does the emphasis on work (and now marriage) continue to dominate the welfare debate? In large part, this is because the poverty "story" of the last 20 years—created and perpetuated by conservative ideologues and politicians—blames poor people for their own poverty. Women supposedly have too many children without husbands, poor black urban dwellers exhibit pathological behaviors, and liberal welfare policies—by expanding government spending and providing an attractive alternative to jobs and marriage—have made matters worse.

At least one group of theorists—feminist economists—says it isn't so. It is women's particular economic role in capitalism—as caregiver—that shapes their relationship to the labor market, men, and the state. Feminist economists have shown how having and caring for children affects the economic status of women—including women who are not mothers but are still relegated to poorly paid care-giving jobs. While their voices are largely ignored in research and policy circles, feminist economists' analyses provide the best understanding of the obstacles low-income families face and the range of policy options that might work.

WOMEN AND POVERTY

Almost everywhere, women are the majority of poor adults. Recently, a group of sociologists from several U.S. universities looked at poverty in eight industrialized nations. Using a relative poverty measure (half of median family income), they found that, in the 1990s, women's poverty rates exceeded men's in all countries but Sweden. Further, they found that single-mother poverty rates—even in countries with deep social welfare systems—are exceptionally high. (See Figure 1.)

In the United States in 2000, women comprised just over half of the adult population but constituted 61% of all poor adults. (The U.S. poverty income threshold is based on an absolute dollar figure determined in the 1960s and since indexed for inflation.) Toss in children, and the data are even grimmer; 16.2% of all children were poor, while over one-third of all single-mother families were poor. Together, women and children comprised 76% of the poor in the United States, far surpassing their 62% representation in the population as a whole.

Since the late 1950s (when the data were first collected), single-mother families in the United States have never constituted more than 13% of all families; however, they form just under half of all poor families. Figure 2 depicts the proportion of all families—and all poor families—that are single-mother families. The steepest increase occurred in the late 1960s on the heels of the War on Poverty, as poverty rates for everyone were falling.

ECONOMIC THEORY AND POVERTY

From Adam Smith onward, most economists have understood poverty by looking at labor markets, labor-market inequality, and economic growth. According to this approach, it is underemployment or the lack of employment—and the resulting lack of income—that causes poverty. A brief summary of the dominant economic theories in the last half of the 20th century illustrates the point.

Keynesian economic theory argues that the lack of demand in the economy as a whole leads to unemployment. When investors and consumers can't jumpstart the economy, we need fiscal or monetary economic stimuli to induce demand. It was this wisdom that has guided economists to promote economic growth as a way to reduce poverty, arguing that "a rising tide lifts all boats"—as, for example, during the Kennedy and Johnson administrations.

Marxian theorists say that, under capitalism, unemployment cannot be totally eliminated because it is a necessary component of capitalist production that serves to "discipline" workers. Unless we make radical changes to the economic system, there will always be families that are without employment and therefore poor.

Like Marxian economists, *institutional* economists also believe that economic outcomes aren't simply the result of pure market forces; cultural, social, and political forces also come into play. In the 1970s, economists Peter Doeringer and Michael Piore identified distinct labor-market segments. Younger workers, workers of color, and women tend to end up in what they call the "secondary labor market"—characterized by low wages, few promotional opportunities, and easy-to-acquire skills—more than other workers. These workers are particularly vulnerable to unemployment and hence more likely to be poor. The way to relieve poverty is to help these workers move into better jobs, or to create policies that make their jobs better.

These understandings of poverty offer little or no gender analysis—presumably what ails men is equally applicable to women. Analyses of insufficient (aggregate) demand, unemployment, and labor-market inequality rarely mention women or discuss how and why gender matters—unless feminist scholars provide them.

Neoclassical (mainstream) economists also argue that poverty is caused by lack of employment and low wages—but they consider workers responsible for their own wage levels. Workers who choose not to pursue education, training, or on-the-job experience will participate in the labor force less often than more highly trained and skilled workers, be less productive, and receive lower wages. Unlike the political economy theorists just discussed, many non-feminist economists—the most well known being Nobel Prize winner Gary Becker—have tackled the topic of women's lower wages. But they consistently conclude that women's lack of employment, or employment at low wages, results from rational individual choice. Only policies that boost incentives for individuals to invest in themselves (like tax credits for education) will alleviate poverty.

GENDER MATTERS

It is true that one reason women are poor is that they are not in the labor force or are underemployed. But while employment is an important underpinning to understanding poverty, it is not the same for women as for men.

Most economists who study labor markets assume that workers in capitalist economies are "unencumbered"—that they don't have significant constraints on their time outside of paid work. Encumbered workers are treated as a "special case"—worthy of examination, but understood and analyzed as an exception rather than the rule.

Since the beginnings of capitalism, however, female workers have almost always been "encumbered." And women's role as caregivers—their main encumbrance—has shaped their participation in the economy, as feminist historians and economic historians have shown. Historically, women's economic opportunities have been severely constricted, with race, age, and marital status sending important market "signals" about where women could or should be employed. For example, until the 1960s, many professional and some clerical jobs had "marriage bars," i.e., employers refused to hire married women on the assumption that they did

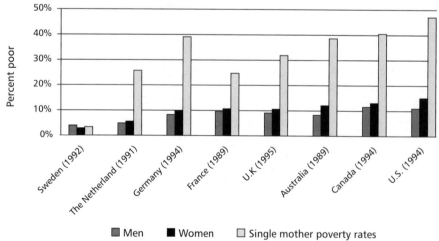

FIGURE 1
Percent of all poor non-elder men and women and single mothers in eight industrialized countries

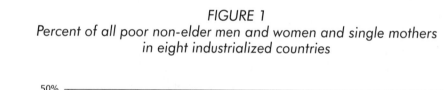

Note: Poverty rates are the proportion of non-elderly adults ages 25-54 whose after-tax and transfer family incomes fall below 50% of the median family income.

Source: Table 1, in Karen Christopher et al., "Gender Inequality in Poverty in Affluent Nations: The Role of Single Motherhood and the State," in Karen Vleminckx and Timothy Smeeding, eds., *Child Well-Being, Child Poverty and Child Policy in Modern Nations* (London: Policy Press, 2001).

not need the salaries these jobs paid, and would not stick around once they had children. Similarly, before anti-discrimination laws were enacted, many workers of color could not get jobs as managers in many professions, or even as sales clerks if the business catered to a white clientele.

For more than a century, this labor market "ordering" has given rise to employment, income, and wage policies that reinforce and reproduce women's political and economic dependence on men (and non-whites' inferior status in relation to whites). These policies assume that the standard family is a heterosexual married couple with a lone male breadwinner employed in industrial production. For example, in order to collect unemployment insurance benefits, workers must work a minimum number of hours and receive a minimum amount of earnings. Because many women work part-time and earn low wages, they are much less likely to qualify for benefits than men. Similarly, Social Security benefits are based on previous earnings over a sustained period of employment. Women who have spent most of their adult lives as caregivers are thus ineligible for benefits on their own, and must rely on their husbands' contributions instead.

Men's and women's employment patterns are very different. Women's labor force participation rates are lower than men's, and women's employment experiences in economic downturns often differ from men's. Women's job options and choices are also highly influenced by care-giv-

ing responsibilities; mothers are more likely than fathers to trade higher-paying jobs for jobs that are closer to child-care, have more flexible schedules, or require fewer hours.

In addition to shaping women's paid labor-market activities, care work has been economically, socially, and politically undervalued, as feminist economists point out. This is true both when that work is done in the home for free and when others do it for low pay. Among the few jobs immigrant women and women of color can almost always find are low-paying care-work jobs, and they are disproportionately represented in those jobs. For example, in 2001, women were 47% of all workers but 97% of child care workers, 93% of registered nurses, 90% of health aides, and 72% of social workers. Black workers comprised 11% of the workforce but were 33% of health aides, 23% of licensed practical nurses, and 20% of cleaning service workers. This type of occupational "stereotyping" reinforces the care-giving roles that women and people of color fill, and the low pay (relative to jobs with similar skill requirements) reinforces women's dependence on men and racial inequality. Economist Nancy Folbre, in her 2001 book *The Invisible Heart: Economics and Family Values*, calls this the "care penalty."

It is because of their low-paid and unpaid care work, then, that women are particularly economically vulnerable and much more likely to be poor than are men. The role of care giving—as distinct from other factors like employment, economic growth, and labor-market inequality—helps to explain not only women's employment patterns but also women's poverty. So theories of poverty that rely on analyses of employment that assume all people are men—or that women are a special case of men—are not only incomplete, they are wrong.

FEMINIST ANALYSES OF POVERTY

It is no coincidence that, when there has been a viable women's movement—in the early part of the 20th century and in the late 1960s—feminists and women researchers have paid particular attention to poor women.

Documenting poor families: early efforts
In the early 20th century, there was a good deal of concern about how women fit into the

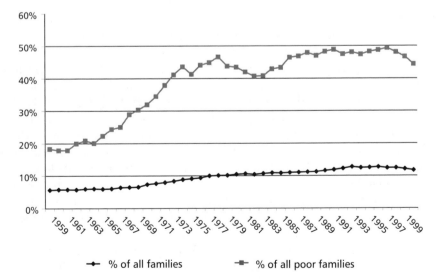

FIGURE 2
Female-headed families with children as a percent of all families and as a percent of poor families, 1995-2000

→ % of all families   ■ % of all poor families

Source: U.S. Bureau of the Census, *Poverty in the United States: 1999* (P60-210), pp. B-11-12 and for 2000: <www.census.gov/hhes/poverty histpov/hstpov4.html>.

capitalist economy. Social scientists living in or near poor communities—often in settlement houses established by women reformers—conducted surveys of women workers, mostly through government-sponsored research. Many of the surveys found that the biggest problems faced by two-parent families were a lack of employment and insufficient wages. Researchers readily recognized that families headed by women were constrained by women's role as caregiver and women's low wages. Instead of advocating more employment for women, they promoted relatively meager levels of public assistance.

In the 1910s and 1920s, women reformers were key players not only in doing research but also in creating policies directed toward poor women and children. These women imposed white middle-class values about child-rearing, hygiene, and education; their construction of "deservingness" replicated and reinforced the ways in which women and men, immigrants and non-immigrants, were supposed to act. At the same time, they successfully implemented income supplement programs for single-mother families at the state level, and they were instrumental in incorporating AFDC (Aid to Families with Dependent Children) into the Social Security Act of 1935. Feminist poverty researchers and reformers did not emerge again until the late 1960s.

Sisterhood may be powerful, but motherhood is not: recent efforts

The women's movement of the late 1960s and 1970s laid some important foundations for understanding women's poverty, even though its main economic strategies were aimed at improving the wages of women who were employed. Feminists fought for affirmative action, which was most successful in creating opportunities for college-educated women. Today, women hold 46% of executive and professional jobs—exactly their representation in all jobs—and comprise just under 30% of all doctors and lawyers. Feminists also organized for comparable worth, which was intended to lift wages for low-income women by recognizing and rewarding the skill level and effort needed to perform low-paying women's jobs (including care-giving ones).

At the same time, feminist scholars called attention to women's "double day" (now called "work/family conflict") and theorized about the role of care work and reproduction in capitalist economies. From the outset, feminist analysts understood that "housework" was work and a vital component of capitalist production. This intellectual work paralleled "wages for housework" campaigns that were launched in Italy, Canada, Great Britain, and the United States.

Using these tools to reinterpret poverty was not hard. Among the first to apply a feminist analysis to women's poverty was sociologist Diana Pearce, in an 1978 article entitled "The Feminization of Poverty: Women, Work, and Welfare." Pearce called attention to the fact that women were disproportionately represented among the poor. Her phrase—"the feminization of poverty"—became very popular in feminist circles as well as in the mainstream press.

Economist Nancy Folbre followed up with a theoretical framework directly linking women's care work as mothers to their poverty. In her 1985 article, "The Pauperization of Motherhood: Patriarchy and Social Policy in the U.S.," she argued that, when the costs of raising children are shifted onto women, women (and children) become dependent on men. Then, when fathers abandon their families, women and children are consigned to poverty. Folbre also argues that public policies around divorce, child support, unemployment insurance, and welfare reinforce this relationship. For example, welfare policies—even before the 1990s reforms—never provided enough income for women to support their families without working "under the table" or getting unreported income, paying a big price for not being married.

Single mothers especially bear the burden of these policies in the form of incredibly high poverty rates. But, Folbre points out, the benefits of care labor—healthy, productive children who become tax-paying adults—are enjoyed by all of society, not merely the mothers who provided the care. If society recognized the value of women's care work and compensated them for it, then fewer women would be poor.

Current trends

Currently, some feminist scholars are addressing the ways that gender influences government allocation of income supports (like pensions, unemployment insurance, and welfare) and non-cash assistance (e.g., education and child care). Sociologist Ann Orloff and political scientists Diane Sainsbury and Jane Lewis argue that state welfare policies (construed broadly) embody deeply gendered notions of citizenship and need. Much of this work is theoretical and does not explicitly address poverty. However, it helps to explain the lack of policies that would correct women's poverty.

Other researchers are focusing on how people's capacity—access to health and education, living conditions, how they are treated in a society—affects their potential to generate income and causes poverty. Building on the work of economist Amartya Sen, feminist economists in the United States have shown that it is unreasonable and unlikely to expect single mothers to "work" their way out of poverty—because women earn lower wages than men, because they have care-giving responsibilities, and because the additional costs associated with caring for children restrict their capacity to be employed even while family needs remain high. For example, Barbara Bergmann and Trudi Renwick developed budgets for low-income families in the 1990s. Chris Tilly and I have demonstrated that the income needs of single-mother families far exceed their earnings possibilities—even with full-time employment. This work refutes the claims of liberals who supported welfare reform in the naïve belief that welfare recipients could easily substitute earnings for public assistance.

Finally, feminist economists are documenting how low-income women—especially single-mother families in which the same adult is both caregiver and breadwinner—relate to the labor market, fathers, and the state. Using longitudinal data, feminist social scientists Roberta Spalter-Roth and Heidi Hartmann found that many poor single-mother families either combine government assistance with wages (under or above the table) or cycle between the two. This research is confirmed and extended by feminist sociologists like Kathryn Edin and Laura Lein, who, through extensive interviews with poor single mothers, documented the particular ways and times that poorly paying jobs as well as men and their incomes drift in and out of women's lives. These studies make it clear that women's employment is not family-sustaining, and that, to survive, single-mother families need a sane combination of earnings, child support, *and* government assistance. In contrast to the narrowly focused, incentive-based literature that characterizes poor women's behavior as pathological, these approaches demonstrate that poor women's lives are dynamic yet fragile, and that the decisions they make are creative, adaptive, and almost always child-centered.

WHO CARES?

Despite their efforts, feminist scholars have not had much impact on the poverty literature—at least not in economics—nor have they influenced policies intended to alleviate poverty. Much (though not all) poverty research is grant-funded, and it tends to focus narrowly on evaluating the individual impact of welfare reform, mostly by looking at welfare "leavers." These factors discourage the use of feminist analysis, since most funding goes either to conservative think tanks with a specific ideological aversion to feminism or to "liberal" think tanks that have made their fortunes in mainstream analysis fitted to their main consumer—the federal government.

Further, these conventional studies often preclude the larger political economy approach taken by feminists. Welfare reform is a mechanism of social control over poor single women—especially women of color—that is part of a larger conservative agenda to justify if not exacerbate economic inequality, assure a large pool of low-wage labor, and silence important political movements. Feminist analysis suggests the need for policies that would not only reduce poverty but also change women's (and people of color's) relationship to the labor market, (white) men, and the state, thus loosening the grip of economic dependence. This isn't in line with the right-wing agenda at all.

However, feminist economic analysis has been very useful to activists who are trying to help poor women. For example, in the mid-1990s, Wider Opportunity for Women (WOW), a feminist group based in Washington, D.C., started conducting family economic self-sufficiency stan-

dard projects. Currently, WOW operates projects in 40 states and D.C. The studies demonstrate how much income a single-mother family needs to survive, and are being used as organizing tools in the states.

During the mid-1990s welfare reform debates and now in discussions about reauthorization of Temporary Assistance for Needy Families (TANF), feminist scholars—connected informally through the "Women's Committee of 100"—have argued that raising children is work and that responsible legislation should recognize unpaid work as work. The Committee has called for a caregiver's allowances (see "Wages for Housework," article 1.5, and <www.welfare2002.org>). And while Congress has not embraced these ideas, a TANF reauthorization bill sponsored by Representative Patsy Mink (D-Hawaii) in the spring of 2002 garnered support from close to 90 members of the House.

Feminist economists argue that the role of economists is to understand how societies do or do not provide for people's needs. Through their research and skills, they provide the tools for activists to argue that women's employment status and care-giving responsibilities place many at the bottom of the economic pecking order. At the same time, feminist economists are connecting their work directly to social movements, lending their expertise—and their own voices—to living wage campaigns, efforts to improve compensation for child care workers and home health aides, and efforts to eliminate poverty, not welfare.

Resources: Kathryn Edin and Laura Lein, *Making Ends Meet: How Single Mothers Survive Welfare and Low Wage Work* (Russell Sage Foundation, 1997); Nancy Folbre, "The Pauperization of Motherhood: Patriarchy and Social Policy in the U.S.," *Review of Radical Political Economics*, vol. 16, no. 4 (1984): 72-88; Nancy Folbre, *The Invisible Heart: Economics and Family Values* (New York: The New Press, 2001); Jane Lewis, "Gender and the Development of Welfare Regimes," *Journal of European Social Policy* 3 (1992): 159-73; Alice O'Connor, *Poverty Knowledge: Social Science, Social Policy, and the Poor in Twentieth Century U.S. History* (Princeton, N.J.: Princeton University Press, 2001); Ann Orloff, "Gender and the Social Rights of Citizenship: The Comparative Analysis of Gender Relations and Welfare States," *American Sociological Review* 58 (1993): 303-28; Diana Pearce, "The Feminization of Poverty: Women, Work, and Welfare," *Urban and Social Change Review* (February 1978); Trudi Renwick and Barbara Bergmann, "A Budget-based Definition of Poverty with an Application to Single-parent Families," *Journal of Human Resources* 28, no. 1 (1993): 1-24; Diane Sainsbury, *Gender, Equality, and Welfare States* (Cambridge: Cambridge University Press, 1996); Amartya K. Sen, *Development as Freedom* (New York: Alfred A. Knopf, 1999); Roberta SpalterRoth et al., *Welfare That Works: The Working Lives of AFDC Recipients* (Washington, D.C.: Institute for Women's Policy Research, 1995); Chris Tilly and Randy Albelda, "Family Structure and Family Earnings: The Determinants of Earnings Differences among Family Types," *Industrial Relations* 33, no. 2 (1994): 151-167; U.S. Census, *Current Population Surveys* <www.census. gov/hhes/income/histinc/histpovtb.html>; Bureau of Labor Statistics, *Employment and Earnings*, Table 11 *www.bls.gov/cps/home.htm#charemp.§§*

CHAPTER 8

International Trade and Finance

INTRODUCTION

When it comes to the global economy, most textbooks line up behind the "Washington Consensus"—a package of "free trade and financial liberalization policies that the U.S. Treasury Department, the International Monetary Fund (IMF), and the World Bank have spun into the prevailing prescriptions for the world's developing economies. Mainstream textbook discussions of exchange rates, international trade, and economic development policies almost always promote a market-dictated integration into the world economy. Outside the classroom, however, popular discontent with the Washington Consensus has spawned a world-wide movement calling into question the myth of self-regulating markets on which these policies rest.

While the doctrines of free trade and financial liberalization are seldom questioned in mainstream economics textbooks, both are scrutinized here. Arthur MacEwan shows how industrialized economies developed by protecting their own manufacturing sectors—never preaching the "gospel of free trade" until they were highly developed. Today, he argues, these countries prescribe free trade not because it's the best way for others to develop, but because it gives U.S. corporations free access to the world's markets and resources, which in turn strengthen the power of business against workers (Article 8.1). Timothy Wise explores the perils of trade liberalization by looking closely at the liberalization-induced crisis faced by Mexican farmers of corn and coffee and their response to the crisis (Article 8.2) Jessica Collins and John Miller expose the deceptive arguments that corporate consultants and economists present to support financial and economic liberalization (Article 8.3). And Jim

Crotty and Kang-Kook Lee look at the East Asian economic crisis. Focusing on Korea, Crotty and Lee explain the causal role of financial liberalization in destabilizing the Korean economy, and the devastating impact of IMF-directed policies on workers (Article 8.9).

In later articles, MacEwan compares the IMF and World Bank (Article 8.5), while Sarah Anderson takes apart these institutions' claims that they are pursuing a new antipoverty mission (Article 8.6). The remaining articles in the chapter consider ways to truly transform the global economy. Ellen Frank examines the forces that have led developing countries into a debt trap and goes on to propose steps to prevent them from accumulating debt again (Article 8.7). In another article, Frank explains the ins and outs of the trade deficit and the threat that a record trade deficit poses for the U.S. economy (Article 8.4). Dara O'Rourke takes up efforts to combat sweatshop conditions in the world's export factories, discussing the difficulties of monitoring production in the global apparel industry (Article 8.8). In Article 8.10, Arthur MacEwan analyzes the role of oil in the U.S. invasion of Iraq. He argues that the war wasn't fought to supply the U.S. market, but to secure U.S. economic interests, including profits for U.S. oil companies.

We close the chapter with a debate about fair trade and farm subsidies (Article 8.11). Gawain Kripke, a senior policy analyst at Oxfam America, argues that fairer trade rules would provide enormous benefits to the world's poorest people. Dean Baker and Mark Weisbrot, co-directors of the Center for Economic and Policy Research, maintain that while ending agricultural subsidies for wealthy nations would make them less hypocritical, but it wouldn't do much to help the developing world.

DISCUSSION QUESTIONS

1) (Article 8.1) MacEwan claims that the "infant industry" argument for trade protection is much more widely applicable than standard theory suggests. To what countries and industries might it apply in today's world economy? Explain your answer.

2) (Article 8.1) Free trade, MacEwan argues, gives business greater power relative to labor. Why is this so? Is it a good reason to oppose free trade?

3) (Article 8.2) What was the impact of liberalization on Mexican farmers of corn and coffee? What does their experience suggest about appropriate policies for promoting agriculture and economic growth in the developing world?

4) (Article 8.3) How does the mixing of performance and policy variables in the Kearney report lead to misleading conclusions about the effects of globalization? What is the relationship of openness and liberalization to economic development and poverty alleviation?

5) (Article 8.4) What is a current account deficit and what

KEY TO COLANDER

E = Economics. M = Macroeconomics.

The articles in this chapter are linked to chapters E32-33 and E21, or M16-M18, which take up macroeconomic policies in developing countries and international policy issues.

Articles 8.7-8.11 fit with chapters E32-33 and E21, or M16-M18.

Article 8.1-8.4 critically balance the advocacy of trade liberalization found in most economics textbooks, and should be read with E21 and E33, or M17-M18.

Articles 8.3-8.5—explorations of what would constitute genuine reform of the IMF and the World Bank—go with E33 or M18.

causes it? When does a current account deficit become a problem? How problematic is the U.S. current account deficit?

6) (Article 8.5) In what ways do the IMF and The World Bank differ? In what ways are they the same?

7) (Article 8.6) Why have the IMF and World Bank felt the need for a "makeover?" Was it successful?

8) (Article 8.7) Why do poor countries find themselves in a debt trap? What are the perils of relying on foreign equity (stock) investors to finance economic development instead?

9) (Article 8.8) The anti-sweatshop movement demands that certain companies (such as colleges selling insignia clothing) see that the goods they sell are manufactured subject to certain labor standards. Explain what this movement is trying to do in terms of consumer sovereignty and solving information problems. When some economists say that the movement is about back-door trade protectionism, what do they mean? Do you agree with them?

10) (Article 8.9) What was South Korea's model of development, and what was its track record? How have the changes of the mid-1990s, and those after the crisis of 1997, affected Korea's economic development? Finally, why do Crotty and Lee doubt that the IMF-directed reforms have created a new Korean miracle?

11) (Article 8.11) Who do you find more convincing in the debate about fair trade, Kripke or Baker and Weisbrot? Do you think fairer trade rules pay off for poor countries? If not, what policies would do a better job of improving the lot of poor people in the developing world?

ARTICLE 8.1   *November/December 1991, updated July/August 2002*

THE GOSPEL OF FREE TRADE

THE NEW EVANGELISTS

BY ARTHUR MACEWAN

In the early 1990s, the passage of the North American Free Trade Agreement marked a new epoch of U.S. economic expansion into the Americas. Today, the chimes of "free trade" are ringing out even more loudly in corporate America, as neoliberal economic policies—such as the Free Trade Area of the Americas—continue to make their way around the world.

With his article, "The Gospel of Free Trade," published in November 1991, Arthur MacEwan helped Dollars & Sense readers to demystify the role of trade in the development of domestic economies. Drawing on the lessons of economic history, MacEwan shows that "free trade" is not the best route to economic prosperity for nations.

Just as British corporations cheered in favor of free trade in the 19th century, the largest U.S. corporations today are pushing to reduce restraints on trade and investment. The result: downward pressure on wages and social welfare programs in both rich and poor countries, and a reduced capacity of citizens across the globe to control their own economic conditions.

—Darius Mehri

Free trade! It's the cure-all for the 1990s. With all the zeal of Christian missionaries, the U.S. government has been preaching, advocating, pushing, and coercing around the globe for "free trade."

While a Mexico-U.S.-Canada free trade pact is the immediate aim of U.S. policy, George Bush has heralded a future free trade zone from the northern coast of Canada to the southern tip of Chile. For Eastern Europe, U.S. advisers prescribe unfettered capitalism and ridicule as unworkable any move toward a "third way." Wherever any modicum of economic success appears in the Third World, free traders extol it as one more example of their program's wonders.

Free traders also praise their gospel as the proper policy at home. The path to true salvation—or economic expansion, which, in this day and age, seems to be the same thing—lies in opening our markets to foreign goods. Get rid of trade barriers, allow business to go where it wants and do what it wants. We will all get rich.

Yet the history of the United States and other advanced capitalist countries teaches us that virtually all advanced capitalist countries found economic success in protectionism, not in free trade. Likewise, heavy government intervention has characterized those cases of rapid and sustained economic growth in the Third World.

Free trade, does, however, have its uses. Highly developed nations can use free trade to extend their power and their control of the world's wealth, and business can use it as a weapon against labor. Most important, free trade can limit efforts to redistribute income more equally, undermine progressive social programs, and keep people from democratically controlling their economic lives.

A DAY IN THE PARK

At the beginning of the 19th century, Lowell, Massachusetts, became the premier site of the country's textile industry. Today, thanks to the Lowell National Historical Park, you can tour the huge mills, ride through thee canals that redirected the Merrimack River's power to the mills, and learn the story of the textile workers, from the Yankee "mill girls" of the 1820s through the various waves of immigrant laborers who poured into the city over the next century.

During a day in the park, visitors get a graphic picture of the importance of 19th-century industry to the economic growth and prosperity of the United States. Lowell and the other mill towns of the era were centers of growth. They not only created a demand for Southern cotton, they also created a demand for new machinery, maintenance of old machinery, parts, dyes, skills, construction materials, construction machinery, more skills, equipment to move the raw materials and products, parts maintenance for that equipment, and still more skills. The mill towns also created markets—concentrated groups of wage earners who needed to buy products to sustain themselves. As centers of economic activity, Lowell and similar mill towns contributed to U.S. economic growth far beyond the value of the textiles they produced.

The U.S. textile industry emerged decades after the industrial revolution had spawned Britain's powerful textile industry. Nonetheless, it survived and prospered. British linens inundated markets throughout the world in the early 19th century, as the British navy nurtured free trade and kept ports open for commerce. In the United States, however, hostilities leading up to the War of 1812 and then a substantial tariff made British textiles relatively expensive. These limitations on trade allowed the Lowell mills to prosper, acting as a catalyst for other industries and helping to create the skilled work force at the center of U.S. economic expansion.

Beyond textiles, however, tariffs did not play a great role in the United States during the early 19th century. Southern planters had considerable power, and while they were willing to make some compromises, they opposed protecting manufacturing in general because that protection forced up the price of the goods they purchased with their cotton revenues. The Civil War wiped out Southern opposition to protectionism, and from the 1860s through World War I, U.S. industry prospered behind considerable tariff barriers.

DIFFERENT COUNTRIES, SIMILAR STORIES

The story of the importance of protectionism in bringing economic growth has been repeated, with local variations, in almost all other advanced capitalist countries. During the late 19th century, Germany entered the major league of international economic powers with substantial protection and government support for its industries. Likewise, in 19th-century France and Italy, national consolidation behind protectionist barriers was a key to economic development.

Only Britain—which entered the industrial era first—might be touted as an example of successful development without tariff protection. Yet, in addition to starting first, Britain built its industry through the expansion of its empire and the British navy, hardly prime ingredients in any recipe for free trade.

Japan provides a particularly important case of successful government protection and support for industrial development. In the post-World War II era, when the Japanese established the foundations for the modern "miracle," the government rejected free trade and extensive foreign investment and instead promoted its national firms.

In the 1950s, for example, the government protected the country's fledgling auto firms from foreign competition. At first, quotas limited imports to $500,000 (in current dollars) each year; in the 1960s, prohibitively high tariffs replaced the quotas. Furthermore, the Japanese allowed foreign investment only insofar as it contributed to developing domestic industry. The government encouraged Japanese companies to import foreign technology, but required them to produce 90% of parts domestically within five years.

The Japanese also protected their computer industry. In the early 1970s, as the industry was developing, companies and individuals could only purchase a foreign machine if a suitable Japanese model was not available. IBM was allowed to produce within the country, but only when it licensed basic patents to Japanese firms. And IBM computers produced in Japan were treated as foreign-made machines.

Today, while Japan towers as the world's most dynamic industrial and financial power, one looks in vain for the role free trade played in its success. The Japanese government provided an effective framework, support, and protection for the country's capitalist development.

Likewise, in the Third World, capitalism has generated high rates of economic growth where government involvement, and not free trade, played the central role. South Korea is the most striking case. "Korea is an example of a country that grew very fast and yet violated the canons of conventional economic wisdom," writes Alice Amsden in *Asia's Next Giant: South Korea and Late Industrialization*, widely acclaimed as the most important recent book on the Korean economy. "In Korea, instead of the market mechanism allocating resources and guiding private entrepreneurship, the government made most of the pivotal investment decisions. Instead of firms operating in a competitive market structure, they each operated with an extraordinary degree of market control, protected from foreign competition."

With Mexico, three recent years of relatively moderate growth, about 3-4% per year, have led the purveyors of free trade to claim it as one of their success stories. Yet Mexico has been opening its economy increasingly since the early 1980s, and most of the decade was an utter disaster. Even if the 1980s are written off as the cost of transition, the recent success does not compare well with what Mexico achieved in the era when its government intervened heavily in the economy and protected national industry. From 1940 to 1980, with policies of state-led economic development and extensive limits on imports, Mexican national output grew at the high rate of about 6% per year.

The recent Mexican experience does put to rest any ideas that free market policies will improve the living conditions for the masses of the people in the Third World. The Mexican government has paved the road for free trade policies by reducing or eliminating social welfare programs. In addition, between 1976 and 1990, the real minimum wage declined by 60%. Mexico's increasing orientation toward foreign trade has also destroyed the country's self-sufficiency in food, and the influx of foreign food grains has forced small farmers off the land and into the ranks of the urban unemployed.

THE USES OF FREE TRADE

While free trade is not the best economic growth or development policy, the largest and most powerful firms in many countries find it highly profitable. As Britain led the cheers for free trade in the early 19th century, when its own industry was already firmly established, so the United States—or at least many firms based in the United States—finds it a profitable policy in the late 20th century.

For U.S. firms, access to foreign markets is a high priority. Mexico may be relatively poor, but with a population of 85 million it provides a substantial market. Furthermore, Mexican labor is cheap; using modern production techniques, Mexican workers can be as productive as workers in the United States. For U.S. firms to obtain full access to the Mexican market, the United States must open its borders to Mexican goods. Also, if U.S. firms are to take full advantage of cheap foreign labor and sell the goods produced abroad to U.S. consumers, the United States must be open to imports.

On the other side of the border, wealthy Mexicans face a choice between advancing their interests through national development or advancing their interests through ties to U.S. firms and access to U.S. markets. For many years, they chose the former route. This led to some development of the Mexican economy but also—due to corruption and the massive power of the ruling party—created huge concentrations of wealth in the hands of a few small groups of firms and individuals. Eventually, these groups came into conflict with their own government over regulation and taxation. Having benefited from government largesse, they now see their fortunes in greater freedom from government

control and, particularly, in greater access to foreign markets and partnerships with large foreign companies. National development is a secondary concern when more involvement with international commerce will produce greater riches quicker.

In addition, the old program of state-led development in Mexico ran into severe problems. These problems came to the surface in the 1980s with the international debt crisis. Owing huge amounts of money to foreign banks, the Mexican government was forced to respond to pressure from the International Monetary Fund, the U.S. government, and large international banks. That pressure meshed with the pressure coming from Mexico's own richest elites, and the result has been the move toward free trade and a greater opening of the Mexican economy to foreign investment.

Of course, in the United States, Mexico, and elsewhere, advocates of free trade claim that their policies are in everyone's interest. Free trade, they point out, will mean cheaper products for all. Consumers in the United States, who are mostly workers, will be richer because their wages will buy more. In both Mexico and the United States, they argue, rising trade will create more jobs. If some workers lose their jobs because cheaper imported goods are available, export industries will produce new ones.

Such arguments obscure many of the most important issues in the free trade debate. Stated, as they usually are, as universal truths, these arguments are plain silly. No one, for example, touring the Lowell National Historical Park could seriously argue that people in the United States would have been better off had there been no tariff on textiles. Yes, in 1820, they could have purchased textile goods more cheaply, but the cost would have been an industrially backward, impoverished nation. One could make the same point with the Japanese auto and computer industries, or indeed with numerous other examples from the last two centuries of capitalist development.

In the modern era, even though the United States already has a relatively developed economy with highly skilled workers, a freely open international economy does not serve the interests of U.S. workers, though it will benefit large firms. U.S. workers today are in competition with workers around the globe. Many different workers in many different places can produce the same goods and services. Thus, an international economy governed by the free trade agenda will bring down wages for U.S. workers.

The problem is not simply that of workers in a few industries—such as auto and steel—where import competition is the most obvious and immediate problem. A country's openness to the international economy affects the entire structure of earnings in that country. Free trade forces down the general level of wages across the board, even of those workers not directly affected by imports. The simple fact is that when companies can produce the same products in several different places, it is owners who gain because they can move their factories and funds around much more easily than workers can move themselves around. Capital is mobile, labor is much less mobile. Businesses, not workers, gain from having a larger territory in which to roam.

CONTROL OVER OUR ECONOMIC LIVES

But the difficulties with free trade do not end with wages. Free trade is a weapon in the hands of business when it opposes any progressive social programs. Efforts to place environmental restrictions on firms are met with the threat of moving production abroad. Higher taxes to improve the schools? Business threatens to go elsewhere. Better health and safety regulations? The same response.

Some might argue that the losses from free trade for people in the United States will be balanced by gains for most people in poor countries—lower wages in the United States, but higher wages in Mexico. Free trade, then, would bring about international equality. Not likely. In fact, as pointed out above, free trade reforms in Mexico have helped force down wages and reduce social welfare programs, processes rationalized by efforts to make Mexican goods competitive on international markets.

Gains for Mexican workers, like those for U.S. workers, depend on their power in relation to business. Free trade and the imperative of international "competitiveness" are just as much weapons in the hands of firms operating in Mexico as they are for firms operating in the United States. The great mobility of capital is business' best trump card in dealing with labor and popular demands for social change—in the United States, Mexico, and elsewhere.

None of this means that people should demand that their economies operate as fortresses, protected from all foreign economic incursions. There are great gains that can be obtained from international economic relations—when a nation manages those relations in the interests of the great majority of the people. Protectionism often simply supports narrow vested interests, corrupt officials, and wealthy industrialists. In rejecting free trade, we should move beyond traditional protectionism.

Yet, at this time, rejecting free trade is an essential first step. Free trade places all the cards in the hands of business. More than ever, free trade would subject us to the "bottom line," or at least the bottom line as calculated by those who own and run large companies.

For any economy to operate in the interest of the great majority, people's conscious choices—about the environment, income distribution, safety, and health—must command the economy. The politics of democratic decision-making must control business. In today's world, politics operates primarily on a national level. To give up control over our national economy—as does any people that accepts free trade—is to give up control over our economic lives.

Resources: The New Gospel: North American Free Trade," *NAC-LA's Report on the Americas* 24(6), May 1991; Robert Pollin and Alexander Cockburn, "Capitalism and its Specters: The World, the Free Market and the Left," *The Nation*, 25 February 1991; P. Armstrong, A. Glyn, and J. Harrison, *Capitalism Since World War II*, 1984.

November/December 2003

FIELDS OF FREE TRADE
MEXICO'S SMALL FARMERS IN A GLOBAL ECONOMY

BY TIMOTHY A. WISE

In Cancún, Mexico, on the stifling afternoon of September 10, Korean farm leader Lee Kyung Hae scaled the police barricades, which were keeping 10,000 protesting farmers from storming the World Trade Organization (WTO) talks, and thrust a knife into his own heart. His self-sacrifice proved to be a catalyst for the disparate protesters and a solemn reminder of the toll trade liberalization has taken on the world's poorest farmers. When the talks collapsed four days later, it became clear that the ship of free trade had foundered badly on the shoals of its captains' hypocrisy on farm policy.

Mexican farmers provided the protests' largest contingent, and not just because the meeting took place on their own embattled soil. Based on their experiences under the North American Free Trade Agreement (NAFTA) and the free-trade model that it embodies, they had a lot to say. Farmers of maize and other grains, who produce for subsistence and for local and regional markets, have been hardest hit by liberalization, with imports from the United States driving prices down to unsustainable levels. But much of the export sector has suffered as well, with gains in industrial tomato farming more than offset by sharp declines in coffee, Mexico's most important export crop in both employment and output.

Mexico's small-scale farmers came together last winter to demand that their government renegotiate NAFTA's agricultural provisions and establish new policies for the countryside. While they have thus far failed to win a commitment from the pro-free trade administration of Vicente Fox to renegotiate NAFTA, last spring they secured new funds for rural development and a promise to assess the agreement's impact on small farmers and to take measures to defend and promote the sector. Whether the movement can hold Fox to those promises remains to be seen, but the farmers' rejection of the neoliberal model is here to stay.

A closer look at the experiences of Mexican farmers of corn and coffee—the country's largest domestic and export crops which directly support some 20 million of the country's 100 million people—illustrates the perils of agricultural trade liberalization. Farmers' responses to the crisis and their policy proposals present a useful starting point for an alternative approach to rural development, one that recognizes the limits of trade, the importance of domestic food sources, and the value of peasant production.

UNREALIZED PROMISES

Although some policy-makers still point to Mexico as a success story, there is a growing consensus that the free trade experiment—which began well before NAFTA's inception in 1994—has not lived up to expectations. Its failures are all the more striking given Mexico's indisputable success in transforming one of the world's most protected economies into one of the most open and in attracting the foreign investment needed to capitalize such a transformation. Since 1985, when Mexico began its rapid liberalization process, exports have doubled and foreign direct investment has nearly tripled. According to the promises of free-trade proponents, with inflation in check, Mexico should have reaped the rewards of liberalization. It hasn't. Growth has been slow, job creation has been sluggish, wages have declined, poverty has increased, and the environment has taken a beating. (See "Free Trade's Unkept Promises," p. 127.)

In many ways, Mexico got what NAFTA promised: trade and investment. Unfortunately, these have not translated into benefits for the Mexican population as a whole or into improvements in the country's fragile environment. And there is little question that rural Mexico has suffered the greatest decline.

NAFTA VERSUS MAIZE

When NAFTA was negotiated, Mexico's leaders promised the agreement would help modernize the countryside, converting low-yield peasant plots into highly productive commercial farms growing fruits, vegetables, and other export crops for the U.S. market. Farmers who could not modernize or export would be absorbed as workers into the rising export industrial sector and the expanding service sector. Sensitive to the important role of corn in Mexico's culture and economy—over 3 million farmers grow corn, triple the employment in the *maquiladora* export assembly sector—NAFTA included a 15-year phase-out period for corn tariffs along with strict import quotas. Such a phased "tariff-rate quota" system was designed to ensure a gradual transition to competition with more developed and highly subsidized U.S. producers.

Farmers were confronted with a far different reality. After negotiating these protections for its corn farmers, the Mexican government proceeded to throw them overboard. Citing supply shortages for basic grains, the government unilaterally approved imports over NAFTA's quotas and then declined to collect tariffs. The decision reflected the growing power of agribusiness interests within Mexico, which coveted access to cheaper and lower-quality U.S. corn. The livestock industry wanted cheap feed, the beverage industry sought inexpensive corn sweetener, and a growing processed-food industry wanted to reduce its input costs for flour.

The result was free-trade shock treatment for corn farmers. Instead of a difficult long-term adjustment to competition with U.S. farmers, they faced the near-impossible challenge of fully liberalized trade just three years into NAFTA. Imports doubled and the price of corn fell nearly 50%. At the same time, the Mexican government was phasing out its price-support system, the final step in bringing Mexico into compliance with the Uruguay Round Agreement on Agriculture (URAA). Though CONASUPO, the main government agency managing supplies and prices, did not fold until 1998, price supports for most crops were eliminated in 1989. Corn and beans saw support into the mid-1990s, though at reduced levels. Facing fiscal pressures after the peso crisis and bailout of the banking sector, the government also reduced other rural support and modernization programs.

Corn farmers and other grain growers responded with an aggressive effort to stay on the land. Their organization, the National Association of Commercial Enterprises (ANEC), brings together over 180,000 producers, mostly small- and medium-scale landowners working 25 acres or less and selling the majority of their produce in local and regional markets. ANEC has bought abandoned state storage facilities, developed its own marketing infrastructure, promoted regional trade, and fostered sustainable agriculture practices. It is estimated that members earn prices 10% to 12% higher than the free market can provide.

"We do not and will not accept that we are mere surplus, that we are not productive, not competitive, that we are a burden for the country," said an ANEC leader at the group's 2000 General Assembly. "We are productive now … we can be more productive in the future … but only if the role of the small and medium peasant producers is revalued." Despite ANEC's success in revaluing the contributions of small farmers, the import flood still threatens to drown many growers, with producer prices below the cost of production.

DISINTEREST AND DISINVESTMENT

The farm crisis is not simply a problem of imports, or even of the structural imbalances between the United States' industrial agriculture and Mexico's more traditional farming. In corn fields, those differences are stark, with the United States farming nearly four times the acreage at over three times the yield, resulting in eleven times Mexico's output. That glut of American corn, which is subsidized at a per-acre level at least triple that of Mexico, sells at less than half the price of Mexico's traditional maize. Such disparities prompted farmers' initial demand to exclude corn from NAFTA, a position the government later watered down to the 15-year tariff-rate quota and a vague U.S. promise to consider reducing its farm subsidies.

At the heart of the crisis, though, is a long-term structural decline in international prices for agricultural and other non-oil commodities. According to the World Bank, real prices for non-oil commodities have fallen by an average of 50% since 1980 to their lowest levels in a century. Global overproduction has been fed by rising productivity in industrial agriculture and the neoliberal mantra to export, export, export. For many developing countries, World Bank and International Monetary Fund policies have mandated a deepening dependency on a few commodities and a turn away from the diversification that characterized Latin American development strategies in the 1960s and 1970s. This dependency, in turn, makes countries particularly vulnerable when commodity prices fall sharply.

Small farmers are even more vulnerable when their government abandons them. True to its neoliberal ideals and its URAA commitments, the Mexican government dismantled most of the agencies that had bought and sold farm produce, provided credit and technical assistance, and administered price supports and subsidies. The percentage of the government budget devoted to agriculture fell by half, to just 4.6% of outlays. Farm subsidies dropped 58% in real terms. The promised modernization of Mexican agriculture through public investment withered on the free-trade vine. New irrigation, an explicit government goal prior to NAFTA, never materialized, with the amount of new irrigated land falling from 100,000 acres in 1991 to a post-NAFTA average of just 17,000 acres per year. Lending by both government and private-sector rural credit programs declined 75% after 1994, when NAFTA took effect, while rural bankruptcies increased sixfold.

Nor did foreign investment, the free-trade elixir for all development ills, step in to slow the bleeding. A paltry 0.2% of the $128 billion in foreign direct investment that flowed into Mexico from 1994 to 2002 went to agriculture. Just three activities—hog farming, horticulture (fruits and vegetables), and flowers—claimed 94% of that total, and almost 90% ended up in the two Mexican states that already had the most modern agriculture.

According to one government-commissioned study, overall investment levels as a percentage of agricultural GDP declined from a healthy 11% in 1980 to 6% in 1985, then dropped to 3% just prior to NAFTA's signing. They have remained under 2% since NAFTA took effect. If its goal was to modernize Mexican agriculture, the liberalization project has been a dismal failure.

WINNING THROUGH EXPORTS?

In a free-trade world it is almost a given that if you're not part of the trading, you're part of the problem. NAFTA's apologists could claim that Mexico's inefficient grain farmers were just not competitive in a market freed of distortions. As the cold logic of comparative advantage separated the high-value wheat (or, in this case, corn) from the uncompetitive chaff, they needed to find more productive uses for their labor or their land. With few prospects for efficiency gains on poor lands suffering disinvestment and a rural credit vacuum, farmers who wanted to stay in agriculture would have to switch crops and export.

For small farmers in Mexico's rugged highlands, coffee might have seemed a likely solution. It was already the country's largest export crop, and the second largest commodity export after oil. Before NAFTA, Mexico was the world's fourth largest coffee producer, and its shade-grown arabica beans were highly valued on the international market. Better still, there would be no competition with U.S. producers.

So much for economic theory. Mexico's coffee farmers have been living their own free-trade nightmare, and it has little to do with NAFTA. In 1989, the U.S. and Mexican governments pulled out of the International Coffee Agreement (ICA), a supply-management arrangement between major producing and consuming countries that had kept supplies and prices at relatively stable and sustainable levels. The target price had been $1.20 to $1.40 per pound. Such "market-distorting" schemes are proscribed by the Organization for Economic Cooperation and Development and the Agreement on Agriculture of the GATT (General Agreement on Tariffs and Trade), the precursor to the WTO.

The result was as predictable as it was devastating to small coffee farmers. Prices plummeted to below the costs of production (about $0.60 a pound in Mexico) as stored coffee flooded the market and free competition among producing countries bid down prices. Five years of low prices (1989-94) ended temporarily when destructive frosts in Brazil in 1994 and 1997 killed off coffee trees in the world's largest producing nation. But when Brazil's new, high-yield coffee plantations came back on the market, prices fell even lower.

The market was further glutted by the entry of Vietnam, which grew from a virtual nonproducer in 1990 into the second largest coffee producer in the world by 2000. The World Bank and other development agencies had heavily promoted coffee as a viable export crop for small farmers in Vietnam and elsewhere, offering loans and other inducements. It worked, but by 2000, depressed prices had even low-cost producers in Vietnam scrambling to survive. By 2002, even the lowest-cost producers were unable to recoup their production costs.

Mexico's coffee farmers were especially hard hit by the price drop. They grow some of the world's best coffee, but at costs higher than many of their competitors. The sector is dominated by small farmers on shady hillside plots, with yields lower than Brazil's ecologically damaging but high-yield plantations. And the Mexican government added neoliberal insult to free-trade injury by eliminating INMECAFE, the Mexican coffee institute that had marketed and promoted Mexican coffee from its 285,000 producers.

In one of Mexico's poorest coffee-growing states, the Coffee Producers of Oaxaca (CEPCO), a grassroots organization of nearly 30,000 small-scale producers from nine indigenous groups, responded to the crisis with an impressive array of independent initiatives designed to "appropriate the production process for the producers." The members created their own credit union, mobilized women farmers, and promoted direct sales from their collective to marketers and consumers in the fair-trade movement. CEPCO campaigns encouraged farmers to produce certified organic coffee, bringing substantially higher prices for some 8,000 member families.

International market prices now hover around $0.50 a pound (and producers usually get far less than that). Organic fair-trade coffee pays producers $1.41 a pound, a dramatic price premium. But while the fair-trade and organic markets are growing quickly, they still account for a very small percentage of the market—currently about 3%. As even the most ardent fair-trade advocates acknowledge, niche markets can't solve a worldwide overproduction prob-

FREE TRADE'S UNKEPT PROMISES

NAFTA took effect in 1994, but the "neoliberal" experiment began in the mid-1980s following Mexico's 1982 debt crisis. Ten years into NAFTA and nearly twenty years into neoliberalism, the track record, drawn from official World Bank and Mexican government figures, is poor:

- Economic growth has been slow. Since 1985, Mexico has seen average annual per capita real growth of just 1%, compared to 3.4% from 1960 to 1980.

- Job growth has been sluggish. There has been little job creation, falling far short of the demand from young people entering the labor force. Manufacturing, one of the few sectors to show significant economic growth, has registered only marginal net job creation since NAFTA took effect.

- The new jobs are not good jobs. Nearly half of all new formal-sector jobs created under NAFTA do not include any of the benefits mandated by Mexican law (social security, vacations, holidays, etc.). One-third of the economically active population works in the informal sector.

- Wages have declined. The real minimum wage is down 60% since 1982, 23% since NAFTA's inception. Wages in all sectors have followed suit.

- Poverty has increased. According to Mexico's most respected poverty researchers, the number of households living in poverty has grown 80% since 1984, with nearly 80% of Mexico's people now below the poverty line, up from 59% in 1984. Income distribution has become more lopsided, making Mexico one of the hemisphere's most unequal societies.

- The rural sector is in crisis. Four-fifths of rural Mexicans live in poverty, over half in extreme poverty. Migration levels remain high despite unprecedented risks due to increased U.S. border patrols.

- Imports surpass exports. The export boom has been outpaced by an import boom, in part due to intrafirm trade within multinationals.

- The environment has deteriorated. The Mexican government estimates that from 1985 to 1999, the economic costs of environmental degradation amounted to 10% of annual GDP, or $36 billion per year. These costs dwarf economic growth, which amounted to only $9.4 billion annually.

lem that affects far more producers than fair-trade consumers could ever sustain.

CEPCO's organic producers aside, most Mexican coffee farmers are in dire straits. Even high-quality arabica beans now receive low prices from international buyers. The national coffee farmer association in Mexico reports a 40% decline in coffee production in the past three years, a 55% decline in coffee exports, and a 70% decline in income from coffee sales. Many producers are letting the beans rot on the trees, since it makes little economic sense to harvest them. Clearly, if there is going to be a solution to coffee farmers' free-trade woes, it will come from a reversal of free-trade policies. An international coalition of coffee farmer organizations has called for a return to supply management and international assistance in keeping the lowest quality coffee off the market.

MOBILIZING FOR CHANGE

CEPCO's and ANEC's efforts have not been enough to reverse the overwhelming impacts of unregulated globalization and the Mexican government's abandonment of small-scale farmers. That is why coffee and corn growers have joined other farmers' groups in demanding policies and trade agreements that recognize and value the social, economic, and environmental contributions of small producers. Their demands are hardly radical, but their implications are entirely subversive to the neoliberal model. The farmers' movement has demanded:

1. A moratorium on the agricultural provisions of NAFTA, if not their renegotiation;
2. Emergency and long-term agricultural development programs;
3. Viable rural credit institutions providing adequate and affordable credit;
4. Government investment in rural infrastructure and communities;
5. Food safety and quality for Mexican consumers (a response to the importation of genetically modified corn from the United States);
6. Recognition of the rights of indigenous communities.

The April 2003 agreement with the Fox administration represented one important battle in a longer war. In the long run, the farmers' movement is demanding a return to an inclusive government development strategy in which trade and foreign investment are but two of many economic means to an end. They are not the ends in themselves.

If the WTO meetings in Cancún are any indication, farmers will continue to be a thorn in the side of the liberalization juggernaut. Via Campesina, an international farmer alliance that claims over 100 million members, put the issue front and center in Cancún. Arguing that agricultural products are more than just commodities and rural communities are more than just laborers, the group demanded that agriculture be removed from the WTO. They advanced the new concept of "food sovereignty"—the right of every country to decide how it will meet the food needs of its people, free of the strictures of WTO rules.

With negotiations on the proposed Free Trade Area of the Americas slated for November, we can look forward to further conflict. Current drafts include significant agricultural liberalization, following through on the U.S. promise that the Free Trade Area of the Americas will be a "NAFTA for the hemisphere." Before signing any deal, the peoples of Latin America and the Caribbean would do well to talk to Mexico's farmers.

Source: Timothy A. Wise, Hilda Salazar, and Laura Carlsen, *Confronting Globalization: Economic Integration and Popular Resistance in Mexico* (Kumarian Press 2003); Timothy A. Wise, "NAFTA's Untold Stories: Mexico's Grassroots Responses to Economic Integration," (Interhemispheric Resource Center, June 10, 2003); Charis Gresser and Sophia Tickell, "Mugged: Poverty in Your Coffee Cup," (Oxfam Int'l, 2002); Alejandro Nadal, "The Environmental and Social Impacts of Economic Liberalization on Corn Production in Mexico," (Oxfam GB and WWF International, September 2000).

September/October 2000

KNOW-NOTHINGS AND KNOW-IT-ALLS

WHAT'S WRONG WITH THE HYPE ABOUT GLOBALIZATION

BY JESSICA COLLINS AND JOHN MILLER

Protesters against globalization have no idea what they are talking about. At least that is the verdict of the mainstream press. According to their coverage, the "protectionist" labor unions and the "privileged, cause-happy" college kids that took to the streets of Seattle and Washington, D.C., were content to accept as gospel "the vaguest snippets of knowledge" about the economics of globalization, the World Trade Organization, the International Monetary Fund (IMF), and the World Bank.

"[The protesters'] tales rarely get fact-checked," complains Paul Krugman, the M.I.T. economics professor and *New York Times* columnist. "Nobody asks whether the moral of the story is really as clear-cut as it seems." Quick to dismiss the protesters' views as uninformed and illegitimate, Krugman would have done better to fact-check the mainstream media, which was itself guilty of recycling data uncritically and accepting as gospel the conclusions of the institutional powers themselves.

Take "Parsing the Protests," an article written by Thomas Friedman, the *Times'* star international reporter turned columnist, in anticipation of the April 16 Washington, D.C., protest. Friedman warned his readers that they would be hearing "much blarney" from the protesters. Under "facts you won't hear," Friedman provided his supposed antidote to the protesters' nonsense: the results from a recent study conducted by the A.T. Kearney Co., an economic consulting firm. The report proves, according to Friedman, that "globalization" promotes faster economic growth, higher standards of living, and greater political freedom. While he does note the downside reported by Kearney—greater inequality, corruption, and pollution—Friedman is quick to point out that, increased inequality notwithstanding, the economic growth he associates with "globalization" still results in decreased poverty.

Despite the appearance of evenhandedness and objectivity, the report contains, to borrow Thomas Friedman's phrase, "much blarney," including "snippets" that Fried-

man passes around uncritically. A.T. Kearney Co. itself is a for-profit research company with corporations for customers. It boasts a "distinguished 75-year history of helping business leaders gain and sustain competitive advantage." But the Kearney Co.'s stake in promoting "globalization" is a fact Friedman never shared with his readers.

INSIDE THE KEARNEY REPORT

To make the pro-globalization case, Kearney's Global Business Policy Council ranked 34 developed and developing countries on a scale from "globalizing slowly" to "globalizing rapidly" based on their scores on ten different indices. The report uses this "globalization ledger" to engage in some crucial sleight of hand. It passes off "the greater integration of the economies around the world," measured by their globalization indices, as the equivalent of free trade. By misrepresenting isolation from the world economy as the only alternative to free trade, the study preordains its pro-globalization (really pro-free trade) conclusions. Opponents of free trade have not endorsed isolation from the world economy as a development strategy since the early days of dependency theory some three decades ago.

The "globalization" debate is not about economic isolation vs. integration into the world economy; but about what policies allow a developing economy to most successfully engage with the world economy. The Kearney Co., Friedman, and other "globalizers" presume that engagement requires complete submission to the neoliberal policy agenda promoted by international capital, economic powers like the United States, and international agencies like the IMF. Opponents of "globalization" argue instead that a different form of engagement with the world economy—based on more democratic control of the economy, more protections for workers and the environment, and greater limits on the movement of capital—is likely to produce a more widespread and equitable form of economic development.

The Kearney globalization ledger fails to distinguish between these two different strategies for economic development in today's international economy. In one way or another, seven of the ten variables in its globalization index measure a country's *degree* of engagement with the world economy, but say little about the policies determining the *manner* of engagement.

TRADE, GROWTH, AND OPENNESS

One of Kearney's indices is a country's level of trade, the

combined value of its exports and imports as a percentage of Gross Domestic Product (GDP). This is an index used in many mainstream studies of globalization. Finding a positive correlation between the levels of trade and economic growth (measured as GDP growth per capita), the report cites this data as support for free-trade policies. All the data really mean, however, is that international trade and economic growth tend to move in the same direction. It says nothing about whether trade *causes* faster economic growth. You might just as well conclude that economies enjoy high levels of trade because other economic policies promote rapid economic growth.

Even if international trade does promote economic growth, this does not mean that "free-trade" *policies* (lower tariffs and non-tariff barriers to trade) cause growth. Japan's export boom during the 1980s would have registered high marks on Kearney's trade index. But Japanese authorities oversaw their boom not with the free-trade policies endorsed by the Kearney study, but with managed-trade policies, such as selective tariffs and export subsidies.

When economists address the current policy debate about globalization properly, the evidence fails to endorse the pro-globalization position touted in the Kearney study. In their exhaustive survey of the major studies on trade policy and economic growth, mainstream economists Francisco Rodríguez and Dani Rodrik find "little evidence that open trade policies—in the sense of lower tariff and non-tariff barriers to trade—are significantly associated with economic growth." By weighing down their globalization index with trade *performance* variables that say little about trade *policies*, the Kearney study manages to obscure this anti-free trade finding.

The same criticisms apply to the Kearney report's claim that "globalization" alleviates absolute poverty (measured as the number of people living on less than US$1 per day). Apart from the problems presented by their use of the World Bank's measure of poverty, the correlation between the report's "globalization" index and reduced poverty tells us little more than that economic growth is associated with lower poverty rates. Over the last 50 years, the most dramatic reductions in poverty have actually occurred in East Asia, among countries such as South Korea, Taiwan, and China, all of which have implemented extensive trade restrictions and relied on government intervention into their economies.

Beyond all the problems with its method, the findings of the Kearney study are downright strange. Their globalization ledger is highly misleading. Look, for instance, at two Latin American countries. Chile, identified as an "aggressive globalizer," has surely embraced liberalization. But at the same time, Chilean authorities restrict the free movement of short-term international capital, requiring financial investors to make a one-year interest-free deposit, in their central banks, equaling 30% of their investments. Mexico, a "stalled globalizer," has during the last two de-

cades adopted neoliberal policies. But when the Mexican economy sank into crisis, its trade performance deteriorated, causing several of its globalization indices to plummet. That hardly constitutes grounds for attributing Mexico's growth problems to a lack of openness.

The Kearney analysis of East Asia yields equally strange results. Part of the problem is that its globalization ledger ranks countries not by their absolute level of globalization but by the change in their globalization index. For instance, China is classified as an "aggressive globalizer" because it has recently liberalized its trade policies. But Singapore, the most global economy on the Kearney list, is only a "strong globalizer." Despite its recent liberalization, China is no poster child for the neoliberal agenda. It does not have a convertible currency, it maintains state control of its banking system, and it allows little foreign ownership in equity markets.

Even Kearney's comparison of different countries' growth rates is problematic. The report looks at two different periods, 1978 to 1982 and 1993 to 1997, and finds that its "rapid globalizers" grew more quickly than the other countries, especially during the later period. Looking over the longer period from 1970 to 1998 eliminates much of the association between a high "globalization" score and rapid economic growth. For instance, five countries from the Kearney report made the IMF's list of fastest-growing developing economies over the last three decades (with per capita income growth over 3.75% a year). Just one, China, is classified a "rapid globalizer" (though inappropriately). The rest came from much further down on the Kearney globalization ledger. Thailand was but a "moderate globalizer"; South Korea, a "passive globalizer"; Indonesia and Malaysia, "stalled globalizers."

ACCEPTING THE CHALLENGE

In its period of most rapid economic development, the half century following the Civil War, the United States imposed import tariffs averaging around 40%, a level higher than those in almost all of today's developing economies. During the 19th and 20th centuries, German and Japanese economic development depended on managed trade, not free trade. Even the World Bank, in its 1993 report *The East Asian Miracle*, acknowledged as much for the Japanese postwar boom. South Korea and Taiwan, whose key growth periods came during the 1960s and 1970s, faced a world economy with far less capital mobility and engaged that world with managed-trade policies—export subsidies, domestic-content requirements, import-export linkages, and restrictions of capital flows, including direct foreign investment.

In his *New York Times* article, Thomas Friedman challenges the critics of "globalization" to name "a single country that has upgraded its living or worker standards, without free trade and integration." As the above list suggests, every single one of today's developed countries did exactly that. You can file that under "facts you won't hear" from the mainstream media.

UNDERSTANDING THE TRADE DEFICIT

BY ARTHUR MacEWAN

Dear Dr. Dollar

Can you explain what trade deficits are? Who owes what to whom or is it just an accounting device?
—*Jack Miller, Indianapolis, Ind.*

I see that the United States has had a negative international trade balance for years. What happens to those dollars we've sent overseas?
—*Bill Clark, Chillicothe, Ohio*

f Americans collectively import more goods and services from foreigners than we export, we are said to have a *trade deficit*. Paying for the things we import accounts for most of the flow of dollars out of the United States. However, money flows out of the country for other reasons as well. The U.S. government provides foreign aid and supports overseas military bases; immigrants to the United States send dollars back to their families; foreigners who own U.S. businesses or financial assets take income out of the country.

When these factors are added to the trade deficit, the net outflow of dollars is called the *current account deficit*. In 2002, the U.S. trade deficit amounted to $418 billion, and the current account deficit totaled $480 billion. Data for 2003 is not yet available, but preliminary reports indicate the current account deficit will be at least $550 billion.

Once the dollars leave the country, three things can happen.

First, foreigners can use dollars to purchase U.S. assets: stocks, bonds, bank deposits, government debt, real estate, businesses. When Toyota buys land and equipment for a factory in the United States, when a British investment fund buys stock in a U.S. corporation, when a German bank purchases U.S. Treasury bonds, then the United States is said to be "financing" its current account deficit

by selling assets. In 2002, foreigners acquired $612 billion in U.S. assets.

The United States has run persistent and increasing current account deficits since the 1980s, and foreigners have used the dollars to stake significant claims on U.S. assets. At the end of 2002, the value of U.S. assets owned by foreigners exceeded the value of foreign assets owned by U.S. residents by $2.4 trillion. This is the reason the United States is often said to be a debtor nation, with a net debt to the rest of the world of $2.4 trillion. But this "debt" is denominated in our own currency. For that reason, it does not pose the same risks for the United States as developing countries with large debts—which must be repaid in dollars or euro—face.

OVER THE PAST FEW YEARS, THE DOLLAR LOST ABOUT ONE-THIRD OF ITS VALUE RELATIVE TO THE EURO.

Foreign central banks provide a second outlet for dollars that leave the United States. The dollar is the most widely used international currency, and many less-developed countries have sizable dollar-denominated debts. Governments sometimes hang on to whatever dollars fall into their hands, parking them in liquid assets like U.S. bank accounts or U.S. government bonds to earn interest. In 2002, foreign governments held almost $95 billion in dollar reserves, which they will use to cover future deficits, repay debts, intervene in financial markets, or simply to exert influence in negotiations with the United States.

If you've followed the arithmetic so

far, you will have figured out that in 2002, on balance, more dollars flowed back into the United States to purchase assets then flowed out. This allowed U.S. companies to buy assets overseas, almost $200 billion worth.

As long as the country's large current account deficit is financed by these capital inflows, it is not necessarily a problem. But a third possible consequence of the massive U.S. current account deficit is that foreigners will lose confidence in the U.S. economy and stop purchasing U.S. assets. If this happens, the supply of dollars in the global banking system will exceed demand and the exchange value of the dollar will fall.

Some people believe this is already happening. Over the past few years, the dollar lost about one-third of its value relative to the euro. This could signify that foreigners are shifting from U.S. to euro-based assets. If the era of dollar supremacy is indeed coming to a close, the value of the dollar will continue to fall. What this would mean for the U.S. and world economies is difficult to predict. A sustained loss of confidence in the dollar could have many potentially serious ramifications.

Imports would grow more expensive, infuriating our trading partners, who depend on the U.S. market for their goods. With less foreign demand for U.S. assets, stock prices might tumble and interest rates rise. United States-based banks and corporations would find it harder to buy foreign assets and expand overseas. The dollar has been in trouble before and, in the past, the U.S. government pressured other countries to buy or hold dollars and prop up its value. Whether other countries agree to this will depend, ultimately, on whether the United States and other major economic powers are still talking to one another.

THE IMF VERSUS THE WORLD BANK

BY ARTHUR MacEWAN

Dear Dr. Dollar:

Who are the people really running the IMF and World Bank? How do they get their money? And what's the difference between the two institutions?
— Charlie Tesch, Somerville, MA

The International Monetary Fund (IMF) and World Bank are run by their member governments, but not on the basis of one-country-one-vote. Instead, governments have votes based on the amount of money they pay in to the organizations. In this sense, they operate much like private corporations, except that the owners of shares are governments instead of individuals.

The U.S. government has by far the largest share of votes in both the IMF and World Bank and, along with its closest allies, effectively controls their operations. In 1998, the U.S. held 18% of the votes in the IMF and 15% in the World Bank. Together, the United States, Germany, Japan, the U.K. and France control about 40% of the shares in both institutions. With the rest of the shares spread among 175 other member governments, some holding a tiny number of votes, the United States is effectively in charge.

So the people running the IMF and the World Bank are the same folks who run the U.S. government and the governments of its closest allies. Since the institutions were founded at the end of World War II, the president of the World Bank has always been a U.S. citizen, and the head of the IMF has always been a European. These are all men, generally coming from the top of the financial industry.

While the IMF and the Bank operate as extensions of the U.S. government's foreign policy, they are well insulated from democratic accountability. Con-

gress, to say nothing of the populace in general, has no role in overseeing their operations, and they operate largely outside the public eye (though Congressional ire sometimes appears in response to a request for more funds).

What the IMF and the World Bank do is lend money to governments. Because many governments, especially governments of poor countries, are often in dire need of loans and cannot readily obtain funds through financial markets, they turn to these institutions. And if the IMF and World Bank will not loan to a country, international banks certainly won't. As a result, the IMF and the World Bank have great power, and are able to insist that governments adopt certain policies as a condition for receiving funds.

The IMF and the Bank make sure that U.S. allies get the financial support they need to stay in power, abuses of human rights, labor, and the environment notwithstanding; that big banks get paid back, no matter how irresponsible their loans may have been; and that other governments continually reduce barriers to the operations of U.S. business in their countries, whether or not this conflicts with the economic needs of their own people.

In the division of functions between the IMF and the World Bank, the IMF provides funds to governments in immediate financial emergencies and the Bank provides funds for long-term development projects. For example, when the financial crisis that developed in 1997 spread through several Asian countries, capital fled to safer havens. The values of local currencies fell drastically relative to the dollar. Governments (and private firms) whose revenues were in their own local currencies could not meet their dollar obligations to international bankers. This forced governments to turn to the

IMF for funds to maintain the values of their currencies and meet their obligations to international banks. Along with the loans, however, came conditions: the IMF's program for economic stability.

The World Bank may receive fewer headlines, not being on the spot in crises, but over the long run it shapes the economies of countries where it makes loans. Its loans cover a wide spectrum of projects, from large hydroelectric dams to local business training programs. Many of the Bank's programs appear desirable in themselves—who would object to clean water facilities, education in animal husbandry, or better roads? Yet the particular projects promote a development strategy that minimizes the role of the public sector, and demands the privatization of communal lands and other public property.

As to the source of their funds, the IMF gets most of its money as subscriptions from member governments—the amount determining the number of votes each government has in running the operation. When, in extreme circumstances, the IMF needs an especially large amount of funds, it can activate a line of credit it has established with governments and large banks.

The World Bank raises its money by taking loans from the private sector, operating through financial markets as would private firms or governments. Because the Bank is backed by funds from member governments, it can obtain private funds at relatively low interest rates. It then turns around and loans this money to the governments of poor countries to support development projects. In effect, the Bank allows governments of poor countries to borrow, through it, on the international capital markets and at lower rates than they could borrow were they to seek funds on their own.

THE IMF AND WORLD BANK'S COSMETIC MAKEOVER

BY SARAH ANDERSON

Medieval doctors always prescribed the same "cure"; no matter what the ailment, they applied leeches to patients and bled them. For the past decade and a half, critics have likened the World Bank and the International Monetary Fund (IMF) to these doctors. The two institutions have thrown millions of people deeper into poverty by promoting the same harsh economic reforms—including privatization, budget cuts, and labor "flexibility"—regardless of local culture, resources, or economic context. Strapped with heavy debts, most developing countries have reluctantly accepted these reforms, known as structural adjustment programs (SAPs), as a condition for receiving IMF or World Bank loans.

In recent years, the doctors' harsh medicine has been exposed in dozens of studies and in increasingly vocal street protests. In response, the World Bank and the IMF have been attempting to revamp their public image into that of anti-poverty crusaders. While the World Bank has long claimed a commitment to helping the poor, this is a real departure for the IMF, which has unrepentantly elevated financial and monetary stability above any other concern. Considering the two institutions' records, it is not surprising that the sudden conversion from crude medieval doctors to institutional Mother Theresas has provoked considerable skepticism.

MAIN ELEMENTS OF THE SAP FORMULA

Reducing the size of the state: The IMF requires that countries privatize public companies and services and fire public sector workers. While this may free up more funds to pay off loans, domestic capacity is crippled as a result. In Haiti, for example, the IMF admits that privatization of schools has seen extreme deterioration in school quality and attendance that will likely hamper the country's human capacity for many years to come. For example, only 8% of teachers in private schools (now 89% of all schools) have professional qualifications, compared to 47% in public schools. Sec-ondary school enrollment dropped from 28% to 15% between 1985 and 1997. Nevertheless, the IMF recommends further privatization in Haiti.

Balancing the government budget: Even though rich country governments commonly engage in deficit spending, the IMF and World Bank believe this is a big no-no for poor countries. Faced with tough choices, governments often must cut spending on health, education, and environmental protection, since these don't generate income for the federal budget. According to Friends of the Earth, Brazil was pressured to slash funding for environmental enforcement by over 50% after accepting an IMF bailout agreement in 1999.

Deregulating the economy: The World Bank and IMF continue to push for the elimination of trade and investment barriers, and for the export-orientation of poor countries' economies. Again, if poor countries increase their foreign currency earnings by boosting exports, they may be more able to repay international creditors. The people, however, will not necessarily benefit. The World Bank's own statistics show that, in many regions of the world, increased exports are not associated with increased personal consumption. For example, while export volume increased by 4.3% in Sub-Saharan Africa between 1989 and 1998, per capita consumption declined by 0.5%.

Weakening labor: The institutions have also ardently promoted so-called "labor market flexibility" through measures that make it easier to fire workers or undermine the ability of unions to represent their members. In the spring of 2000, Argentine legislators passed the harsher of two labor law reform proposals after IMF officials spoke out strongly in support of it. The IMF, backed up by the might of the global financial community, appears to have carried more weight than the tens of thousands of Argentines who carried out general strikes against the reform. Even though a recently released World Bank study shows a correlation between high rates of unionization and lower levels of inequality, the Bank and Fund maintain that they cannot engage in promoting labor rights because this would constitute interference in domestic politics.

Although the Bank and Fund have promoted SAPs as a virtual religion for nearly 20 years, they cannot even claim that they have achieved a reduction in the developing world's debt burden. Between 1980 and 1997, the debt of low-income countries grew by 544%, and that of middle-income countries by 481%.

THE IMF GETS A FACELIFT

In 1999, in response to increasing opposition, the IMF gave its Enhanced Structural Adjustment Facility (through which it made SAP loans) the new moniker of Poverty Reduction and Growth Facility. Both the IMF and World Bank announced that under their new approach, they would require governments seeking loans and debt relief to consult with civil society to develop strategies for poverty reduction. In addition, the institutions vowed an increased commitment to debt relief for the poorest countries. World Bank President James Wolfensohn expressed his pride in these efforts by commenting that he comes in to work every day "thinking I'm doing God's work."

Although most of the new poverty reduction initiatives are in an early stage, the World Bank and IMF have given plenty of evidence to support the skeptics:

Anti-poverty PR stunts: Nongovernmental organizations (NGOs) have raised strong criticism of the civil-society consultation processes that are supposed to take place as governments develop the required Poverty Reduction Strategy Papers. Sara Grusky of the Washington-based Globalization Challenge Initiative (GCI) doubts the value of "consultation" if countries will still have to accept the standard policies to get the IMF's "seal of approval." Carlos Pacheco Alizaga of Nicaragua's Center for International Studies says that civil-society consultation is restricted to narrow discussions of social policy. He argues that the process "tries to dilute the central discussion which is the lack of a new model of development for the impoverished countries and the creation of a new world trade system that should not be controlled by the rich countries of the north and the transnational companies." As of October 2000, only two countries (Uganda and Burkina Faso) had completed a Poverty Reduction Strategy Paper. Another 13 had completed interim drafts, but in several cases civil-society groups have reported either a complete lack of public consultation or mere public relations stunts that excluded groups more critical of Bank and Fund policies.

> THE WORLD BANK AND THE IMF HAVE BEEN ATTEMPTING TO REVAMP THEIR PUBLIC IMAGE INTO THAT OF ANTI-POVERTY CRUSADERS.

Debt rhetoric: A year ago, the World Bank and IMF initiated a joint plan, called the "Heavily Indebted Poor Country" (HIPC) initiative, to provide a measure of debt relief to certain countries that agree to structural adjustment conditions. The World Bank touts HIPC as an example of its "leadership to relieve the unsustainable debt burdens that stand in the way of development and poverty reduction."

The IMF may be more candid about HIPC's true goals. A statement on its web site identifies the main objective not as poverty reduction but rather the reduction of poor countries' debt burdens to levels that will "comfortably enable them to service their debt" and "broaden domestic support for policy reforms." As Soren Ambrose of the Alliance for Global Justice puts it, "HIPC is just a cruel hoax designed to trick developing countries into accepting more structural adjustment."

The World Bank and IMF have tried to tout the HIPC initiative as a permanent solution to the debt crisis by concocting wildly unrealistic predictions of the eligible countries' future economic performance. (As of October 2000, only 10 of the 41 countries had met the rigid HIPC criteria.) They estimate that export, GDP, and government revenue growth will average 7–12% in nominal dollar terms for the next 20 years—optimism that is completely unjustified by the countries' past performance.

Ecuador eruption: There is perhaps no stronger evidence of the continued havoc wreaked by IMF/World Bank orthodoxy than Ecuador. During the past year, indigenous groups, trade unions, and others have organized mass protests against a harsh IMF reform program that shifts the country's economic crisis onto the backs of the poor. In the midst of a general strike against the program in June 2000, a delegation of Ecuadoran human rights, women's, and trade union groups came to Washington, D.C., to ask the World Bank to postpone consideration of a new loan agreement conditioned on further implementation of IMF reforms. The NGOs argued that there had been a total lack of public consultation on the deal, which required low levels of social spending and removal of subsidies for basic goods, while ignoring the country's need for debt relief. Despite their pleas, the World Bank approved the loan package the following week.

Censorship: The dramatic resignations in the spring of 2000 of two high-level World Bank employees raised further doubts about the institutions' commitment to poverty reduction and civil-society participation. Former Chief Economist Joseph Stiglitz claims that U.S. Treasury Secretary Lawrence Summers and IMF bigwigs succeeded in pushing him out of the Bank in retaliation for his charges that the Fund's policies helped precipitate and worsen the global financial crises that erupted in mid-1997. Stiglitz pointed out that while reckless international investors and domestic banks caused the crises, the costs were borne by the workers.

Then in June, the editor of the World Bank's *World Development Report*, Ravi Kanbur, broke his contract, reportedly in protest over demands that he water down content that had been developed through extensive civil-society participation. Once again, Summers and other supporters of "free market" orthodoxy had allegedly intervened to quash the report's calls for economic redistribution, claiming that economic growth was the ultimate solution for poverty.

Although the final report released in September 2000 contains some strong language about the need to empower the poor, there is no indication that the institutions are willing to consider a substantial reform of their policies. One chapter, "Making Markets Work Better for Poor People," attributes all problems of economic collapse and poverty growth to deficiencies in "market access." The report implies that those former Communist countries that have been mired in economic collapse and stagnation should have followed the examples of the countries that implemented reforms "forcefully and early." This contrasts sharply with the findings of many researchers that the most successful former Communist countries were those that adopted a more gradual and cautious approach.

OLD LEECHES, NEW JARS

So far there is little evidence of a genuine conversion on the part of the IMF and World Bank. They have not fundamentally rethought their formula of "structural adjustment," nor their overall commitment to the "free market" model. The medieval doctors have just repackaged their cruel ministrations with warm and fuzzy labels. The challenge for critics is to keep up the pressure, exposing this façade and unifying around a concrete set of meaningful alternative goals and policies—real transparency, real democracy, and a real commitment to fight poverty.

ARTICLE 8.7

DISARMING THE DEBT TRAP

March/April 2001

BY ELLEN FRANK

Question: What if the International Monetary Fund (IMF), World Bank, and G-7 governments canceled the debts of the poorer countries right now, fully and with no strings attached? Answer: Within five years, most would be up to their necks in debt again. While a Jubilee 2000-style debt cancellation would provide short-term relief for heavily indebted countries, the bitter reality of the current global financing system is that poor countries are virtually doomed to be debtors.

When residents of Zambia or Zaire buy maize or medicine from the United States, they are required to pay in U.S. dollars. If they can't earn enough dollars through their own exports, they must borrow them—from the IMF, the World Bank, a Western government agency, or a commercial lender. But foreign currency loans are problematic for poor countries. If CitiCorp loans funds to a U.S. business, it fully expects that the business will realize a stream of earnings from which the loan can be repaid. When the IMF or World Bank makes foreign currency loans to poor countries—to finance deficits or development projects—no such foreign currency revenue stream is generated, and the debt becomes a burdensome obligation that can be met only by abandoning internal development goals in favor of export promotion.

Few poor countries can avoid the occasional trade deficit—of 93 low- and moderate-income countries, only 11 currently have trade surpluses—and most are heavily dependent on imports of food, oil, and manufactured goods. Even the most tightly managed economy is only an earthquake or crop failure away from a foreign currency debt. Once incurred, interest payments and other debt-servicing charges mount quickly. Because few countries can manage payments surpluses large enough to service the debt regularly, servicing charges are rolled over into new loans and the debt balloons. This is why, despite extraordinary efforts by many indebted less-developed countries (LDCs) to pump up exports and cut imports, the outstanding foreign currency debt of developing countries has more than tripled during the past two decades.

Many poorer nations, hoping to avoid borrowing, have attempted recently to attract foreign investor dollars with the bait of high interest rates or casino-style stock exchanges. But the global debt trap is not so easily eluded. A U.S. financial firm that purchases shares on the Thai stock exchange with baht wants, eventually, to distribute gains to shareholders in dollars. Big banks and mutual funds are wary, therefore, of becoming ensnared in minor currencies and, to compensate against potential losses when local currencies are converted back into dollars, they demand sky-high interest rates on LDC bonds. Thailand, Brazil, Indonesia and many other countries recently discovered that speculative financial investors are quick to turn heel and flee, driving interest rates up and exchange rates down, and leaving debtor countries even deeper in the hole.

If plans to revamp the international "financial architecture" are to help anyone but the already rich, they must address these issues. Developing countries need many things from the rest of the world—manufactured goods, skilled advisors, technical know-how—but loans are not among them. A global payments system based on the borrowing and lending of foreign currencies is, for small and poor nations, a life sentence to debtor's prison.

There are alternatives. First, there need to be far greater transfers of technology and productive resources from First World to Third World without expectation of payment. Second, when payment is expected, developing countries should be permitted to pay for foreign goods and services in their own currencies, rather than scrambling endlessly for the foreign currency they cannot print, do not control, and cannot earn in sufficient amounts through exporting. The United States routinely issues dollars to cover a trade deficit that will exceed $300 billion this year. Europe, too, finances external deficits with issues of euro-denominated bonds and bank deposits. But private financial firms will generally not hold assets denominated in LDC currencies; when they do hold them, they frequently demand interest rates several times higher than those paid by rich countries. The governments of the world could jointly agree to hold these minor currencies, even if private investors will not.

The world needs an international central bank, democratically structured and publicly controlled, that would allow countries to settle payments imbalances politically, without relying on loans of foreign currencies. The idea is not new. John Maynard Keynes had something similar in mind in the 1940s, when the IMF was established. Cambridge University economist Nicholas Kaldor toyed with the idea in the 1960s. Recently, Jane D'Arista of the Financial Markets Center and a number of other international financial specialists have revived this notion, calling for a global settlements bank that could act not as a lender of last resort to international banks (as the IMF does), but as a lender of first resort for payments imbalances between sovereign nations. Such a system would take the problems of debts, deficits, and development out of the marketplace and place them in the international political arena, where questions of fairness and equity could be squarely and openly addressed.

The idea is beguilingly simple, eminently practicable, and easy to implement. It would benefit poor and rich countries alike, since the advanced nations could export far more to developing countries if those countries were able to settle international payments on more advantageous terms. A global settlements bank, however, would dramatically shift the balance of power in the world economy and will be fiercely opposed by those who profit from the international debt trap. If developing countries were not so desperate for dollars, multinational corporations would find them less eager to sell their resources and citizens for a fistful of greenbacks. That nations rich in people and resources, like South Africa, can be deemed bankrupt and forced into debt peonage for lack of foreign exchange is not merely a shame. It is absurd, an unacceptable artifact of a global finance system that enriches the already rich.

September/October 2001

SWEATSHOPS 101

BY DARA O'ROURKE

Navy blue sweatshirts bearing a single foreign word, Michigan, and a well-known logo, the Nike swoosh, were piled high in a small room off the main factory floor. After cutting, stitching, and embroidering by the 1,100 workers outside, the sweatshirts landed in the spot-cleaning room, where six young Indonesian women prepared the garments for shipment to student stores and NikeTowns across America. The women spent hour after hour using chemical solvents to rid the sweatshirts of smudges and stains. With poor ventilation, ill-fitting respiratory protection, no gloves, and no chemical hazard training, the women sprayed solvents and aerosol cleaners containing benzene, methylene chloride, and perchloroethylene, all known carcinogens, on the garments.

It used to be that the only thing people wondered when you wore a Harvard or Michigan sweatshirt was whether you had actually gone there. More and more, though, people are wondering out loud where that sweatshirt was made, and whether any workers were exploited in making it. Students, labor activists, and human-rights groups have spearheaded a movement demanding to know what really lies beneath the university logos, and whether our public universities and private colleges are profiting from global sweatshop production.

WHERE WAS THAT SWEATSHIRT MADE?

So far, few universities have been able to answer these questions. Universities generally don't even know where their products are produced, let alone whether workers were endangered to produce them. Indeed, many apparel manufacturers cannot trace the supply chains which lead to the student store, and are blissfully ignorant of conditions in these factories.

As part of a collaborative research project funded by Harvard University, the University of Notre Dame, Ohio State University, the University of California, and the University of Michigan, I joined a team investigating where and under what conditions university garments were being made. Under pressure from student activists across the country, a small group of university administrators had decided it was time to find out more about the garments bearing their schools' names and logos.

The research team was asked to evaluate garment manufacturing for the top apparel companies licensing the logos of these five universities. We looked at factories subcontracted by nine companies, including Adidas, Champion, and Nike. The nine alone outsource university apparel to over 180 factories in 26 countries. That may sound like a lot, but it is the tip of the global production iceberg. Americans bought about $2.5 billion worth of university-logo garments in 1999. Overall, however, U.S. apparel sales accounted for over $180 billion. There are an estimated 80,000 factories around the world producing garments for the U.S. market. The university garment industry is particularly important not for its size, but for the critical opening it provides onto the larger industry.

The university research team visited factories in each of the top seven apparel-producing countries, China, El Salvador, Korea, Mexico, Pakistan, Thailand, and the United States. We inspected 13 work sites in all. I personally inspected factories for the project in China and Korea, and then inspected factories in Indonesia on my own to see what things looked like outside the official process. It was a learning experience I call "Sweatshops 101."

LESSON #1—GLOBAL OUTSOURCING

The garment industry is extremely complicated and highly disaggregated. The industry has multiple layers of licensees, brokers, jobbers, importer-exporters, component suppliers, and subcontractors on top of subcontractors.

The University of Michigan does not manufacture any of the products bearing its name. Nor does Notre Dame nor Harvard nor any other university. These schools simply license their names to apparel makers and other companies for a percentage of the sale—generally around 7% of the retail price for each T-shirt, sweatshirt, or key chain. Until recently, the universities had little interest in even knowing who produced their goods. If they tracked this at all, it was to catch companies using their logos without paying the licensing fee.

Sometimes the companies that license university names and logos own the factories where the apparel is produced. But more often the licensees simply contract production out to factories in developing countries. Nike owns none of the hundreds of factories that produce its garments and athletic shoes.

A sweatshirt factory itself may have multiple subcontractors who produce the fabric, embroider the logo, or stitch subcomponents. This global supply chain stretches from the university administration building, to the corporate office of the licensee companies, to large-scale factories in China and Mexico, to small-scale subcontractor factories everywhere in between, and in some cases, all the way to women stitching garments in their living rooms.

LESSON #2—THE GLOBAL SHELL GAME

The global garment industry is highly mobile, with contracts continuously shifting from subcontractor to subcontractor within and between countries. Licensees can move production between subcontractors after one year, one month, or even as little as one week.

It took the university research team three months to get from the licensee companies a list of the factories producing university-logo garments. However, because the actual factories producing university goods at any one time change so fast, by the time I had planned a trip to China and Korea to visit factories, the lists were essentially obsolete. One licensee in Korea had replaced eight of its eleven factories with new factories by the time I arrived in town. Over a four-month period, the company had contracted with 21 different factories.

Even after double-checking with a licensee, in almost every country the project team would arrive at the factory gates only to be told that the factories we planned to inspect were no longer producing university goods. Of course, some of this may have been the licensees playing games. Faced with inspections, some may have decided to shift production out of the chosen factory, or at least to tell us that it had been shifted.

Some of the largest, most profitable apparel firms in the world, known for their management prowess, however, simply did not know where their products were being produced. When asked how many factories Disney had around the world, company execs guessed there were 1,500 to 1,800 factories producing their garments, toys, videos, and other goods. As it turns out, they were only off by an order of magnitude. So far the company has counted over 20,000 factories around the world producing Disney-branded goods. Only recent exposés by labor, human rights, and environmental activists have convinced these companies that they need better control over their supply chains.

LESSON #3—NORMAL OPERATING CONDITIONS

The day an inspector visits a factory is not a normal day. Any factory that has prior knowledge of an inspection is very likely to make changes on the day of the visit.

In a Nike-contracted shoe factory in Indonesia I visited in June 2000, all of the workers in the hot press section of the plant (a particularly dangerous area) were wearing brand new black dress shoes on the day of our inspection. One of the workers explained they had been given the shoes that morning and were expected to return them at the end of the shift. Managers often give workers new protective equipment—such as gloves, respirators, and even shoes—on the day of an inspection. However, as the workers have no training in how to even use this equipment, it is common to see brand-new respirators being worn below workers' noses, around their necks, or even upside down.

At one factory the university team visited in Mexico, the factory manager wanted to guarantee that the inspectors would find his factory spotless. So he locked all of the bathrooms on the day of the inspection. Workers were not allowed to use the bathrooms until the project team showed up, hours into the work day.

Licensees and subcontractors often try to subvert monitoring. They block auditors from inspecting on certain days or from visiting certain parts of a plant, claim production has moved, feign ignorance of factory locations, keep multiple sets of books on wages and hours, coach workers on responses to interviews, and threaten workers against complaining to inspectors.

LESSON #4—CONDITIONS IN UNIVERSITY FACTORIES

Factories producing university apparel often violate local laws and university codes of conduct on maximum hours of work, minimum and overtime wages, freedom of association, and health and safety protections.

In a 300-worker apparel plant in Shanghai, the university team found that many of the workers were working far in excess of maximum overtime laws. A quick review of timecards found women working over 315 hours in a month and 20 consecutive days without a day off. The legal maximum in China is only 204 hours per month, with one day off in seven. A sample of 25 workers showed that the average overtime worked was 101 hours, while the legal limit is 36 hours per month. One manager explained these gross violations with a shrug, saying, "Timecards are just used to make sure workers show up on time. Workers are actually paid based on a piece rate system."

The factory also had a wide range of health and safety problems, including a lack of machine guarding on sewing and cutting machines, high levels of cotton dust in one section of the plant, several blocked aisles and fire exits, no running water in certain toilets, no information for workers on the hazardous chemicals they were using, and a lack of protective equipment for the workers.

Living conditions for the workers who lived in a dormitory on site were also poor. The dormitory had 12 women packed into each room on six bunk beds. Each floor had four rooms (48 women) and only one bathroom. These bathrooms had only two shower heads and four toilet stalls each, and no dividers between them.

And what of workers' rights to complain or demand bet-

ter conditions? The union in this factory was openly being run by the management. While 70% of workers were "members" of the union, one manager explained, "We don't have U.S.-style unions here." No workers had ever tried to take control of this group or to form an independent union.

LESSON #5—THE CHALLENGES OF MONITORING

Finding a dozen factories is relatively easy compared to the job of tracking the thousands of rapidly changing factories that produce university goods each year. Systematically monitoring and evaluating their practices on wages, hours, discrimination, and health and safety issues is an even bigger challenge.

Most universities don't have the capacity to individually monitor the conditions in "their" factories, so some are joining together to create cooperative monitoring programs. The concept behind "independent monitoring" is to have a consulting firm or non-governmental organization inspect and evaluate a factory's compliance with a code of conduct. Two major monitoring systems, and a number of less influential initiatives, have recently been developed to meet the need for university monitoring. The Fair Labor Association (FLA) now has over 140 universities as members, and the Worker Rights Consortium (WRC) has over 55 member universities.

The FLA emerged from the Clinton-convened "White House Apparel Industry Partnership" in 1998. It is supported by a small group of apparel companies including Nike, Reebok, Adidas, Levi-Strauss, Liz Claiborne, and Philips Van Heusen. Students and labor-rights advocates have criticized the group for being an industry-dominated organization that allows companies to monitor only 10% of their factories, to use monitors that the companies pay directly, to control when and where monitors inspect, and to significantly restrict the information released to the public after the audits.

United Students Against Sweatshops (USAS) and UNITE (the largest garment-workers' union in the United States) founded the WRC in 1999 as an alternative to the FLA. The WRC promotes systems for verifying factory conditions after workers have complained or after inspections have occurred, as well as greater public disclosure of conditions. The WRC differs from the FLA in that it refuses to certify that any company meets some code of conduct. The group argues that because of the problems of monitoring, it is simply not possible to systematically monitor or certify a company's compliance. The WRC has been criticized by some universities and companies as being a haphazard "gotcha" monitoring system whose governing body excludes the very companies that must be part of solving these problems.

Both groups profess to support the International Labour Organization's core labor standards, including upholding workers' rights to freedom of association and collective bargaining, and prohibiting forced labor, child labor, and discrimination in the workplace. The WRC, however, goes further in requiring that workers be paid a "living wage," and that women's rights receive particular attention. Both programs assert a strong role for local NGOs, unions, and workers. However, the two have widely varying levels of transparency and public disclosure, and very different systems of sanctions and penalties.

LESSON #6—HOW NOT TO MONITOR

Corporate-sponsored monitoring systems seem almost designed to miss the most critical issues in the factories they inspect. Auditors often act as if they are on the side of management rather than the workers.

PricewaterhouseCoopers (PwC) is the largest private monitor of codes of conduct and corporate labor practices in the world. The company claims to have performed over 6,000 factory audits in 1999, including monitoring for Nike, Disney, Walmart, and the Gap. PwC monitors for many of the top university licensees, and was hired as the monitor for the university project.

PwC's monitoring systems are representative of current corporate monitoring efforts. The firm sends two auditors—who are actually financial accountants with minimal training on labor issues—into each factory for eight hours. The auditors use a checklist and a standard interview form to evaluate legal compliance, wages and benefits, working hours, freedom of association and collective bargaining, child labor, forced labor, disciplinary practices, and health and safety.

On the university project, PwC auditors failed to adequately examine any major issue in the factories I saw them inspect. In factories in Korea and Indonesia, PwC auditors completely missed exposure to toxic chemicals, something which could eventually cost workers their lives from cancer. In Korea, the auditors saw no problem in managers violating overtime wage laws. In China, the auditors went so far as to recommend ways for the managers to circumvent local laws on overtime hours, essentially providing advice on how to break university codes of conduct. And the auditors in Korea simply skipped the questions on workers' right to organize in their worker interviews, explaining, "They don't have a union in this factory, so those questions aren't relevant."

The PwC auditing method is biased towards managers. Before an inspection, PwC auditors send managers a questionnaire explaining what will be inspected. They prep managers at an opening meeting before each inspection. In the Chinese factory, they asked managers to enter wages and hours data into the PwC spreadsheet. Even the worker interviews were biased towards the managers. PwC auditors asked the managers to help them select workers to be interviewed, had the managers bring their personnel files, and then had the managers bring the workers into the office used for the interviews. The managers knew who was being interviewed, for how long, and on what issues. Workers knew this as well, and answered questions accordingly.

The final reports that PwC delivered to its clients gave a totally sanitized picture of the factories inspected. This is unsurprising, considering PwC stands to make huge amounts of money by providing companies with safe and comfortable audits.

WHERE TO BEGIN?

Universities face increasing public pressure to guarantee that workers are not being injured or exploited to produce their insignia products. They have no system, however, to track apparel production around the world, and often no idea where their production is occurring. Monitoring systems are still in their fledgling stages, so the universities are starting from a difficult position, albeit one they have profited from for years.

What can universities do about this? They should do what they are best at: produce information. They should take the lead in demanding that corporations—beginning with those they do business with—open themselves up to public inspection and evaluation. Universities have done this before, such as during the anti-apartheid campaign for South Africa. By doing this on the sweatshop issue, universities could spur a critical dialogue on labor issues around the world.

To start, the universities could establish a central coordinating office to collect and compare information on factory performance for member universities' licensees. (The WRC has proposed such a model.) This new office would be responsible for keeping records on licensee compliance, for making this information available over the Internet, for registering local NGOs and worker organizations to conduct independent verifications of factory conditions, and for assessing sanctions.

Such a program would allow universities to evaluate different strategies for improving conditions in different parts of the world. This would avoid the danger of locking in one code of conduct or one certification system. In place of sporadic media exposés embarrassing one company at a time, we would have an international system of disclosure and learning—benchmarking good performers, identifying and targeting the worst performers, and motivating improvements.

It is clearly no longer enough to expose one company at a time, or to count on industry-paid consulting firms. The building blocks of a new system depend on information. This fits the mission of universities. Universities should focus on information gathering and dissemination, and most importantly, on learning. If the universities learn nothing else from "Sweatshops 101," they should learn that they still have a lot of homework do to—and that their next test will be coming soon.

July/August 2001

KOREA'S NEOLIBERAL RESTRUCTURING

MIRACLE OR DISASTER?

BY JIM CROTTY AND KANG-KOOK LEE

Over the last two years, Korea's economy has recovered from the 1997 East Asian economic crisis faster than anyone expected. Indeed, Korea has become the new poster child for the "free-market" or "neoliberal" economic restructuring the International Monetary Fund (IMF) is peddling to a suspicious public in the developing world. In early 2000 the IMF touted Korea's "dramatic turnaround" after the crisis. Not only was Korea's output above what it had been before the crisis but, the IMF gleefully proclaimed, "over the past two years bold policies and a commitment to reform have made Korea a more open, competitive, and market driven economy."

There is a more pessimistic interpretation of Korea's experience under IMF and U.S.-sponsored economic restructuring since late 1997. The harsh policies the IMF imposed on Korea immediately after the start of the Asian crisis actually caused the Korean economy's 1998 collapse. Now, three years later, Korea faces an unbalanced recovery of questionable durability and a labor movement badly, perhaps fatally, wounded by neoliberalism, while the majority of its people suffer rising insecurity and falling incomes. If the IMF and the U.S. government succeed in their drive to transform Korea from an East Asian-style state-guided economy to a market-driven, "globalized" economy, future progressive political movements will find it exceedingly difficult to create an efficient, egalitarian economic system designed to meet the needs of the majority of its people.

THE RISE AND FALL OF KOREA'S "EAST ASIAN" ECONOMIC MODEL

Following a 1961 coup, Korea's new military dictatorship adopted the economic development program pioneered by Japan that came to be known as the "East Asian Model."

The government took control over the broad contours of economic life, guiding and regulating markets to achieve government development goals. It decided what new industries and technologies would receive priority, allocated financial capital to support these decisions, and regulated investment spending by powerful Korean conglomerates known as *chaebol*. Most important, the government tightly controlled the movement of money into and out of Korea.

Under state guidance, Korea became one of East Asia's "miracle" economies. Though the authoritarian government severely repressed the labor movement, Korea's economic performance was outstanding. From 1961 through 1996, real GDP growth averaged 8% a year. And the fruits of this incredible growth were widely shared. Real wages grew by 7% a year during this 35-year period. Renowned Cambridge University economist Ajit Singh called the East Asian model "the most successful economic development model in the history of the world."

About a decade ago, under intense pressure from the United States and the IMF, the Korean government began to relinquish its control over key economic processes. By the mid-1990s, it let firms invest as they pleased, reduced regulation of domestic bank activity, and let foreign banks and investors run short-term or "hot" money into and out of the country. Short-term foreign bank loans exploded between 1993 and 1996, fueling an overheated investment boom. When it became clear in 1997 that the boom was over, these banks pulled out, demanding immediate repayment of some $60 billion in short-term loans, which pushed the Korean banking system near bankruptcy. The banks, in turn, cut loans to highly indebted domestic corporations, forcing them toward the brink of insolvency. Korea borrowed money from the IMF to pay its foreign creditors and, in return, the IMF took effective control of the Korean economy, immediately imposing high interest rates and tight budgets to help restore foreign investor "confidence." These policies pushed the weakened economy over the edge, into 1998's state of collapse.

The Korean crisis occurred because the government stopped performing its traditional economic functions, making the economy vulnerable for the first time to volatile international financial flows. Yet the IMF did not urge Korea to restore control over capital flows to protect against another crisis. Instead, it took advantage of Korea's weakness to destroy what remained of its East Asian structure and replace it with a market-driven neoliberal system. Strong laws protecting job security were replaced by fire-at-will legislation. Remaining barriers to the entry of foreign goods, money, and corporate investment were eliminated. In the neoliberal future, global markets would make all important economic decisions without interference from the government.

THE NOT-SO-MIRACULOUS RECOVERY

It is not hard to assemble evidence in support of the IMF's triumphalist view of Korea's recovery. After falling almost 7% in 1998, Korea's real GDP grew over 10% in 1999, and about 9% in 2000. The rate of unemployment, which averaged just 2% prior to the crisis, peaked at over 8% in early 1999, but dipped below 4% again in 2000. In 1996, the trade deficit stood at $23 billion, equal to 5% of GDP. But the collapse of 1998 drastically reduced imports. Korea boasted a trade surplus of $40 billion—a record 13% of GDP—that year, and recorded surpluses of $25 billion and $12 billion in 1999 and 2000, helping restore production and employment levels.

A closer look at the data, however, suggests that the recent Korean "miracle" may not be all that miraculous. In 2000, three years after the crisis hit, consumption was only 3% above its pre-crisis level, while fixed capital investment was still 9% lower than in 1997. What domestic growth did take place in 1999 and 2000 was only possible because the Korean government adopted expansionary interest rate and budget policies after the initial IMF-imposed austerity. But external agencies such as the IMF and the Organization for Economic Cooperation and Development (OECD) are now demanding a return to fiscal and monetary conservatism. And since Korea's public debt has risen from 17% to 39% of GDP in the last three years, the government is not in position to sustain fiscal stimulus much longer.

The recent expansion appears to have petered out in late 2000. Economic growth slowed dramatically in the fourth quarter and equipment investment, which had been growing rapidly (while construction stayed mired in depression), declined in the last two months of the year. The unemployment rate is above 4% again, and climbing. The Korean Development Institute forecasts that GDP growth in 2001 will fall to 4%, and to 3% if U.S. growth slows. Meanwhile, investment is expected to decline and consumption to rise by only 3%.

THE IMPACT OF RESTRUCTURING ON LABOR AND SOCIAL SOLIDARITY

The United States had been trying for decades, with only limited success, to open Korea's prosperous economy to Western multinational firms and banks. The IMF takeover of Korea finally gave multinationals the opportunity they had long sought. However, these companies wanted no part of Korea's militant trade union movement. To attract foreign investment, labor would first have to be drastically weakened. Thus, one of the IMF's key demands was that Korea repeal labor laws protecting workers from being fired and replaced. In February 1998 Korea, for the first time in the country's modern history, legalized mass firings and the creation of firms to lease temporary workers to other companies. Korea's *chaebol* were quick to take advantage of their new legal powers, firing about 30% of their workers. As demand picked up in 1999 and 2000, firms hired mostly part-time or temporary workers. As a result, the percentage of Korean employees with stable permanent or regular jobs, already by far the lowest in the industrialized world before the crisis, fell dramatically, from 58% in 1995 to 48% in 2000.

President Kim Dae Jung promised workers they would be compensated for rising economic insecurity by the creation of a welfare system generous enough to assure an adequate living standard to all Koreans. Given the enormous cost of such a system and the ever-tighter constraint on government spending, this promise will never be kept. Welfare spending did rise after the crisis—from less than 3% of GDP in 1997 to over 7% in 1999—as unemployment, poverty, and homelessness increased and the government broadened coverage. Even under these dire circumstances, however, Korea's welfare spending came nowhere near the Western European levels of 15–20% of GDP.

The militant and democratic Korean Confederation of Trade Unions (KCTU) made valiant efforts to slow the pace of neoliberal restructuring. Strike activity in 1998 and 1999, measured in number of work days lost to strikes, stood at almost three times the 1997 level, and militant labor actions continue to this day. The KCTU even tried to organize nationwide general strikes to break neoliberal momentum in 1998 and 1999. Unfortunately, resistance has thus far been unsuccessful.

President Kim Dae Jung turned against the labor movement immediately upon taking office, responding to worker activism with fierce repression, including the arrest of virtually all union leaders involved in strike activity. Just recently, in February 2001, the government crushed a large strike triggered by the firing of 1,700 Daewoo Motor workers, and issued arrest warrants for the strike's leaders. In April, police attacked union members demanding access to their office at a Daewoo Motor factory. Even the conservative *Korea Times* deplored the scenes of "bloodied unionists being viciously attacked by riot police," and the conservative opposition political party called for the resignation of the Prime Minister.

The labor movement, however, is divided: the more conservative Federation of Korean Trade Unions has refused to join forces with the KCTU in its fight against restructuring, and the widening split in the workforce between permanent and temporary workers makes it difficult to maintain labor unity. The media is universally anti-labor, the middle class fears that labor activism will destabilize the fragile recovery, and the once-powerful progressive student movement no longer exists. While it would be premature to rule out a new outbreak of effective labor militancy, prospects for labor do not look good. Last June, in an interview with one of the authors, KCTU President Dan Byung-Do observed that while resistance to neoliberal restructuring was on the rise, continued government, *chaebol*, and IMF-U.S. offensives against Korean workers were inevitable.

Korea is a country fiercely proud of its tradition of social solidarity. This is reflected in its long-term commitment to mass education and relative income equality. But Koreans have discovered that there are no exceptions to the rule that neoliberalism generates rising inequality wherever it is imposed. The real income of the top fifth of households rose right through the collapse of 1998, the recovery of 1999 and beyond, while the rest of Korea lost income in both 1998 and 1999. The income of the poorest fifth dropped by 18% over these two years. Not surprisingly, poverty has also worsened since the crisis. The household poverty rate, which stood at 5% in 1996, more than tripled by 1999.

OPENING THE KOREAN STOCK MARKET TO GLOBAL INVESTORS DRAMATICALLY INCREASED BOTH FOREIGN OWNERSHIP AND STOCK-PRICE VOLATILITY.

RESTRUCTURING AND RISING FOREIGN ECONOMIC DOMINATION

The first restructuring agreement between the IMF and Korea was signed by outgoing President Kim Young Sam in December 1997. According to the *New York Times*, President Clinton telephoned the wavering Korean president and "told him he had no choice but to accept an international bailout." Incoming President Kim Dae Jung didn't need outside pressure to cooperate with the IMF. Strongly influenced by his American mentors, he has always been a fervent neoliberal. In a 1985 book, he strongly criticized government interference with markets: "Maximum reliance on the market is the operating principle of my program." Resource allocation, he stressed, should be determined solely through unrestricted, globally open financial markets.

Kim believes that foreign investment is the key to future Korean prosperity. "What we need now, more that anything else, are foreign investors," he stated in an address to the U.S. Congress in 1999. "I believe the crisis will be remembered as a blessing," he said, because it will force Korea's economy open to foreign capital. Kim wants Korea to dance to the tune played by foreign stockholders and banks, a group shown by the Asian crisis to be astoundingly fickle.

The most pressing problem facing the incoming Kim government in late 1997 was the imminent collapse of the nation's banks. To deal with this threat, the government injected massive public funds into the banking system, effectively nationalizing most banks. Standard and Poor estimate the ultimate cost at $125 billion, or about 30% of the country's 1999 GDP. President Kim used state control of the banks to dictate structural change to the heavily indebted *chaebol*. He threatened to cut off their credit unless they slashed their indebtedness by 60% within just two years. In near-depression conditions, firms could meet this demand only by the extensive sale of real assets and the large-scale issue of new stock. Since domestic firms were broke, this policy was guaranteed to dramatically increase foreign control of Korea's economy.

Just as President Kim intended, foreign direct investment (FDI) and portfolio investment poured in. After running between $1 billion and $2 billion for most of the 1990s, FDI from 1998 through 2000 totaled over $40 billion, while net portfolio investment in the same period totaled $22 billion. These figures may understate the increase in foreign control, since the collapse of the Korean currency (the won) made asset purchases in foreign currency "fire sale" cheap. Most FDI took the form of acquisitions rather than the building of new facilities. Korea thus gained few additional real assets in return for this unprecedented transfer of corporate control to outsiders.

Opening the Korean stock market to global investors dramatically increased both foreign ownership (which almost tripled between 1997 and 2000, to over 30% of the value of Korean stocks) and stock-price volatility. The main Korean stock price index was 350 in late 1997, rose to near 1000 in mid-1999, and dropped to 500 at the end of 2000, before rebounding to near 600 in April 2001. Yet President Kim continues his effort to impose shareholder-guided capitalism in Korea, a system that forces managers to adapt investment strategies to hyperactive stock-price fluctuations.

These capital inflows have added to Korea's holdings of foreign currencies, but they have a longer-run downside. Korea is losing control of its economic destiny. Major Korean financial institutions, previously used by Korean governments to guide credit in accordance with development plans, have been sold at bargain prices to foreign owners, who have no obligation to cooperate with the government. With the proposed sale of Seoul Bank to foreign interests this summer, control of six of Korea's nine commercial banks will be in the hands of outsiders. The *Korea Times* reports that foreign owned banks are "reluctant to extend loans to Korean enterprises." Meanwhile, the industries most responsible for Korea's export performance—such as semiconductors, telecommunications, and autos—have also fallen under foreign influence. The *Korea Times* reports that foreigners own 44% of Korean semiconductor shares and 21% of telecommunication shares, and are the dominant stockholders in such important firms as Hyundai Motors, Hyundai Electronics, LG Chemical, and Samsung Electronics.

The situation in autos is especially disastrous. In 2000, Daimler-Chrysler gained significant influence over Hyundai Motors through the purchase of over 10% of its shares. And Kim Dae Jung, in his lust for foreign ownership, ordered Daewoo Motors, Korea's second largest auto maker, to be sold to foreign interests, even though Daewoo has become so weak that its sale will bring little money. In April 2001, the *Korea Herald* reported that a General Motors (GM) spokesman "demanded that Daewoo Motor be immediately sold to the U.S. car maker without charge." Daewoo has lost much of its value because government-controlled creditor banks starved it of operating funds to deliberately force management to impose firings and wage cuts on its fiercely militant unions, bringing them to heel. GM refused to make an offer for Daewoo until the unions were broken. Daewoo has cut employment by 6,100 since November, firings the *New York Times* says are designed "to make a deal more desirable to GM." In mid-2000, London's influential *Financial Times* raised "the possibility that the entire [Korean auto] sector, the second largest in Asia, could soon be dominated by foreigners."

KOREA'S ONLY HOPE FOR THE FUTURE IS TO DEFEAT NEOLIBERAL RESTRUCTURING

The widely advertised neoliberal Korean "miracle" is a fraud. The financial system remains fragile and subject to crisis even after the massive injection of public funds. Key corporations remain debt-ridden. Since Korea's financial markets have been liberalized to an even greater extent than in 1997, and foreign financial investment in Korea is both more important and more unstable, a renewed outbreak of financial crisis cannot be ruled out.

The neoliberal restructuring process has dismantled or badly weakened most of the policy tools the government used so effectively to impose social control over the Korean economy in the decades before the crisis. Indeed, this is largely what neoliberal restructuring *is*—the replacement of potentially democratic political control over the economy with market processes dominated by rich individuals and powerful companies. With a "flexible" labor market and weak unions, free cross-border capital flows, unregulated stock and bond markets, corporations independent of government influence, banks guided only by short-term profits, and foreign domination of finance and industry, what policy instruments will be available to future progressive governments to guide Korean economic development so that it meets the needs of all the country's people? This is the most serious long-term problem facing Korea.

The destruction of the policy tools traditionally used to guide the economy is not an easily reversible political process. State-regulated economic systems, whether in the West during in the Golden Age of the 1950s and 1960s or in the East Asian "miracle" economies, were created in the aftermath of depression, revolution, or war. In the absence of a severe economic crisis, it will be extraordinarily difficult to put together the domestic political coalitions necessary to create such a system from scratch, even in the absence of external pressures and constraints. For a country as embedded in the global neoliberal system as Korea will be if the U.S. government, the IMF, President Kim, and their supporters have their way, it might well prove impossible. The battle for a progressive future for Korea has not yet been lost. The government retains powerful economic levers, the union movement remains militant, and public support for neoliberal restructuring, and for President Kim himself, has declined dramatically of late. But time is running short. To have any chance of success, a national offensive to defeat neoliberalism must begin soon.

ONE OF THE IMF'S KEY DEMANDS WAS THAT KOREA REPEAL LABOR LAWS PROTECTING WORKERS FROM BEING FIRED AND REPLACED.

May/June 2003

IS IT OIL?

BY ARTHUR MACEWAN

Before U.S. forces invaded Iraq, the United Nations inspection team that had been searching the country for weapons of mass destruction was unable to find either such weapons or a capacity to produce them in the near future. As of mid-April, while the U.S. military is apparently wrapping up its invasion, it too has not found the alleged weapons. The U.S. government continues to claim that weapons of mass destruction exist in Iraq but provides scant evidence to substantiate its claim.

While weapons of mass destruction are hard to find in Iraq, there is one thing that is relatively easy to find: oil. Lots of oil. With 112.5 billion barrels of proven reserves, Iraq has greater stores of oil than any country except Saudi Arabia. This combination—lots of oil and no weapons of mass destruction—begs the question: *Is it oil* and not weapons of mass destruction that motivates the U.S. government's aggressive policy towards Iraq?

THE U.S. "NEED" FOR OIL?

Much of the discussion of the United States, oil, and Iraq focuses on the U.S. economy's overall dependence on oil. We are a country highly dependent on oil, consuming far more than we produce. We have a small share, about 3%, of the world's total proven oil reserves. By depleting our reserves at a much higher rate than most other countries, the United States accounts for about 10% of world production. But, by importing from the rest of the world, we can consume oil at a still higher rate: U.S. oil consumption is over 25% of the world's total. (See the accompanying figures for these and related data.) Thus, the United States relies on the rest of the world's oil in order to keep its economy running—or at least running in its present oil-dependent form. Moreover, for the United States to operate as it does and maintain current standards of living, we need access to oil at low prices. Otherwise we would have to turn over a large share of U.S. GDP as payment to those who supply us with oil.

Iraq could present the United States with supply problems. With a hostile government in Baghdad, the likelihood that the United States would be subject to some sort of boycott as in the early 1970s is greater than otherwise. Likewise, a government in Baghdad that does not cooperate with Washington could be a catalyst to a reinvigoration of the Organization of Petroleum Exporting Countries (OPEC) and the result could be higher oil prices.

Such threats, however, while real, are not as great as they might first appear. Boycotts are hard to maintain. The sellers of oil need to sell as much as the buyers need to buy; oil exporters depend on the U.S. market, just as U.S. consumers depend on those exporters. (An illustration of this mutual dependence is provided by the continuing oil trade between Iraq and the United States in recent years. During 2001, while the two countries were in a virtual state of war, the United States bought 284 million barrels of oil from Iraq, about 7% of U.S. imports and almost a third of Iraq's exports.) Also, U.S. oil imports come from diverse sources, with less than half from OPEC countries and less than one-quarter from Persian Gulf nations.

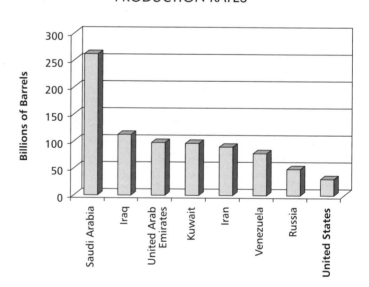

YEARS OF RESERVES AT CURRENT ANNUAL PRODUCTION RATES*

*The number of years it would take to use up existing reserves at current production rate. Past experience, however, suggests that more reserves will be found. In the 1980s, the world's proven reserves expanded by 47%, even as the consumption continued apace. With a more rapid rate of economic growth in the 1990s, and thus with the more rapid rate of oil consumption, the world's reserves rose by almost 5%.

Source: BP Statistical Review of World Energy 2002 <www.bp.com/centres/energy2002>

Most important, ever since the initial surge of OPEC in the 1970s, the organization has followed a policy of price restraint. While price restraint may in part be a strategy of political cooperation, resulting from the close U.S.-Saudi relationship in particular, it is also a policy adopted because high prices are counter-productive for OPEC itself; high prices lead consumers to switch sources of supply and conserve energy, undercutting the longer term profits for the oil suppliers. Furthermore, a sudden rise in prices can lead to general economic disruption, which is no more desirable for the oil exporters than for the oil importers. To be sure, the United States would prefer to have cooperative governments in oil producing countries, but the specter of another boycott as in the 1970s or somewhat higher prices for oil hardly provides a rationale, let alone a justification, for war.

THE PROFITS PROBLEM

There is, however, also the importance of oil in the profits of large U.S. firms: the oil companies themselves (with ExxonMobil at the head of the list) but also the numerous drilling, shipping, refining, and marketing firms that make up the rest of the oil industry. Perhaps the most famous of this latter group, because former CEO Dick Cheney is now vice president, is the Halliburton Company, which supplies a wide range of equipment and engineering services to the industry. Even while many governments—Saudi Arabia, Kuwait, and Venezuela, for example—have taken ownership of their countries' oil reserves, these companies have been able to maintain their profits because of their decisive roles

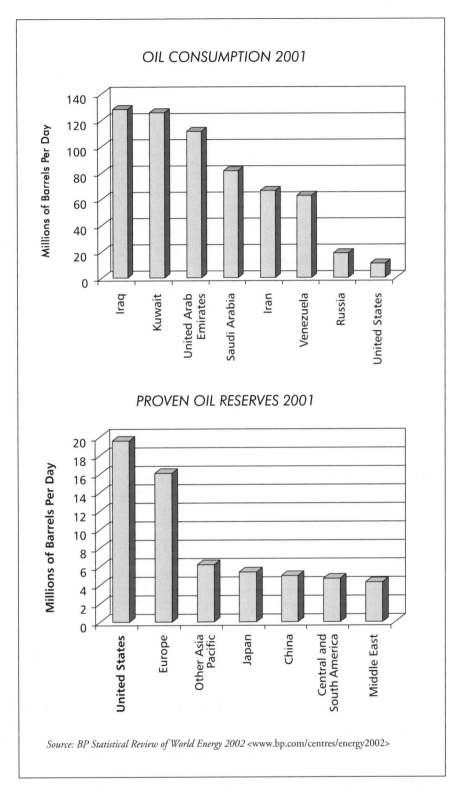

Source: BP Statistical Review of World Energy 2002 <www.bp.com/centres/energy2002>

at each stage in the long sequence from exploration through drilling to refining and marketing. Ultimately, however, as with any resource-based industry, the monopolistic position—and thus the large profits—of the firms that dominate the oil industry depends on their access to the supply of the resource. Their access, in turn, depends on the relations they are able to establish with the governments of oil-producing countries.

From the perspective of the major U.S. oil companies, a hostile Iraqi government presents a clear set of problems. To begin with, there is the obvious: because Iraq has a lot of oil, access to that oil would represent an important profit-making opportunity. What's more, Iraqi oil can be easily extracted and thus produced at very low cost. With all oil selling at the same price on the world market, Iraqi oil thus presents opportunities for especially large profits per unit of production. According to the *Guardian* newspaper (London), Iraqi oil could cost as little as 97 cents a barrel to produce, compared to the UK's North Sea oil produced at $3 to $4 per barrel. As one oil executive told the *Guardian* last November, "Ninety cents a barrel for oil that sells for $30—that's the kind of business anyone would want to be in. A 97% profit margin—you can live with that." The *Guardian* continues: "The stakes are high. Iraq could be producing 8 million barrels a day within the decade. The math is impressive—8 million times 365 at $30 per barrel or $87.5 billion a year. Any share would be worth fighting for." The question for the oil companies is: what share will they be able to claim and what share will be claimed by the Iraqi government? The split would undoubtedly be more favorable for the oil companies with a compliant U.S.-installed government in Baghdad.

Furthermore, the conflict is not simply one between the private oil companies and the government of Iraq. The U.S.-based firms and their British (and British-Dutch) allies are vying with French, Russian, and Chinese firms for access to Iraqi oil. During recent years, firms from these other nations signed oil exploration and development contracts with the Hussein government in Iraq, and, if there were no "regime change," they would pre-empt the operations of the U.S. and British firms in that country. If, however, the U.S. government succeeds in replacing the government of Saddam Hussein with its preferred allies in the Iraqi opposition, the outlook will change dramatically. According to Ahmed Chalabi, head of the Iraqi National Congress and a figure in the Iraqi opposition who seems to be currently favored by Washington, "The future democratic government in Iraq will be grateful to the United States for helping the Iraqi people liberate themselves and getting rid of Saddam.... American companies, we expect, will play an important and leading role in the future oil situation." (In recent years, U.S. firms have not been fully frozen out of the oil business in Iraq. For example, according to a June 2001 report in the *Washington Post*, while Vice President Cheney was CEO at Halliburton Company during the late 1990s, the firm operated through subsidiaries to sell some $73 mil-

> IRAQI OIL COULD COST AS LITTLE AS 97 CENTS A BARREL TO PRODUCE. AS ONE OIL EXECUTIVE PUT IT, "NINETY CENTS A BARREL FOR OIL THAT SELLS FOR $30—THAT'S THE KIND OF BUSINESS ANYONE WOULD WANT TO BE IN."

lion of oil production equipment and spare parts to Iraq.)

The rivalry with French, Russian and Chinese companies is in part driven by the direct prize of the profits to be obtained from Iraqi operations. In addition, in order to maintain their dominant positions in the world oil industry, it is important for the U.S. and British-based firms to deprive their rivals of the growth potential that access to Iraq would afford. In any monopolistic industry, leading firms need to deny their potential competitors market position and control of new sources of supply; otherwise, those competitors will be in a better position to challenge the leaders. The British *Guardian* reports that the Hussein government is "believed to have offered the French company TotalFinaElf exclusive rights to the largest of Iraq's oil fields, the Majoon, which would more than double the company's entire output at a single stroke." Such a development would catapult TotalFinaElf from the second ranks into the first ranks of the major oil firms. The basic structure of the world oil industry would not change, but the sharing of power and profits among the leaders would be altered. Thus for ExxonMobil, Chevron, Shell and the other traditional "majors" in the industry, access to Iraq is a defensive as well as an offensive goal. ("Regime change" in Iraq will not necessarily provide the legal basis for cancellation of contracts signed between the Hussein regime and various oil companies. International law would not allow a new regime simply to turn things over to the U.S. oil companies. "Should 'regime change' happen, one thing is guaranteed," according to the *Guardian*, "shortly afterwards there will be the mother of all legal battles.")

Oil companies are big and powerful. The biggest, ExxonMobil, had 2002 profits of $15 billion, more than any other corporation, in the United States or in the world. Chevron-Texaco came in with $3.3 billion in 2002 profits, and Phillips-Tosco garnered $1.7 billion. British Petroleum-Amoco-Arco pulled in $8 billion, while Royal Dutch/Shell Group registered almost $11 billion. Firms of this magnitude have a large role affecting the policies of their governments, and, for that matter, the governments of many other countries.

With the ascendancy of the Bush-Cheney team to the White House in 2000, perhaps the relationship between oil and the government became more personal, but it was not new. Big oil has been important in shaping U.S. foreign policy since the end of the 19th century (to say nothing of its role in shaping other policy realms, particularly environmental regulation). From 1914, when the Marines landed at Mexico's Tampico Bay to protect U.S. oil interests, to the CIA-engineered overthrow of the Mosadegh government in Iran in 1953, to the close relationship with the oppressive Saudi monarchy through the past 70 years, oil and the interests of the oil companies have been central factors in U.S. foreign policy. Iraq today is one more chapter in a long story.

THE LARGER ISSUE

Yet in Iraq today, as in many other instances of the U.S. government's international actions, oil is not the whole story. The international policies of the U.S. government are certainly shaped in significant part by the interests of U.S.-based firms, but not only the oil companies. ExxonMobil may have had the largest 2002 profits, but there are many additional large U.S. firms with international interests: Citbank and the other huge financial firms; IBM, Microsoft, and other information technology companies; General Motors and Ford; Merck, Pfizer and the other pharmaceutical corporations; large retailers like MacDonald's and Wal-Mart (and many more) depend on access to foreign markets and foreign sources of supply for large shares of their sales and profits.

The U.S. government (like other governments) has long defined its role in international affairs as protecting the interests of its nationals, and by far the largest interests of U.S. nationals abroad are the interests of these large U.S. companies. The day-to-day activities of U.S. embassies and consular offices around the world are dominated by efforts to further the interests of particular U.S. firms—for example, helping the firms establish local markets, negotiate a country's regulations, or develop relations with local businesses. When the issue is large, such as when governments in low-income countries have attempted to assure the availability of HIV-AIDS drugs in spite of patents held by U.S. firms, Washington steps directly into the fray. On the broadest level, the U.S. government tries to shape the rules and institutions of the world economy in ways that work well for U.S. firms. These rules are summed up under the heading of "free trade," which in practice means free access of U.S. firms to the markets and resources of the rest of the world.

In normal times, Washington uses diplomacy and institutions like the International Monetary Fund, the World Bank, and the World Trade Organization to shape the rules of the world economy. But times are not always "normal." When governments have attempted to remove their economies from the open system and break with the "rules of the game," the U.S. government has responded with overt or covert military interventions. Latin America has had a long history of such interventions, where Guatemala (1954), Cuba (1961), Chile (1973) and Nicaragua (1980s) provide fairly recent examples. The Middle East also provides several illustrations of this approach to foreign affairs, with U.S. interventions in Iran (1953), Lebanon (1958), Libya (1981), and now Iraq. These interventions are generally presented as efforts to preserve freedom and democracy, but, if freedom and democracy were actually the goals of U.S. interventions the record would be very different; both the Saudi monarchy and the Shah of Iran, in an earlier era, would then have been high on the U.S. hit list. (Also, as with maintaining the source of supply of oil, the U.S. government did not intervene in Guatemala in 1954 to maintain our supply of bananas; the profits of the United Fruit Company, however, did provide a powerful causal factor.)

The rhetorical rationale of U.S. foreign policy has seen many alterations and adjustments over the last century: at the end of the 19th century, U.S. officials spoke of the need to spread Christianity; Woodrow Wilson defined the mission as keeping the world safe for democracy; for most of the latter half of the 20th century, the fight against Communism was the paramount rationale; for a fleeting moment during the Carter administration, the protection of human rights entered the government's vocabulary; in recent years we have seen the war against drugs; and now we have the current administration's war against terrorism.

What distinguishes the current administration in Washington is neither its approach toward foreign affairs and U.S. business interests in general nor its policy in the Middle East and oil interests in particular. Even its rhetoric builds on well established traditions, albeit with new twists. What does distinguish the Bush administration is the clarity and aggressiveness with which it has put forth its goal of maintaining U.S. domination internationally. The "Bush Doctrine" that the administration has articulated claims legitimacy for pre-emptive action against those who might threaten U.S. interests, and it is clear from the statement of that doctrine in last September's issuance of *The National Security Strategy of the United States of America* that "U.S. interests" includes economic interests.

The economic story is never the whole story, and oil is never the whole economic story. In the particular application of U.S. power, numerous strategic and political considerations come into play. With the application of the Bush Doctrine in the case of Iraq, the especially heinous character of the Hussein regime is certainly a factor, as is the regime's history of conflict with other nations of the region (at times with U.S. support) and its apparent efforts at developing nuclear, chemical, and biological weapons; certainly the weakness of the Iraqi military also affects the U.S. government's willingness to go to war. Yet, as September's *Security Strategy* document makes clear, the U.S. government is concerned with domination and a major factor driving that goal of domination is economic. In the Middle East, Iraq and elsewhere, oil—or, more precisely, the profit from oil—looms large in the picture.

IF FREEDOM AND DEMOCRACY WERE ACTUALLY THE GOALS OF U.S. INTERVENTIONS, THE RECORD WOULD BE VERY DIFFERENT.

FAIR TRADE AND FARM SUBSIDIES: HOW BIG A DEAL?

TWO VIEWS

In September 2003, the global free-trade express was derailed—at least temporarily—when the World Trade Organization talks in Cancún, Mexico, collapsed. At the time, the inconsistency of the United States and other rich countries—pressing poor countries to adopt free trade while continuing to subsidize and protect selected domestic sectors, especially agriculture—received wide attention for the first time. Where does ending agricultural subsidies and trade barriers in the rich countries rank as a strategy for achieving global economic justice? Dollars & Sense *asked progressive researchers on different sides of this question to make their case.*

MAKE TRADE FAIR

BY GAWAIN KRIPKE

Trade can be a powerful engine for economic growth in developing countries and can help pull millions of people out of poverty. Trade also offers an avenue of growth that relies less than other development strategies on the fickle charity of wealthy countries or the self-interest of multinational corporations. However, current trade rules create enormous obstacles that prevent people in developing countries from realizing the benefits of trade. A growing number of advocacy organizations are now tackling this fundamental problem, hoping to open a route out of poverty for tens of millions of people who have few other prospects.

WHY TRADE?

Poor countries have few options for improving the welfare of their people and generating economic growth. Large debt burdens limit the ability of governments in the developing world to make investments and provide education, clean water, and other critical services. Despite some recent progress on the crushing problem of debt, only about 15% of the global South's $300 billion in unpayable debt has been eliminated.

Poor countries have traditionally looked to foreign aid and private investment to drive economic development. Both of these are proving inadequate. To reach the goals of

continued on page 148

FALSE PROMISES ON TRADE

BY DEAN BAKER AND MARK WEISBROT

Farmers throughout the Third World are suffering not from too much free trade, but from not enough. That's the impression you get from most media coverage of the recent World Trade Organization (WTO) meetings in Cancún. The *New York Times, Washington Post,* and other major news outlets devoted huge amounts of space to news pieces and editorials arguing that agricultural subsidies in rich countries are a major cause of poverty in the developing world. If only these subsidies were eliminated, and the doors to imports from developing countries opened, the argument goes, then the playing field would be level and genuinely free trade would work its magic on poverty in the Third World. The media decided that agricultural subsidies were the major theme of the trade talks even if evidence indicated that other issues—for example, patent and copyright protection, rules on investment, or developing countries' right to regulate imports—would have more impact on the well-being of people in those countries.

There is certainly some element of truth in the argument that agricultural subsidies and barriers to imports can hurt farmers in developing countries. There are unquestionably farmers in a number of developing countries who

continued on page 149

MAKE TRADE FAIR

continued from page 147

the United Nations' current Millenium Development campaign, including reducing hunger and providing universal primary education, wealthy countries would have to increase their foreign aid from a paltry 0.23% of GDP to 0.7%. Instead, foreign aid flows are stagnant and are losing value against inflation and population growth. In 2001, the United States spent just 0.11% of GDP on foreign aid.

Likewise, although global foreign direct investment soared to unprecedented levels in the late 1990s, most developing countries are not attractive to foreign investors. The bulk of foreign private investment in the developing world, more than 76%, goes to ten large countries including China, Brazil, and Mexico. For the majority of developing countries, particularly the poorest, foreign investment remains a modest contributor to economic growth, on a par with official foreign aid. Sub-Saharan Africa, with the highest concentration of the world's poor, attracted only $14 billion in 2001.

In this environment, trade offers an important potential source of economic growth for developing countries. Relatively modest gains in their share of global trade could yield large benefits for developing countries. Gaining an additional 1% share of the $8 trillion global export market, for example, would generate more revenue than all current foreign aid spending.

But today, poor countries are bit players in the global trade game. More than 40% of the world's population lives in low-income countries, but these countries generate only 3% of global exports. Despite exhortations from the United States and other wealthy countries to export, many of the poorest countries are actually losing share in export markets. Africa generated a mere 2.4% of world exports of goods in 2001, down from 3.1% in 1990.

Many factors contribute to the poorest countries' inability to gain a foothold in export trade, but the core problem is that the playing field is heavily tilted against them. This is particularly true in the farm sector. The majority of the global South population lives in rural areas and depends on agriculture for survival. Moreover, poverty is concentrated in the countryside: more than three-quarters of the world's poorest people, the 1.1 billion who live on less than one dollar a day, live in rural areas. This means that agriculture must be at the center of trade, development, and poverty-reduction strategies throughout the developing world.

Two examples demonstrate the unfair rules of the global trading system in agriculture.

"IT'S NOT WHITE GOLD ANYMORE"

Cotton is an important crop in Central and West Africa. More than two million households depend directly on the crop for their livelihoods, with millions more indirectly in-

volved. Despite serious social and environmental problems that have accompanied the expansion of cotton cultivation, cotton provides families with desperately needed cash for health care, education, and even food. The cotton crop can make a big difference in reducing poverty. For example, a 2002 World Bank study found a strong link between cotton prices and rural welfare in Benin, a poor West African country.

Cotton is important at a macroeconomic level as well; in 11 African countries, it accounts for more than one-quarter of export revenue. But since the mid-1990s, the cotton market has experienced chronic price depression. Though prices have rebounded in recent months, they remain below the long-term average of $0.72 a pound. Lower prices mean less export revenue for African countries and lower incomes for African cotton farmers.

But not for U.S. cotton farmers. Thanks to farm subsidies, U.S. cotton producers are insulated from the market and have produced bumper crops that depress prices worldwide. The global price of cotton is 20% lower than it would be without U.S. subsidies, according to an analysis by the International Cotton Advisory Committee. Oxfam estimates that in 2001, as a result of U.S. cotton subsidies, eight countries in Africa lost approximately $300 million—about one-quarter of the total amount the U.S. Agency for International Development will spend in Africa next year.

DUMPING ON OUR NEIGHBOR

Mexico has been growing corn (or maize) for 10,000 years. Today, nearly three million Mexican farmers grow corn, but they are facing a crisis due to sharply declining prices. Real prices for corn have fallen 70% since 1994. Poverty is widespread in corn-growing areas like Chiapas, Oaxaca, and Guerrero. Every year, large numbers of rural Mexicans leave the land and migrate to the cities or to the United States to try to earn a living.

The price drops are due to increased U.S. corn exports to Mexico, which have more than tripled since 1994. These exports result in large part from U.S. government policies that encourage overproduction. While Mexican farmers struggle to keep their farms and support their families, the United States pours up to $10 billion annually into subsidies for U.S. corn producers. By comparison, the entire Mexican government budget for agriculture is $1 billion. Between 2000 and 2002, a metric ton of American corn sold on export markets for $20 less than the average cost to produce it. The United States controls nearly 70% of the global corn market, so this dumping has a huge impact on prices and on small-scale corn farmers in Mexico.

To be fair, the Mexican government shares some of the responsibility for the crisis facing corn farmers. Although the North American Free Trade Agreement (NAFTA) opened trade between the United States and Mexico, the Mexican government voluntarily lowered tariffs on corn beyond what was required by NAFTA. As NAFTA is fully phased in, though, Mexico will lose the option of raising tariffs to safeguard poor farmers from a flood of subsidized corn.

WHAT DO POOR COUNTRIES WANT?

Cotton and corn illustrate the problems that current trade regimes pose for developing countries and particularly for the world's poorest people. African countries want to engage in global trade but are crowded out by subsidized cotton from the United States. The livelihood of Mexican corn farmers is undermined by dumped U.S. corn. In both of these cases, and many more, it's all perfectly legal. WTO and NAFTA rules provide near impunity to rich countries that subsidize agriculture, and increasingly restrict developing countries' ability to safeguard their farmers and promote development.

How much do subsidies and trade barriers in the rich countries really cost the developing world? One study estimates that developing countries lose $24 billion annually in agricultural income—not a trivial amount. In today's political climate, it's hard to see where else these countries are going to find $24 billion to promote their economic development.

The benefits of higher prices for farmers in the developing world have to be balanced against the potential cost to consumers, both North and South. However, it's important to remember that many Northern consumers actually pay more for food *because of* subsidies. In fact, they often pay twice: first in higher food costs, and then in taxes to pay for the subsidies. Consumers in poor countries will pay more for food if farm commodity prices rise, but the majority of people who work in agriculture will benefit. Since poverty is concentrated in rural areas, the gains to agricultural producers are particularly important.

However, some low-income countries are net food importers and could face difficulties if prices rise. Assuring affordable food is critical, but this goal can be achieved much more cheaply and efficiently than by spending $100 billion on farm subsidies in the rich countries. The World Bank says that low-income countries that depend on food imports faced a net agricultural trade deficit of $2.8 billion in 2000-2001. The savings realized from reducing agricultural subsidies could easily cover this shortfall.

Each country faces different challenges. Developing countries, in particular, need flexibility to develop appropriate solutions to address their economic, humanitarian, and development situations. Broad-stroke solutions inevitably fail to address specific circumstances. But the complexity of the issues must not be used as an excuse for inaction by policy-makers. Failure to act to lift trade barriers and agricultural subsidies will only mean growing inequity, continuing poverty, and endless injustice.

Sources: Xinshen Diao, Eugenio Diaz-Bonilla, and Sherman Robinson, "How Much Does It Hurt? The Impact of Agricultural Trade Policies on Developing Countries," (International Food Policy Research Institute, Washington, D.C., 2003); "Global Development Finance: Striving for Stability in Development Finance," (World Bank, 2003); Lyuba Zarksy and Kevin Gallagher, "Searching for the Holy Grail? Making FDI Work for Sustainable Development,"(Tufts Global Development and Environment Institute/WWF, March 2003); Oxfam's website on trade issues <www.maketradefair. com>.

FALSE PROMISES ON TRADE

continued from page 147

continued from page 147

have been undersold and even put out of business by imports whose prices are artificially low thanks to subsidies the rich countries pay their farmers. It is also true that many of these subsidy programs are poorly targeted, benefiting primarily large farmers and often encouraging environmentally harmful farming practices.

However, the media have massively overstated the potential gains that poor countries might get from the elimination of farm subsidies and import barriers. The risk of this exaggeration is that it encourages policy-makers and concerned nongovernmental organizations (NGOs) to focus their energies on an issue that is largely peripheral to economic development and to ignore much more important matters.

To put the issue in perspective: the World Bank, one of the most powerful advocates of removing most trade barriers, has estimated the gains from removing all the rich countries' remaining barriers to trade in manufactured and farm products *and* ending agricultural subsidies. The total estimated gain to low- and middle-income countries, when the changes are phased in by 2015, is an extra 0.6% of GDP. In other words, an African country with an annual income of $500 per person would see that figure rise to $503 as a result of removing these barriers and subsidies.

SIMPLISTIC TALK ON SUBSIDIES

The media often claim that the rich countries give $300 billion annually in agricultural subsidies to their farmers. In fact, this is not the amount of money paid by governments to farmers, which is actually less than $100 billion. The $300 billion figure is an estimate of the excess cost to consumers in rich nations that results from all market barriers in agriculture. Most of this cost is attributable to higher food prices that result from planting restrictions, import tariffs, and quotas.

The distinction is important, because not all of the $300 billion ends up in the pockets of farmers in rich nations. Some of it goes to exporters in developing nations, as when sugar producers in Brazil or Nicaragua are able to sell their sugar in the United States for an amount that is close to three times the world price. The higher price that U.S. consumers pay for this sugar is part of the $300 billion that many accounts mistakenly describe as subsidies to farmers in rich countries.

Another significant misrepresentation is the idea that cheap imports from the rich nations are always bad for developing countries. When subsides from rich countries lower the price of agricultural imports to developing countries, consumers in those countries benefit. This is one reason why a recent World Bank study found that the removal of *all* trade barriers and subsidies in the United States would have no net effect on growth in sub-Saharan Africa.

In addition, removing the rich countries' subsidies or barriers will not level the playing field—since there will still often be large differences in productivity—and thus will not save developing countries from the economic and social upheavals that such "free trade" agreements as the WTO have in store for them. These agreements envision a massive displacement of people employed in agriculture, as farmers in developing countries are pushed out by international competition. It took the United States 100 years, from 1870 to 1970, to reduce agricultural employment from 53% to under 5% of the labor force, and the transition nonetheless caused considerable social unrest. To compress such a process into a period of a few years or even a decade, by removing remaining agricultural trade barriers in poor countries, is a recipe for social explosion.

It is important to realize that in terms of the effect on developing countries, low agricultural prices due to subsidies for rich-country farmers have the exact same impact as low agricultural prices that stem from productivity gains. If the opponents of agricultural subsidies consider the former to be harmful to the developing countries, then they should be equally concerned about the impact of productivity gains in the agricultural sectors of rich countries.

Insofar as cheap food imports might have a negative impact on a developing country's economy, the problem can be easily remedied by an import tariff. In this situation, the developing world would gain the most if those countries that benefit from cheap imported food have access to it, while those that are better served by protecting their domestic agricultural sector are allowed to impose tariffs without fear of retaliation from rich nations. This would make much more sense, and cause much less harm, than simply removing all trade barriers and subsidies on both sides of the North-South economic divide. The concept of a "level playing field" is a false one. Mexican corn farmers, for example, are not going to be able to compete with U.S. agribusiness, subsidies or no subsidies, nor should they have to.

It is of course good that such institutions as the *New York Times* are pointing out the hypocrisy of governments in the United States, Europe, and Japan in insisting that developing countries remove trade barriers and subsidies while keeping some of their own. And the subsidy issue was exploited very skillfully by developing-country governments and NGOs at the recent Cancún talks. The end result—the collapse of the talks—was a great thing for the developing world. So were the ties that were forged among countries such as those in the group of 22, enabling them to stand up to the rich countries. But the WTO remedy of eliminating subsidies and trade barriers across the board will not save developing countries from most of the harm caused by current policies. Just the opposite: the removal of import restrictions in the developing world could wipe out tens of millions of farmers and cause enormous economic damage.

AVOIDING THE KEY ISSUES

While reducing agricultural protection and subsidies just in the rich countries might in general be a good thing for developing countries, the gross exaggeration of its importance has real consequences, because it can divert attention from issues of far more pressing concern. One such issue is the role that the IMF continues to play as enforcer of a creditors' cartel in the developing world, threatening any country that defies its edicts with a cutoff of access to international credit. One of the most devastated recent victims of the IMF's measures has been Argentina, which saw its economy thrown into a depression after the failure of a decade of neoliberal economic policies. The IMF's harsh treatment of Argentina last year, while it was suffering from the worst depression in its history, is widely viewed in the developing world as a warning to other countries that might deviate from the IMF's recommendations. One result is that Brazil's new president, elected with an overwhelming mandate for change, must struggle to promote growth in the face of 22% interest rates demanded by the IMF's monetary experts.

Similarly, most of sub-Saharan Africa is suffering from an unpayable debt burden. While there has been some limited relief offered in recent years, the remaining debt service burden is still more than the debtor countries in that region spend on health care or education. The list of problems that the current world economic order imposes on developing countries is long: bans on the industrial policies that led to successful development in the West, the imposition of patents on drugs and copyrights on computer software and recorded material, inappropriate macroeconomic policies imposed by the IMF and the World Bank. All of these factors are likely to have far more severe consequences for the development prospects of poor countries than the agricultural policies of rich countries.

Sources: Elena Ianchovichina, Aaditya Mattoo, and Marcelo Olareaga, "Unrestricted Market Access for Sub-Saharan Africa: How much is it worth and who pays," (World Bank, April 2001); Mark Weisbrot and Dean Baker, "The Relative Impact of Trade Liberalization on Developing Countries," (Center for Economic and Policy Research, June 2002).

APPENDIX 1: GROSS DOMESTIC PRODUCT

(Billions of 2000 dollars, unless otherwise noted)

Year	Real GDP Growth Rate (%)	GDP	Personal consumption spending	Gross private investment	Govt. consumpt. & investment	Exports	Imports	Population (millions)	GDP per capita
	1	2	3	4	5	6	7	8	9
1959		2,441.3	1,554.6	266.7	714.3	77.2	101.9	178	13,728
1960	2.5	2,501.8	1,597.4	266.6	715.4	90.6	103.3	181	13,847
1961	2.3	2,560.0	1,630.3	264.9	751.3	91.1	102.6	184	13,936
1962	6.1	2,715.2	1,711.1	298.4	797.6	95.7	114.3	187	14,556
1963	4.4	2,834.0	1,781.6	318.5	818.1	102.5	117.3	189	14,976
1964	5.8	2,998.6	1,888.4	344.7	836.1	114.6	123.6	192	15,627
1965	6.4	3,191.1	2,007.7	393.1	861.3	117.8	136.7	194	16,423
1966	6.5	3,399.1	2,121.8	427.7	937.1	126.0	157.1	197	17,293
1967	2.5	3,484.6	2,185.0	408.1	1,008.9	128.9	168.5	199	17,536
1968	4.8	3,652.7	2,310.5	431.9	1,040.5	139.0	193.6	201	18,199
1969	3.1	3,765.4	2,396.4	457.1	1,038.0	145.7	204.6	203	18,578
1970	0.2	3,771.9	2,451.9	427.1	1,012.9	161.4	213.4	205	18,395
1971	3.4	3,898.6	2,545.5	475.7	990.8	164.1	224.7	208	18,774
1972	5.3	4,105.0	2,701.3	532.1	983.5	176.5	250.0	210	19,557
1973	5.8	4,341.5	2,833.8	594.4	980.0	209.7	261.6	212	20,488
1974	-0.5	4,319.6	2,812.3	550.6	1,004.7	226.3	255.7	214	20,199
1975	-0.2	4,311.2	2,876.9	453.1	1,027.4	224.9	227.3	216	19,962
1976	5.3	4,540.9	3,035.5	544.7	1,031.9	234.7	271.7	218	20,826
1977	4.6	4,750.5	3,164.1	627.0	1,043.3	240.3	301.4	220	21,570
1978	5.6	5,015.0	3,303.1	702.6	1,074.0	265.7	327.6	223	22,531
1979	3.2	5,173.4	3,383.4	725.0	1,094.1	292.0	333.0	225	22,987
1980	-0.2	5,161.7	3,374.1	645.3	1,115.4	323.5	310.9	228	22,666
1981	2.5	5,291.7	3,422.2	704.9	1,125.6	327.4	319.1	230	23,011
1982	-1.9	5,189.3	3,470.3	606.0	1,145.4	302.4	315.0	232	22,350
1983	4.5	5,423.8	3,668.6	662.5	1,187.3	294.6	354.8	234	23,148
1984	7.2	5,813.6	3,863.3	857.7	1,227.0	318.7	441.1	236	24,598
1985	4.1	6,053.7	4,064.0	849.7	1,312.5	328.3	469.8	238	25,386
1986	3.5	6,263.6	4,228.9	843.9	1,392.5	353.7	510.0	241	26,028
1987	3.4	6,475.1	4,369.8	870.0	1,426.7	391.8	540.2	243	26,668
1988	4.1	6,742.7	4,546.9	890.5	1,445.1	454.6	561.4	245	27,519
1989	3.5	6,981.4	4,675.0	926.2	1,482.5	506.8	586.0	247	28,226
1990	1.9	7,112.5	4,770.3	895.1	1,530.0	552.5	607.1	250	28,435
1991	-0.2	7,100.5	4,778.4	822.2	1,547.2	589.1	603.7	253	28,011
1992	3.3	7,336.6	4,934.8	889.0	1,555.3	629.7	645.6	257	28,559
1993	2.7	7,532.7	5,099.8	968.3	1,541.1	650.0	702.1	260	28,944
1994	4.0	7,835.5	5,290.7	1,099.6	1,541.3	706.5	785.9	263	29,743
1995	2.5	8,031.7	5,433.5	1,134.0	1,549.7	778.2	849.1	267	30,131
1996	3.7	8,328.9	5,619.4	1,234.3	1,564.9	843.4	923.0	270	30,886
1997	4.5	8,703.5	5,831.8	1,387.7	1,594.0	943.7	1,048.3	273	31,891
1998	4.2	9,066.9	6,125.8	1,524.1	1,624.4	966.5	1,170.3	276	32,837
1999	4.5	9,470.3	6,438.6	1,642.6	1,686.9	1,008.2	1,304.4	279	33,908
2000	3.7	9,817.0	6,739.4	1,735.5	1721.6	1,096.3	1,475.8	282	34,759
2001	0.5	9,866.6	6,904.6	1,590.6	1768.9	1,039.0	1,437.1	286	34,554
2002	2.2	10,083.0	7,140.4	1,572.0	1836.9	1,014.2	1,484.7	289	34,938
2003									

APPENDIX 2: TRADE, INVESTMENT, & GOVERNMENT SPENDING

(Billions of 2000 dollars, unless otherwise noted)

Year	Trade Balance on Goods & Services	Nominal Trade-Weighted Value of US $	Gross Business Fixed Investment	Gross Residential Invest-ment	After-tax Corporate Profits	Manufact. Capacity Utili-zation Rate (%)	Govt. Transfer Payments	Federal Expenditures Minus Transfer Payments	State & Local Expenditures Minus Trans. Pmts.
	10	11	12	13	14	15	16	17	18
1959	0.3				154	81.6	126.3	276.6	157.1
1960	16.7				147	80.1	130.7	281.4	169.2
1961	19.7				150	77.3	147.1	289.0	182.3
1962	15.6				182	81.4	149.8	319.0	192.4
1963	19.3				195	83.5	156.4	331.7	204.6
1964	27.2				218	85.6	159.1	341.6	220.1
1965	20.7				250	89.5	170.0	351.9	236.5
1966	12.7				256	91.1	190.7	394.8	257.2
1967	10.9				244	87.2	220.1	433.6	277.5
1968	1.0				238	87.1	238.0	458.4	299.4
1969	0.3				212	86.5	249.0	453.9	322.4
1970	8.2				178	79.3	290.5	439.8	351.9
1971	-4.5				207	77.7	330.3	430.6	377.7
1972	-18.0				231	83.2	370.9	439.2	400.5
1973	6.0				237	87.5	392.2	429.5	422.3
1974	-12.4				181	84.1	419.6	425.1	441.8
1975	32.6				219	73.4	482.9	428.1	463.9
1976	-15.1				244	77.9	493.8	437.4	478.2
1977	-63.7				276	82.3	498.0	455.2	490.7
1978	-65.0				288	84.5	508.6	474.9	498.5
1979	-49.6				269	84.3	513.8	490.2	506.8
1980	-35.9				211	78.8	553.4	530.3	514.8
1981	-27.4				240	77.3	557.4	580.5	516.9
1982	-38.5				228	71.3	572.0	621.3	529.9
1983	-88.6	52.8			282	73.6	587.4	663.1	547.2
1984	-161.2	60.1			327	79.5	586.1	710.4	569.1
1985	-174.8	67.2			331	78.5	601.5	758.7	604.5
1986	-194.4	62.4			294	78.5	624.7	787.2	640.6
1987	-207.2	60.4			326	81.2	618.7	804.3	665.9
1988	-151.4	60.9			384	84.1	636.6	806.9	685.8
1989	-118.6	66.9			357	83.2	664.5	821.7	709.3
1990	-99.1	71.4	886.6	298.9	358	81.6	698.5	837.8	738.8
1991	-36.9	74.4	829.1	270.2	370	78.3	707.7	849.6	754.1
1992	-44.2	76.9	878.3	307.6	383	79.4	832.0	840.3	769.8
1993	-78.3	83.8	953.5	332.7	420	80.3	865.2	827.4	781.6
1994	-107.7	90.9	1,042.3	364.8	450	82.6	885.5	813.1	804.0
1995	-103.2	92.7	1,109.6	353.1	519	82.7	910.9	830.0	825.8
1996	-109.6	97.5	1,209.2	381.3	591	81.1	946.5	828.4	845.2
1997	-112.2	104.4	1,320.6	388.6	652	82.6	963.0	828.1	870.6
1998	-169.1	115.9	1,455.0	418.3	574	82.0	981.1	817.2	907.4
1999	-266.9	116.0	1,576.3	443.6	606	81.4	1007.6	819.0	954.2
2000	-375.4	119.4	1,679.0	446.9	553	81.1	1038.1	826.3	997.8
2001	-349.5	125.9	1,625.7	448.5	556	75.4	1104.3	817.4	1035.7
2002	-402.2	126.8	1,565.8	470.3	682	73.9	1196.2	824.8	1054.0
2003									

APPENDIX 3: WORKFORCE & WAGES

Year	Civilian Labor Force over 16 (thousands)	Total Employment over 16 (thousands)	Female Employment over 16 (thousands)	% of Civilian Jobs Held by Women	Labor Force Unionized (%)		Average Gross Weekly Earnings (1982 dollars)	Change from a Year Earlier (%)
	19	20	21	22	23	24	25	26
1959	68,369	64,630	21,164	32.7	25.0			
1960	69,628	65,778	21,874	33.3	24.5			
1961	70,459	65,746	22,090	33.6	23.1			
1962	70,614	66,702	22,525	33.8	23.5			
1963	71,833	67,762	23,105	34.1	23.0			
1964	73,091	69,305	23,831	34.4	23.0		302.52	
1965	74,455	71,088	24,748	34.8	23.2		310.46	2.6
1966	75,770	72,895	25,976	35.6	23.7		312.83	0.8
1967	77,347	74,372	26,893	36.2	23.7		311.30	-0.5
1968	78,737	75,920	27,807	36.6	24.0		315.37	1.3
1969	80,734	77,902	29,084	37.3	23.6		316.93	0.5
1970	82,771	78,678	29,688	37.7	23.4		312.94	-1.3
1971	84,382	79,367	29,976	37.8	22.8		318.05	1.6
1972	87,034	82,153	31,257	38.0	22.3		331.59	4.3
1973	89,429	85,064	32,715	38.5	22.2		331.39	-0.1
1974	91,949	86,794	33,769	38.9	22.0		314.94	-5.0
1975	93,775	85,846	33,989	39.6	20.9		305.16	-3.1
1976	96,158	88,752	35,615	40.1	20.4		309.61	1.5
1977	99,009	92,017	37,289	40.5	19.9	23.8	310.99	0.4
1978	102,251	96,048	39,569	41.2	19.8	23.0	310.41	-0.2
1979	104,962	98,824	41,217	41.7	19.1	24.1	298.87	-3.7
1980	106,940	99,303	42,117	42.4	18.6	23.0	281.27	-5.9
1981	108,670	100,397	43,000	42.8			277.35	-1.4
1982	110,204	99,526	43,256	43.5			272.74	-1.7
1983	111,550	100,834	44,047	43.7		20.1	277.50	1.7
1984	113,544	105,005	45,915	43.7		18.8	279.22	0.6
1985	115,461	107,150	47,259	44.1		18.0	276.23	-1.1
1986	117,834	109,597	48,706	44.4		17.5	276.11	0.0
1987	119,865	112,440	50,334	44.8		17.0	272.88	-1.2
1988	121,669	114,968	51,696	45.0		16.8	270.32	-0.9
1989	123,869	117,342	53,027	45.2		16.4	267.27	-1.1
1990	125,840	118,793	53,689	45.2		16.0	262.43	-1.8
1991	126,346	117,718	53,496	45.4		16.0	258.34	-1.6
1992	128,105	118,492	54,052	45.6		15.7	257.95	-0.2
1993	129,200	120,259	54,910	45.7		15.7	258.12	0.1
1994	131,056	123,060	56,610	46.0		15.5	259.97	0.7
1995	132,304	124,900	57,523	46.1		14.9	258.43	-0.6
1996	133,943	126,708	58,501	46.2		14.5	259.58	0.4
1997	136,297	129,558	59,873	46.2		14.1	265.22	2.2
1998	137,673	131,463	60,771	46.2		13.9	271.87	2.5
1999	139,368	133,488	62,042	46.5		13.9	274.64	1.0
2000	142,583	136,891	63,586	46.5		13.5	275.62	0.4
2001	143,734	136,933	63,737	46.5		13.4	275.38	-0.1
2002	144,863	136,485	63,582	46.6		13.3	278.91	1.3
2003	146,510	137,736	64,404	46.8		12.9	279.94	0.4

APPENDIX 4: UNEMPLOYMENT

Year	All Civilian Workers	White	White Males	White Females	Black	Black Males	Black Females	All 16–19 Years	Average Unemployment Duration (weeks)
	27	28	29	30	31	32	33	34	35
1959	5.5	4.8	4.6	5.3	10.7	11.5	9.4	14.6	14.4
1960	5.5	5.0	4.8	5.3	10.2	10.7	9.4	14.7	12.8
1961	6.7	6.0	5.7	6.5	12.4	12.8	11.9	16.8	15.6
1962	5.5	4.9	4.6	5.5	10.9	10.9	11.0	14.7	14.7
1963	5.7	5.0	4.7	5.8	10.8	10.5	11.2	17.2	14.0
1964	5.2	4.6	4.1	5.5	9.6	8.9	10.7	16.2	13.3
1965	4.5	4.1	3.6	5.0	8.1	7.4	9.2	14.8	11.8
1966	3.8	3.4	2.8	4.3	7.3	6.3	8.7	12.8	10.4
1967	3.8	3.4	2.7	4.6	7.4	6.0	9.1	12.9	8.7
1968	3.6	3.2	2.6	4.3	6.7	5.6	8.3	12.7	8.4
1969	3.5	3.1	2.5	4.2	6.4	5.3	7.8	12.2	7.8
1970	4.9	4.5	4.0	5.4	8.2	7.3	9.3	15.3	8.6
1971	5.9	5.4	4.9	6.3	9.9	9.1	10.9	16.9	11.3
1972	5.6	5.1	4.5	5.9	10.4	9.3	11.8	16.2	12.0
1973	4.9	4.3	3.8	5.3	9.4	8.0	11.1	14.5	10.0
1974	5.6	5.0	4.4	6.1	10.5	9.8	11.3	16.0	9.8
1975	8.5	7.8	7.2	8.6	14.8	14.8	14.8	19.9	14.2
1976	7.7	7.0	6.4	7.9	14.0	13.7	14.3	19.0	15.8
1977	7.1	6.2	5.5	7.3	14.0	13.3	14.9	17.8	14.3
1978	6.1	5.2	4.6	6.2	12.8	11.8	13.8	16.4	11.9
1979	5.8	5.1	4.5	5.9	12.3	11.4	13.3	16.1	10.8
1980	7.1	6.3	6.1	6.5	14.3	14.5	14.0	17.8	11.9
1981	7.6	6.7	6.5	6.9	15.6	15.7	15.6	19.6	13.7
1982	9.7	8.6	8.8	8.3	18.9	20.1	17.6	23.2	15.6
1983	9.6	8.4	8.8	7.9	19.5	20.3	18.6	22.4	20.0
1984	7.5	6.5	6.4	6.5	15.9	16.4	15.4	18.9	18.2
1985	7.2	6.2	6.1	6.4	15.1	15.3	14.9	18.6	15.6
1986	7.0	6.0	6.0	6.1	14.5	14.8	14.2	18.3	15.0
1987	6.2	5.3	5.4	5.2	13.0	12.7	13.2	16.9	14.5
1988	5.5	4.7	4.7	4.7	11.7	11.7	11.7	15.3	13.5
1989	5.3	4.5	4.5	4.5	11.4	11.5	11.4	15.0	11.9
1990	5.6	4.8	4.9	4.7	11.4	11.9	10.9	15.5	12.0
1991	6.8	6.1	6.5	5.6	12.5	13.0	12.0	18.7	13.7
1992	7.5	6.6	7.0	6.1	14.2	15.2	13.2	20.1	17.7
1993	6.9	6.1	6.3	5.7	13.0	13.8	12.1	19.0	18.0
1994	6.1	5.3	5.4	5.2	11.5	12.0	11.0	17.6	18.8
1995	5.6	4.9	4.9	4.8	10.4	10.6	10.2	17.3	16.6
1996	5.4	4.7	4.7	4.7	10.5	11.1	10.0	16.7	16.7
1997	4.9	4.2	4.2	4.2	10.0	10.2	9.9	16.0	15.8
1998	4.5	3.9	3.9	3.9	8.9	8.9	9.0	14.6	14.5
1999	4.2	3.7	3.6	3.8	8.0	8.2	7.8	13.9	13.4
2000	4.0	3.5	3.4	3.6	7.6	8.0	7.1	13.1	12.6
2001	4.7	4.2	4.3	4.1	8.6	9.3	8.1	14.7	13.1
2002	5.8	5.1	5.3	4.9	10.2	10.7	9.8	16.5	16.6
2003	6.0	5.2	5.6	4.8	10.8	11.6	10.2	17.5	19.2

APPENDIX 5: INFLATION, INTEREST RATES, & DEBT

Year	Consumer Price Index (CPI)	Infla-tion from CPI (%)	Growth of money supply	Prime interest rate (%)	Real prime rate (ex post) (%)	New home mortgage yields (%)	Federal surplus/deficit (billions of 2000 $)	Federal debt held by public, as % of GDP
	36	37	38	39	40	41	42	43
1959	29.1	0.7		4.48	3.79		-61.7	47.9
1960	29.6	1.7	4.9	4.82	3.10		1.4	45.6
1961	29.9	1.0	7.4	4.50	3.49		-15.5	45.0
1962	30.2	1.0	8.1	4.50	3.50		-32.9	43.7
1963	30.6	1.3	8.4	4.50	3.18	5.89	-22.0	42.4
1964	31.0	1.3	8.0	4.50	3.19	5.83	-26.7	40.0
1965	31.5	1.6	8.1	4.54	2.93	5.81	-6.2	37.9
1966	32.4	2.9	4.6	5.63	2.77	6.25	-16.0	34.9
1967	33.4	3.1	9.3	5.61	2.52	6.46	-36.0	32.9
1968	34.8	4.2	8.0	6.30	2.11	6.97	-101.2	33.3
1969	36.7	5.5	3.7	7.96	2.50	7.81	12.2	29.3
1970	38.8	5.7	6.5	7.91	2.19	8.45	-10.2	28.0
1971	40.5	4.4	13.4	5.72	1.34	7.74	-79.6	28.0
1972	41.8	3.2	13.0	5.25	2.04	7.60	-77.6	27.4
1973	44.4	6.2	6.6	8.03	1.81	7.96	-46.8	26.0
1974	49.3	11.0	5.4	10.81	-0.23	8.92	-17.6	23.9
1975	53.8	9.1	12.7	7.86	-1.27	9.00	-140.0	25.3
1976	56.9	5.8	13.4	6.84	1.08	9.00	-183.4	27.5
1977	60.6	6.5	10.3	6.83	0.33	9.02	-125.6	27.8
1978	65.2	7.6	7.5	9.06	1.47	9.56	-129.4	27.4
1979	72.6	11.3	7.9	12.67	1.32	10.78	-82.1	25.6
1980	82.4	13.5	8.6	15.27	1.77	12.66	-136.6	26.1
1981	90.9	10.3	9.7	18.87	8.55	14.70	-133.6	25.8
1982	96.5	6.2	8.8	14.86	8.70	15.14	-204.1	28.7
1983	99.6	3.2	11.3	10.79	7.58	12.57	-318.7	33.0
1984	103.9	4.3	8.6	12.04	7.72	12.38	-274.0	34.0
1985	107.6	3.6	8.0	9.93	6.37	11.55	-304.5	36.3
1986	109.6	1.9	9.5	8.33	6.47	10.17	-310.5	39.5
1987	113.6	3.6	3.6	8.21	4.56	9.31	-204.5	40.6
1988	118.3	4.1	5.8	9.32	5.18	9.19	-205.0	40.9
1989	124.0	4.8	5.5	10.87	6.05	10.13	-194.1	40.6
1990	130.7	5.4	3.8	10.01	4.61	10.05	-271.1	42.0
1991	136.2	4.2	3.0	8.46	4.25	9.32	-318.9	45.3
1992	140.3	3.0	1.6	6.25	3.24	8.24	-336.2	48.1
1993	144.5	3.0	1.5	6.00	3.01	7.20	-288.6	49.4
1994	148.2	2.6	0.4	7.15	4.59	7.49	-225.2	49.3
1995	152.4	2.8	4.1	8.83	6.00	7.87	-178.1	49.2
1996	156.9	3.0	4.8	8.27	5.32	7.80	-114.5	48.5
1997	160.5	2.3	5.7	8.44	6.15	7.71	-23.1	46.1
1998	163.0	1.6	8.8	8.35	6.79	7.07	71.7	43.1
1999	166.6	2.2	6.1	8.00	5.79	7.04	128.3	39.8
2000	172.2	3.4	6.1	9.23	5.87	7.52	236.4	35.1
2001	177.1	2.8	10.4	6.91	4.06	7.00	124.4	33.1
2002	179.9	1.6	6.4	4.67	3.09	6.43	-151.8	34.1
2003	184.0	2.3	4.3	4.12	1.82	5.80	-355.8	36.1

DATA SOURCES AND NOTES

Column
no.

1	Calculated from the *Economic Report of the President 2004 (ERP04)* Table B-3.
2–7	From *ERP04* Table B-2.
8	Calculated from *ERP04* Table B-34.
9	Calculated from 2 and 8.
10	Calculated from *ERP04* Table B-103, adjusted using the GDP deflator (*ERP04* Table B-3).
11	From *ERP04* Table B-110.
12–13	From *ERP04* Table B-2.
14	Calculated from *ERP04* Table B-90, adjusted with GDP deflator (*ERP04* Table B-3). Figures are net of inventory valuation and capital consumption (depreciation) adjustments.
15	From *ERP04* Table B-54.
16	Calculated from *ERP04* Table B-84, adjusted with GDP deflator (*ERP04* Table B-3). Includes federal grant-in-aid.
17	Calculated from *ERP04* Table B-84, adjusted with GDP deflator (*ERP04* Table B-3).
18	Calculated from *ERP04* Table B-85, adjusted with GDP deflator (*ERP04* Table B-3).
19–20	From *ERP04* Table B-35.
21	From *ERP04* Table B-36.
22	Calculated from 20 and 21.
23	From Bureau of Labor Statistics (BLS) *Directory of National Unions and Employee Associations*, which provided union membership data from 1930 to 1980. The directory data were obtained directly from the labor unions and employee associations. The responding organizations provided, through their own determination, the average number of dues-paying members. The dues-paying member definition used here includes unemployed members as well as members on strike, layoff, or retired.
24	From BLS *Current Population Survey*. Figures for 1977–1980 are from May of each year. The 1983–1999 figures are annual averages. Beginning in 1994, data are not strictly comparable with data for 1993 and earlier years because of redesign of the *Current Population Survey* questionnaire and collection methodology. Unlike the data in 23, figures in 24 refer to union membership status of employed persons.
25	From *ERP04* Table B-47.
26	From *ERP04* Table B-47.
27–28	From *ERP04* Table B-42.
29–30	From *ERP04* Table B-43.
31	From *ERP04* Table B-42. Figures in 31 "Black and other" before 1972.
32–33	From *ERP04* Table B-43. Figures in 32 and 33 "Black and other" before 1972.
34	From *ERP04* Table B-42.
35	From *ERP04* Table B-44.
36	From *ERP04* Table B-60.
37	Calculated from 36.
38	From *ERP04* Table B-69.
39	From *ERP04* Table B-73.
40	Calculated by subtracting 37 from 39.
41	From *ERP04* Table B-73.
42	Calculated from *ERP04* Table B-78, adjusted using the GDP deflator (*ERP04* Table B-3).
43	Calculated from *ERP04* Table B-78.

CONTRIBUTORS

Randy Albelda, a *Dollars & Sense* Associate, teaches economics at the University of Massachusetts-Boston.

Sarah Anderson is the director of the Global Economy Program of the Institute for Policy Studies in Washington, D.C.

Dean Baker is co-director of the Center for Economic and Policy Research.

Jim Campen teaches economics at the University of Massachusetts-Boston. He was a member of the *Dollars & Sense* collective from 1974 to 1982.

Jessica Collins is a former *Dollars & Sense* intern.

Jim Crotty teaches economics and is a member of the Center for Popular Economics at the University of Massachusetts-Amherst.

James M. Cypher teaches economics at California State University-Fresno.

Daniel Fireside is co-editor of *Dollars & Sense.*

Ellen Frank, a *Dollars & Sense* collective member, teaches economics at Emmanuel College in Boston.

James K. Galbraith is professor at the Lyndon B. Johnson School of Public Affairs, University of Texas at Austin, and Senior Scholar of the Levy Economics Institute.

Elise Gould is an economist at the Economic Policy Institute, where she specializes in health and labor issues.

Lena Graber is a former *Dollars & Sense* intern.

Kang-Kook Lee is a graduate student in economics at the University of Massachusetts-Amherst.

Gawain Kripke is a senior policy advisor at Oxfam America.

Arthur MacEwan, a *Dollars & Sense* Associate, teaches economics at the University of Massachusetts-Boston.

Ann Markusen is a former Senior Fellow at the Council on Foreign Relations and Professor of Public Policy and Planning at the Humphrey Institute of Public Affairs, University of Minnesota.

Gretchen McClain, a former member of the *Dollars & Sense* collective, is an economic consultant.

John Miller, a *Dollars & Sense* collective member, teaches economics at Wheaton College.

Gina Neff is the associate director of Economists Allied for Arms Reduction.

Amy Offner is a is a former co-editor of *Dollars & Sense.*

Dara O'Rourke is an assistant professor of Urban Studies and Planning at the Massachusetts Institute of Technology (MIT).

Doug Orr teaches economics at Eastern Washington University.

Robert Pollin teaches economics and is co-director of the Political Economy Research Institute at the University of Massachusetts-Amherst. He is also a *Dollars & Sense* Associate.

Nomi Prins is a former investment banker turned journalist. She is the author of *Money for Nothing.*

Alejandro Reuss is former co-editor of *Dollars & Sense.*

Jonathan Rowe is senior fellow at Redefining Progress in San Francisco and a contributing editor at the *Washington Monthly.*

Adria Scharf is co-editor of *Dollars & Sense.*

Ted Schmidt teaches economics at Buffalo State College, SUNY.

Bryan Snyder teaches economics at Kansas State University-Manhattan.

Eoghan Stafford is a former *Dollars & Sense* intern.

Chris Tilly, a *Dollars & Sense* collective member, teaches at the University of Massachusetts-Lowell.

Mark Weisbrot is co-director of the Center for Economic and Policy Research in Washington, D.C.

Timothy A. Wise, former staff editor at *Dollars & Sense*, is deputy director of the Global Development and Environment Institute at Tufts University.